P9-EDR-721

THE BIRTH OF NEW CRITICISM

The Birth of New Criticism

Conflict and Conciliation in the Early Work of William Empson, I.A. Richards, Laura Riding, and Robert Graves

DONALD J. CHILDS

McGill-Queen's University Press
Montreal & Kingston • London • Ithaca

ISBN 978-0-7735-4211-2 (cloth)
ISBN 978-0-7735-8923-0 (ePDF)
ISBN 978-0-7735-8924-7 (ePUB)

Legal deposit fourth quarter 2013
Bibliothèque nationale du Québec

Printed in Canada on acid-free paper that is 100% ancient forest free (100% post-consumer recycled), processed chlorine free

This book has been published with the help of a grant from the Canadian Federation for the Humanities and Social Sciences, through the Awards to Scholarly Publications Program, using funds provided by the Social Sciences and Humanities Research Council of Canada.

McGill-Queen's University Press acknowledges the support of the Canada Council for the Arts for our publishing program. We also acknowledge the financial support of the Government of Canada through the Canada Book Fund for our publishing activities.

Library and Archives Canada Cataloguing in Publication

Childs, Donald J., author
The Birth of New Criticism: conflict and conciliation in the early work of William Empson, I.A. Richards, Laura Riding, and Robert Graves/ Donald J. Childs.

Includes bibliographical references and index.
Issued in print and electronic formats.
ISBN 978-0-7735-4211-2 (bound). – ISBN 978-0-7735-8923-0 (ePDF). – ISBN 978-0-7735-8924-7 (ePUB)

1. New Criticism – History. 2. Empson, William, 1906–1984 – Criticism and interpretation. 3. Richards, I. A. (Ivor Armstrong), 1893–1979 – Criticism and interpretation. 4. Riding, Laura, 1901–1991 – Criticism and interpretation. 5. Graves, Robert, 1895–1985 – Criticism and interpretation. I. Title.

PN98.N4C45 2013 801'.95 C2013-906405-2
C2013-906406-0

This book was typeset by Interscript in 10.5/13 Sabon.

In memory of
Frederick James Luxton (1926–2010)
Donald Childs (1928–2011)

Contents

Acknowledgments

This book has been published with the help of a grant from the Canadian Federation for the Humanities and Social Sciences, through the Awards to Scholarly Publications Program, using funds provided by the Social Sciences and Humanities Research Council of Canada. Part of the chapter "New Criticism," from *Encyclopedia of Contemporary Literary Theory: Approaches, Scholars, Terms*, edited by Irene R. Makaryk © University of Toronto Press, 1993, is reprinted with permission of the publisher.

THE BIRTH OF NEW CRITICISM

Introduction

The story of the origins of New Criticism is fairly well known and fairly well agreed upon, yet it is not accurate: it leaves out Robert Graves. The story really ought to begin with Graves, if for no other reason than that he was the first to practise what we now recognize as close reading. As we shall see, directly from his practice of close reading – and from his early attempts to explain, recommend, and justify this approach to reading poetry – descend a number of New Criticism's most famous and most fundamental aspects. As we shall also see, the line of descent (sometimes as much by dissent as by agreement) runs through the early work of Graves's acknowledged collaborator, Laura Riding, the early work of his acknowledged admirer, William Empson, and the early work of his acknowledged detractor, I.A. Richards.

Even New Critics who did not know Graves's early work directly nonetheless, by mid-century, knew it indirectly through the work of the two major influences on New Criticism most influenced by him: Richards and Empson. Like the less well-known Riding, these two adopt many of Graves's ideas and adapt them to their own purposes in their 1920s works. To tell the story of Graves's role in the development of New Criticism is therefore also to tell the story of the relationship of his work to that of Richards and Empson, and of course Riding, too. All three of them incorporated the work of Graves not always appropriately, but always productively. The story of the conflicts and conciliations among the literary theories they developed and the interpretive practises they deployed deserves a place in literary history.

My own account of New Criticism twenty years ago in *The Encyclopedia of Contemporary Literary Theory* (1993) is typical of the merits and the demerits of the existing stories of this movement's development, especially in terms of the critics it discusses and those it does not.[1] I wrote as follows:

> Never a formal school, New Criticism is an approach to literature extrapolated from the often discrete literary theories and critical practices of British literary critics such as I.A. Richards, William Empson, and F.R. Leavis and American literary critics such as Cleanth Brooks, W.K. Wimsatt, Jr., Allen Tate, Richard Palmer Blackmur, Robert Penn Warren, and John Crowe Ransom, whose book, *The New Criticism* (1941), provided the name for the movement.[2] The New Critical sensibility first received articulation in the 1920s in the essays of the Anglo-American poet and critic T.S. Eliot and subsequently flourished in the pedagogy of North American and British teachers of English literature.
>
> In half a dozen essays published between 1919 and 1923 – from "Tradition and the Individual Talent" to "The Function of Criticism" – Eliot gave voice to a provocative combination of modernist principle and prejudice that was to ground most of the New Critical theory and practice developed during the next thirty years. Against the romantic celebration of the poem as a record of an exceptional person's personality, Eliot argued that "honest criticism and sensitive appreciation is directed not upon the poet but upon the poetry."[3] Similarly, against Walter Pater's impressionism, he argued that attention ought to be directed solely upon the poem, and not upon the critic. In short, he disallowed genetic and affective accounts of the work of art (to become known as the intentional and affective fallacies, respectively) because they compromise the integrity of the work of art *as* art.
>
> Responding to scientific positivism's claim that science alone produces knowledge, Eliot argued that the study of literature ought to strive towards scientific objectivity. Reacting against positivism, however, he claimed that literature contains a unique knowledge not available to science – a knowledge born of the multiple perspectives on experience that the juxtaposition of words in a work of art allows. By marking such an antiscientific use of language as a fact, and by agreeing that knowledge is a matter of fact, Eliot effected an uneasy rapprochement between positivism and literary criticism.

Beginning with Richards's important works of the 1920s (*The Principles of Literary Criticism*, *Science and Poetry* and *Practical Criticism*), New Critics developed these arguments into major axioms about the autonomy of the work of art, its resistance to paraphrase, its organic unity, its inevitably ironic use of language, and its welcoming of close reading.[4]

Like the Russian formalists – largely unknown to the New Critics before René Wellek's *Theory of Literature* (1949) – New Critics rejected the prevailing tendency to substitute another discipline for the study of literature itself.[5] Richards, one of the first and most influential of the critics associated with New Criticism, warns in *Practical Criticism* (1929) that readers ought to refrain from applying to a poem the external standards of the chemist, the moralist, the logician, or the professor. What matters, suggests Cleanth Brooks in *The Well Wrought Urn* (1947), is "what the poem says as a poem."[6] (New Critics generally regard "poem" as a synonym for "literature.")

William K. Wimsatt, Jr, and Monroe C. Beardsley, in "The Intentional Fallacy" (1946), argue that the meaning of a poem is internal, determined by what is public linguistic fact – grammar, semantics, syntax – and not by what poets might reveal in conversation, letters or journals concerning their intentions (often the focus of traditional positivistic or historical scholarship).[7] Even the "I" speaking in a lyric poem is a creation of the poem, they insist, and ought to be regarded as a dramatic persona, and not as the poet. Developing Allen Tate's interest in "Literature as Knowledge" (1941) in the ontology of a poem, Wimsatt and Beardsley suggest that poetry's obligation is not just to convey knowledge but also to *be* knowledge.[8] Even earlier, in *The World's Body* (1938), John Crowe Ransom argues that meaning is always a function of the poem's full linguistic being, for it exists in a tension between its paraphrasable core and its lively local details – the latter being capable of subverting the former – and so the poem can never be reduced to a static and lifeless concept or intention.[9]

Like all New Critics since, Richards recognized the threat to the autonomy and integrity of the poem contained in the habit of reducing the poem to just such a concept or intention – the habit of paraphrase. In *New Bearings in English Poetry* (1932), his student F.R. Leavis deprecates the limitation of a poem's self-sufficiency represented in the shifting of focus away from the poem to something outside it.[10] Yet it was Brooks who most notoriously raised the warning about paraphrase by labelling it a "heresy."[11] Brooks acknowledges that paraphrase is useful as shorthand in describing a poem or pointing to certain aspects of it, but he will not allow that it can ever represent the essential meaning of the poem. It is like scaffolding that can be erected around a building but which ought never to be mistaken for the structure within. For Brooks, as for Ransom, the structure of the poem is a "pattern of resolved stresses."[12] This resolution is not a matter of finding a mean between extremes (a process that might well lend itself to paraphrase) but rather a dramatic balancing and harmonizing of attitudes, feelings, ideas, denotations, and connotations. The analogy between drama and poetry is deliberate: conflict is built into the being of each such that they *become* action instead of a *statement about* action. To paraphrase the poem as a statement about its action, therefore, is to refer to something outside it and so to deny its autonomy. In its extreme form, the argument against paraphrase leads to R.P. Blackmur's conclusion in *The Double Agent* (1935) that, beyond paraphrase, "the rest, whatever it is, can only be known, not talked about."[13]

For New Critics, what is known but difficult to talk about is the experience of the poem as a unified whole. In this experience, the reader perceives the poem as a "Total Meaning" – a blending of many meanings and language tasks simultaneously.[14] Borrowing both from Eliot's concept of the poet as always "forming new wholes" and from Samuel Taylor Coleridge's concept of the imagination as a vital "esemplastic" power, Richards, in *The Principles of Literary Criticism* (1924), defines the poem as an intricate and exquisite reconciliation of experience.[15] The poem, then, is not only an autonomous being, but also – given that this reconciliation is vital and dynamic – an organic being, complete with both internal tensions and structural unity. Each word is a part of the context of interrelated meanings that are fused together as the poem, and the poem's complex totality also infuses the individual words and phrases. In short, the part is a determiner of the meaning as a whole and the meaning as a whole determines the precise meaning of each part. According to Brooks, then, one appreciates "what the poem says as a poem" by reading "the poem ... as a whole."[16]

Poetry depends for its being upon irony. A word used by New Critics in several ways, irony may be understood as represented by a continuum of definitions ranged between "irony is the tendency of any word, but particularly words combined as poetry, to suggest more than one meaning" and "irony is the tendency of a good poem to include a significant number and subtle variety of factors at odds with what is apparently being said in the poem." In "Pure and Impure Poetry" (1942), Robert Penn Warren claims that the poet "proves his vision by submitting it to the fires of irony – to the drama of his structure."[17] In other words, as a dramatic tension – as a balancing and reconciliation – of opposite or discordant qualities, a poem is ironic in structure. The poem is defined by the ironic competition of meanings within it – the inevitably ironic aspect of language having been wrought up to a very high degree in poetry, in which a structural harmony amongst competing meanings is achieved. "Irony," explains Brooks, "is the most general term that we have for the kind of qualification which the various elements in a context receive from the context."[18]

New Critics are virtually unanimous in celebrating irony as the essence of poetry. For Ransom, the effect of the qualification of the poem's various elements by their context is a construction that is a simulacrum of democracy – poetry and democracy allowing freedom to individual words and citizens, respectively. For Tate, poetry is a more general simulacrum of reality: a construction of reality (whatever it be) in language that, as poetry, is a more complete mode of utterance than scientific language. For Brooks, the good poem is a simulacrum of the oneness of reality and so the poet's task is "to unify experience."[19] The instrument for the latter is paradox – for Brooks, a rhetorical strategy that claims to unify opposites. The instrument for representing the manifold variety in reality is ambiguity, the poet's tribute to the diversity in human experience. The particularly democratic consequence of the irony within the poem is contradiction, the celebration of dissension among the words of the poem as the instrument of a complex whole.

Richards's definition in *Practical Criticism* of the four different kinds of meaning possible in a poem (sense, feeling, tone, and intention) invited a new kind of reading: "All respectable poetry invites close reading."[20] Every New Critic acknowledges the importance of close reading, for the concomitant of New Critical praise of irony, paradox, ambiguity, and complexity in general is the requirement that each word of a poem be scrutinized in detail with regard to all relevant denotations and connotations. Attention to detail is necessary if the whole both depends upon accurate perception of the many-sided parts and also reveals in the parts unsuspected sides illuminated only retrospectively by the whole.

In Britain, notable close readers were F.R. Leavis and William Empson. The name of Leavis's literary magazine, *Scrutiny* (founded 1932), implies the line-by-line examination of literature that he favoured.[21] Empson's *Seven Types of Ambiguity* (1930) demonstrates that word-by-word analysis of poems is necessary in order to appreciate the inevitability and meaningful productivity of ambiguity's omnipresence in poetry. His definition of ambiguity as "any consequence of language, however slight, which adds some nuance to the direct statement of prose" was very influential upon American New Critics in general, but particularly upon Cleanth Brooks.[22]

The element of New Critical practice that has established itself most ineradicably is this habit of close reading. Few, if any, contemporary approaches to literature can forego the careful reading for irony, paradox, ambiguity, and contradiction that New Critics offered as the *sine qua non* of literary study.

•

This old essay remains a serviceable account of New Criticism's theory and practice, but obviously I left out any mention of Robert Graves and Laura Riding. As we shall see from my survey of other accounts of the development of New Criticism, nearly everyone else has made the same mistake.

•

As in my account, so in most other accounts: the origin of this movement's assertion of the autotelic status of the work of literature is generally traced to Eliot, and the origin of the practice of close reading is generally traced to Richards and Empson. In *The Concise Oxford Dictionary of Literary Terms* (1990), for instance, Chris

Baldick observes that New Criticism was "a movement in American literary criticism from the 1930s to the 1960s, concentrating on the verbal complexities and ambiguities of short poems considered as self-sufficient objects without attention to their origins and effects ... Influenced by T.S. Eliot's view of poetry's autotelic status, and by the detailed semantic analyses of I.A. Richards in *Practical Criticism* (1929) and Empson in *Seven Types of Ambiguity* (1930), the American New Critics repudiated 'extrinsic' criteria for understanding poems, dismissing them under such names as the affective fallacy and the intentional fallacy."[23] Charles E. Bressler makes the same broad points in *Literary Criticism: An Introduction to Theory and Practice* (2003): "Two British critics and authors, T.S. Eliot and I.A. Richards, helped lay the foundation for this form of Formalistic analysis. From Eliot, New Criticism borrows its insistence that criticism be directed toward the poem, not the poet ... From Eliot's contemporary, I.A. Richards, a psychologist and literary critic, New Criticism borrows a term that has become synonymous with its methods of analysis, practical criticism."[24] M. H. Abrams says something quite similar in *A Glossary of Literary Terms* (1985): the term New Criticism

> came to be applied to a widespread tendency in American criticism, deriving in part from various elements in I.A. Richards's *Principles of Literary Criticism* (1924) and *Science and Poetry* (1926), and from the critical essays of T.S. Eliot ... A poem, it is held, should be treated as such – in Eliot's words, "primarily as poetry and not another thing" – and should therefore be regarded as an independent and self-sufficient object ... The distinctive procedure of the New Critic is explication or close reading: the detailed and subtle analysis of the complex interrelations and *ambiguities* (multiple meanings) of the components within a work ... [T]he distinctive explicative procedure of the New Criticism derives from such books as I.A. Richards's *Practical Criticism* (1929) and William Empson's *Seven Types of Ambiguity* (1930).[25]

It is the question of who deserves credit for the development of close reading (and credit thereby, whether directly or indirectly, for the development of certain theories and practises of literary interpretation related to it) that concerns me most in this study. As we have seen, the question is usually decided in favour of Richards and Empson. Cleanth Brooks himself, called upon to write the entry on

New Criticism for the *Princeton Encyclopedia of Poetry and Poetics* (1974), acknowledges that "One aspect of the [New Criticism] which is often seized upon as central is the 'close reading' of poetry." It cannot be denied, he says, that "The application of semantics to literary study, a development which owes most to men like I.A. Richards and William Empson, has indeed been very important." Brooks recalls Empson again in explaining that "Another aspect of the [New Criticism] is to be seen in its resolute attempt to set up an organic theory of literature": "These critics ... have attempted to take the full context into account and to see each individual word of a work, not only as contributing to the context, but as deriving its exact meaning from its place in the context. Hence the development of terms like irony, plurisignification, ambiguity, etc., to indicate the richness and complication of meanings developed in a poetic context." The promoter of practical criticism, on the one hand, and the anatomizer of ambiguity, on the other – despite the former's "affective bias" in his fixation upon the reader's response to poetry, and despite the latter's "inveterate psychologising about both writer and reader" – are both recognized by Brooks as honoured precursors.[26]

The story of the relationship between the early work of Richards and the early work of Empson usually identifies affiliation (Richards is the teacher; Empson is the pupil) and co-operation (Empson follows Richards's ideas and develops them). In *Modern Literary Theory: An Introduction* (1986), for instance, David Robey, explaining that Richards's influence is seen "most of all ... in the practice of close reading," points out that "Richards's influence in this respect has been much reinforced by the work of his pupil William Empson" via the latter's "practical, analytical development of Richards's theory."[27] David Daiches makes the same observation in *Critical Approaches to Literature* (1984): "One of the pioneers in ... close analytic criticism ... is William Empson, a pupil of I.A. Richards who developed Richards's concern with meaning into a special kind of descriptive technique."[28]

As the example of Brooks shows, some of the earliest and most influential of American New Critics acknowledged the importance of Richards and Empson in the development of their own even more rigorous practice. John Crowe Ransom highlights the teacher-pupil relationship between Richards and Empson. In *The New Criticism* (1941), however critical he happens to be of Richards's scientism in *Principles of Literary Criticism*, Ransom celebrates Richards's subsequent book *Practical Criticism* "as one of the documents of major influence upon the thinking of our age": "In criticizing the students' ability to read the meaning of the poetry, Richards reveals himself as an astute reader. He looks much more closely at the objective poem than his theories require him to do. His most incontestable contribution to poetic discussion, in my opinion, is in developing the ideal or exemplary readings, and in provoking such readings from other scholars."[29] Turning his attention to Empson, Ransom writes: "If Mr. Richards has not offered an extensive treatment of Ambiguity it is because he has got Mr. Empson, at Cambridge, to offer one. A brilliant pupil is presumptive evidence of a brilliant teacher, and Richards' fame would be secure if he had done nothing but inspire Empson." Indeed, Ransom declares the work of Empson and Richards to be the reason there is the need to declare that a "new criticism" has been born:

> Empson's first book, *Seven Types of Ambiguity* ... is a systematic account of the author's readings in English poetry in search of ambiguity. I believe it is the most imaginative account of readings ever printed, and Empson the closest and most resourceful reader that poetry has yet publicly had ... Writings as acute and at the same time as patient and as consecutive as this have not existed in English criticism, I think, before Richards and Empson. They become frequent now; Richards and Empson have spread quickly. That is a principal reason why I think it is time to identify a powerful intellectual movement that deserves to be called a new criticism ... [R]eading will never again be able to be as dull and unimaginative as it must have been before Empson showed its possibilities.[30]

Few dissent from this narrative. Some, however, downgrade the importance of Empson. In *The Penguin Dictionary of Literary Terms and Literary Theory*, J.A. Cuddon celebrates the "immeasurable influence" on "the development of what came to be called New Criticism" of Richards's literary interpretation in *Practical Criticism* "based on close analysis of a text in isolation," his "Detailed, balanced and rigorous examination of a text to discover its meanings and to assess its effects." Apparently, for Cuddon, Empson is a minor rather than a major influence – or at least so he implies by his grudging acknowledgment that "Ever since William Empson published *Seven Types of*

Ambiguity (1930) this term has had some weight and importance in critical evaluation."[31] Similarly, William Van O'Connor allows that "There seems little doubt ... that Empson has helped to teach at least one generation of poetry readers to find more complicated meanings in poetry than they had hitherto been prepared to find," but he does so only after he has suggested that "Empson had been anticipated by Frederick C. Prescott in *The Poetic Mind* (1922)," a book in which the "analyses bring out the same sort of thing that Empson does."[32]

John Paul Russo, Richards's biographer, is an even more determined supporter of Richards and equally determined subordinator of Empson. He asserts not only that Richards is the first close reader, but also that he is the first close reader to recognize the importance of ambiguity in literature: "*Practical Criticism* as a whole can be understood as an attempt to present the 'systematic ambiguity' of the poems based on student responses and Richards' own interpretation."[33] To support this claim, however, Russo thoroughly misreads Richards's observations about "systematic ambiguity" in the "Introductory" chapter to *Practical Criticism*. Richards is actually concerned here about the ambiguities of vague terms popular among the writers of the protocols that he solicited from students for analysis: he wonders just what "the meanings of 'sentimentality,' 'truth,' 'sincerity,' or 'meaning' itself" might be for these students. Richards finds that although his quest "to understand half the opinions which appear in the protocols" requires "no little mental plasticity," the quest itself is not impossible, for "something like a plan of the ways in which the likely ambiguities of any given term or opinion-formula may radiate ... make[s] itself quite apparent. For the hope of a new technique of discussion lies in this: that the study of the ambiguities of one term assists in the elucidation of another."[34] Richards clearly refers to the interconnected meanings of the terms "sentimentality," "truth," "sincerity," and "meaning" as used by his protocol writers – *not* to the meanings of the terms in the poems they analyze. So when he declares that "Ambiguity in fact is systematic," and "the separate senses that a word may have are related to one another," he is talking not at all about the ambiguities to be found in poetry (as Empson would do), but rather about the ambiguities that are to be found in the sloppy terms in his students' discussions of poetry.

Whereas Richards's biographer promotes his man's claims to New Critical fame, Empson's biographer, John Haffenden, prefers his man's claims to be the prime mover of New Criticism's close reading technique. Haffenden notes the inaccuracy of Russo's characterization of Richards's comments about ambiguity, and he also notes the inaccuracy of Russo's characterization of Richards's comments about G.H. Luce's poem in *Practical Criticism* as an emblematic and influential example of close reading. Haffenden will have none of this: "Richards himself well knew – several months before publishing his reluctant gloss on Luce's line (with its incidental ambiguity that Russo belatedly pins down on his behalf) – that Empson had brought forth, at remarkable speed, a sustained argument about seven types of ambiguity, along with detailed analyses ... The first publication of all this work by Empson appeared in February 1929, in the periodical *Experiment* (co-edited by Empson), which prinked itself out in the wonderful analysis of ambiguity of syntax (double meaning) in Shakespeare's Sonnet XVI that would go straight into *Seven Types*: truly, that piece exemplifies the method of close reading as it stood in 1929."[35] Haffenden complains that when it comes to the development of New Criticism, "Russo is keen to give his man the credit for virtually everything – including the machinery of poetic ambiguity that Empson first deployed."[36] Haffenden himself manages to avoid giving his own man credit for virtually everything, although Empson gets more credit than is his due.

Haffenden acknowledges the importance of the influence of Robert Graves on the method of reading literature developed in *Seven Types of Ambiguity* – as, of course, did Empson himself (in what he would many years later describe as a "little compliment to Robert Graves"): "I derive the method I am using from Mr. Robert Graves' analysis of a Shakespeare Sonnet, 'The expense of spirit in a waste of shame,' in *A Survey of Modernist Poetry.*"[37] As Haffenden observes, "The quintessence of the theory of ambiguity according to Empson may have been incited by I.A. Richards, but it actually owes just as much, if not more, to the work of Sigmund Freud and Robert Graves."[38] Haffenden even finds evidence – some of it internal to *Seven Types of Ambiguity*, some of it from an unpublished notebook, some of it from essays published later – to support his conclusion that "Empson's greatest debt to Graves certainly did pre-date *A Survey of Modernist Poetry.*"[39] But he hardly begins to make this case (let alone make it clear and certain), largely because he has hardly begun to appreciate the evidence available to support it.

Of course there is another name to conjure with in this story of New Criticism's method of close reading: Laura Riding's. William Harmon and Hugh Holman mention Riding briefly when they point out in *A Handbook to Literature* (2003) that New Criticism's emphasis on the work of literature as an "object in itself" actually "has varied sources," "among them are I.A. Richards' *The Principles of Literary Criticism* (1924), Laura (Riding) Jackson's criticism that appeared in the later 1920s, William Empson's *Seven Types of Ambiguity* (1930), the work of Remy de Gourmont, the anti-romanticism of T.E. Hulme, the French *explication de texte*, the concepts of order and tradition of the southern Agrarians, and the work of Ezra Pound and T.S. Eliot."[40]

Haffenden considers Riding's claim to have influenced Empson's method of reading poetry for ambiguity, but in this regard is as niggardly as Empson himself in giving credit where it is due. While Empson neglected to acknowledge that *A Survey of Modernist Poetry* was co-written by Laura Riding,[41] Haffenden observes – again, however, without making the case – that "The influence of the 'Graves-Riding' exegesis of Sonnet 129 is everywhere apparent in *Seven Types of Ambiguity.*"[42] His reversal of the unvarying practice of Riding and Graves to order their names with Riding's first and Graves's second (and his rather too quick dismissal of Riding's assertion that "Mr Empson's book applied a method original to that book [*A Survey of Modernist Poetry*], and originating with myself") implies that he follows his own man in discounting the extent of Riding's influence even when he is forced to acknowledge it.[43]

By contrast, Deborah Baker, as Haffenden observes, not only "gives credit to Riding as the initiator of the critical approach used in *A Survey of Modernist Poetry*," but also disparages Empson's achievement: "Being an aspiring mathematician, Empson set out to prove that there were, in fact, exactly seven varieties of linguistic ambiguity ... 'Ambiguity' and 'indeterminacy' remain the language of a critic; a poet would be more likely to insist, as Riding did, on the existence of congruent meanings or 'manifold precision.'"[44] It is as though Baker is channelling Riding's own anger at Empson for his cavalier dismissal of her influence on him.

Similarly, Elizabeth Friedmann, noting that "Empson's book is usually credited with initiating the development of a critical method that would channel modernist poetry into the mainstream of English and American literature" observes (as does Haffenden, as does Empson) that "This approach is recommended in *A Survey* [*of Modernist Poetry*]."[45] In Empson's acknowledgment of the book in question as the inspiration for his method, however, Friedmann notes two mistakes: not just the use of the name "Robert Graves" alone, but also the use of the word "method." First, "The critical 'method' that William Empson acknowledged in his book on ambiguity was not designed by Riding and Graves as a systematic approach to the poem to be followed in order to produce an 'explication'; rather, it commended serious attention to the poet's words and punctuation for the purpose of determining the poem's intended *meaning* as it is transmitted from the poet's mind to the reader's via the printed page ... However, this originally passionate attention to the poem's verbal and syntactical makeup became a kind of end in itself as the New Criticism gathered adherents."[46] Second, "Even though *A Survey of Modernist Poetry* and *A Pamphlet Against Anthologies* are described by their authors as 'word-by-word' collaborations, Laura Riding was the guiding critical intellect in the composition of both books, as Robert Graves himself attested during their literary partnership ... In fact, *A Survey of Modernist Poetry* may be seen as an expansion of the 'short-term view of a single generation of poetry ... and its internal problems and tendencies' offered in the second chapter of Laura's *Contemporaries and Snobs*, the chapter Laura and Robert reworked as their 'Conclusion' for *A Survey*."[47] However, the demonstrable debts of Empson to the work by Graves that pre-dates his collaboration with Riding undermines Friedman's attempt to give her woman credit for virtually everything.

Still, such one-sided accounts of Riding's role in the birth of New Criticism have had their effect. Jahan Ramazani writes that "in *A Survey of Modernist Poetry* (1927), by Laura Riding and Robert Graves, Riding had been perhaps the first to try the experiment of reading a poem apart from any historical or linguistic context: her intense appreciation of the semantic complexities of a Shakespeare sonnet encouraged the young English poet and critic William Empson to discover the value of exploring every nuance of meaning, with the aid of psychology and sociology."[48]

Poor old Graves. Not only has he been largely left out of the prevailing narrative of the origins of New Criticism. New narratives marginalize him even more.

As we can see, then, there is certainly a question to be addressed concerning the origin of close reading. Among those who have addressed it so far, and addressed it most vigorously, if not most comprehensively or most accurately, it begins to look as though everyone has his man or her woman. Because I argue the case for Graves's recognition as the developer of close reading, Graves might come off as my man and insofar as I also urge the case not only for Riding's claim to have influenced Empson but also for her influence on Richards, Riding may come off as my woman. Although there is much about each that I do not admire (in the lives they led, the letters they wrote, and the works they left), both deserve clear and careful study of their roles in the birth of close reading in particular and of New Criticism generally.

Still, rare as it is that Riding and Graves should receive credit, one cannot quite endorse Harold Fromm's casual, unargued claim: "the New Critics carefully took in Graves and Riding's *Survey of Modernist Poetry* (1927), whose close reading of Shakespeare set the model for Empson and his followers while promulgating the view of a poem as an autotelic, self-existent substance unbeholden to the outside world or to history."[49] Or at least one cannot endorse it yet, for no one has done the work that would be required to support it. Certainly Riding was personally acquainted with Allen Tate and John Crowe Ransom in the mid-1920s, Graves and Ransom exchanged letters of admiration for each other's poetry in the mid-1920s, and Brooks – among others – later alludes appreciatively to *A Survey of Modernist Poetry* in his own work, but the case remains to be made that American New Critics "carefully took in" the book by Riding and Graves.[50]

Ironically, however, for all this fuss about who deserves credit for the development of close reading, few actually sought such credit. Initially, Riding was the only one to prefer her claim to be the originator of the close reading method, and it was more than forty years after the publication of the seminal books in the 1920s by Richards, Empson, Graves, and herself that she finally did so publically: "It seems to me appropriate to record that, without public statement of mine, recognition of my intellectually and verbally sensitive hand within the glove of the *Survey* method has been mounting, with perception of its connection, via Mr. Empson's hobby-horse use of it, with the 'New Criticism,' which tried to make real horse-flesh of it."[51]

By contrast, Graves was dismissive of the man who had tried to give him credit for inspiring his method of reading poetry closely for ambiguity: "Empson is as clever as a monkey & I do not like monkeys."[52] As Christopher Norris points out, Empson resented the turn given his method by many American New Critics, especially as his close reading technique became aligned with dogmas about the irrelevance and inaccessibility of authorial intention: "Empson sought to turn back this tide of anti-intentionalist doctrine, serving as it did – and he was quick to perceive the connection – as a prop for religious (anti-humanist) beliefs which could pass themselves off under cover of a professional concern with matters of interpretive method and technique."[53] As Empson himself writes, "if the poem was good, and if I could go at it the way I wanted to, nothing in the poem at all would be irrelevant by the time the critic had finished explaining it ... To say that you won't be bothered with anything but the words on the page (and that you are within your rights, because the author didn't *intend* you to have any more) strikes me as petulant."[54] Before Richards came round in the 1930s to the idea that there was an overdetermination of meaning in poetry and that it was merely superstition to believe that poetry must have "one and only one true meaning," Empson's close readings apparently made him feel something like dizzying illness: "Long ago, when a bound copy of *Seven Types* first reached me ... I used to press it on likely readers with this recommendation: 'It will make you feel you are having a lovely go of influenza – high-fever fireworks, you know.'"[55] Eliot, who was a great influence on the development of New Critical axioms like the intentional fallacy and the affective fallacy but not much of a close reader in his practical criticism, actually mocked the technique in his late essay, "The Frontiers of Criticism" (1956): "The method is to take a well-known poem ... without reference to the author or to his other work, analyse it stanza by stanza and line by line, and extract, squeeze, tease, press every drop of meaning out of it that one can. It might be called the lemon-squeezer school of criticism."[56]

•

For the critics, scholars, and cultural historians who have not taken sides in this investigation, the discussion since the second half of the twentieth century has tended to focus not upon the question of who deserves credit for developing close reading, but rather upon the question of whose interests are served by this development. It is certainly possible to study the history of the origins and development of New Criticism in terms other than personal ones, as well as in terms other than the apparently benign and neutral terms of conceptual and technical influence. Origins can be studied in terms of causes material, formal, efficient, final; causes historical, ideological, discursive; causes social, psychological, biographical, and so on. There can never be one story of New Criticism; there can only ever be stories.

Marxists and other materialist critics of culture, for instance, tend to see New Criticism as a reactionary bourgeois exercise: its origins can be traced to people, powers, purposes on the wrong side of history. From within the hermeneutic tradition, New Criticism can be interpreted as another aspect of the Western technological tradition of turning the world into objects for manipulation. Sociological historians describe New Critics as romantics resistant to positivism or as Christians resistant to secularism. Critics of a more deconstructive bent trace something similar in New Criticism: a metaphysically logocentric and an ideologically conservative exercise dedicated to the preservation of the Christian logos. From the point of view of feminism, gender criticism, and queer theory, one can trace in New Criticism a hetero-normative discourse that practises reverence for and interpretive recovery of phallic oneness: oneness displaced into the unity of the literary text as verbal icon, which incarnates, preserves, and expresses self-sufficiency, reconciliation of opposites, organic wholeness. One could even characterize New Criticism as an expression of homosexual panic. Male poets (Stevens, Pound, and Eliot, for instance) were anxious about Western culture's tendency to regard poetry as a feminine pursuit, so the New Critics – all men – made both the writing and reading of poetry a tough, hard, strong, disciplined, homosocially self-sufficient activity. Postcolonial theory might regard New Criticism as an ideological mystification of imperial economics: a mystification by which the culturally diverse raw materials that are the sources of the poem in material history are manufactured into the aesthetically, interpretively, ontologically finished goods that circulate now in the great tradition of literature, magically independent of material history.

Terry Eagleton's account of a significantly ideological difference between Richards and Empson (the only account of New Criticism dissenting from the narrative that describes affiliation and co-operation between them) shows a Marxist way of accounting for origins. He figures Richards as an agent of ruling-class hegemony insofar as he is associated with the development of "practical criticism" and "close reading," approaches to literature that ostensibly serve bourgeois interests. On the one hand, "Practical criticism meant a method which spurned belle-lettristic waffle and was properly unafraid to take the text apart; but it also assumed that you could judge literary 'greatness' and 'centrality' by bringing a focused attentiveness to bear on poems or pieces of prose isolated from their cultural and historical contexts"; on the other hand, close reading "meant detailed analytic interpretation, providing a valuable antidote to aestheticist chit-chat; but it also … inescapably suggests an attention to *this* rather than to something else: to the 'words on the page' rather than to the contexts which produced and surround them." Richards is thereby complicit in encouraging "the illusion that any piece of language, 'literary' or not, can be adequately studied or even understood in isolation." The emphasis on practical criticism and close reading "was the beginnings of a 'reification' of the literary work, the treatment of it as an object in itself, which was to be triumphantly consummated in the American New Criticism."[57]

Richards, practical criticism, and close reading were all on the wrong side of history. Advancing "literature as a conscious ideology for reconstructing social order … in the socially disruptive, economically decaying, politically unstable years which followed the Great War," Richards posits that "If historical contradictions cannot be resolved in reality, they can be harmoniously conciliated as discrete psychological 'impulses' within the contemplative mind." For Richards, Eagleton observes, "The most efficient kind of poetry is that which organizes the maximum number of impulses with the minimum amount of conflict or frustration. Without such psychic therapy, standards of value are likely to collapse beneath the 'more sinister potentialities of the cinema and the loud-speaker.'" As Eagleton sees it, then, "Organizing the lawless lower impulses more effectively will ensure the survival of the higher, finer ones; it is not far from the Victorian belief that organizing the lower classes will ensure the survival of the upper ones, and indeed is significantly related to it."[58]

Similarly, American New Critics were able to find in poetry "a nostalgic haven from the alienations of industrial capitalism" by developing a form of criticism that would provide "an 'aesthetic' alternative to the sterile scientific rationalism of the industrial north." Eagleton notes that "'Coherence' and 'integration' were the keynotes": "just as American functionalist sociology developed a 'conflict-free' model of society, in which every element 'adapted' to every other, so the poem abolished all friction, irregularity and contradiction in the symmetrical cooperation of its various features," and "through such unity, the work 'corresponded' in some sense to reality itself." And so "Poetry, as an essentially contemplative mode, would spur us not to change the world but to reverence it for what it was, teach us to approach it with a disinterested humility."[59]

According to Eagleton, however, Empson develops Richards's noxious practical criticism and close reading in a way that departs from the reactionary politics that both his mentor and his American admirers promote. Whereas "For I.A. Richards and the New Critics, the meaning of a poetic word is ... a function of the poem's internal verbal organization" (in New Criticism, particularly, "the reader is shut out by a locked structure of ambivalences, reduced to admiring passivity)," Empson, "an old-style Enlightenment rationalist whose trust in decency, reasonableness, common human sympathies and a general human nature is as winning as it is suspect," at least recognizes that "It is the reader's response which makes for ambiguity" and that "this response depends on more than the poem alone," for "the reader inevitably brings to the work whole social contexts of discourse." And so "Empsonian ambiguities ... indicate points where the poem's language falters, trails off or gestures beyond itself, pregnantly suggestive of some potentially inexhaustible context of meaning." Insofar as "Empson's poetics are liberal, social and democratic, appealing ... to the likely sympathies and expectations of a common reader than to the technocratic techniques of the professional critic," Empson is "a remorseless opponent" of New Criticism.[60] Empson's heart is on the right side of history.

Richard Palmer's account of New Criticism nicely outlines broadly hermeneutical concern that "the philosophical base of New Criticism was always shaky and uncertain, vacillating between realism and idealism." Its "formalism, unclear about its ground in experience rather than in the 'form' of the work as an object, too often fell victim to an atemporal and ahistorical conception of interpretation, and interpretations often seemed to be in terms of static knowledge rather than vital experience." Similarly, "to see a work as 'object' rather than as 'work' places the reader at a distance from the text": "Methodical questioning runs the risk of closing to the interpreter the possibility of being led by the work itself. A method will impose a list of questions, thus structuring in advance the encounter one will have with the work." According to Palmer, then, "Such a conception of interpretation tends to equate conceptual mastery with understanding. The work when conceived as an object (instead of a work) becomes simply an entity about which knowledge is acquired through spatializing ideation, dissection, and analysis. Such an approach represents the transposition into criticism of a technological approach to the world, an approach which looks only for such knowledge of an object as will give mastery and control over it."[61]

Of course Palmer also recognizes the positive potential of a New Criticism informed by a Gadamerian and Heideggerian perspective. For instance, Gadamer's argument – in Palmer's words, "The work of art has its authentic being in the fact that, in becoming experience, it transforms the experience: the work of art works. The 'subject' of the experience of art, the thing that endures through time, is not the subjectivity of the one who experiences the work; it is the work itself" – on the one hand agrees with New Criticism's preservation of "the literary work in separation from the author's opinions and creative act, and from the tendency to take the reader's subjectivity as a starting point," and yet on the other hand would have enabled New Critics "to see more clearly the nature of the continuity between the self-understanding attained from literature and the self-understanding in and through which we exist." After all, Palmer points out, "The New Critics sometimes even speak of a 'surrender' to the being of the work; in this they are truly in agreement with Gadamer."[62] And vice versa.

Similarly, Palmer observes, as for Heidegger, so for New Critics: "the poem itself is supreme and not biographical background ... The New Critic and Heidegger would agree on the ontological autonomy of the poem and the heresy of paraphrase." But whereas because for the New Critic "Too easily the text becomes an object and explication a conceptual exercise which works solely with the 'given,' accepting the restrictions of scientific objectivity" (that is, "the New Critic has difficulty making his case for the 'truth' of the poem within the context of his presuppositions"), "Heidegger wants to let the text speak with its own truth and voice."[63]

Gerald Graff, however, outlines an alternative history of the ideas originally animating New Criticism, suggesting that an implicitly Gadamerian and Heideggerian resistance to "the restrictions of scientific objectivity" was fundamental to the earliest expressions of the movement:

> It is odd that the New Critics should be denounced for their scientific empiricism, since this was one of the chief cultural ills which the New Critics themselves sought to combat. The New Criticism

> stands squarely in the romantic tradition of the defence of the humanities as the antidote to science and positivism. The methodology of "close reading" was an attempt not to imitate science but to refute its devaluation of literature: by demonstrating the rich complexity of meaning within even the simplest poem, the New Critic proved to the "hard-boiled naturalist," as Cleanth Brooks referred to him, that literature had to be taken seriously as a rival mode of cognitive knowledge ... To see New Criticism as an expression of "the modern technological way of thinking" ... is to have no way of accounting for the persistent condemnations of just this scientific, technological mentality ... running throughout New Criticism from T.S. Eliot to John Crowe Ransom and Brooks.

Graff further observes that "Instances of ... denigrations of science could be almost indefinitely multiplied by further quotation from Ransom, Brooks, Allen Tate, R.P. Blackmur, W.K. Wimsatt, Robert Penn Warren, and Robert B. Heilman." Even "I.A. Richards, one major New Critic who *did* attempt to apply systematic scientific principles to the analysis of literature, subordinated these principles to the larger aim of redeeming culture from the demoralizing effect of the scientific world view. Richards's scientism ... subserved a romantic esthetic which proposed literature as a compensation for loss of belief."[64]

That being said, Graff also identifies an influence on New Criticism even more original than anti-scientific romanticism. "It was not quasi-scientific empiricism that influenced most New Critics to seek impersonality and objectivity so much as the Christian doctrine of Original Sin"; and it is precisely the Christian *logos* that critics of both a secular humanist and a deconstructive bent recognize, resent, and resist as a cause of New Criticism.[65] Norris, for instance, traces in New Criticism the descent from *Seven Types of Ambiguity* via a kind of dissent "by mystery-mongering critics like Ransom" of both a critical and theological orthodoxy.

> Ambiguity was soon transformed – mainly at the hands of the American New Critics – from a loose (even casually inclusive) term for any kind of multiple meaning into a full-dress critical orthodoxy where "paradox" and "irony" were treated as measures of true poetic worth, and where any hint of heterodox or dissenting ideas ... could be kept out of sight by strict application

> of the relevant critical ground-rules ... In short, it had become a form of surrogate or ersatz theology, along with all the attendant baggage of canonical dogmas and heresies ... There were clear links between the new style of secularized close reading and a long tradition of scriptural hermeneutics in the service of dogmatic or revealed religious truth.

In the hands of New Critics, "Close reading ... became a sure route of access to regions of the soul untouched by the spirit of latter-day secular critique," and so Empson's method was thereby made complicit in "the standard Christian ploy of ignoring the rational *resistance* to paradox and praising the poet for his 'deep' perception of religious truths beyond reach of mere analytic reason."[66]

Similarly, John Guillory – to show how New Criticism's ostensibly objective evaluation of the words on the page actually serves the interests of a literary elite, on the one hand, and "the liberal pluralism which is the regnant ideology of the academy," on the other – traces the descent from Eliot to Brooks in particular and to New Criticism generally of an ideological determination to enforce "the cognitive silence of the literary work, the silencing of difference": "The technique of formalist interpretation subtends the larger ideology, satisfying within a narrower domain of practice the longing for consensus, for a metaphysics of the same – a longing expressed by the posited 'unity' of the literary work."[67]

For others, Eliot's theory of impersonality – so fundamental an influence on New Criticism in its turning of attention from the poet to the poem – turns out to be a strategy for expressing implicitly sexual desire. Following the trail of such desire, critics today can easily turn close reading into the closet reading of queer theory.

Tim Dean, for instance, acknowledging that "defences of his theory of impersonality invite ridicule for their blindness to the cultural situatedness of high modernist aesthetics, its entanglement with reactionary ideologies of all stripes" ("Any literary critic with a modicum of political awareness knows that the only thing to do with impersonality is to demystify it"), reads impersonality quite otherwise: "According to Eliot, the impersonalist poet becomes a medium for others' voices; in this way impersonality provides a means of access to others instead of a means of hiding oneself. To the extent that it clears a space for otherness at the expense of the poet's self, the impersonalist aesthetic should be considered ethically exemplary rather than politically suspect. Approaching impersonality from this different perspective allows us to grasp how Eliot's conception of the poet as a passive medium for alien utterances tacitly feminizes the poet's role."[68] From the point of view of the queer theory to which Dean subscribes, Eliot's imagining himself as ideally penetrated by "otherness" is an exemplary revision of heterosexist culture's understanding of masculinity as impenetrable.

Observations like these could easily be extended by queer theorists to New Criticism as a whole: concentrating upon the words on the page frees the poem from its author's controlling agency, providing a means of access to otherness at the expense of the poet's phallic self. After all, as Palmer points out, some New Critics – and especially New Criticism's precursors Riding and Graves, I would add – speak of poets and readers as surrendering themselves to the being of the poem, opening within themselves a space for the poem to be. And so Dean's conclusions about Eliot might also be applied to New Criticism: "His impersonalist theory of poetry compels Eliot – even in the face of his own conscious intentions – to embrace a passivity and openness that renders him vulnerable to what feels like bodily violation."[69]

Following a similar line of investigation into the ideas of impersonality and organicism in the literary tradition, as Eliot represents these things in his early essays that most influenced New Criticism, Michele Tepper suggests that tracing the genealogy of the essay "Tradition and the Individual Talent" " through Eliot's other 1919 formulations of the individual's relationship to tradition ... demonstrates how Eliot's own closely interrelated anxieties around sexuality and around his own self-perceived debased position as an American writer motivate the formulation of his earliest and most influential critical positions." She suggests "that 'Tradition and the Individual Talent' grew out of Eliot's eroticized formulation of the poet's relationship to the past" and "that this formulation remains in traces in the poet's absorption into the body of tradition, which in turn interacts with the other great 'organic formations' of European literature." In the end, "an analysis of the circulation of bodies and desires in 'Tradition and the Individual Talent' can allow us ... to open up a space for a more fully embodied and historicized understanding of our own critical practices": "a drive toward sensual connection underlies even criticism's most emphatic statements of disinterested impersonality."[70]

And so, even if one regards the impersonalization of poetry (whether by Eliot in particular or by New Criticism in general) as merely what Colleen Lamos calls a "mask of self-abnegation," it remains the case, as Dean puts it, that "from impersonalist practice something fundamental remains to be learned about the relation between transhistorical conceptions of poetic utterance and modern forms of sexuality."[71] For instance, one might develop further Brooks's reading of Donne's poem "The Canonization" in *The Well Wrought Urn* and Guillory's observation that it is determined by a desire to put Christianity at the centre of literary interpretation ("As the urn gestures to the ashes it contains, so the phoenix gestures, by its very allusive density, to the meaning not of any one poem but of poetry: that meaning is to make this allusion, to point to the figure who is historically emblematized as a phoenix, who delivered the *pattern* of resurrection, and who first spoke the paradoxes Brooks cites as exemplary").[72] By close reading of this poem, heterosexual union is made to serve as an image of the unity of this poem in particular, of the unity by reconciliation of opposites of all proper poems in general, of the unity by marriage of Christ and His church, and of the unity implied by a metaphysics of the same.

Similarly, Tepper's observations of Eliot's essays – first, that Eliot's "works speak of nonnormative forms of carnality and eroticism that are not reducible to genital sexuality: the desire to consume and be consumed, the desire to lose oneself in something greater, and the desire to encompass that greater thing within one's own body – to have it in one's bones," and, second, that his "Metaphysical models lived in an era in which desire was not as easily reduced to homo- and heterosexual as it is (even, too often, by queer theory) in the twenty-first century"– might also be extended to New Criticism more generally.[73] Brooks's choice of "The Canonization" for exemplary New Critical close reading can be seen as interesting not just for its foregrounding of straight sexual union as a model of the poem's unity, but also for its foregrounding of what can be seen as the poem's speaker's defensive engagement with an implicitly senior male mentor's chastisement of him for neglecting his opportunities and obligations in the common world of their homosocial bonds (the world of male privilege represented by the king's court, the legal courts, the church, business, and so on). That is, the speaker in "The Canonization" can be seen as responding defensively to the implicit charge by his unheard interlocutor that his lovey-dovey behaviour is not properly manly. Foucault assures us that sex cannot be kept out of these cultural equations, and Sedgwick assures us that homosexual panic is the means of enforcing homosocial order.

Such perspectives can obviously be brought to bear in an investigation of the causes and effects of New Criticism in general, and of close reading in particular.

Urging "a reconsideration of the aesthetics of modernism in a historical light," Patricia Chu argues that by "attaching postcoloniality to the modernity of modernism," one can see that "the new subjectivities of the twentieth century ... emerge from systems of authority and regulation," that "the much vaunted self-consciousness of this era is inextricably bound with anxiety about whether individual decisions, desires and the power to act on them were illusory," and that "modern(ist) self-consciousness expresses uncertainty about the governed self."[74] From this point of view, one can treat the development of New Criticism, in the context of the "state modernization and governmentalization" entailed by global capitalism "across a broad swathe of cultural production" (a context that exposes modernism's expression of new identities and subjectivities as an illusory function of the state's determination to create and sustain just such "administrable identities and subjectivities"), as a displacement of the Anglo-American ideal of the self-governing citizen into the fantasy of the self-governing poem.[75]

•

In this study, I am interested no more in the question of whether New Criticism was on the right side or the wrong side of material, ontological, or sexual history than in the question of whether or not Eliot, Richards, Empson, Riding, and Graves approved of what subsequent New Critics made of their ideas about and approaches to literature. Whatever the politics, ideology, discourse, sexuality, or mystery-mongering with which one might see it as complicit, the development of close reading techniques is fundamental to New Criticism. As understood by Graves, close reading reveals the special nature of literary language (at least in English): first, it is ambiguous, ironic, plurisignificant; second, it is manifoldly precise, organically whole, convergently meaningful, overdeterminedly unified; third, from these facts it follows that to paraphrase literary language is to distort – if not to omit altogether – what is literary about language (heresy!). Graves put all of these ideas into circulation by 1925, and Richards, Empson, and Riding recognized this fact, and so the development of close reading as the foundation of practical literary criticism ought really to be traced back in the first instance to the earliest work of Robert Graves, as he put the cat of close reading amongst the pigeons of the historical, positivist, impressionist criticism prevailing in his day, and also in the second instance to the collaborative work by Riding and Graves that emerged subsequent to Graves's early independent work.

To do so is my interest in this book, and such an interest does not preclude alternative accounts of New Criticism's origins; indeed, it implicitly proposes to help fund them, inviting those interested in any story of the origins of New Criticism to add to it Robert Graves and Laura Riding and an account of their "causes."[76]

•

In the twenty chapters that follow, I show that the influence of Graves and Riding is behind much that is celebrated as fundamentally New Critical in the early work of Richards and Empson. I document, by comparison and contrast of key texts, how the always linguistic – and often psychological – conflict and conciliation in poetry that is their common concern was actually identified, explained, interpreted, and theorized first and foremost by Graves, and then by Riding and Graves.

Chapter 1 recalls the long and increasingly acrimonious dispute between William Empson and Laura Riding about her claim to have been the inspiration for his method of reading poetry and thereby the inspiration for the New Criticism that developed from his method. It shows that Riding's "word by word collaboration" with Graves in *A Survey of Modernist Poetry* was a much more substantial influence on Empson than he ever acknowledged.[77] The extent to which their discussion of modernist poetry influenced *Seven Types of Ambiguity* has not received the attention it deserves.

Chapter 2, however, begins the argument that Empson was nonetheless correct in foregrounding Graves's influence upon the development of his method. It draws attention to the role of Graves's "'conflict' theory of poetry," as Empson referred to it in *Seven Types of Ambiguity*, in the latter's understanding of the psychological and grammatical function of poetic ambiguity – a theory developed prior to Graves's acquaintance with Riding's work, and a theory subsequently rejected by Riding.[78]

Chapter 3 pauses in the making of the case that Graves is the primary influence on Empson to complicate matters by pointing out that key aspects of the work of Riding and Graves that influenced

Empson were themselves inspired by Frederick Clarke Prescott's *The Poetic Mind* (1922). This chapter shows how much of Prescott's prototypically close reading of what he regarded as the psychoanalytically overdetermined word-play of poets from Shakespeare to Keats was mediated to Empson by Graves, on the one hand, and by Riding and Graves, on the other. Neither Riding nor Graves ever acknowledged Prescott's work, but they ought to have.

Chapter 4 shows how Graves's mediation to Empson of the potential of psychoanalysis for literary criticism led to Empson's wrestling in *Seven Types of Ambiguity* with the question of the degrees of conscious control possible in the creation of poetic ambiguity, particularly in relation to his third type of ambiguity. Empson struggles mightily to define a purely conscious use of ambiguity in poetry, but he gives up by chapter's end. Just as Graves argues that genuine poetry approaches its limit as the poet's psychological conflict approaches consciousness, so Empson accepts that poetry approaches its limit as the poet's recourse to ambiguity approaches conscious control of it.

In addition to the influence of Graves's psychoanalytical theories upon Empson, there is also the influence of his practical criticism as a way of demonstrating the relevance and the reach of his literary theory. Chapter 5 shows how closely Empson followed some of Graves's readings, particularly with reference to the psychological conflict that is expressed in the ambiguous language of the religious poems of George Herbert and the romantic odes and allegories of Keats.

Chapter 6 shows how, from his first chapter to his last, Empson follows Graves in his defence of detailed poetic analysis against those who regard it as an emotionally sterile scientism. In response to what he anticipates will be the usual objections in the 1920s to pedantic, overly intellectual analysis of poetry, Empson adopts and adapts for his own purposes Graves's goal of a synthesis between a spontaneous emotional appreciation of poetry and an intellectual analysis of poetry underwritten by psychological and linguistic sophistication.

Empson begins *Seven Types of Ambiguity* in the grip of Eliot's admiration for the metaphysical sensibility and its tendency to be "constantly amalgamating disparate experience," as distinct from the ostensibly dissociated sensibility of poets of the nineteenth century.[79] Chapter 7 shows how in the course of writing his book, Empson comes around to Graves's much more admiring attitude towards the poets of the nineteenth century, particularly the romantics, explaining in detail how Empson came to agree with Graves that the poets of the nineteenth century are not nearly as remote from the semantic duality essential to poetry as Empson had initially been led by Eliot's criticism to believe. Indeed, Graves helps Empson to recognize that Eliot's arch-enemy in "Tradition and the Individual Talent," William Wordsworth, is an exemplary model of at least one of the seven types of ambiguity.

Chapter 8 shows how Graves was the source of the conceptual paradigm central to Empson's understanding of the special associative power residing in the English language generally and in English poetry particularly. By close readings demonstrating how the effect of certain lines of poetry depends upon words with two or three, or even four, meaningful associations – close readings that Empson recalled more than forty years later – Graves convinces Empson of the literary potential of the Freudian idea that language is capable of signifying patterns of meaning beyond the author's conscious awareness and deliberate control. Of all the nudges that Graves gave Empson towards his anatomy of ambiguity, these discoveries of multiply significant meanings in English poetry perhaps constitute the strongest.

And even the taxonomies of type by which Empson's anatomy would proceed are modelled by Graves in his early work. Chapter 9 shows how, just as Empson would, Graves categorizes poetry both in terms of the kind of ambiguity present in poems and in terms of whether or not the poet is conscious of them. Empson, then, could look to this work by Graves not only for an example of the general usefulness of taxonomy in explaining the kinds of multiple meanings that come systematically to be associated in poetry, but also for examples of particular kinds of associated meanings that a more academic and focused critic could explain – at greater length, in greater detail, and with more sophistication – as seven types of ambiguity.

Finally, the tenth chapter considers Empson's new edition of *Seven Types of Ambiguity* in 1947. Acknowledgment of *A Survey of Modernist Poetry* is removed, Graves is mentioned again as the originator of Empson's method of interpretation, and Graves is referred to both in terms of his "'conflict' theory" and in terms of his observations about the phenomenal rather than noumenal nature of the art object. It turns out that the influence of Graves strongly endures more than twenty years after Empson first read him.

•

With Chapter 11, attention in this study turns to the relationship between the theories of Richards, on the one hand, and the theories of Graves, the team of Riding and Graves, and Riding herself, on the other. Chapter Eleven examines the harsh treatment of Graves in *Principles of Literary Criticism* (1924), showing that Richards positions himself on the side of scientifically actual and simple interpretation of literature and sets Graves, and through him psychoanalysis as a whole, on the side of fantastically conjectural and multiple interpretations of literature. Richards regards Graves as simply playing games with literature. It will be some years yet before he develops an appreciation for the kind of "complicated cross-referencing" between images in poetry that Graves celebrates in the early 1920s.[80] It will be some years yet, that is, before Richards will recognize and celebrate overdetermination of meaning as a constitutive principle of poetic language. The chapters that follow rehearse evidence that Graves and Riding helped Richards to this end.

Chapter 12 shows that a number of the ideas advanced in Graves's early books, *On English Poetry* and *The Meaning of Dreams*, and in essays that would become chapters of *Poetic Unreason*, are important stimuli for Richards's account in *Principles of Literary Criticism* of the psychological dimensions of the writing and reading of poetry, particularly his account of poetry as communication and his account of the value of poetry – "the two pillars upon which a theory of criticism must rest."[81] Richards found that Graves had articulated accurate insights, despite their being couched in what he regarded as psychoanalytical mumbo-jumbo. And so, like Empson, Richards found himself systematizing and saying better many things that Graves said first in a rather haphazard and slap-dash way. Also like Empson, it turns out, when Richards was at this revisionary work, he did not bother to mention Graves by name. So there is traced in Chapter Twelve both a pronounced influence of Graves in Richards's early work and a pronounced anxiety about it.

If the imprint that Graves left on Richards's imagination is clear in *Principles of Literary Criticism*, it is even clearer in *Science and Poetry*, where Richards presents the salient points of *Principles of Literary Criticism* in a more accessible and popular form. As we see in Chapter 13, Richards clearly adopts what Graves calls in *The Meaning of Dreams* the "Theory of Double Self" and adapts it to the terms of his own literary theory.[82] He is thereby put on the road to an appreciation of both the overdetermination of meaning in poetry and the systematic reconciliation of meanings within a simultaneously psychological and aesthetic whole.

In Chapter 14, "Riding Corrects Richards (and Graves)," I suggest not only that Riding and Graves know the work of Richards as they write *A Survey of Modernist Poetry*, but also that they organize the book so as to conclude it with a repudiation of the "scientific barbarism" that has crept into modernism.[83] It is likely that Graves knew of Richards's attack on his psychological reading of "Kubla Khan" in *Principles of Literary Criticism* soon after the book appeared. But in *A Survey of Modernist Poetry* he did not take issue with Richards directly, since Riding seems to have persuaded Graves during this first act of collaboration between them that Richards's criticism was a mishandled attack on a scientific barbarism from which Graves suffered just as much as Richards. To collaborate with Riding, Graves had to jettison his conflict theory, his grounding of poetry in personal significance, and his generally psychoanalytical paradigms.

Chapter 15 suggests that with his criticism of H.D.'s poetry in the chapter "Badness in Poetry" in *Principles of Literary Criticism*, Richards implies a method for reading modernist poetry that Riding and Graves repudiate in *A Survey of Modernist Poetry*. In response to Richards's disparagement of H.D. for what they consider to be wrong reasons, particularly his complaint that what results from the "tenuousness and ambiguity" of her poems "is almost independent of the author," Riding and Graves announce that a true poem is precisely the autonomous aesthetic entity, independent of the poet, that Richards fears.[84] According to Riding and Graves, H.D. fails to make her poems into frighteningly autonomous aesthetic entities deserving the label "modernist." On the other hand, however, Chapter 16 points out that although Riding seems to have had nothing good to say about Richards at this time, one can see that in collaboration with Graves in *A Survey of Modernist Poetry* she actually responds positively to a number of the points raised in *Principles of Literary Criticism* without ever acknowledging the fact. Indeed, Riding and Graves together adapt a number of the topics developed by Richards in his work up to1926 to the purposes of their apology for modernist poetry in general, and for Riding's own poetry in particular.

I suggest in Chapter 17 that, second only to *Seven Types of Ambiguity*, Richards's *Practical Criticism* is the founding document of New Criticism that is the most influenced by Riding and Graves. Indeed, in a number of important respects, Richards's report on his experiments with his Cambridge students takes the shape it does because of his reaction to their collaboration, *A Survey of Modernist Poetry*. Like Empson's book, *Practical Criticism* serves as something of a Trojan horse: it was an extremely influential work welcomed by American New Critics like Ransom who either did not notice or chose not to acknowledge that it contains the influence of Riding and Graves within it. Like *Seven Types of Ambiguity*, *Practical Criticism* is thereby a tremendous multiplier of the influence of Riding and Graves on New Criticism.

Chapter 18 explores the ways that for both Richards, on the one hand, and for Riding and Graves, on the other, pedagogy's the thing: does it promote the stock response, the stock feeling, the stock situation, the stock poem, or does it promote the independence and the individuality of the poem, the poet, and the reader? Similarly, Chapter 19 considers the extent to which Richards agrees with Riding and Graves that one of the "chief difficulties of criticism" concerns "the effects of *technical presuppositions*" and the effects of "*general critical preconceptions*."[85] According to Richards, these preconceptions and preconditions are a function of anthology culture. By 1928, there was no issue in contemporary literary criticism more distinctly the preserve of Riding and Graves than this. On both of these fronts, these chapters show, Richards's main concern in *Practical Criticism* is the same as that of Riding and Graves in *A Survey of Modernist Poetry*: how to educate people to become better readers of poetry, for better reading of poetry has the potential to make people better citizens. Each book explores this problem in terms of its implications for classroom culture, literary culture, and political culture. Like Riding and Graves, Richards depicts poetry as calling the reader to an intimate engagement with that reader's own being. From Riding and Graves, Richards gleans his image of the poem as pedagogue of the plastic modern mind: the mind which, in a liberal capitalist democracy, he expects to make the choices that will existentially found and fund the future development of human beings.

Finally, Chapter 20 considers the extent to which Richards cooperates with Riding and Graves in developing the idea that to paraphrase poetry is heresy. On the one hand, their slow reading for sense is fundamental to Richards's concept of close reading in *Practical Criticism*. In fact, what counts for Richards as a *reading* in *Practical Criticism* turns out to be just what Riding and Graves recommend as a reading in *A Survey of Modernist Poetry*: no two-minute perusal, but a time-length of engagement with the poem that enables what Richards calls a growing response to it and what Riding and Graves describe as a seeing of all that one can see at a given point and a taking of it all with one as one goes along (of course this way of reading poetry is also a model for the way of being in the world that the future will demand, according to Richards). On the other hand, neither slow reading for meaning nor close reading for meaning should be confused with summary or paraphrase of the poem. In his chapters on "Figurative Language" and "Sense and Feeling," Richards follows Riding and Graves in their emphasis on the "discrepancy" between what the poem says and any paraphrase of it that might be attempted, whether as a poetical or prose summary.[86] The argument in each case is the same, and so is much of the language by which it is articulated: the logical expansion of the poetic phrase into prose, according to Riding and Graves, and the intuitive expansion of the poetic phrase into a parallel poem, according to Richards, each constitutes a damaging, destructive attack upon poetry. In the end, we can see, Richards adopts the language of Riding and Graves that celebrates in poetry the "principle of self-determination," "its quality of independence from both the reader and the poet," and its "self-explanatory" nature.[87]

1

An Old Anxiety about Influence

When *Seven Types of Ambiguity* was published in the United States in 1931 it was hardly noticed, purchased by just eight people; it sold steadily from the moment it was published the year before in Britain, however, where it was also widely reviewed.[1] It was certainly noticed by Riding. Empson's Dedication (or Preface or Acknowledgments; it is difficult to say how he regarded these sentences) reads: "Mr. I.A. Richards, then my supervisor for the first part of the English Tripos, told me to write this essay, and various things to put in it; my indebtedness to him is as great as such a thing should ever be. And I derive the method I am using from Mr. Robert Graves' analysis of a Shakespeare Sonnet, 'The expense of spirit in a waste of shame,' in *A Survey of Modernist Poetry.*" This immediately gave rise to a dispute with Laura Riding, co-author of *A Survey of Modernist Poetry*, about who deserved credit for inspiring this method of reading literature.[2] The dispute lasted more than forty years and became more intense each time they renewed it, perhaps a sign of the growing importance of New Criticism in literary history.

From the beginning, Riding regarded the method as developed at least as much by her as by Graves, and she ultimately insisted that the analysis of the sonnet in question was mostly hers. Increasingly frustrated by her determination to claim credit for a method of criticism that she seemed to disdain, Empson professed to find her behaviour "puzzling": "if you despise it so much as your letters imply, whyever are you so keen to have priority in it?"[3] Forty years later, after a year of acrimonious and unavailing correspondence with Empson from 1970 to 1971, Riding folded her tent, taking comfort from what she saw as the tide of literary history: "It seems to me appropriate to record that, without public statement of mine, recognition of my intellectually and verbally sensitive hand within the glove of the *Survey* method has been mounting, with perception of its connection, via Mr Empson's hobby-horse use of it, with the 'New Criticism,' which tried to make real horse-flesh of it."[4]

A silly quarrel comes thereby to obscure for eighty years what ought to have been acknowledged quite unambiguously in 1930: first, that Empson owed his method of reading poetry more to Robert Graves than to any other person; second, that although Laura Riding's contribution to the development of this method was not nearly as important as Graves's, neither was it negligible. In the chapters that follow, I will show the sources in Graves's early works of the method that Empson develops: the method by which the close reading of ambiguity in poetry serves to identify the fullest possible range of meaning within it that is able to be reconciled into a coherent psychological and aesthetic whole. I begin by addressing the dispute between Riding and Empson concerning this question of influence: a question that ideologically progressive literary history has subsequently figured more as a question about who deserves blame for the origin of New Criticism than as a question about who deserves credit for it. It turns out that Empson owes a good deal to Riding, but not as much as she thinks he does.

•

In the fall of 1928, while I.A. Richards was writing *Practical Criticism*, his new pupil Empson discussed with him the method of reading literature suggested by *A Survey of Modernist Poetry*. Having completed his Cambridge degree in mathematics in the spring of that year, Empson had enrolled in English as a member of Magdalene College, which led to Richards's becoming his Director of Studies. With regard to the meetings that followed as part of their effort to define a research topic for Empson, Richards recalled in 1940 that "At about his third visit he brought up the games of interpretation which Laura Riding and Robert Graves were playing with the unpunctuated form of 'The expense of spirit in a waste of shame.' Taking the sonnet as a conjuror takes his hat, he produced an endless swarm of lively rabbits from it, and ended by 'You could do that with any poetry, couldn't you?'"[5]

Richards recalls this conversation more than a decade after the fact. Looking back, he seems to have supplied Riding's name only in retrospect to this account of his recollections of that conversation, for Empson – like so many others at the time, many of whom Riding and Graves chastised in their next book *A Pamphlet Against Anthologies* – treated *A Survey of Modernist Poetry* as another book of literary theory by Robert Graves, one that followed logically from the theory of poetry that he was developing in *On English Poetry* (1922), *The Meaning of Dreams* (1924), *Poetic Unreason* (1925), and *Impenetrability, or the Proper Habit of English* (1926).[6] Either Empson had not noticed or he had not taken seriously the fact that there was another name before Graves's on the title page of *A Survey of Modernist Poetry*. Prompted by Richards at the end of the meeting described above to explore this way of reading poetry more thoroughly and more systematically than Riding and Graves had done, Empson immediately went off to write *Seven Types of Ambiguity* – as we have seen, indicating in his introductory note that he thought the book's reading of Shakespeare's sonnet was the work of Graves alone.

When Riding learned in 1931 that Empson had made this mistake, she wrote to inform him of the error and to ask for a copy of the book. Empson duly arranged for a copy to be sent to her, and promptly apologized: "I am sorry not to have mentioned your name with his in the preface ... I had not the book by me and forgot that it was a collaboration."[7] Riding and Graves had been determined from the beginning that their collaboration be acknowledged, prefacing their second book together, *A Pamphlet Against Anthologies* (1928), with a list of the newspapers, magazines, and journals whose reviewers had not properly acknowledged Riding's co-authorship of *A Survey of Modernist Poetry*, many of them referring only to "Mr. Graves's book": "At the beginning of a previous work, *A Survey of Modernist Poetry*, we carefully described it as a word-by-word collaboration. We did this because it was obvious to us that the vulgarity of a certain type of English reviewer would be encouraged by the combined circumstances that the first author was a woman and that the second was a man whose name was perhaps better known to him than that of the first; and because we were interested to see how far this vulgarity would persist in spite of our statement ... We therefore take a statistical pleasure in listing the ... papers which succumbed, through their reviewers, to this vulgarity."[8] So it is not surprising that Riding and Graves did not let the matter drop with what Riding characterised as Empson's "meaningless and useless" personal apology to her: she regarded what he had done as another

YBP Library Services

CHILDS, DONALD J.

BIRTH OF NEW CRITICISM: CONFLICT AND CONCILIATION
IN THE EARLY WORK OF WILLIAM EMPSON, I.A.
RICHARDS,...   Cloth   399 P.
MONTREAL: MCGILL-QUEENS UNIV PRESS, 2013

TITLE CONT: LAURA RIDING, AND ROBERT GRAVES.
AUTH: UNIVERSITY OF OTTAWA.

ISBN 0773542116   **Library PO#** SLIP ORDERS

		List	100.00 USD
6207 UNIV OF TEXAS/SAN ANTONIO		**Disc**	17.0%
App. Date 10/22/14	ENG.APR 6108-09	**Net**	83.00 USD

SUBJ: NEW CRITICISM--HIST.

CLASS PN98   DEWEY# 801.95   LEVEL ADV-AC

YBP Library Services

CHILDS, DONALD J.

BIRTH OF NEW CRITICISM: CONFLICT AND CONCILIATION
IN THE EARLY WORK OF WILLIAM EMPSON, I.A.
RICHARDS,...   Cloth   399 P.
MONTREAL: MCGILL-QUEENS UNIV PRESS, 2013

TITLE CONT: LAURA RIDING, AND ROBERT GRAVES.
AUTH: UNIVERSITY OF OTTAWA.

ISBN 0773542116   **Library PO#** SLIP ORDERS

		List	100.00 USD
6207 UNIV OF TEXAS/SAN ANTONIO		**Disc**	17.0%
App. Date 10/22/14	ENG.APR 6108-09	**Net**	83.00 USD

SUBJ: NEW CRITICISM--HIST.

CLASS PN98   DEWEY# 801.95   LEVEL ADV-AC

instance of the "wilful omission of the first author's name."[9] Publicly exposing this implicitly misogynist vulgarity was important to both authors. Graves wrote a long letter to Empson's publishers the same day as Riding (an "enormous letter," Empson recalled, denouncing him "for a plot against women"), endorsing Riding's request that an erratum slip be added to all further copies sold, indicating the order of authorship as Riding first, Graves second.[10] Riding actually wrote again a month later, asking that she be sent a copy of the erratum slip, for she was not willing to accept as fact a mere account from either the author or the publishers of what they had done.

Yet there was more to the story, although it would not emerge for many years – in further exchanges of correspondence between Empson and Riding. In 1966, when James Jensen reported in the *Modern Language Quarterly* the results of his investigation into the influence of *A Survey of Modernist Poetry* upon *Seven Types of Ambiguity*, the editor of the journal published replies by Empson, Richards, and Graves to his queries about their responses to Jensen's essay – the editor having neglected to consult Laura (Riding) Jackson (as she had since become known), believing that she was dead.[11] She was anything but. With his response to the editors, Graves put the cat amongst the pigeons and set up a second round of correspondence between Empson and Riding: "I was, I believe, responsible for most of the detailed examination of poems in *A Survey of Modernist Poetry* – for example showing the complex implications of Sonnet 129 before its eighteenth-century repunctuations."[12] When Empson read Jensen's essay and Graves's letter several years after they were published, he cited this material in his correspondence with Riding to justify once more his omission of her name from his original preface to the first edition of *Seven Types of Ambiguity*.

Empson wrote to Riding because Chatto and Windus, the publisher of *Seven Types of Ambiguity*, had asked him to take over their correspondence that year with Riding, who had just learned that there had been a revised edition of Empson's book, published in 1947, and that in the Preface to this revised edition Empson had omitted all reference to *A Survey of Modernist Poetry* and thereby retracted his belated acknowledgment via the erratum slip of the dual influence of Riding and Graves upon him: "I ought to say in passing," he writes in the Preface to the second edition, that "Mr. Robert Graves" "is, so far as I know, the inventor of the method of analysis I was using here."[13] Riding was determined that there be no further misattribution of the origin of the method to Graves, emphasizing in her letters to Chatto and Windus that she was "the actual originator of the technique": "The method, as anyone familiar with my work, my thinking, my laborings with other poets for this better attention to the requirements of linguistic responsibility, is of my formation."[14]

Perhaps still nursing wounded pride at the public revelation of his mistake that the erratum slip had marked, perhaps angered by demands for further acknowledgment, Empson tries to justify himself forty years after the fact by two new tactics. First, he attributes the main influence on *Seven Types of Ambiguity* to work by Graves that preceded the latter's collaboration with Riding. He identifies in Graves's *On English Poetry* (1922), which he describes as "mainly concerned" with a "Conflict theory of poetry," "the necessary background for a theory of poetical ambiguity," and he suggests that Graves had "reached it by 1926, with *Impenetrability, or the Proper Habit of English.*"[15] Citing passages from these early works, Empson explains in 1970 the logic of his introductory note in 1930, insofar as he is able to reconstruct it in retrospect: "these passages, I thought, though they were really very decisive looked a bit scrappy, and when I got round to reading *A Survey of Modernist Poetry* (1927) I felt that the treatment of the 'lust in action' sonnet would be the right thing to mention in my acknowledgment. It dealt with a complete poem, as I was by this time trying to do, and it had a cumulative weight and impressiveness. What I thought about the collaborator I do not remember, but I suppose these few pages, so very unlike the rest of the book, seemed to me such an evident further step by the mind of Robert Graves that no collaborator could disagree."[16]

Second, since Graves had recently "confessed" that the reading of the Shakespeare sonnet was his own, and not Riding's, Empson notes that, as it turns out, his original acknowledgment of just Graves's influence in the first edition of *Seven Types of Ambiguity* was actually quite accurate after all.[17] Certainly "The analysis uses the idea of ambiguity of syntax, which may need to be made plain by unusual punctuation; I used this in my book a good deal, and it seems quite possible that I derived it from the analysis of 'lust in action.' If you assure me that you invented it, and not Robert Graves, I grant that I may be in your debt so far; I don't remember any case of Robert Graves using ambiguity of syntax in his previous writing."[18] In the end, though, Empson concedes the possibility of Riding's influence on his awareness of the significance of ambiguity of syntax in 1930 only because he regards it as not worth fighting about, for he has now decided, it seems, that it is not an important ambiguity: "I did use quite a bit of 'ambiguity of syntax,' which I now think a very dubious thing, and perhaps one which cannot occur in the sharp form needed to express a conflict. Anyway it is always a temptation to the analyst, because it gives him a big extra chance of forcing in his own ideas against the surface intention of the poem."[19]

Finally, Riding and Empson ended their discussion of the question of her influence without resolving it. Riding certainly did not buy what she called Empson's "early-Graves alibi."[20] The correspondence eventuated by the *Modern Language Quarterly* article left Riding convinced that Graves was a "liar" and that Empson was "an improviser of fabrications."[21] Empson was nasty too, declaring it impossible that he should ever have been influenced by anything that Riding wrote since "none of your work ever seemed capable of retaining my eye on the page."[22]

•

When they were no longer collaborators and lovers, Riding and Graves each claimed the most celebrated parts of *A Survey of Modernist Poetry* – whether as the one who physically wrote the words, interpreted the literature, or theorized the critical method applied. And even if the analysis of Shakespeare's Sonnet 129 was written wholly or largely by Graves (and it is certainly consistent with, although considerably more sophisticated than, his interpretation of poetic ambiguities in his earlier works), there is still the question of how much of his analysis was directed by Riding's principles and ideas, if not actually dictated by her. Since Graves claims in 1966 responsibility "for most of the detailed examination of poems," but attributes to Riding responsibility for certain of "the general principles," the question of her influence upon Empson clearly remains unresolved.[23] Empson was certainly inspired as much by the theoretical principles that Riding and Graves enunciated as by the practical criticism of the Shakespeare sonnet that they offered.

Similarly, Empson's Pithian arrow about Riding's unreadability begs the question of just how much of the "word-by-word collaboration" in *A Survey of Modernist Poetry* was written by Riding, for even if Graves was entirely responsible for the section on Shakespeare, Empson was certainly also influenced by other sections of the book.[24]

Besides the analysis of the significance of ambiguity of syntax in Shakespeare's sonnet in *A Survey of Modernist Poetry*, for instance, there is a discussion of ambiguity of syntax in an analysis of the poetry of E.E. Cummings that was almost certainly written by Riding. So there are a number of other possible sources of Riding's influence that Empson does not consider, let alone acknowledge.

An important feature of the reading of Shakespeare's Sonnet 129 was the close study by Riding and Graves of changes made to the punctuation of the sonnet since 1609. Their attention to the history of punctuation in this sonnet is designed to suggest that it is the intolerable difficulty of reading Shakespeare "that provoked his editors to meddle with his texts as being too incomprehensible as they were written."[25] Their purpose in invoking Shakespeare's poetry in their discussion of modern poetry is to show that despite the fact that "understanding of … poetry … like Shakespeare's … is taken for granted," Shakespeare's poetry is actually more difficult to understand than that of an apparently difficult contemporary poet like E.E. Cummings.[26] In fact, although one would not know it from the correspondence between Empson and Riding, it is in this analysis of Cummings's work that our attention is first directed to the meaningfulness of ambiguity of syntax.

Riding and Graves do not use either the word "ambiguity" or the word "syntax" in their study of Shakespeare's sonnet, let alone the phrase "ambiguity of syntax." Yet their explanation of how "changes in punctuation do the most damage … to the meaning" of the poem certainly amounts to both an analysis and a defence of the poetic meaningfulness of what Empson calls "ambiguity of syntax," for it is precisely in the suppression of ambiguities in the syntax of the poem that they say editors have done the most to damage a reader's understanding of the poem.[27] They note that in the sonnet's first two lines, the replacement of the first comma with a semicolon ("Th' expence of Spirit in a waste of shame/Is lust in action, [;] and till action, lust") prevents a syntactical ambiguity: "In the second line a semicolon after the first *action* instead of a comma … cuts off the idea at *action* instead of keeping *in action* and *till action* together."[28] The semicolon, that is, prevents the reader's perceiving an instance of parallel construction that the 1609 version allows: "The expense of spirit in a waste of shame is lust in action and is lust till action." In lines six and seven ("and no sooner had [,] Past reason hated"), "particularly serious is the interpolation of a comma after *no sooner had*; for this confines the phrase to a special meaning, *i.e.* 'lust no sooner had is hated past reason,' whereas it also means 'lust no sooner had *past reason* is hated past reason.'"[29] Again, emendation prevents the reader from perceiving the ambiguous parallel construction in the 1609 version. Similarly, they note significant changes and restrictions of meaning for the adverb "well" in the last two lines of the sonnet ("All this the world well knows [;] yet none knows well,/To shun the heaven that leads men to this hell"). This line, "if unpunctuated except for the comma Shakespeare put at the end," is a general statement of a central theme, "that lust as lust *is* satisfiable but that satisfied lust is in conflict with itself": "The man in lust is torn between lust as he well-knows it with the world and lust in his personal experience, which crazes him to hope for more than lust from lust. The force of the second *well* is to deny the first *well*: no one really knows anything of lust except in personal experience, and only through personal experience can lust be known *well* rather than 'well-known.' But separate the second *well* from the first, as in the revised version, and the direct opposition between *world* and *none*, *well knows* and *knows well* is destroyed, as well as the whole point of the word-play between *well knows* and *knows well*; for by the removal of the comma after the second *well*, this is made merely an adverb to modify *To shun* in the following line – *well* here means merely *successfully* with *To shun*, not *well enough* with *knowes*."[30] In each case of interchangeable adjectival or adverbial modification, and in each case of ambiguous parallel construction, Riding and Graves find ambiguous syntax to be meaningful.

That is, the double readings that are possible in the 1609 version of the sonnet produce a pattern of distinctions which is significant precisely in terms of the doubleness it patterns: "All the distinctions in the poem between *lust in action* and lust *till action*, between lust *In pursuit* and lust *in possession* are made to show in the end that there are no real distinctions."[31] Depriving the poem of ambiguous parallel constructions deprives it of this theme that a lust is a lust is a lust. Similarly, the ambiguity as to which words certain adjectives and adverbs modify is systematically patterned, and meaningful in this patterning: "It must be kept in mind throughout that words qualifying the lust-business refer interchangeably to the taker (the man who lusts), the bait (the object of lust), and lust in the abstract." So "*Had* may mean the swallowing of the bait by the taker, or the catching of the taker by the bait, or 'lust had,' or 'had by lust.'"[32]

And so their argument that emendation to change punctuation removes meaning from the poem is indeed, as Empson notes, an observation about the significance of "ambiguity of syntax."

For anyone interested to affirm Riding's influence upon Empson, it is important to note that *A Survey of Modernist Poetry* does not confine discussion of the ambiguity of syntax to Shakespeare's sonnet. In fact, the analysis of Shakespeare is intended to demonstrate that the ambiguity of *his* syntax is even greater than the ambiguity of syntax already identified in Cummings's poem "Sunset." Well before their famous analysis of Shakespeare's sonnet, Riding and Graves demonstrate that one of the virtues of "Sunset" is that it is "able to stave off death by continually revealing, under examination, an unexpected reserve of new riddles" – the most interesting and fruitful source of which is its riddling syntax: "Did we not accept the poem as a non-grammatic construction and make sense of it nevertheless? Could we not show it to be potentially or even actually grammatic and make sense of it because it was grammatic? By reading *swarms* and *chants*, which we have probably been reading as nominative plural nouns, as third person singular verbs, and by reading *silver* and *gold* not as adjectives but as nouns?"[33] Here is where the analysis of ambiguous syntax that Empson once found so interesting in *A Survey of Modernist Poetry* actually begins.

This analysis is quite likely by Riding. Graves writes to T.S. Eliot several times in 1926 about the work that his new collaborator Laura Gottschalk (as Riding was then known) is contributing to the book that will become *A Survey of Modernist Poetry*. Apparently, she was responsible for the book's analysis of American poets: "She is far more in touch with the American side than I am."[34] Graves indicates that she has written an essay on "The H.D. Legend" ("it might do for a part of this prospective book devoted to 'Legends,' e.g. the other Imagists, Sandburg, D.H. Lawrence") and that she has written "on John Ransom and Marianne Moore; principally a preliminary essay on Regionalism as a critical clue in American poetry (i.e. a false clue)."[35] Such was the division of labour that Riding treats even the American poets that Graves does know well: she writes on Ransom, though, by this point, Ransom has published Graves, corresponded with Graves, and even introduced Graves to Riding, and though, at this time, Graves has just passed along a manuscript of Ransom's poems first to Eliot and then to the Woolfs, thereby arranging for Ransom's first publication in Britain.

It is important to note that ambiguity of syntax is presented in both *A Survey of Modernist Poetry* and *Seven Types of Ambiguity* not only as a feature of literary language, but also as a feature of the language of the very best literature. For example, Riding and Graves note that "Shakespeare's punctuation allows the variety of meanings he actually intends; if we must choose any one meaning, then we owe it to Shakespeare to choose at least one he intended and one embracing as many meanings as possible, that is, the most difficult meaning"; they would make the same point about E.E. Cummings in particular and modernist poets in general: "It is always the most difficult meaning that is most final."[36] Analysis of ambiguity of syntax in both the poem by Shakespeare and the poem by Cummings is offered in support of this principle, which will become a fundamental axiom of both Empson's method in particular and the method of New Criticism in general.

In the conclusion to Chapter Two of *Seven Types of Ambiguity* Empson states: "I shall now return to Shakespeare and allow myself a couple of digressions; about the emendations of his text and his use of a particular grammatical form."[37] His survey of the history of emendations to Shakespeare's texts suggests to him that a "conservative attitude to ambiguity" is operative: "it is assumed ... that Shakespeare can only have meant one thing."[38] His phrasing follows that of Riding and Graves here. He follows them further in disavowing the practice of restricting meanings to special interpretations of special words – reversing it, in fact, so as to embrace as many meanings as possible – possibility in each case being determined by plausibility.

When reading Shakespeare for ambiguity, Empson seems to be converting the either/or strategy of "three centuries of scholars and critics" into the both/and strategy of poststructural theorists (he confesses that he has often behaved like the Arden editor: "I have myself usually said 'either ... or' when meaning 'both ... and'"[39]) but he presents his method as a way of recovering what Shakespeare might have meant and what his original audiences might have thought he meant, thereby affirming an intentionality and a referentiality that are anathema to poststructuralism. The Arden editor, he notes, negates a whole host of associations for the word "rooky" in *Macbeth* before declaring the meaning he believes that Shakespeare intended: "This somewhat obscure epithet, however spelt (and it should be spelt *rouky*), does NOT mean 'murky' or 'dusky' ...; NOR 'damp,' 'misty,' 'steamy with exhalations' ...; NOR 'misty,' 'gloomy' ...; NOR 'where its fellows are already assembled' ..., and has NOTHING to do with the dialect word 'roke' meaning 'mist,' 'steam,' etc ... the meaning here ... I THINK, is simply 'rouking' or perching wood, *i.e.*, where the rook (or crow) perches for the night."[40] Embracing all of these meanings as plausible – "these meanings ... might, for all we know ... have seemed plausible to anybody in the first-night audience; might have seemed plausible to Shakespeare himself, since he was no less sensitive to words than they" – Empson argues that "such a note ... makes you bear in mind all the meanings it puts forward" and that "this is the normal experience of readers" of Shakespeare.[41] And so "the reader must hold in mind a variety of things he may have meant, and weight them, in appreciating the poetry, according to their probabilities."[42]

Similarly, fearing that his analysis of ambiguity in two lines from *Macbeth* ("Come what may,/Time, and the Houre, runs through the roughest day") "seems too elaborate," he adds a footnote in 1947 to the second edition of his book, defending himself in terms that again recall Riding and Graves: "I cannot see what else (what less) the line means if it is taken seriously as meaning anything."[43] He has accepted the axiom of Riding and Graves that "if we must choose any one meaning, then we owe it to Shakespeare to choose at least one he intended and one embracing as many meanings as possible."[44] Otherwise, one risks stopping at "less" than he means.

Empson argues that it is simply not the case "that a great deal has been added to Shakespeare by the mere concentration upon him of wrong-headed literary attention."[45] The ambiguity revealed by scholarship and criticism is a function not of our interpretive blindness or wilful perversity, but of the text itself: "Here as in recent atomic physics there is a shift in progress, which tends to attach the notion of a probability to the natural object rather than to the fallibility of the human mind."[46] So Empson's conclusion about the history of Shakespearean emendation is precisely the same as that of Riding and Graves: Shakespeare's "original meaning was of a complexity to which we must now work our way back."[47]

•

This principle that one owes it to the poet to perceive as much meaning as possible in a poem, of course, has practical implications, which Riding and Graves work out for Empson. In fact, his recommendation that one bear in mind, as one reads along, all that words and phrases and lines might mean is a development of the practical approach to reading that Riding and Graves recommend. In the hands of New Critics, this kind of attention to the manifold of meanings presented in a poem will come to be known as close reading.

For "getting out of the prose and into the poetic state of mind," Riding and Graves suggest "developing a capacity for minuteness, for seeing all there is to see at a given point and for taking it all with one as one goes along."[48] Empson locates in Shakespeare a regular syntactical strategy for stimulating precisely this poetic state of mind: "a linguistic form common in Shakespeare's verse, and typical of his method; 'the (noun) and (noun) of (noun)'; in which two, often apparently quite different, words are flung together, followed by a word which seems to be intended to qualify both of them"; since "this form demands that the reader should find a highest common factor of its first two nouns, it implies that he must open his mind to all their associations, so that the common factor may be as high as possible. That is, it is a powerful means of forcing him to adopt a poetical attitude to words."[49]

Riding and Graves's definition of "the poetic state of mind" as a capacity for minute attention to all that words can mean clearly anticipates Empson's definition of the "poetical attitude to words." Empson finds this poetic state of mind described not in their analysis of Shakespeare's sonnet, however, but rather in their analysis of a poem called "The Rugged Black of Anger," which they present without identifying its author. It is, of course, a poem by Riding. Ironically, then, Empson is influenced by a section of *A Survey of Modernist Poetry* that requires him not only to read Riding, but also to read what seems to be Riding's own analysis of her poem, which concludes the book's central chapters on the American poets Marianne Moore, H.D., and E.E. Cummings (American poets having been identified by Graves as Riding's bailiwick).[50] Although he might not have recognized this as Riding's poem and would later tell her that "none of your work has ever seemed to me capable of retaining my eye on the page," Empson seems to have read her so closely as to have accepted that the best way to read all poetry is the way Riding recommends as the best way to read hers!

On the one hand, Empson echoes her in his explanation of why modernist poetry is characterized by ambiguity of the fifth type: "it is in modern poetry, where the range of ideas is great and the difficulty of holding the right ones in the mind becomes acute, that we discover examples of the most advanced numbers of this series."[51] On the other hand, he takes the Riding-focused description of the proper relationship between modernist poem and plain reader and pretends to locate an actual historical model for this relationship in the relationship between Shakespeare and Elizabethan readers. In response to the literary critic's complaint that Riding's poetry suffers from "so-called obscurity," Riding and Graves recommend "increasing the time-length of reading."[52] "The Rugged Black of Anger," a poem whose "'obscurity' ... would probably cause it to be put aside by the critic after he had allowed it the customary two-minute reading (for if the poet has obeyed all the rules, this is long enough to give a rough idea of what the poem is all about – and that is all that is generally wanted),"[53] is the poem they read slowly, repeating lines, inverting lines, making up transitional lines from the poem's own words and phrases until, "as a sufficient illustration of the method of letting the poem interpret itself," "the poem interpreted is practically itself repeated to three times its own length."[54] The time invested in reading is the key to better reading: "The important thing that would be revealed by a wide application of this method to the reading of poems ... would be that much of the so-called obscurity of poems was created by the laziness of the plain reader, who wishes to hurry through poetry as quickly as he does through prose, not realizing that he is dealing with a kind of thought which, though it may have the speed of prose to the poet, he must follow with a slowness proportionate to how much he is not a poet."[55] And so "increasing the time-length of reading is one way of getting out of the prose and into the poetic state of mind, of developing a capacity for minuteness, for seeing all there is to see at a given point and for taking it all with one as one goes along."[56]

According to Empson, Shakespeare could count on just such slow reading:

> One must consider ... that the Elizabethans did not mind about spelling and punctuation; that this must have given them an attitude to the printed page entirely different from ours (so that readers must continually have been left to grope for the right word); that from the comparative slowness, of reading as of speaking, that this entailed, he was prepared to assimilate words with a completeness which is now lost; that it is only our snobbish

> oddity of spelling [that] imposes on us the notion that one mechanical word, to be snapped up by the eye, must have been intended; and that it is Shakespeare's normal method to use a newish, apparently irrelevant word, which spreads the attention thus attracted over a wide map of the ways in which it may be justified.[57]

Similarly, by a "form of ambiguity ... prominent in early Elizabethan writings," "Herbert and the devotional poets" require slow reading: they "use a conceit to diffuse the interest back on to a whole body of experience, whose parts are supposed eventually reconcilable with one another; and the reader must pause after each display of wit to allow the various moods in which it could be read, the various situations to which it could refer, to sink into his mind."[58]

So Empson cannot deny Riding's influence by claiming that the only influence that *A Survey of Modernist Poetry* exerted on him was by means of its initially exciting but apparently wrong-headed attention to ambiguity of syntax in Shakespeare's sonnet, for the book's influence on him was not confined to this single discussion. Empson confesses that he wrote Chapter Two of *Seven Types of Ambiguity* with a certain "excitement" and acknowledges that he was tempted to claim that "this chapter ... casts a new light on the very nature of language, and must either be all nonsense or very startling and new." The principles he discovered in the work of Riding and Graves constituted both a motivating force for beginning his book and an informing presence throughout it, allowing him to convert the critical tradition of editorial either/or into readerly and writerly both/and.[59] "Most of what I find to say about Shakespeare has been copied out of the Arden text," says Empson.[60] Be that as it may, it is also the case that very much of what he has to say not just about Shakespeare, but also about the nature of language, the nature of writing, and the nature of reading has been copied out of Riding and Graves.

•

As Haffenden notes, although "the influence of the 'Graves-Riding' exegesis of Sonnet 129 is everywhere apparent in *Seven Types of Ambiguity*," it is "perhaps nowhere more so than in the discussion of the second type."[61] Haffenden argues that Chapter Two of *Seven*

Types of Ambiguity, about ambiguities of the second type, represents the earliest part of the book to be written:

> it seems likely that in the Michaelmas Term of 1928, when Richards told him to go ahead with his task of gathering together his happy "heap" of ambiguities, Empson first looked at the way in which alternative meanings often manage to become reconciled ... Not only is Chapter 2 the longest in *Ambiguity*, it includes an example that is little different from the first piece he ever printed on the subject, "Ambiguity in Shakespeare: Sonnet XVI" (*Experiment*, February 1929) – which is obviously modelled on the Graves-Riding analysis of Sonnet 129 ... Likewise, the second chapter of *Ambiguity* incorporates another trial piece that came out in 1929, "Some Notes on Mr Eliot," an analysis of the double meanings created by the confusion of past participles and active verbs in passages from *The Waste Land* and "Whispers of Immortality." Since the only other extract Empson printed in advance of the book was a version of the climactic discussion of Herbert's "The Sacrifice," it is reasonable to deduce that he started out by looking at the very extremes of ambiguity – that is, type 2, which manifests reconciliation, and type 7, sheer conflict.[62]

I find Haffenden's argument here persuasive.

Also suggesting that Chapter Two is the earliest part of the book to have been written is the impression that "the excitement with which it was written" seems less appropriate to the particular type of ambiguity discussed (it is "more common than any of the later types") than to the sense of discovery with which Empson set out on his project – the sense of discovery, in fact, with which he arrived in Richards's office.[63] His feeling then (recall that when demonstrating to Richards the way Riding and Graves had dealt with the multiple meanings in Sonnet 129, he declared, "You could do that with any poetry, couldn't you?") seems to be continuous with the feeling of excitement that he confesses in Chapter Two: he has begun to suspect that the method inspired (as he thought) by Graves "casts a new light on the very nature of language"! Similarly, as Haffenden notes of Empson's February 1929 essay, "Ambiguity in Shakespeare," it "opens so briskly that it seems less a poised introduction than an impatient declaration of intent: 'This is taken out of an essay on the *Seven Types of Ambiguity*. It is an example of the second type: "two or more meanings which all combine to a single mood and intention of the writer.'"[64] The state of excitement that Empson mentions in Chapter Two and that he shows in his first published work of literary criticism at the beginning of 1929, that is, matches Richards's description of a student writing obsessively for two weeks after their discussion of the work of Riding and Graves in the fall of 1928 and then returning with "a thick wad of very illegible typescript under his arm – the central 30,000 words or so of the book."[65]

More directly focussed on the ambiguity of syntax than any other chapter in *Seven Types of Ambiguity*, Chapter Two is implicitly the site of the influence by *A Survey of Modernist Poetry* that Empson concedes in his 1970 letter to Laura Riding. Chapter Two is the one most focussed on Shakespeare, devoting most of the first twelve pages to his sonnets and the last twenty-eight pages to his plays (with twenty-eight pages in between of analysis of type two ambiguities in Chaucer, certain eighteenth-century poets, and T.S. Eliot), deploying across these readings of Shakespeare's poetry and plays as a whole the particular strategies deployed by Riding and Graves in their treatment of Sonnet 129. We find in Chapter Two, it seems, the first work produced by a student who has convinced himself that Graves was on to something perhaps bigger than he knew ("Taking the sonnet as a conjuror takes his hat, he produced an endless swarm of lively rabbits from it, and ended by 'You could do that with any poetry, couldn't you?'") and who has sufficiently persuaded his supervisor of this possibility as to have been sent off to test his hypothesis ("You'd better go off and do it, hadn't you?"). Empson is excited because he can see that the method he is developing "casts a new light on the very nature of language."

Empson obviously has Riding and Graves in mind from the beginning of Chapter Two, taking up from where they leave off by extending their reading strategy regarding Sonnet 129 both to other of Shakespeare's sonnets (more than twelve of them) and to his plays. He explains that in Shakespeare's sonnets "ambiguity, not of word, but of grammar ... is mainly used ... to give an interpenetrating and, as it were, fluid unity, in which phrases will go either with the sentence before or after and there is no break in the movement of the thought."[66] In fact, he suggests, "In managing a Sonnet, so as to give it at once variety of argumentation and the close-knit rhythmical unity of a single thought, these devices are more important than they appear."[67]

The analysis of Sonnet 129 by Riding and Graves is seldom far from Empson's thoughts as he writes about the sonnets in general, as one can see by the observation that follows immediately after the sentences above: Empson notes in Sonnet 32 what Riding and Graves note throughout Sonnet 129: "one of those important and frequent subtleties of punctuation, which in general only convey rhythm, but here … amounts to a point of grammar."[68] A few pages later, while carefully unfolding the "variety of meaning … rooted" in the ambiguities of syntax in Sonnet 16, he makes the same complaint against emendating editors as Riding and Graves: "Punctuations designed to simplify the passage all spoil the antithesis."[69]

Chapter Two thus shows how Empson went about working out a general methodology from the particular moves that Riding and Graves make in *A Survey of Modernist Poetry*. For instance, Empson's observation about Shakespeare's "use of a particular grammatical form" is inspired by Riding and Graves, for what Empson says about "the way Shakespeare uses a combination of 'and' and 'of'" is suggested by what Riding and Graves reveal about the occlusion of the syntactical ambiguity of "and" by eighteenth-century emendation of the first two lines of Sonnet 129.[70] Their complaint that in the second line of the sonnet, the emendator's placement of "a semicolon after the first *action* instead of a comma … cuts off the idea at *action* instead of keeping *in action* and *till action* together" is their first example of the general problem they highlight: "The effect of this revised punctuation has been to restrict meanings to special interpretations of special words."[71] Here, that is, the meaning of "and" has been restricted to its meaning "but" or "so that," whereas in what they call the 1609 version it also has its much vaguer function of simply connecting two clauses (to speak in terms of grammar) or two ideas (to speak in terms of theme) that are to be taken together. Combined with their observation that placement of "a semicolon after the first *action* instead of a comma gives a longer rest than Shakespeare gave," this point about the value of "and" in Sonnet 129 looks very much to be the basis of Empson's point about the value of "and" in Shakespeare's work generally: "In so far as it is valuable for a poet to include several rhythms, grammatical forms, or shades of meaning in a single phrase, those linguistic forms are likely to be most convenient which insist on no definite form of connection between words and allow you simply to pass on from one to the other. Thus the word 'and' will be convenient if you are bringing forward two elements of a situation, conceived as of the same logical type."[72] Just as their treatment of one of Shakespeare's sonnets allowed Empson to see how they might all be treated, so the ambiguity of "and" that Riding and Graves recover here alerts Empson to the systematic ambiguity of Shakespeare's "ands" elsewhere.

Riding and Graves even point to the fruitful ambiguity of "of" in the first line, noting "the double meaning of *of shame* as 'shameful,' *i.e.* 'deplorable,' and as *ashamed*, *i.e.* 'self-deploring.'"[73] Whereas "the word 'and' will be convenient if you are bringing forward two elements of a situation, conceived as of the same logical type," according to Empson, "the word 'of' will be convenient if the two elements are related to the situation differently, and stand in some asymmetrical relation to one another."[74] His example from *King Lear* ("The untented woundings of a father's curse") demonstrates the same sort of ambiguity in this double genitive: "The *wounds* may be cause or effect of the *curse* uttered by a *father*; independently of this, they may reside in the *father* or his child. The curse, indeed, might be uttered *against* the father by the child ... All the meanings arrived at by permuting these versions make up one single-minded *curse*."[75] As with the single-mindedness of the many permutations of Shakespeare's wounding curses, as spied out by Empson, so with "the double meaning of *of shame*" and "the double meaning of *shame* itself as 'modesty' and 'disgrace'" spied out by Riding and Graves: "All these alternate meanings acting on each other, and even other possible interpretations, make as it were a furiously dynamic cross-word puzzle which can be read in many directions at once, none of the senses being incompatible with any others."[76]

Of course Riding and Graves demonstrate far more than alertness to "ambiguity of syntax" in their reading of sonnet 129. Having dealt with the changes in meaning produced by changes in punctuation, they take up the interpretation of the sonnet once more, this time concentrating on "a few points ... left uncovered in our typographical survey of the poem ... principally in the first few lines; for these suffer less from emendations than the rest of the poem."[77] They emphasize the double meanings of words themselves, apart from ambiguities of syntax:

> The very delicate interrelation of the words of the first two lines should not be overlooked ... the double meaning of *waste* as "expense" and as "wilderness," the *waste* place in which the Spirit

> is *wasted*; the double meaning of *expense* as "pouring out" and as the "price paid"; the double meaning of *of shame* as "shameful," *i.e.* "deplorable," and as *ashamed*, *i.e.* "self-deploring"; the double meaning of *shame* itself as "modesty" and "disgrace"; again the double meaning of *lust in action* as "lust" unsuspected by man "in his actions" because disguised as "shame" (in either sense of the word) and condemned by him because he does not recognize it in himself, and as "lust in progress" as opposed to "lust contemplated."[78]

So much significance attends these ambiguities that the first line alone hints at much of what is to follow, "the strong parallelism between *expense* and *waste* and *Spirit* and *shame* expressing in the very first line the terrible quick-change from lust as lust-enjoyed to lust as lust-despised."[79] Riding and Graves, that is, find through their close reading of all the meanings implied by the words of the poem that the ambiguities form a complex whole – the meaningfulness of the ambiguities in the first line suffusing the whole, and the meaningfulness of the ambiguities of the poem as a whole infusing the first line.

Although the complex, systematic whole of multiple meanings that comes of what Riding and Graves describe as "this intensified inbreeding of words," "all these alternate meanings acting on each other," "none of the senses being incompatible with any others," will be examined and explained by Empson as what he calls "the second type of ambiguity" in which "in word or syntax" "two or more meanings all add to the single meaning of the author," it is not the case that Empson was first alerted to the poetic meaningfulness of words with such double meanings by *A Survey of Modernist Poetry.*[80] I will show in the chapters that follow that Empson owes this awareness to his reading of Graves's earlier works.

Yet when Empson explains that the multiple "meanings to be extracted" from a poem may emerge from the multiple meanings of constituent words, as in the case of the various meanings of "change" and "earth" in the verse, "Cupid is winged and doth range;/Her country so my love doth change./But change she earth, or change she sky,/Yet I will love her till I die," he spells things out just as Riding and Graves do in *A Survey of Modernist Poetry*:

> I will love her though she moves from this part of the earth to one out of my reach; I will love her though she goes to live under

> different skies; I will love her though she moves from this earth and sky to another planet; I will love her though she moves into a social or intellectual sphere where I cannot follow; I will love her though she alters the earth and sky I have got now, though she destroys the bubble of worship in which I am now living by showing herself unworthy to be its object; I will love her though, being yet worthy of it, by going away she changes my earth into desire and unrest, and my heaven into despair … she may change *my* earth by killing me, but till it comes I will go on loving.[81]

A perfectly suitable, economical way of meeting the demands of an argument that must show that various meanings of a sentence or phrase are both possible and plausible (paraphrase by direct discourse generally requires far fewer words than paraphrase by indirect discourse), such a style of explication is by no means the only one that Empson might have used, yet it is the one that he uses to the virtual exclusion of any other, and one that Riding and Graves modelled for him.

They deploy this strategy in explaining the effects of ambiguous words on interpretation of line twelve of Sonnet 129 ("Before a joy proposed behind a dream"). Although they identify "the final meaning of the line" – "Even when consummated, lust still stands before an unconsummated joy, a proposed joy, and proposed not as a joy possible of consummation but one only to be desired through the dream by which lust leads itself on, the dream behind which this proposed joy, this love, seems to lie" – they emphasize that the line "is inlaid with other meanings" that can be extracted from the various meanings of virtually every word in it. Riding and Graves go on to paraphrase successively within quotation marks each possible reading of such a line in just the way that Empson will: "For example the line may also be read: 'Before a joy (lust) can be proposed, there must be a dream behind, a joy lost by waking' ('So that I wake and cry to dream again'); or: 'Before a joy can be proposed, it must first be renounced as a joy, it must be put behind as a dream; you know in the pursuit that possession is impossible'; or: 'Before the man in lust is a prospect of joy, yet he knows by experience that this is only a dream'; or: 'Beforehand he says that he definitely proposed lust to be a joy, afterwards he says that it came as a dream'; or: 'Before (in face of) a joy proposed only as a consequence of a dream, with the dream pushing him from behind.'"[82] According to Riding and Graves, "all these and even more readings of the line are possible and legitimate"; the same point that Empson will make at chapter's end about the readings of "rooky" as surveyed by the editor of the Arden Shakespeare.[83]

And just as there are aspects of *A Survey of Modernist Poetry* other than its analysis of ambiguity of syntax that influence Empson, so its influence extends well beyond Chapter Two. Just as concerning "ambiguity, not of word, but of grammar," Empson suggests in the second chapter that "where there is a single main meaning" the device of ambiguity "is mainly used, as in the following examples from Shakespeare's Sonnets, to give an interpenetrating and as it were, fluid unity, in which phrases will go either with the sentence before or after and there is no break in the movement of the thought," so also he observes the same Janus-like functioning of phrases in Chapter Four concerning ambiguity of the fourth type in Shakespeare's Sonnet 83: "Line 2 ... goes both with line 1 and line 3," and "the first line may also stand alone, as an introduction ... so that line 2 goes with line 3; for this version one would put a comma after *therefore*."[84]

The complaint that Riding and Graves make about emendation of sonnet 129 is that it has destroyed this unity by breaking up the continuity of ideas: "In the second line a semicolon after the first *action* instead of a comma ... cuts off the idea at *action* ... A comma after *blouddy* separates it from *full* with which it really forms a single word ... Next come several semicolons for commas; these introduce pauses which break up the continuous flow of ideas treading on one another's heels."[85] Just as their phrase "continuous flow of ideas" anticipates Empson's "no break in the movement of thought," so they emphasize – as Empson soon will – the way that, but for emendation, phrases in the sonnet can go either with one idea or another: between lines seven and eight ("Past reason hated as a swallowed bayt,/On purpose layd to make the taker mad"), "a comma is omitted where Shakespeare actually put one, after *bayt*. With the comma, *On purpose layd* – though it refers to *bayt* – also takes us back to the original idea of *lust*; without the comma it merely carries out the figure of *bayt*."[86] Their analysis of other lines highlights again and again the way emendation has robbed the sonnet of similarly meaningful syntactical ambiguities.

•

As is clear from Chapter Two of *Seven Types of Ambiguity*, Empson found in the readings of Sonnet 129 in *A Survey of Modernist Poetry* not "nonsense," but something "very startling and new."[87] Empson was wrong to remove from the second edition of *Seven Types of Ambiguity* his original acknowledgment of the importance for his own work of this reading of Shakespeare's sonnet, and it is unfortunate that he left no reference at all to *A Survey of Modernist Poetry* in his new 1947 Preface. Yet for all the obviousness of the influence of *A Survey of Modernist Poetry* upon *Seven Types of Ambiguity*, and for all the controversy as to whose influence is thereby exerted most upon Empson, *A Survey of Modernist Poetry* is certainly not the book that Empson ought to have acknowledged as either the first, or the main, or the most important source of the method that he developed. And despite his lack of generosity in withholding acknowledgment of the influence of Riding upon him, Empson is not wrong in refusing to award her pride of place.

However much his thesis supervisor I.A. Richards might have determined in his own work to bury the influence of Graves because it represented "current modes of analysis" fraught with "the gravest dangers," Empson was clearly determined in both the first and second editions of *Seven Types of Ambiguity* to praise it.[88] As we shall see, the person that Empson originally sought to credit for the invention of the method that he developed in *Seven Types of Ambiguity* not only deserves such credit as Empson offered, but a good deal more. It turns out that Empson's "early-Graves alibi" is a good one.

2

A Question of Conflict

Empson was correct in foregrounding the importance of Graves's influence upon him and accurate in belatedly acknowledging that this influence began not with *A Survey of Modernist Poetry* (1927) but rather with Graves's earlier books: *On English Poetry* (1922), *The Meaning of Dreams* (1924), *Poetic Unreason* (1925), and *Impenetrability, or The Proper Habit of English* (1926). Graves's claim to have suffered scant acknowledgment by Empson – had he ever been moved to make it – is much greater than Riding's. Of course, before his assertion to the editor of the *Modern Language Quarterly* in 1966 that he was the author of the analysis of Sonnet 129 in *A Survey of Modernist Poetry*, Graves never sought the credit for having inspired Empson and the New Criticism that Riding sought. Indeed, he held Empson in disdain: "Empson is as clever as a monkey & I do not like monkeys."[1]

Haffenden unfortunately muddies matters somewhat when he points to a book review by Empson published in *The Granta* in May of 1928 as evidence that Empson had read *A Survey of Modernist Poetry* by then. Of George Rylands's *Words and Poetry* (1928), Empson observes: "'The Robert Graves' school of criticism is only impressive when the analysis it employs becomes so elaborate as to score a rhetorical triumph; when each word in the line is given four or five meanings, four or five reasons for sounding right and suggesting the right things. Dazzled by the difficulty of holding it all in your mind at once, you feel this at any rate is complicated enough, as many factors as these could make up a result apparently magical and incalculable."[2] According to Haffenden, Empson "was evidently referring to *A Survey of Modernist Poetry*, by Riding and Graves, because in none of his previous works had Graves orchestrated quite such an elaborate analysis as of the Shakespeare sonnet in that volume."[3] It may well be that Empson had read *A Survey of Modernist Poetry* by the time he wrote this review, but Haffenden's argument that the review constitutes evidence for thinking so is by no means persuasive.

When he speaks of Graves's rhetorical triumph in the reading of this or that "line," Empson may be referring not necessarily to the reading of whole poems in *A Survey of Modernist Poetry* but rather to any number of books in which Graves reads the multiple meanings of the words in famous *lines* of poetry. He might be referring to Graves's reading of multiple meanings in the line in Keats's "Eve of St Agnes" in which "Madeleine is described in 'her soft and chilly nest,' 'Clasped like a missal when swart Paynims pray,' where 'clasped' means 'fastened with a clasp of holiness' or 'held lovingly in the hands,' if the Paynims are held to be converted; but also, without prejudice, 'shut and coldly neglected,' if the Paynims are held to be unconverted."[4] Or he might be referring to Graves's explanation of the title of a book that impressed Empson very much, *Impenetrability, or The Proper Habit of English*: "The word 'habit' that heads this paper is serving three senses. It refers to the habilments or dress of English, that is the actual word-forms; to the general behaviour or carriage of the language; and to the habitual processes of thought which govern it. 'Proper,' the adjective qualifying 'habit,' has also three senses. It means 'fitting,' it means 'peculiar,' it means 'distinguished.' It has even a fourth meaning, for all who know the language of heraldry, and that is 'blazoned in more than a single colour.'"[5] Or he might be referring to the *tour de force* reading in *Poetic Unreason* of "How Many Miles to Babylon?" in which Graves reveals just "within the limits of the Christian group to which the associations of Babylon, candlelight, and threescore and ten are common" an "extraordinarily subtle and condensed argument" functioning by an "interaction" of these words' various meanings – words interacting "too closely for coincidence," the effect of which is the presentation "of a number of linked ideas reconciled in a common symbolism."[6] Furthermore, the word "dazzled" in the book review suggests a reading in *On English Poetry* that Empson recalled for Riding in 1970 as an impressive early example of Graves's method: "take Webster's most famous line in his Duchess of Malfi: 'Cover her face; mine eyes dazzle; she died young' spoken by Ferdinand over the Duchess' body; and that word 'dazzle' does duty for two emotions at once, sun-dazzled awe at loveliness, tear-dazzled grief for early death."[7]

So it is quite possible, in fact, that Empson had not read *A Survey of Modernist Poetry* by the time he wrote this review. His reference in the review to "'The Robert Graves' school of criticism" would then substantiate his claim to Riding in 1970 that he had indeed recognized a method of criticism in Graves's early work before he read *A Survey of Modernist Poetry*, would show that he recognized the same method beginning to be picked up by others such as Rylands, and would suggest that even before he read *A Survey of Modernist Poetry* he was indeed predisposed to regard the book by Riding and Graves as another product of the Robert Graves school of criticism, regardless of the fact of its co-authorship. From this point of view, the review in question would corroborate the "early-Graves alibi" that Riding dismissed as disingenuous and incredible.

Empson's problem of finding "the right thing to mention" in acknowledgment of Graves's influence is not one that it is easy to understand or sympathize with today. Even were *Seven Types of Ambiguity* to have been written a little bit later in twentieth century, the scholarly standards that have since come to prevail in the professional criticism of English literature (which was still a relatively new academic discipline in the 1920s) would have led Empson to invoke Graves by name at several points in the book, and to refer to his works by title and page number.

As things stand, Empson refers to very few contemporary critics and theorists, and refers to even fewer of their works by title: Herbert Read's *English Prose Style*, Freud's *Notebooks*, and Richards's *Practical Criticism*. He acknowledges an interpretation of Hopkins's "The Windhover" by Richards, but does not mention the article that contains it or the journal that published it, and he mentions Richards's discussion of poems in terms of Sense, Feeling, Tone, and Intention, but does not identify the book in which Richards makes these distinctions (*Principles of Literary Criticism*). And without explaining where, Empson notes that Shelley's "Skylark" "has received much discussion lately," confessing "I am afraid more points were brought out than I remembered" before implying that it was T.S. Eliot who started the discussion and that it is Eliot's opinion that needs to be corrected.[8] Similarly, he elsewhere vaguely refers to what "Mr. Eliot somewhere says" about bad critics.[9] Here are confessions of a lack of scholarly interest in the citing of sources that would be regarded by scholars and critics today as rather cavalier.

When he revises *Seven Types of Ambiguity* for the second edition in 1947, however, Empson chides himself in a footnote for not having acknowledged even so indirect an influence as G.K. Chesterton's ("I ought to have acknowledged how much I was using … incidental remarks" of Chesterton's that showed his "great powers as a verbal critic").[10] Between the first and second editions of the book, that is, scholarly standards were changing from the belle-lettristic norms at the beginning of the century to norms closer to those we are familiar with today.

Oddly, then, at the very point when he ought to have made his acknowledgment of his debts to Riding and Graves fuller and more precise, Empson not only compounds the problem by omitting any reference to *A Survey of Modernist Poetry* but also makes for a new problem in his fumbled acknowledgment of Graves. Although he notes, "I ought to say in passing that he is, so far as I know, the inventor of the method of analysis I was using here," this acknowledgment is both less prominent and more vague than the original introductory note.[11] It is reduced to parenthetical status, as Empson now cites Graves in support of a different point altogether, and a relatively minor one at that: that "the judgment of the author may be wrong" in regard to his own work.[12]

Although he does not cite it by title, Empson quotes from a passage in *Poetic Unreason* in which Graves accounts for the fluctuating appeal of a poem in terms of the relevance at any particular time of the poem's statement or solution of some sort of human conflict. According to Graves, "We do not and cannot value in a poem a statement of conflict, or a temporary relief, or a final solution which is too far in the future or too far in the past to be real to us."[13] The appeal of the poets of a certain period is explicable in these terms: "Each generation gives a sort of solution to the more deep-seated problems of life, a solution which appears at the time to be as complete and incontrovertible as it is inevitable … The most venerated poet of any period will be the one who embodies in his works the problems and conclusions of the most advanced system of contemporary philosophy accepted by the intellectual aristocracy."[14] Yet "always the appearance of a hitherto unconsidered aspect of reality stultifies" a generation's solutions to its conflicts, and the moment that "a new system of philosophy" discredits the old one, the venerated poets of the old system will find that "their conflicts will be appreciated in outline, but their solutions will no longer be regarded as adequate" – unless here and there a venerated past poet somehow contrives to anticipate the future.[15] It is the passage from the middle of this account that Empson recalls:

> From the reader's point of view it is of course true that in any given age certain poems are of wider appeal than others and therefore by majority rule the best, and that others represent a view which is of extremely limited acceptance but which is one stage advanced in the succession of events from this popular poetry, and being destined to the votes of the majority in the next generation may be "best" in this sense, that it is more progressive ... If a strange poem occurs which everyone, including the poet himself, after mature consideration agrees to damn as being completely banal, meaningless, unrhythmic, immoral, untrue and designed with the most inexcusable motives, it is always possible that this poem if it survives will appear to future historians as a remarkable piece of art, embodying an aspect of reality by neglecting which the age imposed on itself what they may regard as a number of avoidable ills – "the best poem that the age produced," they will write enthusiastically.[16]

Writing his Preface to the second edition of *Seven Types of Ambiguity* in 1947, Empson forgets titles and he forgets collaborators – and in this instance he forgets to quote the subordinate conjunction "that" – but he does not forget observations, arguments, or methods, whether these be grounded in Graves's version of literary history, his psychoanalytical literary theory, or his practical criticism of particular writers and texts.

•

One consequence of his correspondence with Riding in the 1970s was to prompt Empson to recall Graves's prominent role as a literary theorist in the early 1920s. Explaining to Riding that the lack of an erratum slip in copies of *Seven Types of Ambiguity* sold in the United States was of no real consequence because only eight copies of the book were sold there, Empson suggested to her that sales in Britain had been better because Graves's theorizing had prepared readers for a theory of ambiguity: "I am sorry to hear that the

American edition did not carry it, but I think I can explain that. When they sent a statement after the first year only eight people had bought the book; I offered to send each of them a Christmas card but they could not be traced. I was told that most of the edition was not merely remaindered but pulped ... The American public just would not stand the idea, whereas the English reviews were quite lively and there was a small but steady sale till the edition sold out; I suppose the difference arose because the books of Robert Graves had already made the idea familiar in England."[17]

Writing to others at the same time, Empson alluded to the research into Graves's early influence upon him that his correspondence with Riding had prompted, and he explained it more fully to them than he did to her.

> Of course, you know everybody was talking about Freud and things like that. I might have got it from many other people who are now forgotten as well as Graves. But I bet I had read more of Graves than I remember now and I was certainly keen on this stuff and wanted to imitate it. I really don't remember now at all clearly but there's no doubt I was picking it up. But it didn't seem, you know, very out of the way – the idea that you wanted to use Freudian theory on literary criticism somehow was the thing that Graves picked up a generation before me. We all had it knocking about. But I certainly did read Graves. I'm just having to think about that – I mean having to get out some of the books and consider what I remember having read at the time. I had read quite a bit.[18]

Indeed, Graves's influence informs Empson's theory and practice from beginning to end of *Seven Types of Ambiguity*. In Chapter Three, for instance, Empson notes that: "There is a variety of the 'conflict' theory of poetry which says that a poet must always be concerned with some difference of opinion or habit between different parts of his community; different social classes, ways of life, or modes of thought; that he must be several sorts of men at once, and reconcile his tribe in his own person."[19] Empson puts the word *conflict* in quotation marks because it constitutes Graves's main topic in each of his first three books. But he doesn't acknowledge the source, though he paraphrases Graves's assertion in *Poetic Unreason* that "the poet in the fullest sense of the word must stand in the middle of the larger society to which he belongs and reconcile in his poetry the conflicting views of every group, trade, class and interest in that society."[20] As Haffenden observes, "Empson really must have been telling the truth when he said that ... passages from Graves's first writings ... had indeed inspired his interest in ambiguity."[21]

Haffenden does not follow up on this insight. First, he neglects to indicate other points in *Seven Types of Ambiguity* where Empson actually writes from within the "conflict" theory, as when he explains the "great deal of energy" in Yeats's poem "Who Goes with Fergus?" in terms of Yeats's ability to be "several sorts of men at once": "the poet ... contemporaneously living all lives, may fitly be holding before him both lives of Fergus, and drawing the same moral from either of them."[22] Haffenden also neglects to indicate that Graves had worked out this conflict theory in an even earlier book. In *On English Poetry* (1922), Graves defines "the typical poet" in the same terms, but at greater length:

> A poet in the fullest sense is ... an intermediary between the small-group consciousness of particular sects, clans, castes, types and professions among whom he moves. To ... many of these has he been formally enrolled as a member, and to ... many more has he virtually added himself as a supernumerary member by showing a disinterested sympathy and by practicing his exceptionally developed powers of intuition ... But the rival sub-personalities formed in him by his relation to these various groups, constantly struggle to reconciliation in his poetry, and in proportion as these sub-personalities are more numerous, more varied and more inharmonious, and his controlling personality stronger and quicker at compromise, so he becomes a more or less capable spokesman of that larger group-mind of his culture which we somehow consider greater than the sum of its parts.[23]

According to Graves, in the poet as "spokesman" of the "group-mind of his culture," "men of smaller scope ... hear at times in his utterances what seems to them the direct voice of God."[24]

•

Graves bases his conflict theory on the work of W.H.R. Rivers, as Empson recognized. In a notebook entry of 1932, for instance, one finds Empson reminding himself of "Graves social conflict e.g. Rivers" (sic).[25] It is by summarizing Rivers's books *Instinct and the Unconscious* and *Conflict and Dream* that Graves explains in *The Meaning of Dreams* the approach to dreams in particular and to the unconscious generally that underwrites his own literary theory: "Dr. Rivers ... traces the part played in dreams by what is called Dissociation, that is the breaking up of the human individual into two or more rival 'selves' under the stress of difficult circumstances ... [W] hen we are up against a problem that has two possible ways out ... we split up [into] two selves, each self standing for one of these opposing courses of action ... *When a person is in a conflict between two selves, and one self is stronger than the other throughout the waking life, the weaker side becomes victorious in dream.*"[26] By allowing expression to the repressed self, dreams of conflict balance the personality that has split in waking life. Rivers might seem to follow Freud and Jung on this point, so Graves hastens to add that "the so-called 'unconscious self' ... is not the sort of primitive bogey that people think, but is just the self which in conflict happens at the time to be beaten."[27] Further distancing his understanding of dreams from that of Freud and Jung, Graves suggests that "the usual claim of modern dream-interpreters is not justified, when they say that once a dream of conflict is interpreted the conflict thereby ends."[28] A symbol's effectiveness might thereby disappear, according to Graves, but not the conflict: "If a dream of conflict is interpreted and the conflict remains strong, the dream will merely change its symbols and come again in a new guise."[29]

Remarking upon Empson's 1932 notebook reference to "Graves social conflict" (sic), Haffenden suggests that "whereas Graves's dictum was sociological, and even political, Empson stresses in his response a clear psychological note."[30] This suggestion is rather baffling, however, for Rivers's view of conflict is the key to understanding all of Graves's criticism in the 1920s prior to his collaboration with Riding, and of course Rivers's perspective is thoroughly psychological. Furthermore, the point that Graves emphasizes over and over again in *On English Poetry*, *The Meaning of Dreams*, and *Poetic Unreason* is that poetry and dreams represent similar psychological events. Even many years later, in 1971, Empson recalls that it was the Freudian dimension of Graves's literary criticism that drew his attention. So it would be more accurate to say not that the clear psychological note in Empson *departs* from the work of Graves, but rather that it *echoes* the very early work where the same note is sounded – and sounded first (indeed, according to Empson, "a generation before").

In *On English Poetry*, which was dedicated to Rivers, Graves treats romantic poetry as analogous to dream, declaring that "emotional conflict is necessary for the birth of true poetry."[31] Poetry's usefulness for both the writer and the reader consists in the way it deals with emotional conflict. For the poet, poetry is "the unforeseen fusion in his mind of apparently contradictory emotional ideas."[32] After this "spontaneous process ... over which the poet has no direct control," it "becomes the duty of the poet as craftsman to present this nucleus ["the unforeseen fusion in his mind"] in the most effective way possible" so that the poem can function for the reader as it does for the poet: "Poetry ... is a form of psycho-therapy. Being the transformation into dream symbolism of some disturbing emotional crisis in the poet's mind ... poetry has the power of homeopathically healing other men's minds similarly troubled, by presenting them ... with an allegorical solution of the trouble. Once the allegory is recognized by the reader's unconscious mind as applicable the affective power of his own emotional crisis is diminished."[33] The always romantic Graves hybridizes here Wordsworth's Preface to *Lyrical Ballads* and Rivers's version of psychoanalysis.

Poetic Unreason (1925) – to which *The Meaning of Dreams* (1924) "should be read as an introduction" – restates many of these points.[34] After all, it was "intended as a sober development of certain wayward notes on poetic psychology published three years ago in ... *On English Poetry*."[35] So the "conflict theory" is just as prominent here – from the opening pages onward – as it is in the earlier book: "Poetry is for the poet a means of informing himself on many planes simultaneously ... of the relation in his mind of certain hitherto inharmonious interests, you may call them his sub-personalities or other selves ... [T]he writing of poetry ... enables him to be rid of these conflicts between his sub-personalities."[36] In fact, the word "conflict" is everywhere in Graves's theorizing: "Poetry may take the form of merely stating the nature of the conflict between these interests ... it may be a temporary relief, a narcotic, or counter-irritant, which I call poetry of escape; or it may take the completer form of prescribing the cure of the ailment, suggesting how a new common life can be formed between these conflicting interests."[37] And the conflict is clearly, for the poet, a psychological one.

And so it is for the reader, too. According to Graves, "the reading of poetry performs a similar service" to the one it performs for the poet:

> my experience as a reader of poetry is that I value in a poem the solution of the conflict when I am to some extent aware of the nature of the conflict, but that where there is hitherto only vague unrest in my mind I value in a poem the clearly defined statement of the conflict. It is not that as readers we value the conflict on its own account; that is not natural economy. We value the statement of it because this is halfway to a solution ... In any state of the conflict before the solution is possible, we are glad of narcotic poetry of temporary relief; or of a counter-irritant, which, though at first sight a case of conflict valued on its own account, is rather a sparring match where the spectator takes no sides but may see sweat and strain and bloodshed from which he is excused, and feel happier by contrast with his own more secure life.[38]

Graves's "conflict theory" is foregrounded in each of his first three books, and it is clearly a theory that Empson knows quite well.

This conflict theory also appears in *A Survey of Modernist Poetry*, but only indirectly, and not in such a way that Empson or any other reader could have understood from this book alone the role that it played in Graves's practice of criticism before he began his collaboration with Riding. Riding regarded the psychological dimensions of Graves's early literary criticism as a Trojan horse by which the scientist's criterion for determining truth – the accurate representation of reality (in this case, the poet's individual psychological reality) – gained entrance into a poetic domain that ought to be independent of it. According to Riding, as we shall see, psychological approaches to literature – whether the more-or-less Freudian approach of Graves or the more-or-less behaviourist approach of Richards – attempt to ground poetry in the psychological reality of the poet, whereas poetry can properly be grounded only in the unreality of the individual's imagination.

Even if only briefly and indirectly, however, conflict theory surfaces in the reading of Sonnet 129, for, determined to show "what great difference in the sense the juggling of punctuation marks has made in Shakespeare's original sonnet," Riding and Graves argue that revisions to lines eleven and twelve since Shakespeare's time have suppressed the conflict at the heart of the poem: "The punctuated line in the revised version, cut off from what has gone before and from what follows [by a semicolon], can only mean: 'In prospect, lust is joy; in retrospect, a dream.' Though a possible contributory meaning, as the *only* meaning it makes the theme of the poem that lust is impossible of satisfaction, whereas the theme is, as carried on by the next line, that lust as lust *is* satisfiable but that satisfied lust is in conflict with itself. The next line, if unpunctuated except for the comma Shakespeare put at the end, is a general statement of this conflict."[39]

The conflict theory appears here only incidentally and suggests none of the psychoanalytical framework that Graves imported into his literary criticism from Rivers's analysis of dreams. Furthermore, the psychological conflict is defined as a universal condition of the experience of lust rather than as a particular condition from which Shakespeare suffered. Still, in the context of Empson's familiarity with and admiration for the theory of poetry developed in Graves's other early works, this reference to the conflict at the heart of Shakespeare's sonnet helps to explain Empson's impression that this particular part of the book was written by Graves.

Graves was so well known by 1929 for this method of literary analysis, of course, that Empson did not feel that he had to name him as the author of the conflict theory to which he refers at various points in *Seven Types of Ambiguity*. Perhaps also familiar at this time with Riding's *Anarchism Is Not Enough*, published in May of 1928 (Empson refers knowledgeably to Riding's essay "The Damned Thing" from *Anarchism Is Not Enough* during his correspondence with her in the 1970s), Empson may have known of her contempt for the psychological approach to literature and assumed that she did not write this part of the book.[40] This discussion of Shakespeare in terms of the conflict at the heart of his sonnet helps to substantiate Graves's claim at least to have been involved in *Survey*'s analysis of Sonnet 129, if not to have been the sole author of it, for Riding would not have used the language of Graves's conflict theory in writing that was hers alone.

But although he declares Graves's "'conflict' theory of poetry" a "rather limited formula," Empson actually acknowledges that it is relevant to his understanding of several other types of ambiguity.[41] Indeed, simply by pointing out that that "the 'conflict" theory of poetry" applies "*especially* to generalised ambiguity of the third type," he implies that it applies also to at least some ambiguities of other types.[42] In the 1947 Preface to the second edition of *Seven Types of Ambiguity,* he suggests that "good poetry is usually written from a background of conflict."[43] Empson waters down to the status of merely a usual condition of poetry, however, what Graves regards as a precondition of poetry: "emotional conflict is necessary for the birth of true poetry"; "emotional conflict ... I regard as essential for poetry"; "emotional conflict ... is the whole cause and meaning of poetry."[44]

Similarly, his letters to Riding and others in the 1970s indicate that for all the details of his reading of Graves that he had forgotten, Empson remembered very well after more than forty years the inspiring impression Graves's early works had made upon him. With reference to the chapter "Conflict of Emotions" in *On English Poetry* (1922), Empson writes to Riding that he recalls being "greatly struck" by Graves's discussion of the multiple meanings of the word "perfume" spoken by Lady Macbeth and the multiple meanings of the word "dazzle" spoken by Ferdinand in *The Duchess of Malfi*, explaining to Riding that Graves "is mainly concerned in the book with the Conflict Theory of poetry, that is a healing process through the confrontation of opposed impulses. This is the necessary background for a theory of poetical ambiguity, which he was approaching. He had reached it by 1926, with *Impenetrability, or the Proper Habit of English.*"[45] Riding was not much impressed by Graves's reading of these lines, and she was even less impressed by Empson's attempt to locate the inspiration for his method in work by Graves that pre-dated her collaboration with him.

Empson represents his purpose in the original acknowledgment of Graves to have been "to make some wholehearted acknowledgment of the inspiration that he had given me."[46] Although the passages from *On English Poetry* and *Impenetrability* "were really very decisive," Empson suggests that he decided the treatment of Sonnet 129 in *A Survey of Modernist Poetry* "would be the right thing to mention" because "it dealt with a complete poem" (to deal with complete poems being his own ambition in *Seven Types of Ambiguity*) and because "it had a cumulative weight and impressiveness," as against passages in *On English Poetry* and *Impenetrability* that "looked a bit scrappy."[47] And so it would seem to have been very sloppy thinking that led to his implying in the 1930 introductory note that Graves's influence upon him can be accounted for by reference to *A Survey of Modernist Poetry*. Only in the retrospect prompted by Riding's complaints in 1970 does he indicate that he found in Graves's work before *A Survey of Modernist Poetry* his inspiration for insights into the non-syntactical uses of ambiguity that he explains in *Seven Types of Ambiguity*. That is, only in retrospect, it seems, has he identified in its discussion of ambiguous syntax any treatment of ambiguity in *A Survey of Modernist Poetry* distinct from that he found in Graves's earlier works.

Searching off and on for more than forty years to find the right way of mentioning Graves, to say nothing of his desire "to make some wholehearted acknowledgment of the inspiration" Graves had given him, Empson cannot at any point be said to have succeeded. To demonstrate how much more wholehearted an acknowledgment of Graves's influence ought to have been included in the introductory note to and main text of *Seven Types of Ambiguity*, I shall show here some of the ways that the conflict theory influences Empson.

•

Referring explicitly to Graves's conflict theory regularly throughout *Seven Types of Ambiguity*, but never in a way adequately to acknowledge either its author or, more importantly, its influence upon him, Empson even refers to it implicitly on the very first page of the book when he offers a sample sentence that shows that "in a sufficiently extended sense any prose statement is ambiguous."[48] The sentence "The brown cat sat on the red mat" is ostensibly advanced to show that not all ambiguous statements are interesting to literary criticism. Empson translates this sentence into different and more complicated terms ("'This is a statement about a cat. The cat the statement is about is brown,' and so forth") to show how "irrelevant" such trivial ambiguity of this "extended sense" is to literary criticism.[49] It turns out, however, that "two facts about this sentence, that it is about a cat and that it is suited to a child," mean that "to form an ambiguity worth notice," Empson need "only isolate two of its meanings": "it has contradictory associations, which might cause some *conflict* in the child who heard it, in that it might come out of a fairy story and might come out of *Reading without Tears*."[50]

Reading without Tears, or A Pleasant Mode of Learning to Read, is a collection of Victorian nursery rhymes by Favell Lee Mortimer with a tendency to describe, and even to recommend, in its simple, single-syllable words, violence toward animals – for example, "Bill is a big lad./Bill has a bad dog./Get a rod. Hit a dog" – thus leaving readers educated in such a literary tradition experiencing conflict, Empson implies, should they wonder whether a sentence with a rhyme like Mortimer's might also be followed by a reasoning eventuating in recommendations like hers: "Get a bat. Hit a cat."[51] Of course the point to note is that at the beginning of *Seven Types of Ambiguity*, the first ambiguity of interest to Empson is marked by psychological conflict: the engine of Graves's theory of poetry.

Similarly, in the middle of his book, despite characterizing "the 'conflict' theory of poetry" as a "rather limited formula," Empson affirms the broadly psychoanalytical assumption at the heart of Graves's theory and explains how the theory applies "especially to generalised ambiguity of the third type," in which "two ideas, which are connected only by being both relevant in the context, can be given in one word simultaneously": "The mind has compartments holding opinions and modes of judgment which conflict when they come together ... compartments, therefore, which require attention, and one is particularly conscious of anything that mixes them up. If the two spheres of action of a generalization ... involve two such compartments which must be thought of in two ways, we have the conditions for a general ambiguity of the third type."[52] The distinction between, on the one hand, the two "compartments" of Empson's poet's mind and, on the other, the two "sub-personalities" of Graves's poet's mind does not amount to a difference.

Empson demonstrates the "clash between different modes of feeling" in poetry of this kind by the example of the last verse of Nashe's *Summer's Last Will and Testament*:

> Haste therefore each degree
> To welcome destiny;
> Heaven is our heritage,
> Earth but a player's stage.
> Mount we unto the sky;
> I am sick, I must die –
> Lord, have mercy upon us.[53]

Here "the different modes of feeling ... [are] laid side by side so as to produce 'poetry by juxtaposition'": "The first line of the last three gives the arrogant exaltation of the mystic ... The second, sweeping this mood aside, gives the mere terror of the natural man at the weakness of the body and the approach of death. The third gives the specifically Christian fusion of these two elements into ... humility."[54] Such poetry "becomes ambiguous by making the reader assume that the elements are similar and may be read consecutively, by the way one must attempt to reconcile them or find each in the other, by the way the successive ideas act in the mind."[55]

Over the course of the next two pages, however, it emerges that, with certain qualifications, the conflict of "different modes of feeling" at the heart of ambiguity of the third type is also at the heart of other ambiguities – especially the fourth type, in which "two or more meanings of a statement do not agree among themselves, but combine to make clear a more complicated state of mind in the author."[56] And so if you say of the conflicting elements in Nashe's verse that they do not actually represent type-three ambiguity – that is, if you say of the elements of the conflict that "the experience they convey is too strong to be conceived as a series of contrasts; that one is able to reconcile the different elements; that one is not conscious of their difference but only of the grandeur of the imagination which brought them together" – then Empson merely shifts ground: "In so far as this is true, the example belongs to my fourth chapter."[57] The conflict of "different modes of feeling" endures. The question is not about whether or not there is such a conflict of feelings, but whether or not the conflicting feelings are reconciled.

Furthermore, from yet another perspective, this conflict of "different modes of feeling" can be seen at the heart of ambiguities of the seventh type, too, in which there is full contradiction "so that the total effect is to show a fundamental division in the writer's mind."[58] In the last lines of Nashe's poem, "you may say that two opposites – the fear of death and the hope of glory – are here stated together so as to produce a sort of contradiction; and that the humility of the last line then acts as evasion of the contradiction, which moves it out of the conscious mind into a region of the judgment which can accept it without reconciling it. In so far as this is true, the example belongs to my seventh chapter."[59]

Not surprisingly, then, in Chapter Seven, the "conflict" theory emerges once more – this time in connection with the poet George Herbert, whom Empson treats as a person divided in his own mind just as much as the metaphors, symbols, and images are divided in his poems. On the one hand, in a poem like Herbert's "The Sacrifice," "the contradictory impulses that are held in equilibrium by the doctrine of atonement may be seen in luminous juxtaposition"; on the other hand, "in such cases of ambiguity of the seventh type one tends to lose sight of the conflict they assume; the ideas are no longer thought of as contradictory by the author, or if so, only from a stylistic point of view; he has no doubt that they can be reconciled, and that he is stating their reconciliation."[60]

Empson suggests that "to this extent, the poem is outside the 'conflict' theory of poetry," yet it is not really outside the purview of Graves's theory, nor is Empson yet beyond Graves's influence.[61] Just as for Graves "Poetry may take the form of merely stating the nature of the conflict ... or it may take the completer form of prescribing the cure of the ailment, suggesting how a new common life can be formed between these conflicting interests," so for Empson "The Sacrifice" "assumes, as does its theology, the existence of conflicts" and "the various sets of conflicts in the Christian doctrine of the Sacrifice are stated with an assured and easy simplicity," "but its business is to state a generalised solution of them."[62]

One notes that the idea of conflict is at the heart of the definition of ambiguity of the seventh type (this type, "the most ambiguous that can be conceived, occurs when the two meanings of the word, the two values of the ambiguity, are the two opposite meanings defined by the context, so that the total effect is to show a fundamental division in the author's mind") and one recalls that, according to Haffenden, Empson seems to have started his work on *Seven Types of Ambiguity* with analysis of the second and seventh types. Sure enough, Graves is just as much an obvious presence in Chapter Seven as he is in Chapter Two.[63] Speculating that "the idea of 'opposite' is a comparatively late human invention," and invoking the example of "primitive languages on the authority of Freud" (his example of a language that unites opposites in one word is Ancient Egyptian), Empson concludes that "words uniting two opposites are seldom or never actually formed in a language to express the conflict between them; such words come to exist for more sensible reasons, and may then be used to express conflict."[64] Contemplating the role of opposites "in the Freudian analysis of dreams," but wishing to consider "more serious cases" of opposition than the "dissatisfaction" with which he associates "a Freudian opposite," Empson soon turns his thoughts to Graves's conflict theory: "In more serious cases, causing wider emotional reverberation, such as are likely to be reflected in language, in poetry, or in dreams, it marks a centre of conflict; the notion of what you want involves the notion that you must not take it ... that you want something different in another part of your mind. Of course, conflict need not be expressed overtly as contradiction, but it is likely that those theories of aesthetics which regard poetry as the resolution of a conflict will find their illustrations chiefly in the limited field covered by the seventh type."[65]

Graves's conflict theory shapes Empson's reading of Gerard Manley Hopkins's poem "The Windhover": "in the first three lines of the sestet we seem to have a clear case of the Freudian use of opposites, where two things thought of as incompatible, but desired intensely by different systems of judgments, are spoken of simultaneously by words applying to both; both desires are thus given a transient and exhausting satisfaction, and the two systems of judgment are forced into open conflict before the reader."[66] We have seen all of these points made by Graves: for the poet, poetry is "the unforeseen fusion in his mind of apparently contradictory emotional ideas"; "Poetry is for the poet a means of informing himself on many planes simultaneously ... of the relation in his mind of certain hitherto inharmonious interests, you may call them his sub-personalities or other selves ... Poetry may take the form of merely stating the nature of the conflict between these interests ... it may be a temporary relief."[67]

In his extension of the relevance of the conflict theory into his definition of the seventh type of ambiguity, Empson contradicts his observation in Chapter Three that "it is especially to generalised ambiguity of the *third* type that this rather limited formula will apply."[68] Furthermore, the limit that encumbers the theory is differently conceived here: it is not the conflict theory as formula that is limited but rather the field covered by ambiguity of the seventh type. The seventh type of ambiguity can no more be found everywhere than the third type of ambiguity can be found everywhere, but it begins to look as though a direct or indirect conversation with Graves about conflict can be found virtually everywhere in *Seven Types of Ambiguity*. As the chapter on the sixth type of ambiguity begins, for instance, Empson observes of one of his first examples that "contradiction as to the apparent subject of the statement seems very complete ... But it cannot be said to represent a conflict in the author's mind."[69] Clearly, he continues to work out his own theory with reference to Graves's.

Recalling that he explained to Riding that "the Conflict Theory of poetry" was "the necessary theory for a theory of poetical ambiguity," one can see that Empson was led to explore the roots of conflict in the nature of language itself, whether that of Ancient Egypt, that of the English Renaissance or that of contemporary poetry.[70] As he says in Chapter Two, "some readers of this chapter ... will have felt that it casts a new light on the very nature of language."[71] And so the influence of Graves's conflict theory extends from the beginning to the end of *Seven Types of Ambiguity*.

3

Mediating *The Poetic Mind*: "as many meanings as possible"

In collaboration, Riding and Graves influenced certain aspects of the development of Empson's method; on his own, Graves influenced others. Before proceeding further in making the case for Graves's claim to have been the most important influence on Empson's *Seven Types of Ambiguity*, I must explain that Riding and Graves are both inaccurate in their accounts of who was responsible for what in their close reading of Shakespeare's Sonnet 129. Certain of the principles and certain aspects of the method that they apply are original to neither of them. It is clear that they misremembered the experience of composing their book, for they forgot a decisive influence upon the development of their method.

When William Van O'Connor casually mentions that "Empson had been anticipated by Frederick C. Prescott in *The Poetic Mind* (1922)," he is not as accurate as he might have been, for Prescott's understanding of the poetic mind and its method of reading literature are mediated to Empson first by Graves, and then by Riding and Graves. Yet neither Riding nor Graves ever gives Prescott the credit he is due.[1]

Riding, as Laura Gottschalk, was a fourth-year undergraduate studying English at Cornell University when Prescott's book came out in February of 1922. The Department of English at Cornell today boasts that she studied with Prescott and that, according to M.H. Abrams, she applied Prescott's ideas in *A Survey of Modernist Poetry*.[2] It is clear, however, that Riding could no more have tolerated Prescott's thoroughly Freudian understanding of poetry than Graves's Rivers-inspired "conflict theory." From her point of view, that kind of work subordinates the poem to a reality outside it, the poet's psychological experience, and is therefore wrong. Yet Prescott, like Graves, was very good at showing how the multiple meanings of words in poems worked together in profoundly significant ways – something that Riding found very interesting, indeed.

Graves had certainly read Prescott before his initial acquaintance with Riding, by letter, sometime after mid-1925, and well before meeting with Riding in person at the end of 1925. Citing correspondence between Graves and Prescott from earlier in 1925, Friedmann observes that Graves had "engaged in a friendly correspondence with Frederick Prescott of the Cornell University English department, in whose recently published book, *The Poetic Mind*, Graves had found elements of support for the psychological theories in his own book, *On English Poetry*. So he decided to seek Prescott's assistance in procuring a teaching job at the American university, expressing interest in assisting Prescott in his research in 'aesthetic psychology.'"[3]

There is considerable overlap between the literary theory and the practical criticism articulated in *On English Poetry* and *The Poetic Mind*, published respectively in May and February of 1922. This fact is not surprising, given the authors' attempts to develop a theory of literature and a practical method of literary interpretation based on a similar source: psychoanalytical theory. Although Graves was developing the ideas of Rivers and Prescott was developing the ideas of Freud and Jung, they shared many ideas, values, assumptions, and insights.

Like Graves, Prescott discusses the differences between "two modes of thought": "voluntary or purpose thought" and "associative thought": "our ordinary prosaic thought is of the first of these kinds, dream and poetic vision of the second."[4] Like Graves, Prescott regards "associative, imaginative, poetic thought" as "the primary one" – practical, voluntary, prosaic thought having grown out of it, after it.[5] Like Graves, Prescott stands on guard against the prejudice that the more primitive mode of thought is inferior: "the older faculty in many respects is still the better."[6]Also like Graves, Prescott regards the spontaneous poetry that comes from the unconscious as superior to intellectual poetry.[7] So it is no wonder that Graves was not only able to recognize a kindred spirit in Prescott, but also able to imagine collaborating with him on research into "aesthetic psychology."

The impact of Prescott's work on Graves is evident not in any change of mind by Graves about the nature of literature or how to interpret it, but rather in how Graves lifted everything from turns of phrase to interpretations of literature out of Prescott's work to make more consistent and coherent, and to express more clearly, the theory and practice that had appeared in his earliest work in a rather helter-skelter fashion. Making Graves's theory and practice clearer and more coherent is the project that Empson professed to have recognized as necessary, and in part to have undertaken by means of his own work. Graves borrowed significantly from Prescott, as would Empson from Graves, and thereby from Prescott, too.

In the following pages from *Impenetrability, or The Proper Habit of English* (1926), Graves writes in terms that are consistent with those he had been developing since 1921, yet he also lifts quite a bit of material from *The Poetic Mind*:

> When particular words very highly charged with meaning in their context occur in English literature, this is counted a great virtue. In logical literatures it is a vice, by the rule of "one word, one meaning." For instance, in Keats' *Eve of St. Agnes*, Madeleine is described in "her soft and chilly nest," "Clasped like a missal when swart Paynims pray," where "clasped" means "fastened with a clasp of holiness" or "held lovingly in the hands," if the Paynims are held to be converted; but also, without prejudice, "shut and coldly neglected," if the Paynims are held to be unconverted ...
>
> This, then, is the constant practice of those English poets who achieve the most admired phrases. The reader is not rationally aware of the principle underlying such phrases: he knows that they delight him but does not in the act of reading poetry dissect them. In prose a similar method of concentrated meaning is used and known as "wit," but in this case the reader gets pleasure from a clear rational analysis of the different senses in which the witty phrase is to be read. Here is a passage from a superior society novel:
>
> > On departure our hero clicked his heels politely and acknowledged the salty hospitality of his host: for the old marquis had enjoyed the youth's discomfiture hugely, and had been thus lavish in heaping him with all manner of delicacies and honours only because he knew that they afforded his guest no enjoyment at all.
>
> This word "salty" is the point where opposing senses unite in wit. To "acknowledge salty hospitality" is in one sense to

> acknowledge the social obligation of good manners which eating of a host's salt implies in most countries. But it is also to comment on the absence of goodwill, in the sense that "salty" means "sterile." In a third sense it is to comment on the host's dry humour in recognising and making fun of the guest's discomfiture, for "Attic salt" is a well-known synonym for wit itself. When such a concentration of forces can be exerted at a single point in literature, then, in Humpty-Dumpty's words, "there's glory for you!"[8]

Compare these pages to the central pages of Prescott's chapter on "The Imagination: Condensation and Displacement," where he explains that the role of condensation in what Freud calls "Dream work" is similar to its role in what Prescott calls "Poetic work"[9]:

> Each word will be apt to have two, three, or even many meanings or implications, corresponding to the multiple associations of the mental imagery which it represents ... [O]ften the surface meaning will be of less importance than the latent ones ... [T]he real poetry will be between the lines ... A poem will be "poetical" or "imaginative" in proportion as its language is overcharged with meanings ...
>
> Let us take ... a line from the "Eve of St. Agnes" which has probably given the critics as much trouble as any other in Keats. It represents Madeline, in "her soft and chilly nest," as
>
> Clasp'd like a missal where swart paynims pray.
>
> On this Leigh Hunt comments: "Clasp'd like a missal in a land of pagans, – that is to say, where Christian books must not be seen, and are, therefore, doubly cherished for the danger." This comment R. Garnett calls "entirely wide of the mark," insisting that whereas Hunt takes "clasp'd" to mean "clasp'd to the bosom," its true meaning is "fastened with a clasp." "Clasp'd missal may be allowed to suggest holiness which the prayers of swart paynims neglect," says another comment. "Missal, a prayer book bearing upon its margins pictures of converted heathen in the act of prayer," says still another ... I should think most if not all of the puzzled annotators were right ... I have dwelt on this line because it illustrates a principle which is most important in all reading of poetry, and which is inherent in its very nature – namely, that whereas in true prose words should have one

> meaning and one meaning only, in true poetry they should have as many meanings as possible, and the more the better, as long as they are true to the images in the poet's mind ...
>
> In wit the same fusion of words and images often results in a condensed or "over-determined" expression ... In wit, as in poetry, the fusion often unexpectedly throws together images not ordinarily associated, and brings to light unexpected likenesses, giving thus a kind of poetical pleasure ... In wit the fusion will often result in new verbal formations. "Indeed, he would sometimes remark," Disraeli writes in *Lothair*, "when a man fell into his anecdotage it was a time for him to retire from the world." The meaning compressed into the telescoped word would if expanded require a sentence. Oftener the wit will lie in an ordinary word taken in two senses, in a pun or paronomasia. Two meanings, which might be expressed separately by two unambiguous words, are fused, and the fusion represented by an ambiguity...
>
> [With regard to the question of whether Pope, or Keats, or Shakespeare meant to pun on the word "die" in various works, or whether readers need to be conscious of the possible pun, Prescott avers that] a poet, like a dreamer, may use a symbol of this kind ... without consciously recognizing it; as a reader may unconsciously get its effect. Perhaps indeed the unconscious effect is stronger, for poetry ceases to be poetry where all the effects are conscious and explicable ... An immature or thoughtless reader will of course overlook it. But a reader or an audience that has been carried away by the dramatic feeling will have a sense of it, and will feel too a vague emotional satisfaction ... The satisfaction will be of the nameless and unexplained kind that is the truest mark of poetry ... The thoughtful reader ... will go on to comprehend and explain it ...
>
> [T]he imagination plays with every word that it touches, fills it with meanings and suggestions, colours and brightens it, borrowing lights and colors too from other words and from the context, until the whole expression becomes illuminated, and the glorified utterance becomes a fitting expression of the imaginative mind.[10]

I have quoted a great deal from each book, but this strategy is necessary if one is to appreciate the extent of Prescott's impact on Graves.

Graves clearly cribs his analysis of Keats's line in "The Eve of St Agnes" from Prescott's analysis of the same line. But there is much more to notice here. Graves also echoes many of Prescott's most important phrases, and does so over several pages in the same order in which they occur in Prescott's pages: "language ... overcharged with meanings" becomes "words very highly charged with meaning"; the observation that "in true prose words should have one meaning and one meaning only" becomes the observation that logical languages disapprove of manifold meanings "by the rule of 'one word, one meaning'"; the assertion that a reader need not be conscious of a pun, yet "may unconsciously get its effect," and that "a reader or an audience that has been carried away by the dramatic feeling will have a sense of it, and will feel too a vague emotional satisfaction ... of the nameless and unexplained kind that is the truest mark of poetry," becomes the observation that "the reader is not rationally aware of the principle underlying such phrases [with multiple meanings]: he knows that they delight him but does not in the act of reading poetry dissect them"; the claim that "In wit, as in poetry, the fusion [of meanings in a pun] often unexpectedly throws together images not ordinarily associated, and brings to light unexpected likenesses, giving thus a kind of poetical pleasure," is echoed in the claim that "in prose a similar method of concentrated meaning is used and known as 'wit,' but in this case the reader gets pleasure from a clear rational analysis of the different senses in which the witty phrase is to be read"; finally, both discussions move to a celebration of the "glory" of this aspect of poetic language. None of these ideas or observations is necessarily new to Graves, but as the extensive quotations above show, Graves's recollection of several pages of Prescott's book organized several pages of his own.

Quoting Graves's analysis in *Impenetrability* of both the very passage above about "The Eve of St Agnes" and the very "salty" passage above about the superior society novel in question, Empson declares to Riding that in these "decisive" passages Graves "had reached" finally the "theory of poetical ambiguity" implicit in *On English Poetry*.[11]

•

But there is more. For Prescott, of course, found analysis of Shakespeare's word-play irresistible, and so not surprisingly he enunciated his most fundamental rules for the reading of all literature in the context of his particular readings of Shakespeare – as would Riding and Graves, and then Empson. Prescott's analysis of a line from *Hamlet* reveals his impact on these critics in terms of their shared concern not just to recover Shakespeare's meaning, but also to recover for the contemporary reader the ability to understand the poetic state of mind:

> Hamlet's soliloquy is dramatically the expression of a mind at high tension, filled with more confused images than it can find words for ... The broken and turbid expression itself suggests the mental situation. It is not strange therefore that this speech, when subjected to languid analysis by the verbal critics, should have given a great deal of trouble, and that it should have required ten closely printed pages in the Variorum Shakespeare even to summarize the observations that have been made upon it. Readers who wish to get an idea of what learned German criticism may do for Shakespeare should read Elze's discussion of the line
>
> When we have shuffled off this mortal coil.
>
> Here editors suggest "clay," "vail," "soil," and "spoil," and they try to decide between the possible meanings of "coil." Now it is well in reading Shakespeare, first to avoid emendations as far as may be, and secondly, where two or more meanings are possible and congruous with the context, not to dispute between them, but to understand them all. These two rules of course will not solve all the difficulties, but they will dispense with a great deal of the annotation. In the line just quoted Shakespeare probably had first an image of the turmoil and confusion of this mortal life, and then an image of the body as the wrapping or covering of the soul – both of which might be shuffled off in the "sleep of death." The second image is very closely related to the first, is a little more specific, and more figurative. Both can be fused and condensed in the word "coil," which kills two birds with one small stone. This line again will not bother any reader whose imagination has been awakened by the context. To such a reader the line is alive with meaning; it is not made up of dead or inert words, with definite and exclusive denotations. The real difficulty is that, as we no longer have the imagination to write poetry, we lack even the imagination to read it.[12]

Riding and Graves, and Empson, too, take as their point of departure Prescott's rules: do not emend Shakespeare; understand all of Shakespeare's meaning. The purpose of Riding and Graves in invoking Shakespeare in their discussion of modern poetry is to show that despite the fact that "understanding of ... poetry ... like Shakespeare's ... is taken for granted," Shakespeare's poetry is actually more difficult to understand than that of a contemporary poet like E.E. Cummings.[13] According to Riding and Graves, it is the intolerable difficulty of reading Shakespeare "that provoked his editors to meddle with his texts as being too incomprehensible as they were written."[14] In effect, they echo Prescott's observation that contemporary readers lack the imagination to read it: "The failure of imagination and knowledge in Shakespeare's emendators has reduced Shakespeare to the indignity of being easy for everybody."[15]

•

Other of Prescott's passages on Shakespeare are devoted to the genre preferred by Riding and Graves (and by Empson, too, in much of *Seven Types of Ambiguity*): the sonnets. These passages are equally instructive with regard to how Riding and Graves, and thereby Empson, were invited by Prescott to consider the complexities arising from the proper verbal functioning of the poetic state of mind:

> I have spoken so far as if two things only were fused and represented by figures. In fact, three, four, or more things are often so fused, and the expression strives to represent the resulting complex image. Image *a* suggests image *b* by resemblance, and this in turn image *c*; and from these results a compound image *abc*, which is expressed by some choice from the terms *A*, *B*, and *C*. This compounding of three images occurs in Shakespeare's sonnet (where the third image enters in l. 4):
>
> That time of year thou mayst in me behold
> When yellow leaves, or none, or few, do hang
> Upon those boughs which shake against the cold,
> *Bare ruined choirs*, where late sweet birds sang.[16]
>
> Another sonnet in which Shakespeare uses the word *state* three times, with shifting meaning, closes
> That then I scorn to change my *state* with kings.
> Here the word *state* might mean "condition," or "estate," or "royal splendour," and probably means all of those – not successively, but all at once. In other words, the three meanings are

> fused in the mind, and this word *state* is a kind of triple figure. Sometimes the different meanings are not thus definitely assignable. Shakespeare in writing
>
> When to the sessions of sweet silent thought
> I summon up remembrance of things past,
>
> has probably first in mind legal sessions, but this calls up other associations and the word therefore has other meanings ... Shakespeare always meant more than he intended.[17]

Prescott's suggestion that Shakespeare's words mean all sorts of things at once, rather than merely meaning a sequence of single things in succession, and that these various meanings are fused in the mind, is reproduced in very similar terms by Riding and Graves in their analysis of sonnet 129: "All these alternate meanings acting on each other, and even other possible interpretations of words and phrases, make as it were a furiously dynamic cross-word puzzle which can be read in many directions at once, none of the senses being incompatible with any others."[18] It all leads to Riding and Graves's practical advice for "getting out of the prose and into the poetic state of mind": readers are responsible for "developing a capacity for minuteness, for seeing all there is to see at a given point and for taking it all with one as one goes along."[19] Prescott's provocative suggestion here that "Shakespeare always meant more than he intended," along with his equally provocative suggestion above that "in true poetry [words] ... should have as many meanings as possible, and the more the better," is worked out more fully by Riding and Graves: "The effect of ... revised punctuation has been to restrict meanings to special interpretations of special words. Shakespeare's punctuation allows the variety of meanings he actually intends; if we must choose any one meaning, then we owe it to Shakespeare to choose at least one he intended and one embracing as many meanings as possible, that is, the most difficult meaning. It is always the most difficult meaning that is most final."[20]

•

A brief recapitulation of what Empson took from Riding and Graves shows how much of that influence was also Prescott's influence. In the conclusion to Chapter Two of *Seven Types of Ambiguity*, he takes up Riding and Graves's subject, and treats it in their terms: "I shall now return to Shakespeare and allow myself a couple of digressions; about the emendations of his text and his use of a particular grammatical form."[21] He concludes from his survey of the history of emendations to Shakespeare's texts that a "conservative attitude to ambiguity" is operative: "it is assumed ... that Shakespeare can only have meant one thing."[22] His phrasing follows that of Riding and Graves here. He follows them further in disavowing the practice of restricting meanings to special interpretations of special words – reversing it, in fact, so as to embrace as many meanings as possible – possibility in each case being determined by plausibility. Embracing all of the meanings that the Arden editor lists for the word *rooky* – "these meanings ... might, for all we know ... have seemed plausible to anybody in the first-night audience; might have seemed plausible to Shakespeare himself, since he was no less sensitive to words than they" – Empson argues that "such a note ... makes you bear in mind all the meanings it puts forward" and that "this is the normal experience of readers" of Shakespeare.[23] And so "the reader must hold in mind a variety of things he may have meant, and weight them, in appreciating the poetry, according to their probabilities."[24] These are Prescott's "two rules": "first to avoid emendations as far as may be, and secondly, where two or more meanings are possible and congruous with the context, not to dispute between them, but to understand them all."[25]

•

If it is really the case that the credit for formulating the principles articulated in their reading of Shakespeare's sonnet 129 belongs more to Riding than to Graves, as Graves himself suggested in 1966, then Riding knew Prescott's work well, for there is no doubt that the Prescott principle informs the book's treatment of Shakespeare – and much else, besides. Certainly Graves knew Prescott's work very well, so the fact that a habit of borrowing without acknowledgment not just Prescott's ideas but certain of his phrases, as well, is common to both *Impenetrability* and *A Survey of Modernist Poetry* may be evidence that Graves did indeed write much of the analysis of Shakespeare's sonnet.

Ironically, then, the dispute between Riding and Graves about their "word-by-word collaboration" comes down to the question, in part, "Which of them was the one applying Prescott's rules and recycling his words?" – a question that leads to another: "How could whoever wrote the analysis of Shakespeare's sonnet in *A Survey of Modernist Poetry* ever have pretended that either its principles or its methods were invented exclusively by him or her?"

4

The Limits of Poetic Consciousness

It is clear, then, that Empson knows Graves's pre-Riding work very well before meeting with Richards and discussing with him the method of the "'Robert Graves' school of criticism," and we can see that he has paid particular attention to Graves's theories about the conflicted nature of human consciousness in general and of poetic consciousness in particular. One of Graves's main interests in his early work is to explain the limits of conscious control in the creation of poetry, as it is for Empson in many parts of *Seven Types of Ambiguity*, and in Chapter Three especially. For Graves, of course, conflicting meanings in a poem are a sign of conflicted consciousness in the poet. And his understanding of the relationship between conflict and poetry precludes the possibility of the poet's becoming completely aware of his conflict if his poetry is to remain true. In Chapter Three of *Seven Types of Ambiguity*, however, Empson strives to identify a type of ambiguity that is entirely conscious, implicitly in opposition to Graves's claims for the comprehensiveness of his conflict theory. And in Chapter Seven, he offers in "a doctrinal poem by George Herbert," "The Sacrifice," an example of conflict so thoroughly impersonalized as theological doctrine as to prevent the expression of personal conflict in the poem: "the theological system is accepted so completely that the poet is only its mouthpiece ... [T]o this extent, the poem is outside the 'conflict' theory of poetry."[1]

The persuasiveness of Graves's account of conflict in poetry, however, seems to leave Empson conceding by each chapter's end that the extreme kind of poetic consciousness he places outside of Graves's conflict theory is merely a theoretical limit. It is perhaps impossible of actualization: "'trying not to be ambiguous' is itself very indefinite and treacherous; it involves problems of all kinds as to what a poet can try to do, how much of his activity he is conscious of, and how much of his activity he could become conscious of if he tried."[2] And such a degree of poetic consciousness would certainly be difficult for the critic to discern and determine: "Certainly it is hard to say whether a poet is conscious of a particular implication in his work, he has so many other things to think of."[3] It seems that ambiguous meanings in a poem are always potentially, even if indeterminably, a sign of at least minimally conflicted consciousness in the poet.

•

Early in *Poetic Unreason*, in a chapter called "A Theory of Consciousness," Graves explains the need to revise the distinction that he had assumed in *On English Poetry* between the conscious and the unconscious:

> Hitherto I held that there were two varieties of action and two varieties of thought, in either case known as conscious and unconscious, and that in consciousness and unconsciousness, thought and action derived from each other. In action I distinguished between the "conscious" or *deliberate* action of, say, striking a golf ball in a particular manner, and what is called the "unconscious" or *unwitting* action of, say, slightly frowning when an opponent holes an unlikely putt. In thought, I distinguished between, say, a *deliberate* poetic allegory in the established tradition and an *unwitting* uprush of inspired poetry when in an actual state of dream. These certainly are distinctions with a meaning, but my fault as it appears now was that of believing all mental activity to belong to one or the other category.[4]

Graves now asserts that there is another degree of unconsciousness, a state of non-consciousness beyond the *unwitting*: "I now hold that consciousness and un- or non-consciousness can be distinguished, but in a wider sense than merely as the *unwitting* and *deliberate*; that the nature of non-consciousness is that we can never have any knowledge of its character as we may eventually have knowledge of the *unwitting*."[5] Finding that "consciousness is not an even flow like a looking-glass vista," "in any series of action – knowledge – thought ... there is continuous discrepancy between like units," Graves introduces this new aspect of non-consciousness to explain gaps in consciousness: "to me the only way of accounting for these discrepancies is the intervention of a continuously interrupting and continuously interrupted sequence of non-conscious activity, of which knowledge can never, as I have suggested, appear, but which must be postulated if the logical concatenation of cause and effect is to be maintained."[6]

Graves's reasoning is of the sort that poststructuralists would call "logocentric": discrepancy in meaning is taken to be a sign of that in which discrepancy is resolved. Yet his observation that the failure of signifiers to converge upon a single signified is an inescapable fact of life is consistent with the same sort of insight into sign systems that Saussure offered a generation earlier, and that Derrida would offer a generation or two later. As it is, Graves's thinking here preserves a vaguely theological meta-narrative in which non-consciousness is the first and transcendent signifier: "Action does not directly proceed from thought, nor knowledge from action, nor thought from knowledge, but these phases of consciousness are each derived from moments of non-conscious activity, a sort of invisible property-shifting between each phase."[7] Non-consciousness is effectively a construct that Graves invents to preserve order in the midst of the disorder he cannot otherwise explain.

In his concluding chapter, Empson reasons along very similar lines but much more self-consciously. Empson's encounter with interpretive disorder is framed in terms of a theoretical question about "the problem as to belief in poetry," that is "whether it is necessary to share the opinions of the poet if you are to understand his sensibility,"[8] and is answered in terms of vaguely sociological observations:

> In the last few generations literary people have been trained socially to pick up hints at once about people's opinions, and to accept them, while in the company of their owners, with as little fuss as possible; I might say, putting this more strongly, that in the present state of indecision of the cultured world people do, in fact, hold all the beliefs, however contradictory, that turn up in poetry, in the sense that they are liable to use them all in coming to decisions. It is for reasons of this sort that the habit of reading a wide variety of different sorts of poetry, which has, after all, only recently been contracted by any public as a whole, gives to the act of appreciation a puzzling complexity, tends to make

> people less sure of their own minds, and makes it necessary to be able to fall back on some intelligible process of interpretation.[8]

In such a context, Empson suggests, "any intellectual framework that seems relevant is very encouraging ... whether it actually 'explains' anything or not; if you feel that your reactions *could* be put into a rational scheme that you can roughly imagine, you become willing, for instance, to abandon yourself to the ecstasies of the Romantic Movement ... with much less fear for your critical self-respect."[9] Empson duly considers his own practice: "The same machinery of reassurance, I suppose, is sought for in my use of phrases like 'outside the focus of consciousness,' meaning something imagined as other than the pre-, the un-, the sub-, the non-, and the half-, conscious, but defensible in the same sorts of ways."[10] By his own contribution of an "outside-consciousness" to a list that includes Graves's "non-consciousness," Empson clearly recognizes both that Graves defines his property-shifting non-consciousness as a reassuring dodge in the direction of that which is intellectually explicable and that he himself has performed the same dodge for the same reassurance; indeed, he argues that "To give a reassurance of this kind ... is the main function of analytical criticism."[11]

•

Graves's hypothesis of a variously and multiply signifying non-consciousness becomes the engine of Graves's conflict theory of poetry: "When we say that two experiences are continuous, we mean no more than this, that we do not know what the new experience is going to be, but that when it has come, we have to say that it is continuous with its predecessor. The nature of the particular continuity can only be given after the event. In the same way a poem will never be a copy of the poet's past life. It will be a new experience, but it will be continuous with his past life in the sense that but for this, it could itself never have come into existence. The precise form the poem will take cannot be known until it has taken that form. Non-conscious experience can never be dictated to by a predicting consciousness."[12] This hypothesis allows him to explain both how so much more meaning than the poet deliberately intends can get into a poem and how so much more meaning than the poet can ever understand remains always to be discovered in the poem by future readers, including the poet himself.

The "continuous discrepancy between the units" "in any series of action – knowledge – thought," on the one hand, and the ostensibly necessary postulate of a continuous non-consciousness within which such units cohere, on the other, leaves consciousness constructing a narrative of continuity after the event.[13] The only element that Graves rules out of such a narrative is identity: "no action is merely reproduction of a previous action"; "no thought or mental picture can recur identically"; "a poem will never be a copy of the poet's past life."[14] And so a poem can never be identical with a poet's conscious intention, whether consciousness of that intention precedes the composition of the poem ("Non-conscious experience can never be dictated to by a predicting consciousness"), or whether consciousness of that intention seems coincident with the composition of the poem ("The precise form the poem will take cannot be known until it has taken form").[15]

•

Riding re-presents these ideas in terms of the distinctive critical and philosophical idiom she developed in *Contemporaries and Snobs* (1927) and *Anarchism Is Not Enough* (1928), books that she was writing while collaborating with Graves on *A Survey of Modernist Poetry* and *A Pamphlet Against Anthologies* from 1926 to 1928. Her work at this time shows, like Empson's, how Graves's early work established the question of the relationship between the poet's intention and the poem itself as a topic for contemporary theorists to consider.

In *Contemporaries and Snobs*, Riding repudiates "poetry whose only subject is the psychology of the poet and whose final value is scientific."[16] Such poetry gives rise to the false poem – a poem that, in Graves's terms, is imagined as attempting to copy the poet's past life, to reproduce a previous action, to re-present a mental picture. In Riding's terms, "False poems … are those written to respond to tests of reality imposed by the contemporary mind and are therefore able to satisfy them better than any true one. The creative history of the false poem is the age, the author sensible of the age and the set of outer circumstances involved in his delicate adjustment to the age at a particular moment, in a particular place. Nothing remains beyond this, no life, no element, as in the true poem, untranslatable except in the terms provided by the poem itself. In the true poem these terms form a measurement that did not exist, and the test of the poem's reality is: to what degree is it a new dimension of reality?"[17] Riding's "true poem" is essentially Graves's poem that "cannot be known until it has taken form."

In terms of the history of New Criticism, Riding's great contribution to the development of Graves's idea is to assert that this new reality, non-identical with any other aspect of reality, is effectively a person: "The only difference between a poem and a person is that in a poem *being* is the final state, in a person the preliminary state. These two kinds of realities, that of the person, that of the poem, stand at one end and the other of the poet's mind, which is but progressive experience made into a recurrent sequence circulating between one kind of reality and the other without destroying one reality in the other."[18] And so "the poem itself is supreme, above persons; judging rather than judged ... it is even able to make a reader of its author. It comes to be because an individual mind is clear enough to perceive it and then to become its instrument."[19] Riding recognizes that discrepancy between the meaning of the poem and the meaning intended by the author not only makes the author a reader of the poem, but also makes the poem a being with a mind of its own.

If one consults (and perhaps prefers) the obscurer terms of *Anarchism Is Not Enough*, one finds that the poem is "nothing," but a "nothing" in Jean-Paul Sartre's existential sense, according to which the singular distinction of the human being is to be no such thing as a tool or a constructed object whose essence precedes its existence in the mind of its creator, for the human being's existence is prior to its essence.[20] According to Riding, "A poem is nothing ... Why is it nothing? Because it cannot be looked at, heard, touched or read ... It is not an effect ... of experience; it is the result of an ability to create a vacuum in experience – it is a vacuum and therefore nothing ... Since it is a vacuum it is nothing for which the poet can flatter himself or receive flattery. Since it is a vacuum it cannot be reproduced in an audience. A vacuum is unalterably and untransferably a vacuum – the only thing that can happen to it is destruction."[21] Riding's vacuum takes the place of Graves's non-consciousness. She recognizes the implications of Graves's representation of the poem as non-identical with any element of the world from which it emerges – whether poet's intention, poet's experience, or world's event. Riding's admirer Auden, who often echoes her poetry, echoes this aspect of her literary theorizing when he declares that "Poetry makes nothing happen," such that a line from "In Memory of W.B. Yeats" that might seem defeatist or quietist is from Riding's existential point of view positively triumphant.[22]

Like Riding, Empson is suspicious of Graves's psychological explanation of poetry. He complains at the beginning of Chapter Three about the unhelpfulness in literary matters of certain oppositions between the terms "conscious" and "unconscious": "one must continually feel doubtful about antitheses involving the idea of [the] 'unconscious,' which, like the infinities of mathematics, may be a convenient fiction or a product of definition."[23] In Graves's new theory "on the much debated and very complicated subject of 'Consciousness,'" "non-consciousness" certainly emerges as what Empson would call a "product of definition" – just as an idea of non-good might emerge from a definition of good.[24] It is also what Empson would call a most "convenient fiction," since, although its existence cannot be demonstrated otherwise than by definition, it fortunately maintains at least narratively the logical concatenation of cause and effect. It is "the only way of accounting for ... discrepancies," says Graves; it "must be postulated."[25]

Empson, as we have seen, ultimately agrees – he characterizes his own parallel concept of an "outside the focus of consciousness" as a conveniently reassuring fiction – yet in Chapter Three, looking down on the unconscious by characterizing a certain "variety of the 'conflict' theory of poetry" as a "rather limited formula," he makes clear just whose antitheses about conscious and unconscious ideas make him doubtful.[26] Empson implies, that is, that the antitheses involving the idea of the unconscious about which he personally feels doubtful are to be found in the work of Graves rather than the work of Freud. He clearly has nothing against psychoanalysis as Freud presents it: he refers to Freud approvingly every time he mentions him in *Seven Types of Ambiguity*. Furthermore, he rather boldly supplements his then anti-Freudian supervisor's 1926 essay on Hopkins's contradictory impulses in "The Windhover" ("I am indebted to Dr. Richards for this case; he has already written excellently about it") with a pointedly Freudian perspective on the psychological state implied by such contradiction: "in the first three lines of the sestet we seem to have a case of the Freudian use of opposites, where two things thought of as incompatible, but desired intensely by different systems of judgments, are spoken of simultaneously by words applying to both."[27]

We can see that Empson's recollection in the 1970s that he was very keen on Freud in the 1920s is accurate insofar as he stands up for Freud in the face of his supervisor's hostility, but insofar as he echoes his supervisor's complaint that Graves's conflict theory is inadequate, he seems a long way from acknowledging what he would later tell Riding: that he regarded Graves's conflict theory as "the necessary background for a theory of poetical ambiguity."[28] These passages reveal Empson's anxiety about not only whether his commitment to Graves's method of reading involves him in a psychological paradigm that his thesis director regards with condescension and disdain, but also whether it aligns him with a critic Richards regards as representing "the gravest" psychoanalytical danger.[29] Empson undoubtedly has Richards in mind when he says that "one must continually feel doubtful" of "antitheses involving the idea of 'unconscious.'"[30] His description of the unconscious as, at times, a "convenient fiction" clearly echoes Richards's claim that "an unconscious mind is a fairly evident fiction."[31] To have Richards in mind on this point is also to have Richards's criticism of Graves in mind: "Mr Graves has attempted to analyse *Kubla Khan* ... The reader acquainted with current methods of analysis can imagine the results of a thoroughgoing Freudian onslaught"; "the attempt to display the inner working of the artist's mind by the evidence of his work alone must be subject to the gravest dangers."[32]

•

From the beginning of his discussion of ambiguity of the third type, Empson foregrounds the distinction between the conscious and the unconscious. We learn that "an ambiguity of the third type, considered as a verbal matter, occurs when two ideas, which are connected only by being both relevant in the context, can be given in one word simultaneously."[33] That the ideas are connected only by being both relevant in context is crucial – "they are two pieces of information, two parts of the narrative" – for the point of this type of ambiguity "is the sharpness of distinction between two meanings, of which the reader is forced to be aware."[34] By definition, ambiguity of the third type requires the reader to be conscious of it as ambiguity. Awareness is all: "I am not using the word 'ambiguity' in a logical, but in a psychological sense; the notion of relevance is necessary to pick out cases of it, and it is conceived as always conscious in one mode or another."[35]

For the reader not to be conscious of the two meanings is to miss part of the poem's story or information. Similarly, for the poet not to have become conscious of the one word that does the work of two is to have made a poem longer, less elegant, and less efficient than it need be. Furthermore, for the reader to be conscious of "an additional effect" beyond the connections between the meanings of a pun, and for the poet to express more than narrative information in the two meanings of the pun (for example, to make it also an intimate "expression of sensibility"), is to create a different type of ambiguity.[36] In ambiguity of the third type there can be no meaning for reader or writer that is surplus to this narrow informational focus of consciousness.

Clearly Empson would like to confine ambiguity of the third type to one's being "mainly conscious of the pun, not of its consequences"; to one's being conscious of its providing two meanings of strictly narrative consequence, that is, rather than one's being conscious of the further possible meanings that the pun might present concerning the mood or state of mind of the poet (or mood or state of mind of the character) who speaks the pun. His interest is in the poet's controlling the device of ambiguity and the reader's appreciating it; that is, in its function as a practical device for providing narrative information only: "I want to insist that the question is not here of 'consciousness' of a device as a whole, but of consciousness of a particular part of it ... [C]lear or wide distinction between the two meanings concerned is likely to place the ambiguity at the focus of consciousness ... [to] make it more obvious to the reader, more dependent on being overtly observed, and less intimately an expression of sensibility."[37]

Of course Empson's language of degree here – this part of the device is *more* conscious, that part *less* – is ambiguous in precisely the ways he defines ambiguity throughout his study and so implicitly engages the question that Graves raises: whether a nonconscious activity surplus to the activity of consciousness can ever be escaped or eliminated.

As we have seen, wrestling in his early work with this question of the role of consciousness in poetic creation, especially as seen in his revision of his distinction between "a *deliberate* poetic allegory in the established tradition and an *unwitting* uprush of inspired poetry when in a state of actual dream," Graves no longer believes that such a distinction can be maintained: "Between the 'deliberate' and the 'unwitting' there is, so far as I can see, only this distinction, that the 'deliberate' is in the present tense, the 'unwitting' in the past."[38] Funded by and founded upon the non-conscious, the conscious and the unconscious are always already interpenetrated, a fact that needs only a change of perspective to show itself. The impact upon Empson of Graves's explicit claim in *Poetic Unreason*, and of his implicit claim throughout his early work, that there is always, necessarily, a meaning that is surplus to consciousness in every true poem is evident in Empson's failure to convince himself that he has ever identified a pure example of type-three ambiguity. As he writes Chapter Three, Empson finds himself always quite adept at the change of perspective that reveals the unconscious within his examples of ambiguity of the third type.

•

The worry for Empson is that if it is not possible for the poet or the reader to limit consciousness to the particular part of a pun that is its narrative information, and if the pun always already has a meaning in addition to the conscious one and so is justified in other literary terms, then his reader "may say that, in so far as an ambiguity is justified, it is moved upwards or downwards on my scale out of the third type," or may say that "if the pun is producing *no* additional effect it has no function and is of no interest."[39] Empson concedes that "if this were true, the type would gain in theoretical importance but contain no examples of interest to the reader of poetry."[40] In other words, it would be no more than a product of definition. It would posit a circumscription of language by consciousness never realizable to the degree of pureness or completeness required by the definition of this type of ambiguity.

Empson initially resists the hypothesis that ambiguity of the third type has no poetic function and is of no poetic interest: "I think it is not true, because the matter is complicated by questions of consciousness, of the direction of the reader's attention, of the interaction between separated parts of his mind, and of the means by which a pun can be justified to him."[41] That is, he implies that a reader can, in practice, identify and respond to type-three ambiguity. As Empson explains, "I mean by the conscious part of the effect the most interesting part, the part to which it is most natural to direct your attention."[42] Of course, the reader's consciousness can change, so it can change the nature of the ambiguity in the poem. In "The Temple," for instance, Herbert "has put to extraordinary uses these dry and detached symbols," has made them "apply to three different situations, and from this point of view the poem belongs to my third type."[43] The reader initially finds this aspect of the poem most interesting and naturally directs attention towards it, but he eventually experiences the poem differently: "One may say ... that in ordinary careful reading this poem is of the third type, but when you know it sufficiently well, and have accepted it, it becomes ambiguity of the first or (since it is verbally ingenious) of the second type."[44]

At least for a little while, it seems, the reader experiences ambiguity of the third type, yet Empson himself remains unconvinced that he has ever isolated a pure example of this: "I consider that I have shown by examples how an ambiguity can approach the third-type definition, which is perhaps rather like a limit."[45] The language is mathematical: in mathematics, a "limit" is a quantity which a function or sum of a series can be made to approach as closely as desired. The problem is that the limit at infinity of the function of type-three ambiguity, from the point of view of literary criticism, is zero: at its limit, this type of ambiguity "has no function and is of no interest."[46]

And so Empson ambiguously suggests that ambiguity of the third type, as the "connection between the two halves of an ornamental comparison, the two meanings of a pun," approaches zero (the state of "no connection"), seems to give only "trivial" pleasure.[47] He chooses this word advisedly, for in mathematics the word *trivial* describes something that gives rise to no difficulty and so, in Empson's words, "is of no interest."[48] It denotes objects that have a very simple structure (such as an empty set, a set containing no numbers) and proofs or solutions (to an equation) that are very simple but for the sake of completeness cannot be ignored. This is precisely what Empson wishes to acknowledge about ambiguity of the third type: at its limit, this type of ambiguity is indeed "trivial" ("it has no function and is of no interest"), yet it retains "theoretical importance." There is also some value in the "formal satisfaction" of "a connection between two ideas" even as they approach the limit of "no connection" and the set of type-three ambiguity thereby becomes empty of literary import: "there is at least the pleasure ... in seeing the shell even when it is empty."[49]

•

The mathematical analogies by which Empson proceeds throughout Chapter Three constitute another hint that it is suffused with anxiety about the influence on him of Graves's theories about the unconscious. Early in the chapter, Empson links hypotheses about the unconscious to hypotheses about infinity: "one must continually feel doubtful about antitheses involving the idea of [the] 'unconscious,' which, like the infinities of mathematics, may be a convenient fiction or a product of definition."[50] It is possible that this analogy is suggested to Empson by Graves's having introduced mathematical language into his own account of the conscious and the unconscious.

Graves frequently mentions mathematics; in fact, he concludes the chapter "A Theory of Consciousness" by pointing to mathematics as a mode of thought that shows it is a mistake to use "the words 'primitive' and 'fantastic' and 'childish' and 'imaginary' as qualifying the emotional mode of thought as opposed to the intellectual mode."[51] But the most interesting mathematical aspect of his writing consists of his use of a vocabulary that is often meaningfully ambiguous in mathematical ways: "Consciousness is a term capable of vertical and horizontal subdividing, vertically into *deliberate* and *unwitting*, horizontally into *action*, *knowledge* (or 'pure consciousness') and *thought* ... In any series of action–knowledge–thought; action–knowledge–thought; action–knowledge–thought, there is continuous discrepancy between the units."[52] The words "term," "series," and "sequence" all have a special mathematical meaning in addition to their more general meanings. In mathematics, the word "term" means each quantity in a series; the word "sequence" indicates an ordered set of terms; the word "series" indicates a set of terms constituting a progression or having values determined by a common relation, or it can mean the sum of a sequence of terms.

Graves uses these words in a way that is faithful not just to their ordinary general sense, but also to their particular, specialized mathematical sense: the terms "action," "knowledge," and "thought" are ordered in the sequence "action–knowledge–thought," and a "series of action–knowledge–thought; action–knowledge–thought; action–knowledge–thought" is the progression of a consciousness that "is not an even flow."[53] He presents the partial sums of the series "action–knowledge–thought; action–knowledge–thought" as pointing to a whole of non-consciousness, for "these phases of consciousness are each derived from moments of non-conscious activity."[54] Concerning this whole, however, Graves declares that "we can never have any knowledge of its character," that it is an activity "of which knowledge can never ... appear."[55] In the mathematical context that his terms evoke, this "continuously interrupting and continuously interrupted sequence of non-conscious activity" resembles less the sort of infinite series that converges to a certain value called its limit (as 1/2 + 1/4 + 1/8 + 1/16 + ... converge to the value 1) than the sort of series that diverges – having no value that its partial sums approach (as 1/2 + 1/3 + 1/4 + 1/5 + ... approach no knowable, nameable value, for even though the terms become infinitely smaller, enough of them added together will always give a value greater than any number that can be named).

And so Graves not only uses mathematical words to account for the manifold meaningfulness of poetry, but he also does so ambiguously – a double incentive for someone recently reading mathematics at Magdalene College, under the supervision of the famous mathematician A.S. Ramsay, to read this material closely. Extraordinarily alert to ambiguity of all sorts, the mathematician Empson cannot have failed to notice that Graves uses what he would call ambiguity of the first type (in which "a word, a syntax, or a grammatical structure, while making only one statement, is effective in several ways at once") in explaining his theory of consciousness.[56]

Graves's purpose in availing himself of an implicitly mathematical vocabulary is ironic: he observes that consciousness cannot be known in the way a mathematical sequence can be known. In mathematics, a sequence can be said to be known if a formula can be given for any particular term by reference to the preceding terms or by reference to the particular term's position in the sequence. In the case of consciousness, the sequence of the terms "action," "knowledge," and "thought" simply does not obey a formula. No term can be known from any of the others by the application of a formula: "Action does not proceed from thought, nor knowledge from action, nor thought from knowledge."[57] Neither poetry nor life is amenable to formulaic representation. Just as "a poem will never be a copy of the poet's past life," so "no thought or mental picture can recur identically," and so "no action is merely a reproduction of a previous action."[58] Graves and Zeno agree that there is a great gulf between the finite sequences of life and the infinite sequences of mathematics: "if only two actions of a given sequence were identical in cause and effect, this sequence would achieve perpetual motion, which, in this finite universe, is not to be hoped."[59] Graves's point is that the prediction of the next item in a sequence that mathematics enables in the context of a principle of order is precisely what life disables because it subscribes to no principle of order.

Empson's mathematical training provides him with terms and analogies to explain the intricate theoretical relationships amongst elements that he identifies in ambiguous poetic language. He uses words like the ones that Graves uses, and he uses them in the same way Graves does – that is, ambiguously. He translates words and concepts from the mathematical contexts in which he has learned them to the new literary critical contexts that he is trying to develop, all the while encouraging the reader to keep in mind both their general and their more particular mathematical meanings.

For instance, a mathematical and logical conceptual framework helps him to explain how ambiguity of the seventh type fits into the "series" of ambiguities that he defines: "An example of the seventh type of ambiguity, or at any rate the last type of this series ... occurs when the two meanings of the word ... are the two opposite meanings defined by the context ... One might say, clinging to the logical aspect of this series, that the idea of 'opposite' ... admits of a great variety of interpretation."[60] Here Empson adds a footnote: "$-a .b$ is contrary to a for all values of b."[61] In any such pair of opposites, he suggests, "you are only stating, for instance, a scale, which might be extended between any two points, though no two points themselves are opposites."[62]

Recognizing that the idea of opposition in poetry has logical, psychological, mathematical, and grammatical dimensions, Empson finds it easiest to explain the way the ambiguity of opposition ranges between the potential to condense two statements into one, on the one hand, and the potential to make extractable from one statement an indefinite number of meanings, on the other, by figuring this range of potentials in terms of a formula:

> When a contradiction is stated with an air of conviction it may be meant to be resolved in either of two ways, corresponding to thought and feeling, corresponding to knowing and not knowing one's way about the matter in hand. Grammatical machinery may be assumed which would make the contradiction into two statements; thus "p and $-p$" may mean: "If $a=a_1$, then p; if $a=a_2$, then $-p$." If a_1 and a_2 are very different from one another, so that the two statements are fitted together with an exhilarating ingenuity,

> then I should put the statement into my sixth type [of ambiguity]; if a_1 and a_2 are very like one another, so that the contradiction draws attention both to the need for and the difficulty of separating them, then I should regard the statement as an ambiguity of the seventh type ... If "*p* and – *p*" could only be resolved in one way into: "If $a=a_1$, then *p*; if $a=a_2$, then – *p*," it might fairly be called an ambiguity, containing two separate statements under the appearance of one ... But it is evident that any degree of complexity of meaning can be extracted by "interpreting" a contradiction; any ${}_xa_1$ and ${}_xa_2$ may be selected, that can be attached to some ${}_xa$ arising out of *p*; and any such pair can then be read the other way round, as "If ${}_xa={}_xa_2$, then *p*; if ${}_xa={}_xa_1$, then – *p*." The original contradiction has thus been resolved into an indefinite number of contradictions: "If $a={}_xa_y$, then *p* and –*p*," to each of which the same process may again be applied.[63]

Empson and Graves agree: the limit of contradiction and the limit of discrepancy is the same – indefinite.

Like Graves, Empson acknowledges a gulf between the formulas of mathematics and logic and the messy facts of life and poetry, and he invokes an "outside-consciousness" similar to Graves's non-consciousness by which to preserve a convenient fiction of order. In life and literature, he observes,

> contradictions are often used ... when the speaker does not know what a_1 and a_2 are; he satisfies two opposite impulses and, as a sort of apology, admits that they contradict, but claims that they are like the soluble contradictions, and can safely be indulged; by admitting the weakness of his thought he seems to have sterilised it, to know better already than anyone who might have pointed the contradiction out; he claims the sympathy of his audience in that "we can none of us say more than this," and gains dignity in that even from the poor material of human ignorance he can distil grace of style ... [H]uman life is so much a matter of juggling with contradictory impulses (Christian-worldly, sociable-independent, and suchlike) that one is accustomed to thinking people are probably sensible if they follow first one, and then the other, of two such courses; any inconsistency that it seems possible to act upon shows that they ... have a fair title to humanity.[64]

Graves's interrupting nonconsciousness serves the same purpose: it explains discrepancy in any explanation of our thoughts and actions as the human condition; we cannot know the non-conscious activity which is at the core of each of us. The Graves who says in his own words that "knowledge can never appear" of the continuously interruptive, non-conscious source of discrepancies in consciousness becomes the figure in Empson's text who from the poor material of human ignorance can gracefully and sympathetically affirm, "we can none of us say more than this."

•

Conceding that with "two notions ... most sharply and consciously detached from one another" in type-three ambiguity "one finds oneself forced to question its value," Empson concludes Chapter Three with a *tour de force* of ambiguous words, until he can no longer suppress the mathematician within, at which point numbers and mathematical notations explicitly supplement words in search of a value that seems to be as much numerical as aesthetic.[65]

Of type-three ambiguity of the special sort (the connection of two ideas by a single word) he suggests that "it must seem trivial to use one word with an effort when there is time enough to say two more simply; even if time is short it seems only twice as useful, in a sort of numerical way."[66] Concerning not this special sort of ambiguity, but rather "general ambiguity of the third type" (associations "concerning whole states of minds" implied by "several different topics, several universes of discourse, several modes of judgement or of feeling"), Empson finds that "the value of the general variety of ambiguity of the third type is no more obvious."[67] He suspects that the duality at the heart of ambiguity may be the key to its value: "You remember how Proust, at the end of that great novel, having convinced the reader with the full sophistication of his genius that he is going to produce an apocalypse, brings out with pathetic faith, as a fact of absolute value, that sometimes when you are living in one place you are reminded of living in another place, and this, since you are now apparently living in two places, means that you are outside time, in the only state of beatitude that he can imagine. In any one place (atmosphere, mental climate) life is tolerable; in any two it is an ecstasy. Is it the number two, one is forced to speculate, which is of this encouraging character?"[68] The mathematician cannot resist putting this insight more generally: "Is to live in *n* + 1 places necessarily more valuable than to live in *n*?"[69]

Empson's answer is "yes." He believes that two is always better than one and, more generally, that a higher number of mental events is always better than any lesser number of mental events. The number two is fundamental to aesthetic value: to make "a connection between two ideas, even when they are merely both relevant and need not have been particularly connected," is still "to connect things in an illuminating way."[70] And so "Proust's belief, as a matter of novel-writing, is very convincing ... the pleasure of style is continually to be explained by just such a releasing and knotted duality, where those who have been wedded in the argument are bedded together in the phrase."[71] As Graves puts it in *Impenetrability*, "When particular words very highly charged with meaning in their context occur in English literature, this is counted a great virtue. In logical literatures it is a vice, by the rule of 'one word, one meaning' ... When such a concentration of forces can be exerted at a single point in literature, then, in Humpty-Dumpty's words, 'there's glory for you!'"[72] For Humpty-Dumpty Graves, to have meaning + 1 is always better than to have one meaning only. According to Empson, "one must assume that *n* + 1 is more valuable than *n* for any but the most evasively mystical theory of value."[73] Ambiguity of the third type, then, which posits the barest possible connection between two ideas, marks the theoretically minimum expression of knotted duality from which any release of literary pleasure can be achieved.

For Empson, the basic insight of Graves's conflict theory consists of its recognition of the philosophical, psychological, and poetic virtue of two. As Graves explains, "My contention is that where a conflict between any two interests occurs, one cannot finally supplant the other; the ruin of this interest will inevitably spell the ruin of that."[74] Whether the binary opposition involves "the fervour of the prayer-meeting" and "the desire for sexual expression," or "sin and grace," or the conscious and the unconscious, Graves's point is constant: they "seem to alternate in equal force."[75] Recall that "between the 'deliberate' and the 'unwitting' there is ... only this distinction, that the deliberate is in the present tense, the 'unwitting' in the past."[76] The deliberate and the unwitting, or the conscious and the unconscious, are always already a part of each other: "when we speak of a deliberate mode of action we mean that the deliberate mode is at the time dominating the unwitting mode which cannot consequently appear."[77] According to Graves, duality is fundamental to consciousness. Even he seems to recognize that his state of nonconsciousness is simply a product of definition, a postulate of theoretical importance with no practical relevance for a reader of poetry.

The poet is society's agent for – and the poem is the occasion for – the reconciling expression and experience of this duality. As Grave presents it, duality is expressed and experienced as one's being two or more persons at once. One can see that what Empson presents as largely his own insight into the value of duality is evident more obviously and more insistently in Graves than in Proust. Empson represents Proust's insight in rather awkward geographical terms: living in more than "one place (atmosphere, mental climate) … is an ecstasy."[78] The point is psychological, not geographical; art provides the psychological place for the experience of two mental places (the present and the past), two mental atmospheres, two mental climates, and so on. And the point is Graves's.

•

Not surprisingly, then, given its role in alerting Empson to the poetic virtue of duality, Graves's modified theory of consciousness plays a part in Empson's definition of the fourth and seventh types of ambiguity as well – definitions that depend on distinctions concerning how much poets know about their own meaning and to what degree they control it. The difficulty Empson has in finding examples of type-three ambiguities stems from his agreement with Graves that poetry cannot be predicted or constrained by the poet's conscious intention.

On the one hand, Empson finds a "curious ambiguity" in a couple of poems by Dryden – "a full-blown pun, such as Restoration poets would normally have been aware of, and made, if they had used it, into an ambiguity frankly of the third type, and yet the reader seems meant to absorb it without realising it is there."[79] Similarly, there are "puzzling" ambiguities elsewhere: "he seems to claim only to be saying one thing, even when one does not know which of two things he is saying."[80] (Graves would find here the distinction between the "deliberate" and the "unwitting.") On the other hand, even in his list of eighteenth-century puns demonstrating "self-consciousness," Empson cannot bring himself to limit the consciousness of the poet to that of a punster: "to join together so smartly a business and a philosophical notion, a nautical and a gastronomical notion, with an air of having them in watertight compartments in your own mind (each such subject has its rules which save a man from making himself ridiculous, and you have learnt them), so that it seems to you very odd and agile to have jumped from one to the other – all this belongs to the light-weight tattling figure (it is very odd it should have been Dr. Johnson's) ... the man quick to catch the tone of his company, who knows the talk of the town."[81] The conditions ought to be right for ambiguity of the third type: "The mind has compartments which hold opinions and modes of judgment which conflict when they come together ... compartments, therefore, which require attention, and one is particularly conscious of anything that mixes them up. If the two spheres of action of a generalisation, or the two halves of an ornamental comparison, involve two such compartments which must be thought of in two ways, then we have a general ambiguity of the third type."[82] Yet in the case of Johnson's writing, it is difficult to explain whose is the controlling consciousness and just what it controls in the writing by which it manifests itself: that the mind's compartments are separate is only an "air"; the air is imparted by a "figure"; the discrepancy between "Doctor Johnson's" poetic figure and his actual person is remarked. Ambiguity of the third type cannot be maintained in the midst of such an array of supplementary ambiguities.

In contrast to Graves's suggestion that "between the 'deliberate' and the 'unwitting' there is ... only this distinction, that the 'deliberate' is in the present tense, the 'unwitting' in the past," Empson increasingly limits to the reader, rather than the poet, the possibility of limiting awareness to "consciousness of a particular part of" the punning device.[83] At the beginning of the chapter, the "questions of consciousness" are focused first, and most explicitly, on the "the direction of the reader's attention" and the "interaction between separated parts of his mind." The poet's consciousness is treated much less explicitly ("its most definite examples are likely to be found, in increasing order of self-consciousness, among the seventeenth-century mystics who stress the conscious will, the eighteenth-century stylists who stress rationality, clarity, and satire, and the harmless nineteenth-century punsters who stress decent above-board fun").[84] The poet's consciousness, it seems, just cannot be presumed to be as simple as the reader's: unable to claim that the poet is ever free of the "unconscious," Empson confines himself to the claim that the pun as narrative device "is less intimately an expression of sensibility."[85] Expression of sensibility is not entirely a matter predicted or constrained by deliberation. No more than Graves does Empson believe that the poet can create "*deliberate* poetic allegory," and deliberate poetic puns, uncomplicated by the "*unwitting* uprush of inspired poetry."[86]

Graves demonstrates this point in *On English Poetry* in his discussion of the same sort of satirical and didactic verse that baffles Empson. According to Graves, "only the theory that a conflict of emotional ideas is a necessary ingredient of verse to make it poetry, will satisfactorily explain why many kinds of verse, loosely called Poetry, such as Satire and Didactic verse are yet popularly felt not to be the 'highest' forms of Poetry."[87] There is too much deliberation here and not enough unwitting inspiration. Graves therefore relates "mere verse" to poetry "as chimpanzee to man."[88] Occasionally, however, in one case out of a hundred, chimpanzee versifiers write a poem (if not *Hamlet*) "in spite of themselves": "Where the writer is dominated by only one aim, in satire, the correction of morals; in didactic verse, instruction; there is no conflict and therefore no poetry. But in rare cases where some Juvenal slips through feelings of compunction to a momentary mood of self-satire and even forgets himself so much as to compliment his adversary; or in didactic verse where a sudden doubt arises and the teacher admits himself a blind groper after truth (so Lucretius time and time again) and breaks his main argument in digressions after loveliness and terror, only then does Poetry appear. It flashes out with the surprise and shock of a broken electric circuit."[89] Empson notes something similar in his observations about the "puzzling" ambiguities that ought not to appear in the satirical and didactic verse of Dryden, but nonetheless somehow do.[90]

For Graves, "the power of surprise ... marks all true poetry."[91] He defines two limits: on the one hand, "Poetry over which the poet has no direct control"; on the other hand, "Poetry over which he has a certain conscious control."[92] At the limit marked by the poet's "conscious control," the element of "the unforeseen fusion in his mind of apparently contradictory emotional ideas" disappears, for nothing is unforeseen.[93] That is, the possibility of surprise disappears. And so "the weakness of originally unspontaneous poetry seems to be that the poet has only the very small conscious part of his experience to draw upon, and therefore in co-ordinating the central images, his range of selection is narrower and the links are only on the surface."[94] Surprise "seems to result from a foreknowledge of certain unwitting processes of the reader's mind, for which the poet more or less deliberately provides."[95] Neither can the processes of the reader's mind be completely witting, nor can the processes of the poet's writing be completely deliberate, for such wit and such deliberation mark the limit at which surprise – and with it, poetry – disappears.

Empson agrees. On the way to demonstrating both the poet's control of ambiguities of the third type and the reader's awareness of the deliberateness with which the poet invokes these ambiguities, Empson always finds that he is on the verge of another type of ambiguity – one of which the poet is not conscious or the poet's consciousness of which cannot clearly be determined. Thus the shift from his declaration at the beginning of the chapter that "it is not true" that ambiguities of the third type "contain no examples of interest to the reader of poetry" and so have only "theoretical importance," to his concession at the end of the chapter that the third type indeed seems to be a trivial product of definition.[96] Reviewing his literary analysis throughout Chapter Three, and returning "to the notion ... put at the beginning of the chapter, that in so far as an ambiguity is valuable, it cannot be purely of the third type," Empson concedes that there can be no pure example of ambiguity of the third type: "I consider that I have shown by examples how an ambiguity can approach the third-type definition, which is rather like a limit, and yet remain valuable."[97] Ambiguity of the third type turns out to be a convenient fiction postulated as the limit of a series of progressively self-conscious uses of ambiguity.

5

Models of Practically Ambiguous Criticism

For Graves, then, the necessary and inevitable discrepancy between the consciousness of the poet and the subsequent, and always larger, non-conscious experience of writing the poem (which may include the poet's intention but also inevitably exceeds it) guarantees ambiguity. The reader (and indeed the poet himself) is left to give an account after the fact of the "invisible property-shifting" that constitutes the simultaneously continuous and non-identical nature of the relationship between the poet's experience, the words of the poem, and the reader's experience of the poem. In many ways, *Seven Types of Ambiguity* is Empson's anatomy of this poetic property-shifting. Like Northrop Frye in his account of archetypes in *Anatomy of Criticism*, and like structuralist theorists after mid-century generally, Empson is less interested in a metaphysical, psychological, or neurological accounting for the patterns of semantic property-shifting that he discerns in literature than in a taxonomically exhaustive accounting of the patterns themselves. However much Graves's conflict theory was "the necessary background for a theory of ambiguity," perhaps the biggest nudge that Graves gave Empson came in the form of his practical criticism in support of his theory.[1] Much of what we think of as Empson's way of reading poetry is actually Graves's way, as Empson always said and yet always managed to say quite ineffectively.

Empson was perhaps most impressed by Graves's practical application of his "'conflict' theory of poetry" to readings of the conflicts at the heart of religious poetry. In fact, Empson's appropriation of Graves's point of view on such poetry shows how he went about the extrapolation of a systematic treatment of ambiguity from Graves's always provocative – and sometimes outrageous – observations about how poems express conflict. It also shows the source in Graves's work of features that Empson would use to distinguish ambiguities of the third, fourth, and seventh type.

Empson brings his analysis of ambiguity to bear on the same kind of poetry, and on many of the same poets. In due course Allen Tate and Cleanth Brooks, among other American New Critics, would do the same.[2] In *Poetic Unreason*, Graves presents Herbert's "The Bag" as "an interesting case" of the "Jekyll and Hyde" poetry that expresses "conflicts between sub-personalities": "Poetry of the Jekyll and Hyde variety, that is poetry where the manifest content and the latent content represent opposite sides of a conflict, finds many instances in 'so-called' religious poetry."[3] According to Graves, "between Jekyll and Hyde there is necessarily conflict," and in the case of religious poetry, "The more Dr. Jekyll hates Mr. Hyde, the more frequent will be the manifestations which trouble the ecclesiastic mind, 'Sin,' 'Temptation,' 'Hypocrisy.'"[4] In Herbert's "The Bag," the general conflict, as in "many instances of so-called 'religious' poetry," is between the sacred and the secular, the spirit and the body, divine love and earthy love; in particular, "The Divine Figure in *The Bag* is fused with the figure of the temptress and at the end of the poem subordinate to her, where it has distinct feminine characteristics."[5]

Graves says that he puts this particularly outrageous reading of Herbert's poem early in the book so that if readers "do not shut up *Poetic Unreason* at this point, they will have no occasion to do so at any later provocation."[6] Designing in all his early books to be provocative (in his "Note" prefacing *On English Poetry*, he indicates "that when putting a cat among pigeons it is always advisable to make it as large a cat as possible"), Graves develops in his prose the same strategy developed in his talks on poetry at Oxford when he was studying there in the 1920s for his B. Litt. degree. Miranda Seymour describes a "well-attended" talk in 1922: "The talk was based on the old nursery rhyme 'How Many Miles to Babylon?'… He started with his theory, taken from Rivers, that all poems emerged from a state of mental conflict. He used the old rhyme to illustrate his case. The author of the poem – it is anonymous – was conjured up by him with a mass of circumstantial detail which left his audience shouting and applauding."[7] The circumstantial detail in question is information that Graves recovered from the denotations and connotations of the words of the poem and from the patterns of associations they form.

Graves understands as axiomatic the principle articulated a generation later by Wimsatt and Beardsley: "even a short lyric poem is dramatic, the response of a speaker (no matter how abstractly conceived) to a situation (no matter how universalized)."[8]

A version of this talk is distilled into a dialogue between Graves and a "Friend" ("a synthetic version of conversations on the same subject with several friends, English and American") published first as an essay in *The Spectator* in July of 1922 and then as part of the first essay of *Poetic Unreason:* the essay that Empson recalls in his preface to the second edition of *Seven Types of Ambiguity* (in fact, the dialogue begins on the very page from which Empson quotes Graves).[9] The nursery rhyme runs as follows:

How many miles to Babylon?
Threescore miles and ten.
Can I get there by candle-light?
Yes, and back again.[10]

Crafting an imaginary Socratic dialogue out of the various talks about "How Many Miles to Babylon?" that he gave in the early 1920s, Graves argues that at the heart of the poem is "the old dialogue ... between body and soul" evoked, on the one hand, by a contrast between "innocence, as expressed in 'candlelight,'" and the Biblical association of Babylon with magnificence, exile, and "world, flesh and devil," and, on the other hand, by a contrast between the child and the adult, linked by Biblical association of the phrase "threescore and ten" with the length in years of a human life. And so, "It is a dialogue, the man who has gone astray after the lusts of the world, addressing a child who lies innocently in bed. When the child asks the question, the man feels that, in spite of the child's apparent helplessness and ignorance of the determinate side of life, he himself, with all his strength and worldly wisdom, is far inferior in power to the child ... 'Keep innocency,' it preaches, 'and you can pass through the Babylon of manhood, and return safe and sound with as much ease as in childhood you visited that magnificent city in your dreams and came back before the candle had burned to its socket.'"[11]

Could the original version of the rhyme have used the word "Babyland" instead of "Babylon," the similarity of their sound leading through the oral tradition to the corruption of the one into the other? No: "That *Babylon* is the original version seems proved by the interaction of the other symbols too closely for coincidence."[12] Will the Biblical associations of "Babylon, candlelight, and threescore and ten" prompt the same associations in everyone?[13] No: "As there are degrees of implication, so there are degrees of perception. There is a common core of experience, certainly, but each individual has, for instance, different personal associations with candlelight, which alter the force of the conflict, whether the candle is thought of more particularly as a friendly charm against darkness, or whether the short flickering life of the candle may associate itself more nearly with the threescore and ten idea."[14]

The talk at Oxford and the synthesized conversation in *Poetic Unreason* contain the essence of Graves's theory and practice. Perhaps had this sophisticated analysis not focused on a nursery rhyme, Empson might have cited it, rather than the study of Shakespeare's sonnet, as the source of his method. Certainly he seems to have noticed it, since he begins his most important chapter (on the second type of ambiguity) with the same strategy: showing how an apparently simple poem may in fact be extraordinarily complex. He quotes an anonymous poem:

> Cupid is winged and doth range;
> Her country so my love doth change.
> But change she earth, or change she sky,
> Yet I will lover her till I die.

How many ways are there of reading the ambiguities here?

> I will love her though she moves from this part of the earth to one out of reach; I will love her though she goes to live under different skies; I will love her though she moves from this earth and sky to another planet; I will love her though she moves into a social or intellectual sphere where I cannot follow; I will love her though she alters the earth and sky I have got now, though she destroys the bubble of worship in which I am now living by showing herself unworthy to be its object; I will love her though, being yet worthy of it, by going away she changes my earth into desire and unrest, and my heaven into despair; I will love her even if she has both power and will to upset both the orderly ideals of men in general (heaven), and the system of society in general (earth); she may alter the earth and the sky *she* has now by

> abandoning her faith or in just punishment becoming outcast, and still I will love her; she may change *my* earth by killing me, but till it comes I will go on loving.[15]

Anticipating objections that he should derive such complex meaning from so simple a poem, Empson says: "This may look as if I were merely writing down different sorts of change, which would not, of course, show direct ambiguity; but *change* may mean 'move to another' or 'alter the one you have got,' and *earth* may be the lady's private world, or the poet's, or that of mankind at large. All meanings to be extracted from these are the immediate meaning insisted upon by the words, and yet the whole charm of the poem is its extravagant, its unreasonable, simplicity."[16] He plays the same game as Graves, for the same effect.

Although friends agreeing that "How Many Miles to Babylon?" is a good poem can initially offer no explanation of its merits beyond the fact that "it's so simple," Graves can show them a pattern underneath the surface of the poem that persuades them otherwise: "I invariably found that when I asked people to think of this poem as composed of a number of linked ideas reconciled in a common symbolism, so as to be emotionally felt but not intellectually classified by the reader, they admitted that … it was a poem of extraordinary subtle and condensed argument."[17] Just like Empson, that is, Graves claims to be revealing in his practical literary criticism the actual associations made unconsciously by properly qualified readers of poetry.

In terms of Graves's cat-and-pigeons figure, the cat is his conflict theory, suspect because of its descent from the ostensibly "scientific assumptions" of psychological theories by Freud and Rivers, causing outrage because promulgated by occasional "overstatements"; the pigeons are "literary enthusiasts" who "seem to regard poetry as something miraculous, something which it is almost blasphemous to analyze."[18] Not everyone in his audience, in other words, applauded Graves when he interpreted literature by means of his conflict theory. In Tom Matthews's account of the reaction of those who attended Graves's Oxford talks, for instance, the dons resent Graves's blasphemous accounts of canonized poetic miracles:

> [The] moment he stopped, they were on him. His first attacker was an older man, evidently one of a strong scatteration of dons among us. This academic, in a voice of mingled scorn and fury,

> wished Mr. Graves to enlighten us, if he would be so kind, on the conflict in Tennyson's mind which produced "The Charge of the Light Brigade." Mr. Graves did so – to general applause, if not to the satisfaction of his questioner. "The Sinking of the Royal George"? "Tyger! Tyger! Burning Bright"? Kipling? Eyes rolling with mischief, smiling almost apologetically, Graves fielded these hard-hit questions with deft ease, and no runs were scored by the other side. This was a game at which he excelled any of his present competitors, and it was a pleasure to watch him play.[19]

Graves alludes to this "game" that he plays at such talks in his discussion of other religious poems in *Poetic Unreason*:

> I was challenged recently to say how far the religious poetry of Francis Thompson was of this Jekyll and Hyde variety … I answered that *Love in Dian's Lap* was applicable to more poems than the heading covers, and that where Thompson writes "The Blessed Virgin" we know that she has a human prototype … I was next particularly asked, "What about the Hound of Heaven?" I had not considered the question, but going home and re-reading the poem, I found *Love in Dian's Lap* written large across it … I gave this analysis to my objector who accepted it, or said he did, but further asked me, "What about Thompson's address to the dead Cardinal?" I said that the position there is much more painful because there is no solution to the trouble, which appears to be a later phase of *The Hound of Heaven* conflict.[20]

Because of the books that he was publishing, Graves's standing amongst those interested in literary theory in the 1920s was high, yet his performances not just at Oxford but also as far afield as the University of Leeds also helped to spread his fame. Years later, when Richards, recalling his first conversation with Empson about *A Survey of Modernist Poetry*, refers to "the games of interpretation which Laura Riding and Robert Graves were playing with the unpunctuated form of 'The expense of spirit in a waste of shame,'" it is easy to assume that he is being dismissive of their method as *mere* games-playing, just as he is dismissive in *Principles of Literary Criticism* of what he characterizes as Graves's Freudian method.[21] Yet it is also the case that anyone familiar with either Graves's work or his reputation could quite matter-of-factly, and not necessarily insultingly (or at least not as insultingly as one might at first think), refer to Graves's practical readings of poetry as "games of interpretation."

Richards was dismissive of Graves's games of interpretation, and he was clearly not alone in this disdain. Graves himself recognized the offence that his readings could occasion: "In writing this of Thompson I hope that I am not giving offence to such of his friends as survive, and will be grateful for any fresh evidence either for or against my view; but I protest that I have not written lightly or without much more detailed research than I have given proof of here."[22] His cat, then, is not always "as large a cat as possible," but only because some of the pigeons were friends, or friends of friends, whose feathers he did not want to ruffle over-much.[23] Graves hastens to reassure readers that he speculates only about Herbert's dream life, not his actual sex life: "I want to emphasize that I do not think that the context that gave rise to the poem could have been a direct encounter with the temptress whom I postulate."[24] Instead, Graves presents the fusion of the divine figure and the figure of the temptress "on the analogy of St. Theresa's visions and a great many other similar records of dreams."[25]

According to Graves, the first eight lines of Herbert's poem are ecclesiastically circumspect, but thereafter there is a pattern of sexual allusion beneath the story of the life of Jesus. In the surface story, Jesus leaves his heavenly home, along the way removing his "azure mantle" and "robes of glorie," finally "undressing all the way," to "repair unto an inne," where he declares that his "doore/Shall still be open," and that he will be listening so intently within his room that "Sighs will convey/anything to me."[26] Graves identifies a subtext about prostitution, which he presents "in the form of a story of what I am convinced occurred, filling in the bare outline with lively trifles of my own invention" (the invention consisting of Graves's imagining Herbert in a dream conversing with his friend John Donne, once the rakish Jack Donne but "now a reformed character," who recounts his experience of having been solicited by a prostitute in "a low tavern in Penny-Farthing Lane"): "I had retired to my chamber ... and was now abed and dozing to sleep, when behold the door opens, and in walks a blue mantled wench. As one who cannot believe his eyes I watched her disrobe and set her clothes neatly upon this chair and that ... 'I am a minister of Christ,' I began ... [S]he went at last, but first she said, 'Man of God, mine is the room lying opposite, and the door is ajar. If you repent your unkindness, I shall hear you sigh and be with you again.'"[27] According to Graves, "the first stanza of the piece and the next two lines is a chapter of the Jekyll life of Herbert the saint, the remainder of the piece is a chapter of the Hyde life of Herbert the sinner."[28]

Graves's other examples of Jekyll and Hyde religious poetry make the same point about the split in the author's mind that such poetry reveals. He offers a medieval example:

> It is customary for modern writers to eulogize the religious lyrics of the Middle Ages as being so full of true religious passion that they are almost erotic. This is a queer way of putting it. A poem like that of the medieval Irish nun beginning:
>
> > Jesukin, my Jesukin,
> > Dwells my little cell within.
> > What were wealth of clerics high?
> > All is lie, but Jesukin.
>
> denotes a positive rebellion in phantasy against the formal system of abstinence to which her life is devoted and a hankering after a lover and child.[29]

There is also "the curious contrary case to *The Bag* ... that of Burns' ballad *John Barleycorn*."[30] Ostensibly "a simple allegory of very easily discernible meaning" (the life and death of John Barleycorn corresponds "with the history of the planting and reaping of barley and its distillation and eventual appearance in the tavern as whiskey"), the poem's "allegorical symbolism goes a little queer," according to Graves, and so reveals "a second allegory working beneath."[31] In this second allegory, "from the beginning to the end, but in the haphazard order of events which one is accustomed to find in allegorical dreams ... the allusions are appropriate to the story of the life, death, and resurrection of Jesus Christ."[32] Burns's conscious interest being the whiskey, his submerged interest being the Gospels, "here it is Jekyll who is recessive and Hyde who is dominant."[33] Faced with Allen Upward's suggestion that "it is most improbable that Burns had the Gospels in his mind" when he wrote the poem and that one must therefore postulate a race memory such as that outlined in *The Golden Bough* to account for the religious dimensions of the poem, Graves disagrees: "The conflict theory accounts for the unwitting interweaving of religion with praise of drink, and if details of the Gospels are enough to account for the form John Barleycorn has taken, it is not necessary to postulate a racial memory which can store up such close ceremonial detail through the centuries."[34] For Graves, Burns's nonconscious activity suffices to explain the continuity within the discrepancy in "John Barleycorn" between the "*deliberate* poetic allegory" and the "*unwitting* uprush of inspired poetry."[35]

On a number of occasions, and at considerable length, and in connection with several types of ambiguity, Empson presents religious poetry – primarily that of Nashe, Richard Crashaw, and Herbert – in precisely these terms. Although it is in reference to the pun as an example of verbal ambiguity of the third type that Empson promises that he will discuss the "self-consciousness" of the puns "among the seventeenth-century mystics who stress the conscious will," it is in fact not until he turns from discussion of ambiguity of the third type "as a verbal matter" to discussion of "ambiguity of the third type ... as a matter concerning whole states of mind" that he actually discusses these poets.[36] It is the conflict in their psyche that is revealed by the conflict in the meanings of their words that really interests him.

Of this ambiguity Empson says:

> one might call this a general ambiguity of the third type ... what is said is valid in, refers to, several different topics, several universes of discourse, several modes of judgment or of feeling ... It may make a single statement and imply various situations to which it is relevant; thus I should call it an ambiguity of this type when an allegory is felt to have many levels of interpretation; or it may describe two situations and leave the reader to infer various things which can be said about both of them; thus I should call it an ambiguity of this type when an ornamental comparison is not merely using one thing to illustrate another, but is interested in two things at once, and is making them illustrate one another mutually.[37]

Empson explains that "Herbert and the devotional poets ... use a conceit to diffuse the interest back on to a whole body of experience, whose parts are supposed eventually reconcilable with one another; and the reader must pause after each display of wit to allow the various moods in which it could be read, the various situations to which it could refer, to sink into his mind."[38]

We are in Graves's territory again, as Empson acknowledges when he suggests that "it is especially to generalised ambiguity of the third type that ... [the] rather limited formula" of a certain "variety of the 'conflict' theory of poetry ... will apply."[39] According to Empson, Herbert is the type of poet who is able to be "several sorts of men at once," able to "reconcile his tribe in his own person."[40] The reader must pause to allow the various relevant moods and situations to sink into his mind because "the mind has compartments holding opinions and modes of judgment that conflict when they come together ... and one is particularly conscious of anything that mixes them up."[41] Compartments of the mind in conflict versus sub-personalities in conflict: where is the difference?

Not surprisingly, perhaps, Empson's central concern in this analysis is not the ambiguous potential of the pun, but rather the ambiguous potential of allegory. On the one hand, "it is not, of course, the normal use of allegory to make a statement which is intended to have several interpretations. The normal use is to tell a homely story and make clear that it means something else ... so that there is only one real meaning, which the first meaning is frankly a device to convey."[42] This is what Graves means by "a *deliberate* poetic allegory in the established tradition," and it is precisely the possibility of deliberately predicting or intending one real meaning, effectively constraining poetry to one real meaning, that he denies. Graves suggests that without ambiguous potential, allegory is not poetry. Empson implicitly agrees, given the examples of allegory that he discusses, but he also explains that he finds two ambiguous potentialities in allegory: the first, although "not, of course, the normal use of allegory," by means of "a statement which is intended to have several interpretations," and the second, according to a footnote added to the second edition, by means of "effects which are undoubtedly ambiguous" even in the absence of a statement intended to have several interpretations.[43]

In fact, Empson's understanding of "ambiguity of the third type ... as a matter concerning whole states of mind" "when an allegory is felt to have many levels of interpretation" can be seen to have been inspired by Graves's observations in *The Meaning of Dreams* about the nature of romantic allegory. Noting that to say "that *La Belle Dame* is a symbol of death by consumption" and "To say that *La Belle Dame* is at the same time symbolic of the Fanny Brawne affair is likely to offend the logically minded," Graves explains that "the double allegory is extremely common in Romantic Poetry, occurring when two conflicts are in progress at the same time in the poet's mind and are closely bound up with and aggravating each other."[44]

So of course Empson acknowledges that "it is especially to generalised ambiguity of the third type" that the "rather limited formula" of "the 'conflict' theory of poetry" will apply, for Empson's definition of generalised ambiguity of the third type descends from Graves's practical criticism of romantic allegory.

•

As we have seen, in Nashe's *Summer's Last Will and Testament*, whether the conflict between the "arrogant exaltation of the mystic" and the "terror of the natural man at ... the approach of death" eventuates in the "Christian fusion of these two elements into ... humility" is unclear.[45] The poem might offer two apparently unconnected meanings that the poet self-consciously presents "in one word simultaneously," alternative meanings that "combine to make clear a complicated state of mind in the author," or a full contradiction that marks "a fundamental division in the writer's mind" (ambiguities of types three, four, and seven, respectively), but at the heart remains the fundamental conflict in these Christian poets between the spirit and the body, the question being to what extent the poet is conscious of these ambiguities and in control of their presentation.[46]

For a clearer example of type-three ambiguity, therefore, Empson turns to Crashaw's "Caritas Nimia," a poem "strictly of the type in question": "Sacred and profane love (in a devotional setting which would consider them very different) are seen as one."[47] According to Empson, Crashaw understands that he engineers a mutual comparison between different kinds of love ("he is well enough aware that they belong to different worlds"): "In this case, though not always in Crashawe, it seems a matter of conscious ingenuity and artifice that Cupid and the love of Christ should so firmly be used to interpret one another."[48] Empson advances Herbert's poem "The Temple" as another poem that consciously contrasts sacred and profane love in order "to treat them as the same, or to explain one by the other."[49] As he explains in a note to the revised edition of 1947, "Herbert keeps the symbols apart with the full breadth of the technique of allegory; though the contrast in question is the same as that of the

Crashaw example."[50] In this kind of devotional verse, recourse to allegory is a sign of the poet's awareness of the differences between the kinds of love that the poem involves.

Insofar as he accepts that "the 'conflict' theory of poetry" applies to religious poetry, Empson accepts that Crashaw and Herbert are able to "be several sorts of men at once" – in this case, saint and sinner – and that they are aware of being both, reconciling in their poems the reconciliation in their persons of these two ways of life.[51] Yet Empson's phrase, "*seems* a matter of conscious ingenuity" (emphasis added), on the one hand, and his later confession in a note to the 1947 edition regarding "The Temple" ("I am not sure that Herbert did not mean the poem dramatically as said by a foolish character"), on the other hand, show once again that Empson remains unconvinced that ambiguity can be predicted or constrained by the deliberating consciousness of either poet or reader.[52]

As with Crashaw, so with Herbert: it is not always the case that he *consciously* uses sacred and profane love to interpret each other. In a verse from Herbert's "Pilgrimage," Empson finds ambiguity of the third type because in juxtaposing angels as coins and angels as messengers of God "its methods, allegory and the overt pun, are the most conscious of all devices to produce ambiguity." He has evidence that Herbert is self-consciously determined to "reconcile his tribe in his own person," yet he admits that it is also the case that "the various meanings are felt as a coherent unit," suggesting that "we have thus practically arrived already at the fourth type, in which the ambiguity is less conscious, because more completely accepted, or fitted into a larger unit."[53]

This transition from ambiguity of type three to ambiguity of type four is explained by Graves: "Hyde and Jekyll co-exist in an individual as possibilities, but in relation to any given situation only one will appear at a time while the conflict continues. If a situation occurs in which they *can* sink their differences, the action of the individual will be neither Hyde-ish nor Jekyllesque but of such a nature thereafter Hyde will no longer be Hyde or Jekyll, Jekyll, but a single individual will emerge not predominantly Jekyll or Hyde, or merely Jekyll plus Hyde, but a new creation making the continuance of the conflicting elements unnecessary."[54] So it would seem that a certain variety of the conflict theory of poetry applies equally "especially" to ambiguity of the fourth type: a "less conscious," "more completely accepted" ambiguity, an ambiguity "fitted into a larger unit."[55]

Graves says of this variety of conflict just what Empson says of seventh-type ambiguity:

> What has happened in poetry where there is disagreement between manifest statement and latent content seems to be this, then: that on the intellectual level either Jekyll or Hyde has already, before the poem appears, expressed an objection to the other or acted against his interests; on the emotional level that position is reversed; when the poem appears there is an outburst in symbolism against the victor. When this outburst now recorded on paper is referred to the intellectual level, in which the position is still unfavourable to the party employing the symbolism, there is no understanding on the part of the victor for the complaints of his opponent in the emotional mode, but the victor either interprets the symbolism in a sense pleasing to himself or views the poem as impersonal and inspired and has at any rate no conflict with it.[56]

Similarly, Empson says that in "cases of ambiguity of the seventh type … the ideas are no longer thought of as contradictory by the author, or if so, then only from a stylistic point of view; he has no doubt that they can be reconciled, and that he is stating their reconciliation."[57]

Graves says of the "Jekyll life" and the "Hyde life" that "neither of these conflicting lives has any respect for the rights of the other," and suggests with regard to the dream that he imagines as inspiring "The Bag" that "if Herbert had understood his dream he would have called his Hyde a blasphemer of the most abandoned character."[58] Herbert's not understanding the conflict between his sub-personalities is a necessary feature of this poem, for just as "direct solicitation" in "a direct encounter with the temptress" in question "would have been sternly met by the good man and the poem would have taken another form," so the poem would have taken another form "if Herbert had understood his dream."[59] Empson's point about the contradiction in Nashe's poem between "the fear of death and the hope of glory" is the same: "you may say … that the humility of the last line … acts as evasion of the contradiction, which moves it out of the conscious mind into a region of the judgment which can accept it without reconciling it" – making the poem an example of the same seventh type of ambiguity as found in Herbert's poem "The Sacrifice."[60]

Empson agrees with Graves about the psychological preconditions necessary for such conflicted poetry: "necessary if so high a degree of ambiguity is to seem normal" to the poet is the "releasing and reassuring condition" "in which the theological system is accepted so completely that the poet is only its mouthpiece."[61] Another device of "incidental convenience" toward this end is allegory: "In devotional verse it is often used ... to impose calm on the writer and allow him to evade his own habits of reticence; almost all sexual language, too ... is a hierarchy of devices of this kind."[62]

•

One can also detect the influence of Graves – no doubt reinforced by the example of Riding and Graves in *A Survey of Modernist Poetry* – in Empson's readiness to ascribe a persona to the speaking voice in a poem somewhat different from, and perhaps quite contradictory of, the voice associated with the known personality of the poet. Just as Riding and Graves acknowledge that the anti-Jewish prejudice in "Burbank with a Baedeker, Bleistein with a Cigar" may or may not belong to Eliot, but assuredly belongs to a point of view expressed in the poem, so Empson insists that in Herbert's poem "The Temple" there is a point of view from which someone can be seen (in the last line, "I did expect a ring") to express the expectation of receiving "the halo of a saint": "Herbert would not have meant that he himself expected the halo of a saint ... And yet after all, though I want to give full weight to this point of view [that the expected ring suggests "the perfect figure of Heaven or of eternity, marriage with God, or a halo,"] I am not sure that Herbert did not mean the poem dramatically as said by a foolish character, so that the halo could poke up its head quite prominently."[63] As we have seen, Empson implies the same question about the relationship between the poet and the speaking persona in eighteenth-century poetry generally, and between Doctor Johnson himself and his literary personae particularly.

Graves regularly presents his readings of poems in terms of the dialogues between conflicting points of view that he perceives within them. And so when Empson concludes his discussion of whether the last verse of Nashe's poem represents ambiguity of type three or type four, or even type seven, with the observation that he regards it as an example of the third type of ambiguity because he "cannot forget the difference" between the three "modes of feeling" and so finds that he must "read it aloud 'dramatically,' as a dialogue between three moods," one is tempted to conclude that he has been inspired in myriad ways by his reading of Graves's early work.[64] For Empson to read poetry out loud to himself as a dialogue between the poet's moods is clearly to follow the example of Graves in his paraphrasing of religious poems as sometimes outrageous dialogues between the poet's spiritual and sexual moods.

In defining ambiguity of the seventh type, Empson shows that he has paid close attention not just to Graves's speculations about the conflicted inner dialogues of religious poets but also to his speculations about the conflicted inner dialogues suggested by Keats's poetry. Empson explains that "an example of the seventh type of ambiguity ... occurs when the two meanings of the word, the two values of the ambiguity, are the two opposite meanings defined by the context, so that the total effect is to show a fundamental division in the writer's mind."[65] The point of Graves's analysis of "La Belle Dame sans Merci" is to show such a division in Keats's mind: "The *Merciless Lady* ... represents both the love that he feared and the death that he feared."[66] In fact, Graves affirms, "I know of no poem in any language which is ... apparently simple and even conventional ... yet opens up longer vistas of torment and horror and self-reproach and despair. Anyone can see that the restlessness of the poet's mind in a setting of this sort makes it impossible for him to marshal his feelings carefully and fully and logically; his agony if it ever finds expression beyond a beating of the breast and a tearing of the hair will use phrases of the most condensed and perverse imagery ... If *La Belle Dame* had not been bound by Keats' regard for the poetic conventions of the men he admired ... the whole thing might have appeared as a confused and disintegrated nightmare."[67]

Empson accepts Keats's mind as a good example of the divided mind, and finds in poetry from "St Agnes' Eve" to "Ode on Melancholy" that Keats uses "ambiguities of this type to convey a dissolution of normal experience into intensity of sensation."[68] To illustrate his point, Empson provides an extensive analysis of "Ode on Melancholy." In this analysis, he duplicates the points made in Graves's analysis of "La Belle Dame sans Merci" in *On English Poetry*.

Graves presents the poem as an expression of "suppressed emotional conflict": Keats's "growing passion for ... Fanny Brawne ... comes into conflict with the apprehension, not yet a certainty, of his own destined death from consumption, so that the merciless Lady, to put it baldly, represents both the woman he loved and the death he feared, the woman whom he wanted to glorify by his poetry and the death that would cut his poetry short."[69] In *The Meaning of Dreams*, Graves expands his analysis to include the suggestion that "*La Belle Dame* may represent also the figure of poetry ... [T]he close connection of this conflict of poetic ambition on the one hand and the inability to write on the other, with the Fanny Brawne conflict and the Death by Disease conflict can be clearly shown."[70] Graves presents evidence for his biographical assumptions from Sidney Colvin's *Life of Keats*, Rossetti's *Life*, and Keats's own letters to his brother George. His purpose is to suggest "the peculiar value of the ballad for speculation on the birth of poetry."[71] Comparing "Keats' two descriptions of Fanny as he first knew her with the lady of the poem" leads Graves to wonder whether a biographical incident can account for the multiple meanings in the poem: "did the natural thinness and paleness which Keats noted in Fanny's full-face form the association-link between his thoughts of love and death? What was the real reason of the 'kisses four'? Was it not perhaps four because of the painful doubleness of the tragic vision – was it extravagant to suppose that two of the kisses were more properly pennies laid on the eyes of death?"[72] To paraphrase Empson, Graves is attempting by such psycho-biographical analysis to trace the verbal path by which one of Keats's experiences dissolves into the multiple intensities of sensation that is the poem.

Empson identifies the same multiple meanings in "Ode on Melancholy": "Opposite notions combined in this poem include death and the sexual act ... the conception of the woman as at once mistress and mother, at once soothing and exciting, whom one must master, to whom one must yield; a desire at once for the eternity of fame and for the irresponsibility of oblivion; an apprehension of ideal beauty as sensual; and an apprehension of eternal beauty as fleeting."[73] Of course, the terms that Graves and Empson introduce are staples in criticism of Keats. The evidence that Empson follows Graves here comes from his observation that "Biographers who attempt to show from Keats's life how he came by these notions are excellently employed, but it is no use calling them in to explain why the poem is so universally intelligible and admired; evidently these pairs of opposites, stated in the right way, make a direct appeal to the normal habits of the mind."[74] The poet's abnormal psyche is not necessary to explain the response to the poem by readers with normal psyches. Not only does he in a general way recall the biographical manoeuvres by Graves, but he also recalls more particularly Graves's insistence that "for the reader, without necessarily any direct detailed regard to the history of the poet, the reading of poetry" – as it does for the poet – "enables him to be rid of ... conflicts between his sub-personalities."[75]

Empson and Graves both see a *psychological* "pattern underneath" the *semantic* "pattern underneath" the surface text, but Empson pays much more attention to its verbal manifestations than to its biographical source. Still, Empson incorporates into his definition of "the normal habits of the mind" a good deal of Graves's "conflict theory."[76] Conflict theory underwrites a good deal of Empson's concluding observation about "the most important thing about the communication of the arts": "the way in which opposites can be stated so as to satisfy a wide variety of people, for a great number of degrees of interpretation."[77]

Reconciliation of opposites, contradictions held in tension, "bearing all the elements in mind" when reading – Empson is inspired on all these fronts first by Graves, then by Riding and Graves, and on all these fronts he inspires in turn American New Critics from Ransom to Tate and Brooks.

6

Defence of Poetic Analysis

One of the most interesting ways that Empson follows Graves in *Seven Types of Ambiguity* is his defence of the kind of detailed poetic analysis that he offers throughout the book. Before *Seven Types of Ambiguity,* he had published only poems and reviews in *Granta* and two essays carved out of the book in *Experiment*, so he was not answering criticism of his own practices when he took up this defence. Instead, he implicitly declares solidarity with critics who have preceded him and upon whom abuse had been heaped. He launches a pre-emptive strike against the reaction to his own work that their prior example had taught him to expect.

For example, T.S. Eliot was criticized for his overly intellectual poetry and criticism. In response to "a usual objection to what is clearly part of [his] programme for the *métier* of poetry … that the doctrine requires a ridiculous amount of erudition (pedantry)," he begins his most famous essay, "Tradition and the Individual Talent," by chastising the English nation for being "more oblivious of the shortcomings and limitations of its critical habits than of those of its creative genius" ("we are such unconscious people" that we believe that "the French are 'more critical' than we, and sometimes even plume ourselves a little with the fact, as if the French were the less spontaneous").[1] Similarly, Graves prefaces his first book with the observation that "literary enthusiasts seem to regard poetry as something miraculous, something which it is almost blasphemous to analyse."[2] In *Poetic Unreason*, he devotes a whole chapter, "Defence of Poetic Analysis," to an explanation of "the strength of [his] position": a strength that lies in the "synthesis suggested between modern analytic psychology and the reading of poetry 'emotionally.'"[3]

Empson knew that he would face the usual objections to intellectual analysis of poetry, and that both his critical method and his psychological and linguistic paradigms owed so much to Graves that he would face the same objections that had already been launched against Graves's work.

In fact, Empson follows Graves in his defence of detailed poetic analysis from his first chapter to his last. In the first, he observes that "people suspect analysis, often rightly, as the refuge of the emotionally sterile."[4] In the last, he points out that the emotionally sterile analyser of poetry is paralleled by the emotionally fragile appreciator of poetry: "many works of art give their public a sort of relief and strength," so much so that "such a public cannot afford to have them analysed."[5] According to Empson, the sterile analyst and the fragile reader are both incompetent – because incomplete – readers of poetry: "On the face of it, there are two sorts of literary critic, the appreciative and the analytical; the difficulty is that they have all got to be both."[6] In reading poetry, "the act of knowing is itself an act of sympathising."[7] Anticipating the usual objections to erudite analysis, Empson follows Graves in attempting a synthesis between spontaneous emotional appreciation of poetry and intellectual analysis of poetry underwritten by psychological and linguistic sophistication.

Empson's synthesis between emotion and analysis certainly maintains the psychotherapeutic dimension that Graves highlights in his conflict theory: "Many works of art give their public a sort of relief and strength, because they are independent of the moral code which their public accepts and is dependent on; relief, by fantasy gratification; strength, because it gives you a sort of equilibrium within your boundaries to have been taken outside them, however secretly, because you know your own boundaries better when you have seen them from both sides."[8] This point is a generalization of Graves's description of poetry "as a record of the conflicts between various pairs of Jekyll and Hyde," in which "the terms Jekyll and Hyde … are rather more than synonyms for 'deliberate' and 'unwitting' because Jekyll is always used in the restricted sense of action in conformity with the dominant social code of the community, while Hyde is the outlaw."[9]

Empson seems to have been quite accurate when recollecting in the 1970s that one of the things that most interested him about Graves's work in the 1920s was the way it introduced Freud's concepts into literary criticism: one sees here that they both accept the

Freudian parallel between dream and literature as wish-fulfilment fantasies, gratifications of socially transgressive desires that the reality principle would stifle but for the disguised expression of these desires that dream and literature afford and effect. Empson's account of the split between poetry's analysers and appreciators also duplicates Graves's simple bifurcation of the mind into intellectual and emotional camps. Like Graves, Empson eschews the more sophisticated terminology and concepts of Freud's own work for the layperson's approach favoured by Graves in his explanation of his conflict theory. The latter suggests that "in the period of conflict, poetry may be either a partisan statement in the emotional or in the intellectual mode of thought of one side of the conflict; or else a double statement of both sides of the conflict, one side appearing in the manifest statement, that is, in the intellectual mode, the other in the latent content, that is, in the emotional mode, with neither side intelligible to the other."[10] Both are necessary: "Both modes are of equal importance since we could not do without either of them."[11]

Like Graves, Empson battles a bias against intellectual analysis – often a bias that amounts to no more than what he calls "a snobbery" in writer and reader.[12] He demonstrates the presence always already of emotional response in properly intellectual analysis of poetry and also the presence always already of intellectual analysis in properly emotional appreciation of poetry. In defence of analysis, he even argues that the prosaic knowledge derived from intellectual analysis can actually lead to the recovery of a form of poetic knowledge and emotional appreciation otherwise inaccessible, because the knowledge that such analysis provides is historically remote from the contemporary reader and must be recovered through scholarship and criticism: "it often happens that, for historical reasons or what not, one can no longer appreciate a thing directly by poetical knowledge, and yet can rediscover it in a more controlled form by prosaic knowledge."[13]

Yet Graves and Empson both give the spontaneous emotional appreciation of poetry its due. Graves observes that "the generalizations of modern science ... are more than usually inadequate for the analysis of poems of emotional conflict."[14] If "the rhythmic hypnotism of the verse" is not effective, or if the "symbolism" is not "intuitively understood," then "the subject for analysis will never have been a poem."[15] Empson agrees: "so far as poetry can be regarded altogether dispassionately, so far as it is an external object for examination, it is dead poetry and not worth examining."[16] According to Graves, "emotional poetry demands that if the rhythmic hypnotism of the verse is to be effective or the symbolism intuitively understood ... then the reader must be in a mood analogous to the poet's when he wrote the poem."[17] Empson again agrees: in reading poetry, "the act of knowing is itself an act of sympathising; unless you are enjoying the poetry you cannot create it, as poetry, in your mind."[18] Their frustration with the bias against intellectual analysis of poetry in no way reduces their respect for emotional appreciation of poetry to mere lip-service.

In respect of the "intuitively understood" poem, Graves notes that "such understanding is not capable of a scientific registration that will enable students of poetry to re-create that mood at will."[19] Empson acknowledges the same great gulf between appreciation of poetry and analysis of poetry: "An appreciator produces literary effects similar to the one he is appreciating, and sees to it ... that his version is more intelligible to the readers he has in mind. Having been shown what to look for, they are intended to go back to the original and find it there for themselves ... The analyst is not a teacher in this way; he assumes that something has been conveyed to the reader by the work under consideration, and sets out to explain ... why the work has had the effect on him that is assumed. As an analyst he is not repeating the effect; he may even be preventing it from happening again."[20]

Having similarly observed that analysis "often destroys what it pretends to explain," Graves suggests that "this is not, however, sufficient reason for refusing to allow emotional or intellectual poetry to be scrutinized in an indirect manner."[21] Analysis of a poem ought to proceed "by comparing the context from which it arose with the context in which it is appreciated" – by comparing, that is, the "mood" of the reader to "the poet's when he wrote the poem."[22] In other words, "to put it plainly, the only hopeful study of poetry is by examining the phase of mental conflict in the reader which allowed him to appreciate by analogy the emotional force of certain symbols and rhythms, and by then comparing this phase analytically with a phase of conflict in the mind of the poet, which historic research suggests as having given birth to the poem."[23] Graves describes a process of getting to know a poet by intuitive appreciation or emotional sympathy, and also a process of getting to know by intellectual analysis that the appreciation or sympathy is objective. Aiming at objectivity, such analysis can never be complete and comprehensive: "The result will only be an equational outline, but without it our intellectual understanding of a poem will be limited: as limited as that of a man born blind who, gaining sight in middle age, sees movement and colour, but has no correlating power to help him distinguish visually between his best friend and a flying piece of paper."[24]

Empson applies all these ideas – the reader as someone getting to know a poet, the mathematical language implied by the phrase "equational outline," and the analogy comparing the poet to a person adjusting his sight to unfamiliar, ambiguous visual stimuli – to his explanation of the reader's experience of and response to ambiguity in the words and sentences of a poem. In any reading experience, he notes, "there is a preliminary stage of uncertainty; 'the grammar may be of such or such a kind; the words are able to be connected in this way or that.'"[25] And so "a plausible grammar is picked up at the same time as the words it orders, but with a probability attached to it, and the less probable alternatives, ready, if necessary, to take its place, are in some way present at the back of your mind."[26] This continually evolving equational outline of possible meanings is a psychological and linguistic constant in the reading experience generally. The reading of poetry inevitably involves the same sort of provisional syntactical, grammatical construct, but "in poetry much less stress is laid on such alternatives; 'getting to know' a poet is largely the business of learning to control them."[27] The mind's construction of an "equational outline" of a poem's meaning parallels the mind's provisional outline of a visual field: "Under some drugs that make things jump about you see any particular thing moving or placed elsewhere in proportion as it is likely to move or be placed elsewhere, in proportion to a sort of coefficient of mobility which you have already given it as part of your apprehension."[28] Similarly, "to take another coefficient which the eye attaches to things, as you have an impression of a thing's distance away, which can hardly ever be detached from the pure visual sensation, and when it is so detached leaves your eye disconcerted (if what you took for a wall turns out to be the sea, you at first see nothing, perhaps are for a short time puzzled as with a blur, and then see differently), so the reading of a new poet, or of any poetry at all, fills many readers with a sense of mere embarrassment and discomfort, like that of not knowing, and wanting to know, whether it is a wall or the sea."[29]

Observing that "it would seem obvious that for emotional poetry the emotional approach is the most fitting one," Graves insists that "the understanding thereby obtained may always be broadened by subsequent intellectual analysis," and that intellectual analysis cannot be confined to such a "subsequent" phase of the reading experience: "Complete dissociation from the manifest statement of poetry is impossible for the reader; true, he may completely mistake the outline of sense that the poem had for the poet, but even when reading dithyrambic poetry of advanced grammatical disintegration, the eye will skip and snatch at random phrases."[30] Empson sees the same process of trial and error deeply embedded in the poetry reading experience of a being that thinks "not in words but in directed phrases": "It is the faint and separate judgments of probability which unite, as if with an explosion, to 'make sense' and accept the main meaning of a connection of phrases."[31]

Although he would claim to Riding in the 1970s that he was constitutionally resistant to influence – "My capacities for absorption are restricted by nature, and I know that much good work cannot enter my mind" – it is clear that he absorbed a great deal of Graves, and that the good work by Graves that enters his mind ranges from major points to minor ones.[32] To correct readers who argue against intellectual analysis of poetry, for instance, Empson even takes up Graves's use of Swinburne in the same cause. Graves complains that "the emotional approach theory is often carried so far that we hear it said that the best way to read Swinburne is to disregard the sense entirely and enjoy the glorious rush of sound and rhythm: not only does this seem hard on Swinburne, who prided himself a good deal on the thought contained in his verse, but it is a counsel reminiscent of the old catch, 'If you can see a piebald horse and not think about its tail you can have a wish.' Complete dissociation from the manifest statement of poetry is impossible for the reader."[33] Empson agrees: "People are oddly determined to regard Swinburne as an exponent of Pure Sound with no intellectual content. As a matter of technique, his work is full of such dissolved and contrasted reminiscences as need to be understood; as a matter of content, his sensibility was of the intellectual sort which proceeds from a process of analysis."[34]

One wonders if Empson's use of the word "reminiscences" here is merely a coincidence, or itself a reminiscence of the passage in Graves. Empson often absorbs not just Graves's line of argument, but also his turns of phrase, metaphors, and analogies. In his defence of poetic analysis, Graves figures the poems threatened by analysis as flowers disturbed in their bed: "There has been a considerable opposition to these analyses of poetry from some of my friends who are poets by profession, and this is not only based on the fear that I or my collaborators may uncover by these means their secret sorrows or repressed vices: nor are they afraid only on my behalf, though they put it this way, that by digging too deep into the flower-bed of my mind I may turn up soil that will kill the flowers already planted; they are equally afraid on their own account that if they acquire this habit from me their occupation will be gone, their poetry will be killed."[35] Empson counters the same concerns by the same figure: "critics have been perhaps too willing to insist that the operation of poetry is something magical ... like the growth of a flower, which it would be folly to allow analysis to destroy by digging the roots up and crushing out the juices into the light of day ... [W]hile it may be true that the roots of beauty ought not to be violated, it seems to me very arrogant of the appreciative critic to think that he could do this, if he chose, by a little scratching."[36] Graves is even more confident: "if this analytic spirit is rife among the reading public, the poet must be analyst, too, and if the reader digs deep and undermines the poet, the poet must countermine even deeper ... I hold that analysis so far from killing poetry gives it greater complexity, richness and, to use a metaphor from thermo-dynamics, entropy."[37]

His method of literary analysis fully explicated, and having proudly established his claim to be one of the critics who, "as 'barking dogs' ... relieve themselves against the flower of beauty, and ... afterwards scratch it up," Empson revisits this question of the relationship between analysis, on the one hand, and poetic inspiration and craft, on the other, in his concluding chapter:

> An ambiguity ... is not satisfying in itself, nor is it, considered as a device on its own, a thing to be attempted; it must in each case arise from, and be justified by, the peculiar requirements of the situation. On the other hand, it is a thing which the more interesting and valuable situations are more likely to justify. Thus the practice of "trying not to be ambiguous" has a great deal to be said for it ... it is a necessary safeguard against being ambiguous without proper occasion, and it leads to more serious ambiguities when such occasions arise. But, of course, the phrase "trying not to be ambiguous" is itself very indefinite and treacherous; it involves problems of all kinds as to what a poet can try to do, how much of his activity he is conscious of, and how much of his activity he could become conscious of if he tried.[38]

Here Empson channels Graves's concerns about the impact of analysis of the poet's conflicts upon the poet's own creativity and the question of just how much of his poetic activity the poet can be conscious of. In the essay Empson cites in his preface to the second edition of *Seven Types of Ambiguity*, Graves emphasizes that "the poet never knows what he is going to write, and very seldom can give a rational account of what he has written even after a long time."[39] The question immediately arises as to the impact upon what the poet is going to write of a rational outline of his poetry – whether his poetry in prospect, or his poetry in retrospect. On the one hand, "No poet, a Dante even or a Virgil, composing pen in hand knows before he writes exactly the form that his carefully prepared scheme will take; and that is why after giving a full account in conversation with a friend of the poem he intends to write, the poem is impossible to write in that form. The knowledge of the outline has started a new phase of the story ... so either the scheme is abandoned altogether ... or it takes a step forward and becomes much more significant and exciting."[40] The case is the same with respect to analysis of a poet's work: "Poetry contains a record of the fears, the aspirations and the philosophy of a poet's other selves, and any knowledge gained by analysis of this record will be helpful to him in future writing. When such analysis is possible the resultant knowledge will not bring a complete end of all conflict ... As a result of the analysis there will be a renewed working of conflict, translated eventually into poetry of a very different character from what passed before."[41] In fact, so far as individual poets are concerned, "Analytic thought is the best preventive against writing by formula, which means only that the same conflict persists over a long period without altering its outline appreciably."[42] We might even expect the same effect upon poetry as a whole:

> A further objection raised against poetic analysis is that "once we become conscious through analysis of the meaning of a piece of poetic symbolism, we can never again get that curious thrill which means an unconscious apprehension of a latent allegory." But in Japanese poetry, where the latent allusory content is understood and systematized, the poetic value is found I understand in the layer of secondary allusion below the layer of which the reader is expected to have rational knowledge. A further development of poetry beyond even that secondary level may in time occur, and for this reason I hold that analysis so far from killing poetry gives it another complexity, richness.[43]

Empson's last paragraph in *Seven Types of Ambiguity* sounds a similar note in his "apology for many niggling pages": "for those who find this book contains novelties, it will make poetry more beautiful, without their ever having to remember the novelties, or endeavour to apply them."[44]

Similarly, the "notion of unity" found in Empson's concluding observation that "anything (phrase, sentence, or poem) meant to be considered as a unit must be unitary, must stand for a single order of mind," develops arguments presented first by Graves, and then by Riding and Graves, concerning differences between the prose state of mind and the poetic state of mind.[45] In *On English Poetry* Graves argues: "Prose in its most prosy form seems to be the art of accurate statement by suppressing as far as possible the latent association of words ... In poetry ... the underlying associations of every word are marshalled carefully ... [S]tandard prose-writing seems to the poet very much like turning the machine guns on an innocent crowd of his own work people."[46] Empson says the same thing, more temperately: "a poetical word is a thing conceived in itself and includes all its meanings; a prosaic word is flat and useful and might have been used differently."[47]

Empson goes on to suggest that in "the process of apprehension, both of the poem and of its analysis ... one wants as far as clarity will allow to say things in the form in which they will be remembered when properly digested."[48] He effectively generalizes the recommendation of Riding and Graves about the way to proceed with a poem like "The Rugged Black of Anger" – the kind of poem "that really seems to mean what it says": "All we can do is to let it interpret itself, without introducing any new associations or, if possible ... without introducing any words not actually belonging to the poem, without throwing any of the poem away as superfluous padding and without having recourse to a prose version."[49] Empson seems to agree with the principle that Riding and Graves announce: "If ... the author of the lines beginning 'The rugged black of anger' were asked to explain their meaning, the only proper reply would be to repeat the lines, perhaps with greater emphasis."[50] As he explains, "in so far as an ambiguity sustains intricacy, delicacy, or compression of thought ... it is to be respected (in so far, one is tempted to say, as the same thing could not have been said so effectively without it, but, of course, in poetry the same thing could never have been said in any other way)."[51]

Riding and Graves understand themselves to be countering the prevailing assumption among critics and readers "that prose ideas have their exact equivalents in poetry," and that the "categories representing the stages of the poem from creation to criticism" trace, first, a process from the "Poet's prose idea" to the "Poem" and, second, a process from the "Poem" to the "Reader's prose summary" (except in the case of modern poetry, where "the real poem, apparently unwritten," is "suppressed," replaced by the "Prose idea as poem," eventuating in the "Reader's poetical summary" of the latter).[52] They insist that in this approach to the interpretation of poetry, we have between "the poem as it stands" and the reader's "summary" of it "not two equivalent meanings but one meaning and another gratuitous meaning derived from it."[53] There is a "discrepancy," for there is "an insurmountable difference between prose ideas and poetic ideas, prose facts and poetic facts."[54]

In explaining why apprehension of the poem requires that "one ... say things in the form in which they will be remembered when properly digested," Empson makes the same point about the discrepancy between, on the one hand, "detailed analysis" of facts and judgements, and on the other, the complex unified feeling prompted by reading poetry:

> People remember a complex notion as a sort of feeling that involves facts and judgments; one cannot give or state the feeling directly ... But to state the fact and the judgment (the thought and the feeling) separately, as two different relevant matters, is a bad way of suggesting how they are combined; it makes the reader apprehend as two things what he must, in fact, apprehend as one thing ... This notion of unity is of peculiar importance ... [T]o say a thing in two parts is different in incalculable ways from saying it as a unit ... When you are holding a variety of things in your mind, or using for a single matter a variety of intellectual machinery, the only way of applying all your criteria is to apply them simultaneously; the only way of forcing your reader to grasp your total meaning is to arrange that he can only feel satisfied if he is bearing all the elements in mind at the moment of conviction; the only way of not giving something heterogenous is to give something which is at every point a compound.[55]

He develops here a view of the poem as self-contained whole elaborated by Riding and Graves. The poem that "really seems to mean what it says," they say, should be "complete without criticism."[56] In fact, "without the addition of any associations not provided in the poem, or of collateral interpretations," the poem should "reveal an internal consistency strengthened at every point in its development."[57] For the reader to read "with a slowness proportionate to how much he is not a poet ... is one way of getting out of the prose and into the poetic state of mind, of developing a capacity for minuteness, for seeing all there is to see at a given point and taking it all along with one as one goes along."[58]

According to Riding and Graves, the poem's "internal consistency strengthened at every point in its development and free of the necessity of external application" establishes the "insurmountable difference between prose ideas and poetic ideas, prose facts and poetic facts," indicating "the independence of poetic facts, as real facts, from any prose or poetical explanation in the terms of practical workaday reality which would make them seem unreal, or poetical facts."[59] Empson makes the same distinction between poetical and prosaic facts and ideas:

> You may know what it will be satisfying to do for the moment; precisely how you are feeling; how to express the thing conceived clearly, but alone, in your mind. That, in its appreciation of, and dependence on, the immediate object or state of mind, is poetical knowledge ... You may, on the other hand, be able to put the object known into a field of similar objects, in some order ... you may know several ways of getting to the thing, other things like it but different ... the thing can be said to your neighbours, and has enough valencies in your mind for it to be connected with a variety of other things into a variety of different classes. That, from its administrative point of view, from its desire to put the thing known into a coherent structure, is prosaic knowledge. Thus a poetical word is a thing conceived in itself and includes all its meanings; a prosaic word is flat and useful and might have been used differently.[60]

Riding and Graves make these distinctions before Empson takes them up, and Riding would go on to hammer away at them in *Contemporaries and Snobs* and *Anarchism Is Not Enough* well before Empson started the first chapter of *Seven Types of Ambiguity*. But the first to make these points, and to do so in defence of poetic analysis, was Graves alone.

Thinking of Graves more as a mentor than as a rival, and regarding him less as a contemporary than as a precursor (one who worked out the relevance of Freud for literary criticism "a generation before me," he recalled), Empson positions himself as successor to Graves in the contest with what the latter called the "literary enthusiasts" who "seem to regard poetry as something miraculous, something which it is almost blasphemous to analyse."[61] Assuming his mentor's mantle, with more than double portion of his art, Empson self-consciously applies Graves's method and brings his own artillery to bear in defence of poetic analysis.

7

The Ambiguous Grammar of Romantic Psychology

So thoroughly does Empson absorb Graves's early work that this influence can even be found complicating his account of the failings of nineteenth-century poetry. According to Eliot, whereas the metaphysical poets were "constantly amalgamating disparate experience," "trying to find the verbal equivalent for states of mind and feeling," for a "thought to Donne was an experience," it seems "something ... happened to the mind of England between the time of Donne ... and the time of Tennyson and Browning," for the latter "do not feel their thought."[1] Following Eliot's lead, Empson initially tries to explain why "the poets of the nineteenth century ... are so little ambiguous in the sense with which I am concerned."[2] He focuses on the disjunction between poetry and science that saw poetry conceived as a refuge from science: "For a variety of reasons, they found themselves living in an intellectual framework with which it was very difficult to write poetry, in which poetry was rather improper, or was irrelevant to business, especially the business of becoming Fit to Survive, or was an indulgence of one's lower nature in beliefs the scientists knew were untrue. On the other hand, they had a large public which was as anxious to escape from this intellectual framework, on holiday, as they were themselves."[3]

But these ideas are not original to Empson. They may all be found at the beginning of "Defence of Poetic Analysis," where Graves warns of the danger for the twentieth century "if the analytic interest developed by this scientific-industrial age is deliberately neglected by myself or my contemporaries as unsuitable for poetic treatment."[4] There is not just the disjunction between poetry and science generally, but also the association of poetry with the old pulse of the primitive within one's lower nature: "The new Poetry, if it is ever written in our age, if the conflict and cleavage between the groups is not always too great ... must be a reconciliation of scientific and philosophic theory on the one hand and the old pulse of love and fear on the other."[5] There is also the figure of arch-"Fit to survive"-scientist Darwin, one whose work in the scientific-industrial age has left him stranded beyond the reach of poetry: "Charles Darwin ... deplored that his mind had been working along scientific lines so long that he found himself unable to appreciate poetry any more."[6] And there is the scientist's suspicion – and even disapproval – of poetry: "there is an interesting figure, Sir Ronald Ross, who is famous for a very valuable scientific discovery in bacteriology and to whose poetic work a cordial greeting is given by a liberal group of critics and writers ... On the other hand more than one distinguished scientist has in talk with me disowned Sir Ronald as not a scientist at all according to the ethics of the profession, but has branded him as a man of imagination who goes for this or that particular problem with a preconceived aim of social service instead of disinterestedly advancing the bounds of scientific knowledge without a thought for the consequences."[7] There is the poets' recourse to beliefs that science knows to be untrue: "There was, of course, Francis Thomson, a poet with a passion for science, but ... latterly he has got somewhat shy of the Beast, and I believe inclines to the mystic idea of outside control by spirits accounting for the genesis of poetry."[8] And so there is also the flight by poets and readers alike to poetry as an escape from science: "Mr. De la Mare has been for years predominantly a poet of escape and when his name is put forward by our leading literary journal, *The Times Literary Supplement*, as the greatest of the modern lyricists it means ... that modern society is in such confusion that the greatest service a poet can do is to provide a temporary escape to the Lubberland of fantasy."[9] When Empson wrings his absorbent mind of its thoughts on the situation of poetry in the nineteenth century, the drops pool together and reveal a pronounced tincture of Graves.

Of course Empson and Graves were not alone in characterizing the poetry of the previous century as escapist. T.E. Hulme called romanticism "spilt religion," a sloppy hankering after the infinite: "The romantic, because he thinks man infinite, must always be talking about the infinite," "is always flying, flying over abysses, flying up into eternal gases," pantheistically collates "all beauty to an impression of the infinite in the identification of our being in absolute spirit."[10] Ford Madox Ford complained that nineteenth-century poets were cowards who could not face the problems of their own day: "It is a charming thing, it is a very lovely thing, it is a restful thing, to lose ourselves in meditations upon the Isles of the Blessed, and very sweet songs may be sung about them. But to do nothing else implies a want of courage. We live in our day, we live in our time, and he is not a proper man who will not look in the face his day and his time."[11] Eliot diagnosed in the poets of the nineteenth century a dissociated sensibility, which meant that "they thought and felt by fits, unbalanced" – not only unable "to find the verbal equivalent for states of mind and feeling," but also unable to comprehend and express the "great variety and complexity" of their civilization – unable, that is, "to force, to dislocate if necessary, language into ... meaning" the way the metaphysical poets had.[12]

Empson does not want to be too harsh on the poets of the nineteenth century: "fantasy gratification and a protective attitude towards one's inner life are in some degree essential for the production of poetry."[13] In particular, he "has no wish to pretend the Romantics were not great poets."[14] Yet one has to draw the line somewhere, and for Empson the line is drawn wherever he finds nineteenth-century poets exploiting "the possibilities of never growing up," preferring romantically to dwell in infantile fantasies.[15] This tendency marks the morbid psychology that Empson regards as destructive of poetically meaningful ambiguity.

In other words, Empson finds nineteenth-century poets in general, and romantic poets in particular, interesting both psychologically and grammatically, but since "their distortions of meaning" tend to "belong to darker regions of the mind," "the mode of approach to them should be psychological rather than grammatical."[16] Is Empson attempting here to distinguish his critical practice – if not his critical theory – from that of Graves? Although neither ignores the role of psychology or grammar in the special workings of poetry, Graves's conflict theory might seem to be psychological first and grammatical second, regarding the doubleness of the poet's psychological state as the thing represented by the doubleness of grammar, whereas Empson's theory of ambiguity might seem to be grammatical first and psychological second, regarding the doubleness of the grammar as the meaningful event in its own right and the poet's psychological state as observable only by inference. So to emphasize that poetic meaning resides in grammar rather than psychology could be seen as a revision of Graves's work in the direction of Eliot's effort in "Tradition and the Individual Talent" to focus "honest criticism" upon the poem and not the poet.[17] Even so, however, we have here a distinction without much practical difference for the literary criticism they practise: for both Empson and Graves, the ambiguity analysable on the page is the key to poetic meaning.

According to Empson, "those who enjoy poems must in part be biographers, but ... it is not all significant ambiguities which are relevant."[18] He makes this point with reference to two lines in a poem by Ben Jonson that "say the opposite of what is meant"; since "there are no other two-faced implications of any plausibility" in the poem, the ambiguous meaning of the lines is not relevant grammatically but only – if at all – in terms of the mind of the poet, an accident by which an unimportant grammatical ambiguity appears in the poem.[19] And so his declaration: "I am talking less about the minds of poets than about the mode of action of poetry."[20] Yet Empson's criterion for determining the relevance of an ambiguity – that the poem demonstrates "other two-faced implications" of some "plausibility" – recalls Graves's vision of "the thought-machinery that with greater luck and cunning may produce something like Poetry": "I had a vision in my mind of the God of Poetry having two heads like Janus."[21] If Empson is tweaking Graves's conflict theory in his distinction between the mind of the poet and the mode of action of poetry, it is still Graves's description of poetry as two-faced that Empson recalls in his definition of poetry's grammatically – rather than psychologically – ambiguous mode of action.

In another explanation of the two-headed God of Poetry, Graves begins with a psychological perspective: "it is hardly necessary to quote extreme cases of morbid psychology or to enter the dangerous arena of spiritualistic argument in order to explain the presence of sub-personalities in the poet's mind. They have a simple origin, it seems, as supplying the need of a primitive mind when confused. Quite normal children invent their own familiar spirits, their 'shadows,' 'dummies' or 'slaves,' in order to excuse erratic actions of their own which seem on reflection incompatible with their usual habits or code of honour."[22] Yet he quickly elides the difference between the grammar of the unconscious and the grammar of poetry:

> "Multiple personality, perhaps," says some one. "But does that account for the stereoscopic process of which you speak, that

> makes two sub-personalities speak from a double head, that as it were prints two pictures on the same photographic plate?" The objector is thereupon referred to the dream-machinery on which poetry seems to be founded. He will acknowledge that in dreams the characters are always changing in a most sudden and baffling manner. He will remember for example that in "Alice in Wonderland" ... the duchess' baby is represented as turning into a pig ... That is a commonplace of dreams ... When there is a thought-connection of similarity or contrast between two concepts, the second is printed over the first on the mental photographic plate so rapidly that you hardly know at any given moment whether it is a pig or a baby you are addressing ... One image starts a sentence, another image succeeds and finishes it, almost, but the first reappears and has the last word. The result is poetry – or nonsense.[23]

It can certainly be said that Graves is talking here as much about the mode of action of poetry as he is about the minds of poets.

At times, in fact, Graves is interested less in the psychological conflict supposed to have existed in the poet's mind than in the grammatical conflict that constitutes the mode of action of poetry, as is clear in his close reading of "the rhyme to remember the signs of the Zodiac by":

> The Ram the Bull, the Heavenly Twins,
> And next the Crab, the Lion shines,
> The Virgin and the Scales,
> The Scorpion, Archer and He Goat,
> The Man who carries the Watering Pot,
> The Fish with glittering tails.[24]

Contemplating the way language might otherwise be used to achieve the mnemonic purpose of this verse, Graves contrasts the language of science in particular and the language of prose in general with the distinctive language of poetry:

> The language of science makes a hieroglyphic, or says "The sign of Aquarius"; the language of prose says "A group of stars likened by popular imagery to a water Carrier"; the language of Poetry converts the Eastern water carrier with his goatskin bag or pitcher,

> into an English gardener, then puts him to fill his watering pot from heavenly waters where the fish are darting. The author of this rhyme has visualised his terrestrial emblems most clearly; he has smelt the rankness of the goat, and yet in the "Lion shines" and the "glittering tails" one can see that he has been thinking in terms of stars also. The emotional contradiction lies in the stars' remote aloofness from complications of this climatic and smelly world, from the terror of Lion, Archer, Scorpion, from the implied love-interest of Heavenly Twins and Virgin, and from the daily cares of the Scales, Ram, Bull, Goat, Fish, Crab and Watering Pot.[25]

Rather than the mind of the poet or the illogic of the dream, it is here the "language of Poetry" that "converts" one person into another, and it is the language of poetry that converts one form of shining into another and one form of glittering into another.[26] Empson makes the same point in the same terms in a passage quoted above: "a poetical word is a thing conceived in itself and includes all its meanings; a prosaic word is flat and useful and might have been used differently."[27]

In fact, the mode of action of the language of poetry here is the only evidence of the mind of the anonymous author. And so Graves must extrapolate: "in the 'Lion shines' and the 'glittering tails' one can see that he has been thinking in terms of stars also."[28] As Graves notes in *Poetic Unreason*, where he develops this point further (in "protest against the myopic literary historian who denies that we know anything at all about the author of an anonymous poem"), "the fact is that when we come to examine *Chevy Chace* or any other poem whose author is either unknown or nothing but a name, we find that our knowledge of the poet's politics, culture, nationality, his attitude to war, to love, to virtue, to truth, in fact all his important characteristics, is considerable."[29] (As noted earlier, when Graves reconstructed the characters of anonymous authors on the basis of their works during his talks at Oxford, many in his audiences applauded.)

So although Empson indicates that he is "talking less about the minds of poets than about the mode of action of poetry," it is the same sense of poetry as a special language representing a distinct thinking experience that leads Empson also to allow that "those who enjoy poems must in part be biographers."[30] He recurs to the same point in his preface to the second edition: "If critics are not to put up some pretence of understanding the feelings of the author in hand they must condemn themselves to contempt."[31] That is to say, as Graves himself says, "Appreciation of a poem means nothing less than a certain intimate knowledge of the author."[32] Close reading inevitably reveals a human compound of thinking and feeling that a romantic reader will attribute to the writer and that a New Critic will attribute to a dramatic speaker or persona.

In terms of the relationship between the mind of the poet and the mode of action of poetry, then, Graves and Empson are usually on the same page – largely because Empson concentrates into a system what Graves scatters as provocative *aperçus*.

•

Graves also agrees with Empson that romantic poets are interesting psychologically. His foregrounding of the romantic poets to demonstrate his conflict theory no doubt constitutes one of the psychoanalytical perspectives on the romantics that Empson represents as ubiquitous in the 1920s. As we have seen, Graves observes in *On English Poetry* that Keats's "Merciless Lady ... represents both the woman he loved and the death he feared, the woman whom he wanted to glorify by his poetry and the death that would cut his poetry short," an observation developed further in *The Meaning of Dreams*: "*La Belle Dame* may represent also the figure of Poetry. Again, the close connection of this conflict of poetic ambition on the one hand and inability to write on the other, with the Fanny Brawne conflict and the Death by Disease conflict can be clearly shown."[33] Noting in "Ode on Melancholy" "the conception of the woman as at once mistress and mother, at once soothing and exciting, whom one must master, to whom one must yield," Empson sums up psychoanalytical approaches to Keats in terms of Freud's thanatos and Oedipus: "Keats's desire for death and his mother ... has become a byword amongst the learned."[34] Graves also reads Wordsworth's poetry psychoanalytically, remarking that Wordsworth uses his memory of daffodils "as a charm to banish the spectres of trouble and loneliness."[35] Empson generalizes such psychoanalytical approaches to Wordsworth as follows: "Wordsworth frankly had no other inspiration than his use ... of the mountains as a totem or father-substitute."[36]

Graves finds romantics interesting psychologically because they write closer than most to the dream experience that he regards as the origin of spontaneous poetry: "dreams are illogical, and spontaneous undoctored poetry, like the dream, represents the complications of adult experience translated into thought-processes analogous to, or identical with, those of childhood."[37] He not only regards romantic poetry as childish, but regards its childishness as evidence that it is as close to the archetype of poetry as any poetry can be:

> it explains, to my satisfaction at any rate, a number of puzzling aspects of poetry, such as the greater emotional power on the average reader's mind of simple metres and short homely words with an occasional long strange one for wonder ... also the very much wider use in poetry than in daily speech of animal, bird, cloud and flower imagery, of Biblical types, characters and emblems, of fairies and devils, of legendary heroes and heroines, which are the stock-in-trade of imaginative childhood; also, the constant appeal poetry makes to the childish habits of amazed wondering, sudden terrors, laughter to signify mere joy, frequent tears and similar manifestations of uncontrolled emotion which in a grown man and especially an Englishman are considered ridiculous.[38]

And so Graves explains "the strict Classicist's dislike of the ungoverned Romantic," "the dislike being apparently founded on a feeling that to wake this child-spirit in the mind of a grown person is stupid and even disgusting, an objection that has similarly been raised to the indiscriminate practice of psychoanalysis, which involves the same process."[39]

In Empson's comments on the romantics, one can see that he agrees with Graves that conceiving things childishly and conceiving things poetically are related: "Almost all of them ... exploited a sort of tap-root into the world of their childhood, where they were able to conceive things poetically."[40] Their recourse to childhood effectively primed the poetic pump. Yet there is a problem here, according to Empson, insofar as that "whatever they might be writing about they would suck up from this limited and perverted world an unvarying sap which was their poetical inspiration."[41] Characterizing the romantic's world of childhood as "limited and perverted," Empson not only fits the profile Graves provides of the classicist who dislikes the ungoverned indulgence of the child-spirit, but also seems to act out this profile rather theatrically in his introduction to *Seven Types of Ambiguity*: infantilising romantic poets by the indiscriminately sexualizing psychoanalysis that he and Graves both abjured. He writes that although "Coleridge, it is true, relied on opium rather than the nursery," "Wordsworth frankly had no inspiration other than his use, when a boy, of the mountain as a totem or father-substitute," "Byron only at the end of his life ... escaped from the infantile incest-fixation upon his sister," and Keats's poetry is all about "desire for death and his mother."[42] Empson trashes romanticism and psychoanalysis whereas Graves defends them.

In his essay on the "Secondary Elaboration" of spontaneous poetry, for example, Graves explains how his own poem "The Bedpost" came to represent a conflict between what his "poet-friends" criticized as "nursery sentimentalities," on the one hand, and Freud's attitude toward childhood, on the other. During his revising of the poem, Graves explains, first, "I had been deeply interested in Freudian psycho-analysis as being a possible corrective for my shell-shock, which had just returned, and I was thinking of putting myself under treatment," and, second, "I was very anxious on [my daughter's] behalf owing to a belief that her nervous system had been undermined ... by the neurotic condition of her nurse." And so, he says, "It will be seen that my love of my child and my own nervous condition ... were associated with the thought of psycho-analysis as a possible relief for both; and yet there was a resistance in my mind against being psycho-analysed. The poem is scattered thick with very bold and definite sex-symbolism ... It will be seen that the conflict between my friends and myself ... was being reconciled in this piece, my nursery sentimentality balanced with its very opposite, the cynical Freudian view of childhood."[43]

Similarly, arguing that "there is no form poetry can take unworthy of our consideration, even our admiration," Graves nominates Edward Lear's "nonsensical" songs as worthy of anthologization alongside "other romantic poetry": "the song of *Calico Pie* presenting grief in terms of childish invention is to me as poignant as the idea of Hamlet played by Burbage the actor as a comic part. Adoption of this pseudo-infantility must surely denote suffering in an extreme form."[44] In fact, "of the romantic-escape poets ... Lear himself, poised humpty-dumpty-wise on the precarious ledge of nursery rhyme, is the chief."[45] Complaining that "Romanticism ... has long been banished to the nursery or the 'primitive' community," Graves works to rehabilitate not so much Lear in particular as the "associative method of thought" (or "the illogical element in poetry") in general.[46] And so Graves objects not just to "the strict Classicist's dislike of the ungoverned Romantic" but also to the implicitly denigrating attitudes towards the associative method of thought and the illogical element in poetry betrayed by Freud, Jung, and even, on occasion, Rivers himself:

> Since the nursery is the one place where there is an audience not too sophisticated to appreciate ancient myths and so-called nonsense rhymes of greater or lesser antiquity, it happens that when we remember a dream, or write a poem in which we afterwards discover this emotional mode we say we are regressing to childhood ... It is just here that psycho-analysis has been at its weakest; the theory of this childish survival has led the doctors of the Vienna school to ascribe to children the particularized passions of grown men and women; and the doctors of the Zurich school to ascribe to civilized man the particularized memory of a savage state enjoyed by his ancestors. Both ascriptions are due to this (to me) false idea that the Romantic or emotional mode of thought has no place in civilized life and is merely a survival of the child or the savage ... A great advance from the scientific side on these theories is made by the late Dr. Rivers ... but his admirable observations on the mechanism of dreams ... are disappointing where they do not allow that associative thought is as modern and reputable a mode as intellectual thought, and regard it as a return to infantility.[47]

Graves insists that a distinction be drawn "between the infantile or primitive *content* of certain dreams and poems, and the emotional or romantic *mode of thought* often employed by sophisticated adults, which need not necessarily have an infantile or primitive content."[48] According to Graves, one of "the most unsatisfactory features hitherto of English psycho-analysis" has lain in "the supposed reference of Romanticism to a primitive or infantile content."[49]

Empson's attitude toward romanticism, infantilism, and psychoanalysis is, in fact, very similar. His complaint is not that the darker regions of a romantic's mind could never have inspired grammatical ambiguity, but rather that the romantic poet's determination to use everyday language made for an aesthetic bias against grammatical ambiguity: "the cult of simplicity moved its complexity back into the subconscious ... and stated as simply as possible the fundamental disorders of the mind."[50] According to Empson, "the badness of much nineteenth-century poetry" comes from the attempt by "critically sensitive" but poetically limited writers to take short-cuts: "They admired the poetry of previous generations, very rightly, for the taste it left in the head, and failing to realise that the process of putting such a taste into the reader's head involves a great deal of work which does not feel like a taste in the head while it is being done, attempting, therefore, to conceive a taste in the head and put it straight on their paper, they produced tastes in the head which were in fact blurred, complacent, and unpleasing."[51]

Empson also echoes here a point that Richards makes in one of his earliest essays, "Emotion and Art" (1919), concerning the difference between "the emotions which accompany the reading of any tragedy" and "the emotions which ensue as the import of the tragedy is understood": "The first will probably be painful, will almost certainly be constricting; the second will be emotions of expansion and release. There is a certain uniformity about the latter emotions, which has helped to mislead theorists to the conclusion that the function of art is to arouse these emotions. That this is a mistake becomes plain when we consider that we can imaginatively and actually arouse these emotions ... as a sentimental exercise. With a little practice this becomes quite easy."[52] Empson concludes his critique of the nineteenth-century's aesthetic by complaining that the poetry of Wordsworth, Coleridge, Byron, Shelley, and Keats offers "imposed excitement, a sense of uncaused warmth, achievement, gratification."[53] Again he follows Richards, who observes of the easy practice of arousing emotions as a sentimental exercise that "such feelings owe their ridiculousness not to any defects as feelings, but to the absence of their really valuable appropriate causes."[54]

According to Empson, romantics "were making a use of language very different from that of their predecessors."[55] Like Graves, Empson expects a poet to express "the complexity of the order of his mind" through the ambiguous order of his words.[56] But he contends that the romantics avoided complexity in two ways. First, what Graves calls conflict and what Empson calls ambiguity was not experienced and expressed poetically as a mode of two-faced thought; rather, it was self-consciously and deliberately contemplated as a topic and expressed as a conclusion (whether about melancholy, dejection, loneliness, or what have you): they "stated as simply as possible the fundamental disorders of the mind."[57] In Graves's terms, according to Empson's analysis, they turned romanticism as mode into romanticism as content. And so romantics did "not need to use ambiguities of the kind I shall consider to give vivacity to their language, or even ambiguities with which the student of language, as such, is concerned."[58] "Wordsworth," Empson baldly declares, "was not an ambiguous poet."[59] Second, romantics repressed any complexity that they could not express according to their aesthetic of grammatical simplicity – short-circuiting romanticism as mode in favour of romanticism as content: "the cult of simplicity moved its complexity back into the subconscious, poisoned only the sources of thought, in the high bogs of the mountains" – leaving the poetry grammatically as much parched as pure.[60] They thereby hurt themselves as much as their poetry: both were made psychologically morbid by the distortions that repression gives rise to. And so "the mode of approach to them should be psychological rather than grammatical," for "their distortions of meaning" do not belong to the realm of poetry proper, but rather "belong to darker regions of the mind."[61]

•

For all of Empson's huffing and puffing about the "limited and perverted" nature of the work of certain poets, his explanation as to why nineteenth-century poets "are so little ambiguous in the sense with which I am concerned" turns out, once again, to have its origin in Graves. This time he is influenced by Graves's attempt to distinguish between the infantile or primitive as the content of romanticism, on the one hand, and the infantile or primitive as a type of romanticism's adult and sophisticated associative mode of thought, on the other.[62]

In his preface to the second edition of *Seven Types of Ambiguity*, Empson clearly agrees with Graves that this associative mode of thought underwrites the ambiguity that is a part of all good poetry, ambiguity that arises as a function of the attempt to name the unnamed: "As I understand it, there is always in great poetry ... an appeal to a background of human experience which is all the more present when it cannot be named."[63] According to Empson, ambiguity ought to be a function of "proper occasion" – "it is a thing which the more interesting and valuable situations are more likely to justify" – and the more proper the occasion, the more "serious" the ambiguity.[64] Graves's chapter on "The Illogical Element in Poetry" in *Poetic Unreason* makes precisely this point – that only the emotional or associative mode of thought can deal with human experience that is beyond language dominated by logic: "Logic only likes one meaning for every word. If it finds the phrase somewhere written 'The Hound of Heaven' there must be only one significance to this Hound idea or to this Heaven idea, not three or four: that is considered illogical."[65] The experience that Empson believes that the poem makes present without naming is explained by Graves as follows: "the secondary meanings of words, however remote, react on each other in moments of passion if there is any similarity of emotional disturbance between the associations these meanings conjure up."[66] According to Graves, "in emotion logic gives place to this associative method of thought, the effect being a stringent condensation of the circumlocution otherwise necessary, the substitution of symbol, for grammatic phrase."[67] Empson makes the same point in his preface to the second edition of *Seven Types of Ambiguity* when he suggests that what moves a reader in "an apparently simple line" are "traces of … his past experience and … his past judgments," and that "the cause of so straddling a commotion and so broad a calm" in the reader must be the "implications" "of such lines."[68] In great poetry, the lines are never simple, for the associative mode of thought that produces "an *apparently* simple line" guarantees that simplicity always belies the complexity of ambiguity.[69]

Tracing the pattern of such emotional associations is the staple of Empson's practical criticism, as in his extended analysis of ambiguity of the fifth type in John Ford's *'Tis Pity She's a Whore* (concerning the lines by Giovanni: "let not the curse/Of old prescription rend from me the gall/Of courage, which enrols a glorious death:/If I must totter like a well-grown oak,/Some undershrubs shall in my weighty fall/Be crushed to splits"):

> *Gall* is first used as "spirit to resent insults" … By the next line *galls* have suggested oak-galls (the reactions of an *oak* to irritations), and the idea of proper retaliation is transferred to its power of *falling* on people, whether they are guilty of wrongs against it or not. But in between these two definite meanings the curious word *enrolled* seems a blurring of the focus; he is thinking of the situation itself, rather than either metaphor … A *glorious death* may be *enrolled* on the scroll of fame, so that the word

> could stand by itself; or, looking backwards, one may gain strength for a *glorious death* by being bathed in, sustained by, a spurt of bitterness, so that *gall* has been *rent* (now with the opposite consequences) from its boundaries in the orderly mind, by being *rolled* in, or around about by, *gall*; or, looking backwards, it may be the *oak* itself which *rolls* down, both to death and upon its victims. You may say this is fanciful, and he was only looking for a word that contained the letter "r" which kept up the style, but in that case it is these associations which explain how that particular word came into his mind.[70]

This last sentence reads as though Empson were countering Richards's over-confident identification of what seems to him the single source of Coleridge's "Kubla Khan" and his subsequent, disdainful dismissal of Graves's reading of "Kubla Khan" in *The Meaning of Dreams* as representing "the gravest dangers" of a fanciful Freudianism. For Empson agrees with Graves: multiple associations bring poetry to be. When discussing ambiguity of the seventh type, which, like ambiguity of the third type, he explicitly links to Graves's conflict theory, Empson declares that he has sought through his discussion of "the identity of opposites" in ancient and modern languages as "a rather sophisticated state of language and feeling" "to cast upon the reader something of the awe and horror which were felt by Dante arriving finally at the most centrique part of earth," for in examining this way of associating words we "are approaching the secret places of the Muse."[71] In the end, Empson's complaint about nineteenth-century poets in general, and romantic poets in particular, is that they too often belie proper romanticism – which is to say that he accepts the very argument that Graves is at pains to make about the romantic nature of all true poetry.

•

Graves has entered Empson's mind in so many ways that even Empson's imagined interlocutor is often the same as Graves's imagined interlocutor: one who says of the associations revealed, "this is fanciful" (for the poet "was only looking for a word containing the letter 'r' which kept up the style"); one who says of analysis of Shakespeare's sonnets that a "slender Sonnet ought not to take so much explaining"; one who says of a poem that even if its associational "wealth of reference and feeling ... is true" then the poet "wrote without properly clarifying his mind."[72] Even when he invokes T.S. Eliot as interlocutor, Empson implicitly accounts for Eliot's obtuseness (about the anatomical accuracy of Shelley's reference in "Hellas" to a snake's shedding of its skin) by imputing to him the same constricting veneration of the clarified mind shared by the other imaginary interlocutors whom both he and Graves would refute. That is, he imagines Eliot dismissing Shelley with the remark, "a seventeenth-century poet would have known his own mind on such points."[73]

Going back to the ancient Egyptians for an example of sophisticated people who know their own minds differently from Europeans who have been educated in the Greco-Roman tradition, Empson follows Graves in blaming the Greeks both for Western literary criticism's veneration of the clear mind and for its equally longstanding neglect of the "illogical" (or emotional or associational) element in poetry. As Graves explains:

> In treating of the illogical aspects of poetry ... "illogical" I am using here in a narrower sense as meaning poetry which does not conform with those principles of logic which govern what I have been calling intellectual as opposed to emotional thought. This logic is a system slowly deduced from the broadest and most impersonal analyses of cause and effect, capable always of empiric proof ... Poetry of the kind which we recognize as Romantic or Fantastic or Inspired being ... dependent on associative thought, its symbolism intimately bound up with a vast number of logical false premises, a defiance of the ordered spatio-temporal structure which the civilized intellect has built for its habitation – this Poetry when Logic was first achieving pre-eminence under the Greeks, either had to be banned altogether from the ideal republic of the philosophers as Plato wished it banned, or had to submit itself to a severe examination and systematization – hence Aristotle's Poetics. For centuries since, philosophic speculation about emotional poetry, dreams and phantasy has been silent or has found only illogic in them.[74]

Aristotle is particularly culpable for the Western critic's expectation that lyric poetry should constitute "logically harmonious and rational statement": "He was intending to make poetry conform to an absolute system, to weed it of all the symbolic extravagances and impossibilities of the dream state from which romantic poetry has always originated, and to confine it within rational and educative limits."[75] And so Graves complains that for "the method of Romantic Poetry and the method of thought in fantastic dreams ... logic has had for centuries nothing but the sneering patronage of the self-respecting citizen for the grotesque but cheerful village idiot. It is this superior intellectual attitude inherited from the logical revival of the eighteenth century that causes a deal of confusion in contemporary literary criticism."[76] Graves then invokes an anecdote told by the proverbial English scholar as illustration of the limits of the proverbial German scholar: "The Aristotelian tradition for literary criticism survives strongly to-day, particularly, it is supposed, in Germany. The traditional English view of German Shakespearean scholarship is enshrined in the tale of the commentator who amended Duke Senior in *As You Like It* from: 'But this our life exempt from public haunt/Finds tongues in trees, books in running brooks,/Sermons in stones and good in everything' to: 'Finds leaves on trees, stones in the running brooks,/Sermons in books and good in everything' ... But instead of grimacing, 'Lo, the poor German,' let us pause to consider whether the traditional English comment on Shakespeare's Romantic method has been any more valuable than the Teuton's."[77] Against critics concerned to explain away Shakespeare's "psychological inconsistencies," his tendency to introduce "details which cause us to lose the sense of a connected whole," and his neglect of "Aristotelian standards," Graves nominates Shakespeare as a standard-bearer of romantic values: "This very inconsistency of plot, the development of this emblem or that in unforeseen directions, has and must always have a necessity and beauty which the context of the author's life would make apparent. Poetry is not as some people want it to be, a condensation and rearrangement of past events, according to a preconceived logical structure, not merely a combination of historic strands, but a new entity whose past is past; even intellectual verses are not recognized as conforming to any principles until after they have found their expression on paper."[78] Whether as the Englishman's caricature of the German scholar or as Graves's caricature of the contemporary English critic, the figure of fun here is the same literary stick-in-the-mud that Empson regularly imagines objecting to associational patterns of ambiguity as "fanciful" and "not properly clarifying."[79] And Graves's conception of the nature of poetic language as a thinking and feeling in process is also the same as Empson's.

Graves grounds poetic language in a more primitive mode of thought capable of identifying opposites in the way that Empson highlights by reference both to the ancient Egyptian language and to contemporary Arabic. Graves complains that "the scholastic tradition as finally systematized in the textbooks ... ridicules the ancient notion that medical bane and salve are always to be found growing together."[80] Empson makes the same observation in his discussion of ambiguity of the seventh type, the kind of ambiguity that will support "theories of aesthetics which regard poetry as the resolution of a conflict."[81] Citing Freud's *Notebooks*, he observe that

> early Egyptians, apparently, wrote the same sign for "young" and "old," showing which was meant by an additional hieroglyphic, not to be pronounced ... They only gradually learnt to separate the two sides of the antithesis and think of the one without conscious comparison with the other ... In so far as opposites are used to resolve or to soften conflict, so that an ageing man is not forced suddenly to find that a new and terrible word will apply to him, or can speak of himself as a young man by an easy and forgivable alteration of tone; to this extent there seems to be nothing peculiarly primitive about the sentiment, or the delicacy which allows it to be phrased ... This discussion is in some degree otiose because I really do not know what use the Egyptians made of their extraordinary words, or how "primitive" we should think their use of them if we heard them talking.[82]

Empson has taken on board the distinction that Graves is at pains to make in *Poetic Unreason* between primitive as something "childish" (and therefore contemptible) and primitive as something "of ancient origin" (but possibly still quite intelligent and sophisticated). Conceding that the ancient Egyptian identification of opposites "has, perhaps, something primitive in its weakness of hold on external truth, and its honesty in voicing desires" – to this extent, it may seem childish – Empson emphasizes that the so-called primitive identification of opposites can be conceptually a very sophisticated business: instancing Arabic as "a striking case of the mental sophistication required to use a word which covers its own opposite," Empson declares that he believes "that though such words appeal to the fundamental habits of the human mind, and are fruitful of irrationality, they are to be expected from a rather sophisticated state of language and feeling."[83]

•

Empson's explanation as to why nineteenth-century poets "are so little ambiguous" in Empson's sense of the term is a warning to readers that they ought not to expect his analysis of ambiguity to rely on examples from nineteenth-century poetry.[84] Yet far from scanting nineteenth-century poets, Empson devotes about 13% of his book to analysis of the role of ambiguity in their work, putting them in a respectable fourth place in this regard (after Shakespeare first, the Renaissance generally second, and the eighteenth century third). Empson devotes especially extensive analyses to Wordsworth, Shelley, and Keats. In fact, contrary to what the introductory chapter leads one to expect, they actually enjoy a certain prominence as exemplars of several different types of ambiguities. So the talk was anti-romantic, but the walk was not.

Empson returns to the topic in his 1947 preface, apologizing for spending so much time on these poets and the question of their aesthetic theory and practice, explaining that he had been led away from verbal analysis by the "cross-current" created at the time by "Mr. T.S. Eliot's criticism in particular, and the Zeitgeist in general" – a situation "calling for a reconsideration of the claims of the nineteenth-century poets so as to get them in perspective with the newly discovered merits of Donne, Marvell, and Dryden. It seemed that one could only enjoy both groups by approaching them with different and incompatible presuppositions, and that this was one of the great problems which a critic ought to tackle."[85]

One of the ways in which *Seven Types of Ambiguity* continues to be interesting is that it records the development of Empson's discoveries about poetic ambiguity between 1928 and 1930 as though he were creating ambiguity of the fifth type, which "occurs when the author is discovering his idea in the act of writing, or not holding it all in his mind at once ... Any fortunate muddle would be included in this, such as occurs in the course of digesting one's material."[86] Neither edited out before first publication, nor any subsequent edition, is evidence that Empson's thinking about nineteenth-century poetry changes during the writing of the book to the extent of contradicting and retracting in later chapters a good deal of what has been said in earlier ones. And so Shelley can be dismissed in the first chapter as one of those nineteenth-century poets "hugging to oneself a private dream-world" who did not keep a sharp enough "distinction between the world he considered real and the world from which he wrote poetry," whose "uncaused," "imposed" emotions obviate the "need to use ambiguities," and yet he can appear later as the central figure in discussion of ambiguity of the fifth type, a veritable virtuoso of this form of poetry.[87] In fact, we learn from the 1947 preface that Shelley is even more central to chapter five than might at first have appeared, for the discussion of Swinburne that follows the discussion of Shelley turns out to have been enabled by the latter ("looking for a puzzle" in Shelley "made me discover something about Swinburne").[88] In addition, the discussion of Marvell that concludes the chapter is designed to show the continuity between, on the one hand, Shelley and Swinburne, who establish the "subdued conceits and ambiguities" that proliferate in the nineteenth century and, on the other hand, Marvell and "the later metaphysical poets," who "came to take the conceit for granted ... till they were writing something like nineteenth-century poetry."[89] It seems that "Marvell was admired both by his own generation and by the nineteenth century," which is understandable since "the nineteenth-century technique" of ambiguity "is in part the metaphysical tradition dug up when rotten."[90] And so Empson concludes his observations about the development of ambiguity of the fifth type by emphasizing that it culminates in "the Romantic Movement's technique; dark hair, tidal water, landscape at dusk are dissolved in your mind, as often in dreams, into an apparently direct sensory image which cannot be attached to any of the senses."[91] From beginning to end, chapter five is Empson's defence of Shelley in particular and nineteenth-century poetry in general. So it is not surprising that Empson concludes it with a nod in the direction of Graves, whose insistent alignment of romanticism with fantastic dreams – it is virtually the *sine qua non* of his early criticism – is echoed here: "dark hair, tidal water, landscape at dusk are dissolved in your mind, as often in dreams."

As indicated above, Empson took note of Graves's reading of "La Belle Dame sans Merci," developing Graves's observations about romantic allegory into his definition of ambiguity of the third type. He also recalls the psycho-biographical exercise in criticism that

Graves conducts by research into Keats. Noting the "opposite notions combined in this poem" ("death and the sexual act," "pain and pleasure," "the conception of woman as at once mistress and mother," "a desire at once for the eternity of fame and the irresponsibility of oblivion"), Empson suggests that "biographers who attempt to show from Keats's life how he came by these notions are excellently employed, but it is no use calling them in to explain why the poem is so universally intelligible and admired; evidently these pairs of opposites, stated in the right way, make a direct appeal to the normal habits of the mind."[92] Graves makes this very point: "appreciation rises in the reader's mind as the result of the same imaginative thinking that produced the poem, without the need of any long-winded translation into a more logical form."[93] Graves believes that explanations of lived experience and associational logic lie behind all poems, but no more than Empson does he believe that awareness of them is necessary for the aesthetic enjoyment of poetry.

In Empson's first extended discussion of Wordsworth, "Tintern Abbey" is offered as an example of a poem demonstrating ambiguity of the fourth type, which "occurs when two or more meanings of a statement do not agree among themselves, but combine to make clear a more complicated state of mind in the author."[94] But it turns out that Wordsworth was simply in a muddled, rather than a complex, state of mind: Empson concludes that his analysis of "Tintern Abbey" "may show how these methods can be used to convict a poet of holding muddled opinions rather than to praise the complexity of the order of his mind."[95] Yet in his later discussion of Wordsworth, Empson apologizes for this evaluation, noting that he was not only harsh but misguided. Considering whether or not "Tintern Abbey" offers evidence of type-four ambiguity is beside the point, for he has now discovered that it exemplifies the more complex state of mind represented by ambiguities of the sixth type!

Empson's promotion of Wordsworth from muddled type-four wannabe to master exemplar of type six also owes a good deal to Graves. For instance, Empson's initial discussion of (attack on) "Tintern Abbey" is largely mapped out by Graves in his discussion of Wordsworth's related poem, "Intimations of Immortality." Contrasting his own conflict theory with the attitude of the scholar devoted to logic, Graves suggests that "the scholastic critic finds the chief value of Wordsworth's 'Intimations of Immortality' in the religious argument ... [I]f he ... suspected Wordsworth of reasoning from a wrong premise he would have serious doubts as to whether it was a good poem after all."[96] Empson initially presents himself as just such a critic of Wordsworth's reasoning from wrong premises. He points to the lines that speak of learning to look on nature in such a way as to perceive the spirit that "rolls through all things" and declares: "Wordsworth seems to have believed in his own doctrines and wanted his readers to know what they were. It is reasonable, then, to try to extract from this passage definite opinions on the relations of God, man, and nature … The reason why one grudges Wordsworth this source of strength is that he talks as if he owned a creed by which his half-statements might be reconciled, whereas, in so far as his creed was definite, he found these half-statements necessary to keep it at bay. There is something rather shuffling about this attempt to be uplifting, yet non-denominational."[97] Half-statements keep "muddled opinions" at bay.[98] On revisiting "Tintern Abbey" after two more chapters, however, Empson arrives at a new conclusion about Wordsworth's psychological and verbal achievement in the poem: the discussion of "Tintern Abbey" as "the last example of my fourth chapter belongs by rights to the sixth; I gave a rather nagging and irrelevant analysis of one of the great passages of Wordsworth, and complained that his theological statements were … a sort of generalization from theological opinions; Wordsworth is concerned with the resultant sentiments rather than the source of belief from which they are drawn. So one cannot say that he is contradicting himself, even by implication, because the theological ideas he has to invoke are not, so to speak, what he wants to make a statement about."[99]

In just the same way, after rehearsing the "scholastic" quarrel with Wordsworth's theology that Graves rehearsed and dismissed, Empson dismisses it too.[100] He has arrived at Graves's point of departure in studying poetry generally (and "Intimations of Immortality" in particular): to the doubt that a poem "reasoning from a wrong premise" can be "a good poem after all," Graves avers, "even the most pagan and revolutionary bard would raise a furious protest; if the poem holds together, if the poet has said what he means honestly, convincingly and with passion – as Wordsworth did – the glory and the beauty of the dream are permanently fixed beyond the scientific lecturer's pointer."[101] The scholastic critic, says Graves, "would not be interested to be told that the poet is being disturbed by a melancholy contradiction between his own happy childhood, idealistic boyhood and disappointed age."[102] Empson is no such scholastic critic, of course, for he is very interested to be told this – in fact, he tells himself pretty much the same thing in Chapter Six, and so tells himself off for having got interpretation of Wordsworth so wrong in Chapter Four.

Extended reflection on Wordsworth's "Tintern Abbey" during the writing of *Seven Types of Ambiguity* thus leads Empson not just to insights into the sixth type of ambiguity, but also to insights into the seamlessness with which mental conflict and verbal ambiguity merge in the best poetry: "In a sense, the sixth class is included within the fourth ... The criterion for the sixth class is more verbal ... But the criterion for the sixth class is not merely verbal, in contrast with the psychological criterion of the fourth; indeed, if a poet is using language properly, it ought to be impossible to maintain such a distinction."[103] Empson gives up the attempt to blame Wordsworth for muddled thinking because he accepts that Wordsworth has used language properly (not in a way different from his predecessors, as he originally claimed) and that he has thereby made it impossible for the reader to distinguish (as Empson originally tried to do) between his state of mind and his use of words.

In writing *Seven Types of Ambiguity*, Empson begins in the grip of contemporary prejudice against the romantics. Eliot had announced that poets must "force ... dislocate if necessary, language into meaning," and he had reported that the poets of the nineteenth century had been inadequate to the task.[104] Empson initially discovered in their work "distortions of meaning" that held promise of the meaning that he and Eliot valued, but he concluded that romantic grammar belongs "to the darker region of the mind" and so advised that the approach to it "should be psychological rather than grammatical."[105] Yet he develops through the tutelage of Graves's close readings not just a theory of criticism but also a practice of criticism – especially in Wordsworth's case – that leaves him pleasantly surprised by ambiguity where his own presuppositions had told him it would not be found. Allowing the ferment of this process of discovery to remain in *Seven Types of Ambiguity* may have struck Empson as the best way to bring along with him readers who begin the book with the same Eliotic prejudice as he did: that nineteenth-century poetry cannot be reconciled with the associational virtues of the poetry of Donne, Marvell, and Dryden.

8

Associations

Another important way Graves influenced Empson was that he emphasized the special power that resides in the English language and that English poetry flaunts so spectacularly: the multiple, contradictory, supplementary, historical, and dynamically developing associations amongst the meanings of words. Empson concludes *Seven Types of Ambiguity* with a consideration of "the conditions under which ambiguity is proper," and in doing so he foregrounds the word "associations": "The methods I have been using seem to assume that all poetical language is debauched into associations to any required degree."[1] He introduces the word via a passage by W.H. Auden and Cecil Day-Lewis in their preface to *Oxford Poetry, 1927*: "there is a 'logical conflict, between the denotatory and connotatory sense of words; between, that is to say, an asceticism tending to kill language by stripping words of all associations and a hedonism tending to kill language by dissipating their sense under a multiplicity of associations.'"[2]

The word "associations," like the word "conflict," is especially associated in the 1920s with Graves, who fights all decade long to earn poetry's "associative method of thought" a standing equal to that of the logic of "standard prose-writing," which "only likes one meaning for every word ... not three or four."[3] The word "association" is the one that Graves uses over and over again to explain the special nature of poetic language. In "The Illogic of Stoney Stratford and of Poetry" and "How Many Miles to Babylon?" (essays published in *The Spectator* in July of 1922), respectively, he defines poetry as "based on associative thinking" and asks readers to think about poems "on the lines of conflicting ideas reconciling themselves in symbolism by means of associative thought."[4] In his prefatory Note to *On English Poetry*, he describes "most scientists" as "insensitive to the emotional quality of words and their associative subtleties."[5] In his chapter on "Definitions," he explains that "In poetry the implication is more important than the manifest statement; the underlying associations of every word are marshalled carefully."[6] He later describes the poet's task as "the business of controlling the association-ghosts which haunt in their millions every word of the English language."[7] His chapter in *Poetic Unreason* on "The Illogical Element in Poetry" is a sustained criticism of the "scholastic system" that "makes no allowance for associative thinking, finds no virtue in a spoonerism or a pun suggested by the homophonic association of, say, 'horse' and 'hoarse,' or in fantastic slips either of pen or tongue."[8] He celebrates romantic poetry as "dependent on associative thought," although he knows that from the point of view of the classical sensibility such poetry offers too many "illegitimate associations."[9] In a university textbook's examples of breaches of logical rules, he finds "a clear example of associative thinking" and delights in identifying the "hidden associative tangle" caused by "the secondary meanings of words" and "the associations these meanings conjure up."[10] His point is that "associative thought is as modern and reputable a mode as intellectual thought."[11]

Empson understands this associative mode of thought to be enacted and invoked in the "linguistic form common in Shakespeare's verse ... 'the (noun) and (noun) of (noun)' ... in which two, often apparently quite different, words are flung together, followed by a word which seems to be intended to qualify both of them."[12] According to Empson, this linguistic form "is a powerful means of forcing [the reader] to adopt a poetical attitude toward words," for "since this form demands that the reader should find a highest common factor of its first two nouns, it implies that he must open his mind to all their associations, so that the common factor may be as high as possible."[13] The often quite different words flung together by Shakespeare "have got to be associated by the constructive imagination of the reader."[14]

Of course Coleridge – whose work Graves knew well and admired greatly – makes similar claims for the associative powers of the imagination, so Graves is by no means the first to champion associative thought. The contemporary figure who incites him to consider the virtues of associative thought, as Graves's celebration of the meaningfulness of "fantastic slips either of pen or tongue" shows, is Freud.[15] And as Empson points out, Freud's ideas were available to young people interested in literary criticism from a number of sources: "Of course, you know everybody was talking about Freud and things like that. I might have got it from many other people who are now forgotten as well as Graves."[16] But certainly the most notorious theorist of associative thought in the 1920s was Graves, and everyone knew it. All of Graves's books before his collaboration with Riding champion a psychoanalytical approach to the interpretation of literature, and even Richards pilloried him as representing the "gravest" dangers of Freudianism. "We all had it knocking about," says Empson; but "the idea that you wanted to use Freudian theory on literary criticism somehow was the thing that Graves picked up a generation before me."[17]

The tension between denotation and connotation to which Empson, Auden, and Day-Lewis refer is a version of the tension that Graves describes between the logic of standard prose writing and the associative mode of thought. He also describes it as the tension between logic and illogic, "analyses of cause and effect" and "associative thinking," "intellectual thought" and the "emotional mode of thought," classicism and romanticism.[18] The ideal for the one sensibility is poetry that is a "logically harmonious and rational statement," embodying thinking as "a logical process of one continuous strand": "the poetry recommended was to pursue a steady course in which every image was to be deduced from the previous one, the whole scheme was to work out according to the logic of human nature and other universal characteristics, and there was no place to be left for caprice."[19] The ideal here is "direct grammatic statement" and "self-aware allegory"; ultimately, "one meaning for every word."[20] The ideal for the other sensibility is "secondary meanings" for every word, poetry whose grammar is "of sibylline obscurity," and allegory that is "latent."[21] The "secondary meanings of words, however remote, react on each other in moments of passion if there is any similarity of emotional disturbance between the associations these meanings conjure up"; "the grammatic construction is continually being interrupted by fresh images before the others have submitted themselves for logical classification"; poetry of this sort, "appearing in a capricious unforeseeable way," is "bound up with allegories interlacing by homophonic and other [logically] illegitimate associations."[22]

So must it be in poetry that is not "a condensation and rearrangement of past events, according to a preconceived logical structure," but rather "a new entity": new because it expresses a conflict that is in the process of being experienced and expresses opposed ideas that are in the process of being linked. And this linkage takes place not by means of a timeless relationship supported by the logic of cause and effect but according to a temporal relationship emerging from the poet's experience and supported by the illogic of homophonic caprice and tongue-slipping accident, or any number of other aspects of the two-faced machinery of poetic language.[23] Such poetry evidences "inconsistency of plot" ("things happen which realistically-minded strangers find difficult to understand"), "geographical confusion," "inconsistent character" ("characters are continually changing from what they at first represented into something else"), and "the development of this emblem or that in unforeseen directions."[24]

Auden and Day-Lewis are concerned to find a way between "an asceticism tending to kill language by stripping words of all association and a hedonism tending to kill language by dissipating their sense under a multiplicity of associations."[25] Similarly, Empson is concerned to balance, on the one hand, the impression that by his method "all poetical language is debauched into associations to any degree required" with, on the other hand, the impression that he offers a "decent homage to the opposing power."[26] All three reflect Graves's concern in *Poetic Unreason* to find the middle way between the same extremes: "if it be ... claimed that the logical method is the only right method, and all others useless because illogical, I would point out that the romantic method has a similar scorn for the logical method: both may therefore be suspect when they advance these mutually exclusive claims."[27]

According to Graves, every poet – whether of the classical logical tradition or the romantic associative tradition – depends on both modes of thought. Although the devotee of logic expects statements to be "empirically confirmable by certain sensuous tests based on a view of the absolute reality of the spatio-temporal structure," and the associationalist nurtures the "madness and contradiction" of "poetic metamorphosis" by which one thing becomes another "so that the reality of the spatio-temporal structure being challenged ceases to be absolute reality," their scorn for each other belies what is common in their world of experience:

> the Spatio-temporally-minded logician will theorize about ghosts and fairies as subjective phenomena while denying their objective

existence, and the romantic or mystic will employ spatio-temporal formulae in an account of his visions while denying the adequacy of the senses to record the experience. And in the same way as a poet or transcendentalist will be dependent on the railway time-table as the most cramped logician, so this logician will night after night permit himself a series of the most fantastic dreams, and unwittingly derive as much benefit from them in aid of his spatio-temporal logic as the time-table gives the transcendental in regulating his journey to some grand conference of international mystics.[28]

And so despite the apparent rivalry between classical and romantic, logical and illogical, denotative and connotative sensibilities, the history of English poetry has always involved the expression of both sensibilities:

> though they are both expressions of a mental conflict, in Classical poetry this conflict is expressed within the confines of waking probability and logic … in Romantic Poetry the conflict is expressed in the illogical but vivid method of dream-changings … The dream origin of Romantic Poetry gives it … a naturally hypnotic effect. [Classical] poetry … feels the need of this easy suggestion to the audience for ideal thinking; and finds it necessary to avoid realism by borrowing shreds of accredited metamorphic diction and legend and building with them an illusion of real metamorphism … The borrowed Metamorphism is hardened to a convention and a traditional form … Sometimes, however … a nation's Classical tradition is broken by popular ridicule and the reappearance of young Metamorphic Poets. But after a little paper-bloodshed … the Classical tradition reappears, dressed up in the cast-off finery of the pioneer Metamorphics … This complicated dog-eat-dog process is cheerfully called "The Tradition of English Poetry."[29]

The way forward is to recognize that these two modes of thought are complementary strategies for dealing with conflict:

> once it is admitted by philosophers that though Romantic thought cannot be exactly foreseen, neither any more can intellectual thought; and further, when they admit that emotional poetry and thought, once it has appeared, has discernible an orderly orientation and inevitability; and when further they observe that

> such poetry and thought is not so primitive in the popularly accepted sense that it cannot use intellectual formulae for its own purposes, but is a method constantly employed unknown to themselves by the most sophisticated and Aristotelian minds, and of great service to them – then, finally, the clash between Classical and Romantic can end and these terms can be used to qualify the forms of poetry alternately appearing as either one or other method of thought employed for dealing with any conflict.[30]

Conflict is a human condition, and so is the fact that our minds proceed by both the emotional and the intellectual modes of thought. Just as poetic language cannot confine itself to either of these extremes, neither can the common language of the person in the street.

Empson agrees. He recognizes contemporary fears "about a break-up of the English language now visible on the hoardings, where words abandon grammatical distinction and work by association,"[31] but is not worried: "This may be alarming but it is not a novelty; it may restore to the language a flexibility it has not possessed since the days of its greatest triumphs."[32] The Elizabethans enjoyed a golden age of English, and he offers the relationship between Shakespeare and his Elizabethan readers as a model of the proper balance between the associative and the intellectual modes of thought in the English language. Shakespeare, he says, will allow him "To show how extremely flexible it [language] was then; how much, so long as it can be combined both with the possibility and encouragement of intellectual precision, an extreme flexibility of language is to be valued."[33]

•

Graves emphasizes the special powers of the English language for comprehending and expressing this double aspect of the English sensibility even before he publishes his first book of literary theory. He concludes *On English Poetry* by reproducing his 1921 letter to the editor of the Tracts of the Society for Pure English in which he argues that a lack of associations among words is as dangerous to accurate expression as an excess: "I would like to sound a warning against the attempt to purify the language too much – 'one word, one meaning' is as impossible to impose on English as 'one letter, one sound.'"[34] Of course "one word, one meaning" is the extreme that Graves associates with scientists, philosophers, and logicians, and his books and essays will soon campaign vigorously against the hegemony of these linear thinkers. Nonetheless, Graves agrees that "a common-sense precision in writing is clearly necessary."[35] Without a certain degree of precision, something so simple as contemplating an orange can lead to a chaos of competing sounds and meanings: "Old gentlemen usually *pare* their oranges, but the homophonic barrage of puns when Jones *père* prepares to pare a pair of – even oranges (let alone another English-grown fruit), has taught the younger generations either to peel a norange or skin their roranges."[36] Still, Graves insists that "over-definition" of a word "discourages any progressive understanding of the idea for which it acts as a hieroglyph."[37]

This "progressive understanding" of an idea comes from the word's associations. The orange can be anatomized in terms of "seeds," "calix," "*exocarp*, *carpel*, and *ovule*," and it can be eaten by "*paring* the *integument* and afterwards removing the *divisions* of the fruit for *mastication*."[38] Yet there is an other than "literary and semi-scientific language" for oranges according to which seeds are pips; the withered calyx is kim; the white part under the rind is the blanket or kill-baby. Anatomizing and eating an orange according to this more homely language, one must peel the "*skin* off the *rind*, ignoring the *kim* and scraping away the *kill-baby*, then pull out the *pigs*, *chew* them decently, and put the *pips* to their proper use."[39] Reducing the definition of "orange" to scientific denotation leaves out of account the way the word is now embedded in non-scientific networks of meaning and potentially prevents its progressive association with other networks of meaning not yet anticipated. And so, "the more precisely circumscribed a word, the less accurate it is in relation to other closely-defined words" – or, in other words, "good English surely is clear, easy, unambiguous, rich, well-sounding, but not self-conscious; for too much pruning kills."[40]

Empson develops very similar points about the vibrancy of contemporary English in the last chapter of *Seven Types of Ambiguity*. Perhaps remembering the particular complaint that Graves makes about the scientist who is so inaccurate in his use of language as to give a grub a hand by describing it as *manufacturing* a channel (the scientist, says Graves, uses words as "lifeless counters, weights, measures, or automatic engines wrongly adjusted"), but certainly remembering at least the general kind of debate that the Society for Pure English was stirring, Empson observes that "people sometimes say that words are now used as flat counters, in a way which ignores their delicacy; that English is coming to use fewer of its words, and those more crudely."[41] Oranges and grubs alike suffer from the poor language skills of Graves's scientist: oranges should be described by more words; grubs should be described by more accurate words.

Empson perhaps recalls Graves's picture of the "good English" anatomy of an orange being displaced by "semi-scientific language" in his own comments on science's general impact on language: "The sciences might be expected to diminish the ambiguity of the language, both because of their tradition of clarity and because much of their jargon has, if not only one meaning, at any rate only one setting and one point of view. But such words are not in general use; they act only as a further disturbing influence on the words used already."[42] Graves's phrase for the scientist's ambition for language – "one word, one meaning" – echoes here in Empson's emphasis on the "one meaning," "one setting," and "one point of view" that science prefers. Similarly, Empson's suggestion that the singular definition of a scientific term nonetheless becomes part of the network of words in a language so as potentially to "act ... as a further disturbing influence on the words used already" echoes Graves's point that the "secondary meanings of words, however remote, react on each other in moments of passion if there is any similarity of emotional disturbance between the associations these meanings conjure up."[43]

Empson grants that what he calls ambiguity (and what Graves calls secondary meaning) is not just a property of poetic language. He points to the typical newspaper headline ("given particular meaning" by ambiguous words that "can be either nouns or verbs, and would take kindly to being adjectives") and general "journalistic flatness" (in which "the word is used ... to stand for a vague and complicated mass of ideas and systems which the journalist has no time to apprehend") as the context for his suggestion that "it would be easy enough to take up an alarmist attitude, and say that the English language needs nursing by the analyst very badly indeed."[44] Yet like Graves, who complains that "It is no longer practical to coin words, resurrect obsolete ones and generally to tease the language as the Elizabethans did," Empson argues that the headline can be "a very effective piece of writing" because

> it conveys its point ... with a compactness which gives the mind several notions at one glance of the eye, with a unity like that of metaphor ... Nor can I feel that it will be a *disaster* if other

> forms of English literature adopt this fundamental mode of statement, so interesting to the logician; it is possible that a clear analysis of the possible modes of statement, and a fluid use of grammar which sets out to combine them as sharply as possible into the effect intended, may give back something of the Elizabethan energy to what is at present a rather exhausted language. But this is by the way; I have only used the headline to insist on the value of a detached and willing attitude to grammar, to show that the grammatical sentence is not the only form of statement in modern English.[45]

Whether in the secondary meanings that attend talk about oranges or in the syntactical and semantic ambiguities of newspaper headlines, Graves and Empson find a potential pattern of associations awaiting only the wit of a modern Elizabethan to spy out and express.

•

The key idea that Graves passes along to Empson concerns the pattern of associations that secondary meanings constitute. This idea is the basis of Empson's distinction between "accidental ambiguity" ("English is becoming an aggregate of vocabularies only loosely in connection with one another, which yet have many words in common, so that there is much danger of accidental ambiguity, and you have to bear firmly in mind the small clique for whom the author is writing") and "two-faced implications of any plausibility."[46] On the one hand, "An ambiguity is not satisfying in itself, nor is it, considered as a device on its own, a thing to be attempted; it must in each case arise from, and be justified by, the peculiar requirement of the situation."[47] On the other hand, each ambiguity must support a larger whole: "all the subsidiary meanings must be relevant, because anything (phrase, sentence, or poem) meant to be considered as a unit must be unitary, must stand for a single order of mind."[48] As Graves writes in explanation of the emotional conflict at the heart of poetry, "I plead the rule that 'Poetry contains nothing haphazard,' which follows naturally on the theory connecting poetry with dreams. By this rule I mean that if a poem, poem-sequence or drama is an allegory of genuine emotional experience and not a mere cold-blooded exercise, no striking detail and no juxtaposition of apparently irrelevant themes which it contains can be denied at any rate a personal significance – a cipher that can usually be decoded from another context."[49] There is always at least the unity of a psycho-biographical associational logic recoverable from every proper poem. But the fact that an element in a poem has more than one meaning is interesting only if there is a whole within which the various meanings cohere.

As early as his 1921 letter to the editor of the Society for Pure English, Graves declares his belief that language is a living entity and implicitly an organic whole. Reviewing proposals made in the Society's first five tracts, he figures the English language as a thriving eco-system (comprising weeds, flowers, birds, and bees) and warns against a pedantic, mechanical, technological attitude toward language that could prove lethal: "By all means weed out homophones, and wherever a word is overloaded and driven to death let another bear part of the burden; suppress the bastard and ugly words of journalese or commerce; keep a watchful eye on the scientist, take necessary French and Italian words out of their italics to give them an English spelling and accentuation; call a bird or flower by its proper name, revive useful dialect or obsolescent words, and so on; that is the right sort of purification, but let it be tactfully done, let the Dictionary be a hive of living things and not a museum of minutely ticketed fossils."[50] Since "too much pruning kills," the pruners ought at least to be the ones with green thumbs and not those "using words ... as lifeless counters, weights, measures, or automatic engines wrongly adjusted."[51] Auden and Day-Lewis follow the same argument: too much pruning in favour of denotation kills; a choking growth of connotative weeds also kills.

Graves is certainly interested in language understood diachronically – he is curious about the derivation of words and their changing uses over time (of the word "pig" as used for the divisions of an orange, he wonders, "is the derivation from the tithe- or parson's pig known by its extreme smallness?") but he is more interested in the way words are implicated synchronically in the living system of the English language: "As one rather more interested in the choice, use, and blending of words than in the niceties of historical grammar, and having no greater knowledge of etymology than will occasionally allow me to question vulgar derivations of place-names, I would like to sound a warning against the attempt to purify the language too much – 'one word, one meaning' is as impossible to impose on English as 'one letter, one sound.'"[52]

According to Graves, any verbal expression is a temporal and temporary event. It harnesses the various meanings available in the service of the expression of an idea, but such an idea is no more fixed and final than the meanings of each of the individual words or the particular combination of words by which it has come to be expressed. Understanding is always in progress, and its progress is enabled by the connections between ideas revealed by the connections between the words that express these ideas. And so: "Over-definition ... discourages any progressive understanding of the idea for which it acts as hieroglyph. It even seems that the more precisely circumscribed a word, the less accurate it is in relation to other closely-defined words."[53]

As we have seen, the Society for Pure English letter culminates in a demonstration of the "progressive understanding of the idea" represented by the word "orange." Graves begins by telling the "story of a governess" who is "suspicious" of her female charges' "scientific" elder brother's description of the earth as "an oblate spheroid" and suggests to them that it "is *nicer* for little girls to say that the earth is more or less the shape of an orange." His paragraph's *tour de force* deserves quoting at length:

> From [this] fruit ... can be drawn our homely moral of common sense in the use of words. As every schoolboy I hope doesn't know, the orange is the globose fruit of that rutaceous tree the *citrus aurantium*, but as every schoolboy certainly is aware, there are several kinds of orange on the market, to wit the ordinary everyday sweet orange from Jaffa or Jamaica, the bitter marmalade orange that either comes or does not come from Seville, the navel orange, and the excellent "blood," with several other varieties. Moreover the orange has as many *points* as a horse, and parts or processes connected with its dissection and use as a motorcycle. "I would I were an Orange Tree, that Busie Plante," sighed George Herbert once. I wonder how Herbert would have anatomized his Orange, then a rarer fruit than today when popular affection and necessary daily intercourse have wrapped the orange with a whole glossary of words as well as with tissue-paper ... *Peel* (subst.) is ousting *rind*; a pity because there is also *peal* as a homophone; but I am glad to say that what used to be called *divisions* are now almost universally known as *fingers* or *pigs* ... the seeds are "pips," and quite rightly too, because in this

> country they are seldom used for planting, and "pip" obviously means that when you squeeze them between forefinger and thumb they are a useful form of minor artillery; then there is the white pithy part under the outer rind; I have heard this called *blanket*, and it is pretty good, but I have also heard it called *kill-baby*, and that is better; for me it will always remain *kill-baby*. On consulting *Webster's International Dictionary* I find that there is no authority or precedent for calling the withered calix on the orange the *kim*, but I have done so ever since I can remember, and have heard the word in many respectable nurseries (it has a fascination for children), and I can't imagine it having any other name. Poetical wit might call it "the beauty-patch on that fairy orange cheek"; heraldry might blazon it, on *tenne*, as a *mullet*, *vert*, *for difference*; contemporary slang would probably explain it as that "rotten little star-shaped gadget at the place where you shove in your lump of sugar"; but *kim* is obviously the word that is wanted, it needs no confirmation by a Dictionary Revisal Committee or National Academy. There it is, you can hardly get away from it.[54]

According to Graves, the idea of just what an orange has been, is, and shall be makes itself available continually and continuously to the progressive understanding of speakers of English – from schoolboys to correspondents of the Society for Pure English – by the fact that it is circumscribed (not overly precisely, but precisely enough) by so many ordinary words with so many associations and secondary meanings.

In conclusion, Graves epitomizes the "clear, easy, unambiguous, rich, well-sounding" way that good English works by proper instruction on how to eat such an orange. Such instruction must find the mean between the extremes of the "pedantic scientist," on the one hand, and "contemporary slang," on the other. It certainly ought not to be offered in the form of a "self-conscious" and "semi-scientific language" "insisting on *paring* the *integument* and afterwards removing the *divisions* … for *mastication*." Rather, the instruction should be in the form of a language as common to the boys and girls of the "respectable nurseries" as to "the man in the street."[55]

•

In *On English Poetry*, written at about the same time as this letter but with a publication date a year later (1922), Graves explains the application of this perspective on "good English" to poetry. In a prefatory comment to his letter to the Society for Pure English, he indicates that it "explains [his] attitude to the careful use of English by prose writers as well as by poets," and he suggests that the letter be "read in conjunction with" his chapter on poetic diction: "the poet will be best advised to choose as the main basis of his diction the ordinary spoken language of his day; the reason being that words grow richer by daily use and take on subtle associations which the artificially bred words of literary or technical application cannot acquire with such readiness."[56]

Elsewhere in *On English Poetry*, as we have seen, he declares that these subtle associations form patterns in good poetry:

> The underlying associations of each word in a poem form close combinations of emotion unexpressed by the bare verbal pattern ... In this way the poet may be compared with a father piecing together a picture-book puzzle for his children. He surprises them at last by turning over the completed picture, and showing them that by the act of assembling the scattered parts of "Red Riding Hood with the Basket of Food" he has all the while been building up unnoticed underneath another scene of tragedy – "The Wolf eating the Grandmother" ... The analogy can be more closely pressed; careless arrangement of the less important pieces or wilfully decorative borrowing from another picture altogether may look very well in the upper scene, but what confusion below! ... The possibilities of this pattern underneath have been recognized and exploited for centuries in Far Eastern systems of poetry. I once even heard an English Orientalist declare that Chinese was the only language in which true poetry could be written, because of the undercurrents of allusion contained in every word of the Chinese language. It never occurred to him that the same thing might be unrecognizedly true also of English words.[57]

Graves's early criticism is devoted to making this *recognizedly* true.

His clearest formulation of the special poetic nature of the English language appears in the book that Empson later said had most influenced him: *Impenetrability: Or The Proper Habit of English* (1926).

Graves regards English as a language that employs "the imaginative method," unlike the "more logical languages" such as French, which is now "steady enough and secure enough against imaginative interruption."[58] He shows what he means by considering the adjective "brazen": "All the qualities ... which the imagination can give to brass are latent in the word."[59] "'Brazen' may mean 'shining with a metallic glare' ... Or it may mean 'strident,' by recollection of the noise that a brazen trumpet or bugle makes ... Or it may mean 'cased with brass,' and therefore 'shameless and insolent' ... It may mean 'of less worth than gold.'"[60] According to Graves, "It is the persistent use of this method of '*thought by association of images*' as opposed to '*thought by generalised preconceptions*' that distinguishes English proper from the more logical languages."[61] The method of English as a language, therefore, is fundamentally cognate with the special nature of poetic language.

In *Impenetrability*, Graves makes explicit his belief that language – especially English – is capable of signifying patterns of meaning beyond the author's conscious awareness and deliberate control. Although "for French prose-writers and many celebrated French verse-writers the conceits of the words they use are dulled and show no rebellious tendency to form illicit assemblies that might affect the argument," the situation in English literature is quite the opposite: "For English writers of prose or verse, so soon as a gust of natural feeling snatches away the typographical disguise in which their words are dressed, the conceits appear in all freedom: at first they enliven and enforce the argument, but after a while, if the author is not wary, they desert it and begin a digressive dance of their own."[62]

In the passage of Graves's close literary analysis that Empson pointed out to Riding more than forty years after he first read it, Graves articulates the attitude toward language and literature that Empson explains at greater length in *Seven Types of Ambiguity*. Graves begins by comparing English to Latin and its derivative vernaculars such as Italian and French, observing that "When particular words very highly charged with meaning in their context occur in English literature, this is counted a great virtue. In logical literatures it is a vice, by the rule of 'one word, one meaning.'"[63] Empson was clearly paying attention, eventually saying virtually the same thing: "a poetical use of ambiguity ... has some claim to be considered native to the language. I really do not know what importance it has in other European languages ... my impression is that while it is frequent in French and Italian, the subsidiary meanings are nearly always bad grammar, so that the inhabitants of those countries would have too much conscience to attend to them."[64] Graves then proceeds to explicate the highly charged meanings of the word "clasped" in Keats's "The Eve of St Agnes," the example that Empson later recalled for Riding, and concludes: "English is strong enough to bear any weight so long as the load is properly packed and adjusted. Its greatest virtue as a literary language is its readiness to absorb foreign and technical words, and words from the better sort of slang, and to extemporise not only new imaginative phrases but distinguishable varieties of any overworked or ambiguous word."[65]

Having demonstrated how the effect of certain lines of poetry depends upon words with two or three meanings, Graves declares that "This ... is the constant practice of those English poets who achieve the most admired phrases. The reader is not rationally aware of the principle underlying such phrases: he knows that they delight him but does not in the act of reading poetry dissect them."[66] Empson's point is the same: "I have been trying to analyse verses which a great variety of critics have enjoyed but only described in terms of their effects; thus I have claimed to show how a properly-qualified mind works when it reads verses, how those properly-qualified minds have worked which have not at all understood their own working."[67]

•

As always, one can trace Graves's influence on Empson in ways both big and small. For example, Graves observes that "English proper has always been very much a language of 'conceits'; that is, except for the purely grammatic parts of speech, which are in general colourless enough, the vocabulary is not fully dissociated from the imagery from which it developed: words still tend to be pictorial and not typographic ... For English writers of prose or verse, so soon as a gust of natural feeling snatches away the typographical disguise in which their words are dressed, the conceits appear in all freedom: at first they enliven and enforce the argument, but after a while, if the author is not wary, they desert it and begin a digressive dance of their own."[68] Empson identifies the same special claim for English as a poetic language, he notes the same danger that the unwary face in the handling of it, and he even avails himself of the same metaphor:

"All languages are composed of dead metaphors as the soil of corpses, but English is perhaps uniquely full of metaphors of this sort, which are not dead but sleeping, and, while making a direct statement, colour it with an implied comparison. The school rule against mixed metaphor ... is largely necessary because of the presence of these sleepers, who must be treated with respect; they are harder to use than either plain word or metaphor because if you mix them up you must show you are conscious of their meaning, and are not merely being insensitive to the possibilities of language."[69]

Similarly, at three different points in *On English Poetry,* Graves characterizes conflict within the poet as analogous to conflicts like war and civil disturbance: "The mind of a poet is like an international conference composed of delegates of both sexes and every shade of political thought, which is trying to decide on a series of problems of which the chairman has himself little previous knowledge"; "I have ... attempted to show Poetry as the Recorder's précis of a warm debate between the members of the poet's mental Senate on some unusually controversial subject"; "new ideas troop quietly into [the poet's] mind until suddenly every now and again two of them violently quarrel and drag into the fight a group of other ideas that have been loitering about at the back of his mind for years; there is great excitement, noise and bloodshed, with finally a reconciliation and drinks all round. The poet writes a tactful police report on the affair and there is the poem."[70] And here again it is clear that Empson paid close attention, writing in his turn: "In Shakespeare's great parades of associations the attendants are continually quarrelling among themselves"; and "The Folio's comma ... heightens the civil war in the line by dividing it in two."[71]

9

Taxonomies of Types

Finally, one can see that Empson found in Graves's early work the model for his taxonomical strategy of systematically classifying as seven types the dynamic of multiple significations. Such significations are multiple not only because of meanings that historical research recalls from the past, but also because of meanings that new ways of interpreting literature make available in the present and will continue to make available in the future.

In his essay on "Classical and Romantic" sensibilities in *Poetic Unreason*, Graves shows how "we can catalogue a number of distinguishable psychological forms in which poetry can occur."[1] He proposes to do this by "embroidering on the theme" of "two dreams of a typical war-neurosis, the one characteristic and the other fantastic" (that is, the agents, objects, and events "can be confirmed by the senses as possible" in the one, but not in the other).[2] The one dream imitates realistically the actual incident that prompted "a complete breakdown": "A war-weary soldier lies asleep in a deep dug-out; he suddenly awakes to find a bomb hissing on the floor beside him, about to blow him to pieces. The bomb is between him and the door, so that he cannot escape, nor can he kick it out, because the entrance shaft comes down too steeply."[3] The other dream is a fantastic version of the same event, "a dream of grotesque character, the central terror of which is an enormous and half-human cat hissing and about to spring at the dreamer and cutting off his escape from a lift which is waiting to ascend."[4]

Graves proceeds to work out the implications of his declaration that "In the period of conflict, poetry may be either a partisan statement in the emotional or in the intellectual mode of thought of one side of the conflict; or else a double statement of both sides of the conflict, one side appearing in the manifest statement, that is, in the intellectual mode, the other in the latent content, that is, in the emotional mode, with neither side intelligible to the other."[5] The first form of poetry that he describes arises when the poet is unaware of the symbolism latent in his statement: "If the bomb-dream was related as a historic experience, 'At the foot of the shaft John Tompkins lay,/The bomb rolled hissing down,' by someone who did not feel the analogy between the bomb and trench-warfare, that would be direct poetic statement."[6] The second form of poetry arises when the poet is in the emotional mode, unaware of the intelligible potential of his statement: "the cat-dream is fantastic, and might produce a poem of this style: 'The great cat booted and spurred with nails/Flayed him with his nine long tails,/He could not flee by the upward-moving stair,' where the associations of *cat* combine in a psychological unity which cannot be accepted as probable by any empiric test."[7] The third form of poetry that he describes is very similar to the first – in fact, superficially identical to it – but the allegorical symbolism is even more remote from consciousness: "If the soldier at the same time as he was having these unhappy military experiences was involved in a commercial fraud that was in danger of being exploded, the bomb-dream might well serve for his two predicaments at once without further distortion."[8]

Graves clearly categorizes poetry here both in terms of the kinds of ambiguity present in the poems and in terms of whether or not the poet is conscious of them. The bomb-dream and the cat-dream overlap because there are multiple kinds of hissing, multiple kinds of ascent, and so on, all of which enable the kinds of displacement and condensation that Graves outlines. The war experience and the financial experience can both be expressed in the bomb-dream because a word like "explode" is a node for what Graves calls "multiple reference."[9] In Graves's poetic universe, there are always at least two meanings. The question is whether the various meanings can be known and to what extent they are known, both from the poet's and from the reader's point of view. As Jensen points out, *Seven Types of Ambiguity* regularly exhibits the same kind of bifurcation of its analysis between the poet's and the reader's point of view.[10]

Graves begins *Poetic Unreason* by introducing this necessarily double perspective: "I will ask you to think of Poetry in two very different capacities without for a moment confusing them – Poetry as it fulfills certain needs in the poet, and Poetry as it fulfills certain needs in the reader."[11] Empson does the same. As Jensen observes, Empson's concentration on semantic and grammatical ambiguities in his discussion of the first three types is supplemented by focus "on the mind and intention of the author" in types four, five, and seven and by focus on "the reader's conscious recognition" of ambiguity in type six (although "in none of the types is any of the dimensions independent").[12]

Empson derives from his first three ambiguities further types distinguishable in terms of the writer's or the reader's consciousness of multiple references: "I put in the third type cases where one was intended to be mainly conscious of a verbal subtlety; in the fourth type the subtlety may be as great, the pun as distinct, the mixture of modes of judgment as puzzling, but they are not in the main focus of consciousness"; "An ambiguity of the fifth type occurs when the author is discovering his idea in the act of writing, or not holding it all in his mind at once"; ambiguities of the seventh type "show a fundamental division in the writer's mind," the result for the person responding to this context being "at once an indecision and a structure" that draws one "into the stasis of appreciation."[13] Similarly Graves defines further forms of poetry in terms of the poet's developing consciousness of the phenomenon of multiple reference. He derives a fifth type of poetry from the arrival of consciousness upon the scene of poetry otherwise of the second type described above:

> If the poet becoming aware of the allegory comprised in the Cat dream wrote a poem which though logical enough to disregard the verbal associations of cat and cat-o'-nine-tails was to embody the various allegorical settings, it might appear something like this:
>
> War held me: like a mouse, I seemed.
> War, the great cat played with my life,
> Hissing and torturing with delay.
> Or it seemed that war, a nine-thonged whip,
> Flayed me, fast fettered to the ground.
> I could not fly, nor show my torturer fight,
> I felt like some poor lift-boy when masked thieves
> Threaten him and he casts a longing eye
> At the waiting lift across the hotel lounge.

> Here there is nothing unconfirmable by the sense; a man can be held by war and can record his sensations by this or that analogy. But there is a distinction between poetry in which the use of allegory is static, confined to a single consistent theme (as the bomb dream used as an allegory of war) and poetry in which a variety of allegories occur, as in the cat dream.[14]

Graves in fact imagines as a sixth type of poetry the very poetry of the "fundamental division in the writer's mind" that Empson defines as a seventh type of ambiguity: "if there is a conflict in the individual, one interest will be likely to appear on the higher [intellectual] and one on the lower [emotional] level, so that the soldier who was alternately militarist and pacifist, with the militarist dominant on the higher level, would either disregard the cat dream, if he remembered it, as being nonsensical, or if he was versed in these methods of dream analysis would fail to interpret it in the pacifist sense, or in a third case he would even misinterpret it in a sense suitable to the militarist claim."[15] Empson says that of conflicting ideas in "ambiguity of the seventh type one tends to lose sight of the conflict they assume; the ideas are no longer thought of as contradictory by the author"; in this type of ambiguity, there is occasionally "an evasion of the contradiction, which moves it out of the conscious mind into a region of the judgment which can accept it without reconciling it."[16] Here again, Empson's anatomy of the divisions possible in the writer's mind is virtually the same as Graves's.

In a chapter on poems that present "Problems for Classification," Graves even offers an example of what Empson will call an ambiguity of the fifth type, which occurs "when the author is discovering his idea in the act of writing, or not holding it all in the mind at once":

> There is a poem by Wordsworth called *Nutting*, which makes an interesting problem for classification because it is difficult to know how far Wordsworth realized its emotional significance, and how far he was deliberately trying to divert the attention of his readers from an incident in his life which did little credit to his social reputation … It seems most probable that Wordsworth wrote the Nutting poem with all but the "dearest Maiden" passage as part of the Childhood book of the Prelude: later, on arrival at the ninth book he suddenly saw its significance to the Annette Vallon romance. He intended to incorporate it at that

> point as an allegory with the "dearest maiden" ending, and probably an introduction giving the story of his unhappy romance. Dissuaded by considerations of caution he printed *Nutting* separately ... *Nutting* begins then as a romantic poem; but the poet becomes aware of the latent meaning when he has emerged from the mood that made it necessary ... [T]he poet has on the higher level recognized the allegory of a poem on the lower level, so that by deliberate additions and substitutions he can turn it into a solution of one phase at any rate of the conflict.[17]

Writing similarly of "the transitional simile" (rather than of the transitional poem that Graves identifies) – a "simile which applies to nothing exactly, but lies half-way between two things when the author is moving from one to the other" – Empson describes such literary events as "a fortunate confusion."[18]

A similar poem, discovering itself in the act of writing in just the way that Empson describes, is "John Skelton's poem, *Speke, Parot* ... a very interesting example of the development of a poem by accretion of different moods."[19] It offers itself as a fortunate confusion not holding all of its moods together at once. On the one hand, "the actual parrot itself on which the poem has been based is very accurately drawn"; on the other hand, the poem is an allegory: "moral censure of the age crops up here and there throughout the piece"; "in most respects the parrot is Skelton"; "but where the poet thinks of the parrot as being the bird which is always picking up shreds of learning and producing them at the wrong occasion the parrot is his enemy Wolsey."[20] So in the course of Skelton's writing of the poem, there is a "shifting of the latent meaning."[21]

Empson, then, could look to this work by Graves not only for an example of the general usefulness of the taxonomical tactic in explaining the kinds of multiple meanings that come systematically to be associated in poetry, but also for examples of particular kinds of associated meanings that a more academic, disciplined, and focused critic could explain – at greater length, in greater detail, and with more sophistication – as seven types of ambiguity.

10

Remembering Graves in Revision

Between Riding's protests that he failed to acknowledge her influence on *Seven Types of Ambiguity* and their lengthy, angry, and inconclusive correspondence on this topic in 1970 and 1971, Empson revised the book for the publication of a second edition. Should the reference to *A Survey of Modernist Poetry* remain, supplemented by the correct attribution of authorship to both Riding and Graves (as on the erratum slip)? Or should the original acknowledgment of Graves as the sole source of his method stand, with the reference to *A Survey of Modernist Poetry* quietly dropped? Addressing these questions involved reflecting on whether he found the real source of his inspiration to have been the work by Graves in collaboration with Riding that he originally mentioned, or the early work by Graves preceding Riding's influence upon him, work Empson had not mentioned.

The revised preface to *Seven Types of Ambiguity* includes a reference to Graves's conflict theory. Empson had originally mentioned the conflict theory – without attributing it to Graves – only in the main text of the first edition; by foregrounding it in this fashion, he makes it clear that he still considers Graves to have been the chief influence upon him. Moreover, he removes any reference to *A Survey of Modernist Poetry* from the second edition of the book, effectively dismissing Riding's belief that she also deserved acknowledgment.

Yet Empson also declines to replace his reference to the famous book by Riding and Graves with a reference to any particular work by Graves as the source of the method in question. So his acknowledgment of influence becomes simultaneously more accurate in one way and less precise in another. Perhaps just as interesting, however, is the fact that the new preface finds new ways to affirm both Graves's original influence on Empson's method in the late 1920s and his continuing relevance to Empson's thinking about the nature of poetic language in 1947. It turns out that Graves was still a lively presence in Empson's thinking about literature twenty years after his first encounter with his work.

•

In the following passage from the 1947 preface, for instance, Empson alludes both to Graves's assumption that mental conflict underlies all poetry and to Graves's experience of shell-shock following the Great War: "I want now to express my regret that the topical interest of Freud distracted me from giving adequate representation in the seventh chapter to the poetry of straightforward mental conflict ... I believe that rather little good poetry has been written in recent years, and that ... the effort of writing a good bit of verse has in almost every case been carried through almost as a clinical thing; it was done only to save the man's own sanity. Exceedingly good verse has been written under these conditions in earlier centuries as well as our own, but only to externalise the conflict of an individual. It would not have been sensible to do such hard work unless the man himself needed it."[1] However much Empson regrets the implication that he allowed in the first edition that some examples of the seventh type of ambiguity were rooted in Freudian "neurotic disunion," his vocabulary here – his talk of "mental conflict," of poetry as "a clinical thing," as something done because the poet "needed it" (done "to save a man's sanity," to "externalise the conflict of an individual") – remains determinedly psychological and shows that he still accepts Graves's conflict theory. Furthermore, he affirms that conflict theory remains the basis for the work on ambiguity in contemporary poetry that he imagines that he might have done but, he confesses, "if I tried to rewrite the seventh chapter to take in contemporary poetry I should only be writing another book."[2]

Empson presumably has Graves's work in mind when he refers to contemporary verse "carried through almost as a clinical thing ... done only to save the man's sanity."[3] In *On English Poetry*, Graves says that "poetry ... is a form of psycho-therapy."[4] In *The Meaning of Dreams*, he says that his 1921 poem "The Gnat" "has many attributes that connect it with a war-neurosis" and so explains its therapeutic function: "I can say now definitely that I understand what the whole conflict was about. I was at the time suffering badly from so-called shell-shock, the result of prolonged trench service, wounds and a fear that war might break out all over again. Nineteen hundred and twenty-one was a very anxious year, there being wars and rumours of wars in Russia, Ireland, the Near East and elsewhere, and my nervous condition got worse. I did not at the time realise that the fear of war was giving me all this trouble."[5] In *Poetic Unreason*, he explains revisions to one of his poems between 1918 and 1921 as having a therapeutic function because during this time he was "deeply interested in Freudian psycho-analysis as being a possible corrective for [his] shell-shock," and he even suggests that his approach to the criticism of poems has a therapeutic function: "I have been led to take an interest in this analysis business … partly to find relief from a war neurosis from which I still officially suffer."[6] Certainly when his correspondence with Riding in the 1970s prompted Empson to reconsider yet again Graves's influence upon him, he recalled the connection between his mentor's literary theory and shell-shock: "It all began with shell-shock from the First War, of course … He had developed a Conflict Theory of poetry, soon after the war, and went on to consider the verbal means by which conflict finds expression."[7]

Yet however much Empson is thinking of Graves's post-war, post-traumatic poetry here, it is clear that he has "conflict theory" in mind once more as he writes his 1947 preface. In fact, Empson's paragraph about how "the impact of Freud" "distracted" him from properly discussing "poetry of straightforward mental conflict" reprises the main features of Graves's first chapter in *Poetic Unreason* – more than twenty years after Empson first read it.[8] Empson's poet "needed" "to externalise the conflict of an individual"[9]; so does Graves's: "Poetry is for the poet a means of informing himself … of the relation in his mind of certain hitherto inharmonious interests, you may call them his sub-personalities or other selves … [I]t enables him to be rid of these conflicts between his sub-personalities."[10] For Empson's poet, poetry is a "clinical thing" in response to "mental conflict"[11]; so it is both for Graves's poet and his reader: "a well-chosen anthology should be a medicine chest against all ordinary mental disorders … Poetry may take the form of merely stating the nature of the conflict between these [sub-personalities'] interests, a diagnosing of the ailment, in the form of pity, doubt, resentment, or merely a cry of pain; it may be a temporary relief, a narcotic or counter-irritant, which I call poetry of escape; or it may take the completer form of prescribing for the cure of the ailment, suggesting how a new common life can be formed between these conflicting interests by the intervention of some medicating influence."[12]

Most of the 1947 preface – about two-thirds of it – is taken up with a long-delayed response to James Smith's 1931 *Criterion* review of *Seven Types of Ambiguity*, from which Empson quotes at length. Interestingly, an important part of his quarrel with Smith implicitly concerns Graves's conflict theory: "Quite a number of Mr. Empson's analyses ... are interesting only as revelations of the poet's, or of Mr. Empson's, ingenious mind. Further, some of Mr. Empson's analyses deal, not with words and sentences, but with conflicts supposed to have raged within the author when he wrote. Here, it seems to me, he has very probably left poetry completely behind."[13] Smith also complains that because Empson finds ambiguity "everywhere in the drama, in our social experience, in the fabric of our minds, he is led to assume it must be discoverable everywhere in great poetry," a thesis of which Smith doubts that the reader "is even prepared to be convinced."[14]

In answering each charge – that he indulges in suppositions about the mental state of poets and that he believes that ambiguity is omnipresent in great poetry because it is omnipresent in life itself – Empson invokes the work of Graves. That he should do so is not surprising, for Smith presumably alludes by his reference to "conflicts supposed to have raged within the author" to the influence of Graves on Empson. Smith makes it clear that no more than Richards does he accept all this unverifiable nonsense about conflicts supposedly raging within writers. Smith, in fact, is the type of critic of his method that Empson had anticipated from the beginning.

Perhaps just as interesting is the possibility that Empson's response to Smith's criticism of *Seven Types of Ambiguity* serves, in part, as a long-deferred response to Riding's insults about the book. For Smith's *ad hominem* observation in 1931 that "Quite a number of Mr. Empson's analyses ... are interesting only as revelations of the poet's, or of Mr. Empson's, ingenious mind" anticipates a much more vituperative version of the same charge in a letter from Riding. According to Miranda Seymour,

> On February 24, 1939, Laura Riding wrote to William Empson from France, shortly before she went with Graves to America. In this letter, held in a private collection, Miss Riding took Empson to task. She told him, to paraphrase, that his delight in ambiguity

> represented no fundamental ambiguity in meanings but an ambiguity in himself. All of his seeming precision in the midst of apparent ambiguity was an inexactness of himself, in inexact apprehension of truth offered as criticism. Slightly wrong, she went on, was not almost true. He behaved as if he was the teacher, "and you are not that." This "feeling" about him had crystallised and it was her duty to tell him. No answer was desired.[15]

Seymour wonders whether "this letter perhaps contribute[d] to Empson's decision to delete any acknowledgment to Graves or to Riding in the 1947 edition, and all subsequent ones, of his book."[16] In point of fact, of course, acknowledgment of and references to the work of Graves endures, but Riding is done and dusted as far as Empson is concerned.

•

Smith claims that "a poem is not a mere fragment of life" ("a bundle of diverse forces, bound together only by their co-existence"), for a poem "is a fragment that has been detached, considered, and judged by a mind."[17] In response, Empson suggests that a poet "has to judge what he has written and get it right."[18] Empson's point is that Smith's exaltation of the poem as noumenally transcending its phenomenal beginning – its beginning as an experience that is no more than "a bundle of forces, bound together only by their co-existence," a beginning transcended because this fragment of the poet's life has been "judged by a mind" – ignores an important fact: "the judgment of the author may be wrong."[19] To illustrate this point, Empson says that "Mr. Robert Graves ... has remarked that a poem might happen to survive which later critics called 'the best poem the age produced,' and yet there had been no question of publishing it in that age, and the author had supposed himself to have destroyed the manuscript ... This has no bearing on any 'conflict' theory; it is only part of the difficulty as to whether a poem is a noumenon or a phenomenon. Critics have long been allowed to say that a poem may be something inspired which meant more than the poet knew."[20]

Graves's first work of critical theory, *On English Poetry*, defines poetry in terms of these tensions. On the one hand, poetry is "the unforeseen fusion ... of apparently contradictory emotional ideas ... Every poem worthy of the name has its central idea, its nucleus, formed by this spontaneous process."[21] On the other hand, "later it becomes the duty of the poet as craftsman to present this nucleus in the most effective way possible, by practising poetry more consciously as an art"; this entails "the more-or-less deliberate attempt ... to impose an illusion of actual experience on the minds of others."[22] And so, the poet "creates in passion, then by a reverse process of analyzing, he tests the implied suggestions and corrects them on common-sense principles so as to make them apply universally."[23]

Practising poetry consciously as an art, the poet must make many judgments: "One of the chief problems of the art of poetry is to decide what are the essentials of the image that has formed in your mind; the accidental has to be eliminated and replaced by the essential. There is the double danger of mistaking a significant feature of the image for an accident and of giving an accident more prominence than it deserves."[24] No less important are judgments more local: "One of the most embarrassing limitations of poetry is that the language you use is not your own to do entirely what you like with. Times actually come in the conscious stage of composition when you have to consult a dictionary or another writer as to what word you are going to use."[25] The danger of making a mistake is continuous from the first ideas and images in the mind to the final words and punctuation marks on the page.

In *Poetic Unreason*, Graves notes that poetry has always been written "to externalise the conflict of an individual" for "It would not have been sensible to do such hard work unless the man himself needed it"; in his preface to the second edition of his book, Empson repeats Graves's point that "the act of composition is primarily not communication between the individual poet and his neighbours, but an inter-communication of the different selves formed within the individual."[26] The poet's judgment is required "when the poet wakes up to the poem as a poem" and it moves from the private and personal sphere to the public and universal sphere:

> Although there are a number of poems in which the communicative spirit is present from the start as a factor in the conflict, where the poet has missionary intentions or wishes to use the poem as a social weapon, yet in a vast number of cases the poem as it appears in its first draft has no communicative intention at all ... [M]y experience of the first drafts of other poets' work and my own is that generally while the poem is what I might call a

> private poem not yet dispassionately viewed as a marketable commodity, the neat hand-writing, cleanliness, and orderliness of the communicative spirit are conspicuously absent. But when the poet wakes up to the poem as a poem, and if he considers it as entitling him to a certain dignity as its author, he begins the secondary or tertiary elaboration ... But by then the poem has already fulfilled its primary function and has become a commodity or a record, nothing more.[27]

Judgment is required in the secondary or tertiary elaboration of the poem, and judgment can be wrong. Consciousness cannot always make sense of the spontaneous fusion of contradictory emotional ideas: "spontaneous poetry untested by conscious analysis has the ... weakness of being liable to surface faults and unintelligible thought-connections," thought-connections that can be "so free as to puzzle the author himself."[28] As a craftsman, the poet must correct surface faults and make thought-connections intelligible. Proper craft displays "a foreknowledge of certain unwitting processes of the reader's mind, for which the poet more or less deliberately provides."[29] In the crafted poem faithful to the spontaneous process from which it emerged, "the underlying associations of each word ... form close combinations of emotion unexpressed by the bare verbal pattern."[30] As we have seen, "In this way, the poet may be compared with a father piecing together a picture-book puzzle for his children. He surprises them at last by turning over the completed picture, and showing them that by the act of assembling the scattered parts of 'Red Riding Hood with the Basket of Food' he has all the while been building up unnoticed underneath another scene of tragedy – 'The Wolf eating the Grandmother.'"[31] The poet who is too deliberate, the poet who "has only the very small conscious part of his experience to draw upon, and therefore in co-ordinating the central images, his range of selection is narrower and the links are only on the surface," can make a mess of things: "careless arrangement of the less important pieces or wilfully decorative borrowing from another picture altogether may look very well in the upper scene, but what confusion below!"[32]

Empson and Graves agree that literary judgment itself – whether the poet's, the reader's, or the critic's – is itself phenomenal. Graves denies that "there is somewhere already written a wholly good poetry ... that is always good poetry and always good medicine for any age."[33] And he denies that "there is a kind of poetry which does not and cannot serve any possible need either for the poet or the reader."[34] "Aesthetic canons of good and bad" are relative (a function of time and place) and pragmatic (a function of usefulness): "One age values emotional intensity, another values sophistication and emotional restraint; one age demands a high standard of craftsmanship, another demands an anarchic abandon of grammatical or logical control ... My suggestion is that these criteria are not accidental or foreseeable; they represent a need on the part of critics for poetry that will repair certain deficiencies or maintain certain successes not only in poetry of the past, but also in the social, religious and scholastic conditions at the time obtaining."[35] This is the context within which Empson's quotation of Graves in response to Smith's criticism arises.

And so immediately following his reference to Graves's observation in *Poetic Unreason* about the poem that "everyone ... agrees to damn" at one time but at a later time agrees to regard as "the best poem that the age produced," Empson duplicates these arguments by Graves about the relative and pragmatic nature of the canons of aesthetic criticism.[36] They inform his observations about an art show in 1946, "a grand semi-government exhibition of the painter Constable in London ... starring only two big canvasses, both described as 'studies'": "Constable painted them only as the second of three stages in making an Academy picture, and neither could nor would ever have exhibited them. I do not know how they survived. They are being called by some critics (quite wrongly, I understand) the roots of the whole nineteenth-century development of painting. It seems obvious to many people now that they are much better than Constable's finished works ... Of course, the present fashion for preferring [them] may be wrong, too; the point I am trying to make is that this final 'judgment' is a thing which must be indefinitely postponed."[37]

Empson recalls not just Graves's observation about "the best poem of the age," then, but also the fact that it was part of Graves's consideration of whether either a poem or any judgement about it is a noumenon or a phenomenon: "Would Mr. James Smith say that the 'study,' which is now more admired than the finished work, was a noumenon or a phenomenon? I do not see any way out of the dilemma which would leave the profound truths he was expressing much importance for a practical decision."[38]

Empson's observations regarding the Constable exhibition also develop another observation by Graves, this one concerning analogies between painting and poetry in terms of their origin in mental conflict and their subsequent development as discovery of this conflict. According to Graves,

> Art of every sort ... is an attempt to rationalize some emotional conflict in the artist's mind. When the painter says "That's really good to paint" and carefully arranges his still life, he has felt a sort of antagonism between the separate parts of the group and is going to discover by painting on what that antagonism is founded, presenting it as clearly and as simply as he knows how, in the slightly distorting haze of the emotion aroused. He never says, "I think I'll paint a jug or bottle, next," any more than the poet says "I've a free morning on Saturday; I'll write an ode to the moon or something of that sort, and get two guineas for it from the *London Mercury*." No, a particular jug or bottle may well start a train of thought which in time produces a painting, and a particular aspect of the moon may fire some emotional tinder and suggest a poem.[39]

Similarly, although Empson acknowledges that "it seems obvious to many people now that they [Constable's 'studies'] are much better than Constable's finished works," he emphasizes that in the course of Constable's production of his paintings over time, the very process that Graves outlines occurred: a process of secondary and tertiary craftsmanship via deliberate judgments made after "he got an idea," a process that Graves describes as attempting "to rationalize some emotional conflict in the artist's mind."[40] "Nobody pretends that they were an uprush of the primitive or in some psychological way 'not judged' by Constable. When he got an idea he would make a preliminary sketch on the spot, then follow his bent in studio (obviously very fast), and then settle down on another canvas to make a presentable picture out of the same thing."[41] Constable follows the process of composition that Graves outlines for "art of every sort," from "the unforeseen fusion in his mind of apparently contradictory emotional ideas" to "the duty ... as craftsman to present this nucleus in the most effective way possible."[42]

Insisting that the studies are better than the finished Academy pictures, "you could defend the judgment of Constable by saying that he betrayed his art to make a living, but this would be absurdly unjust to him";[43] as absurd as thinking that poets write odes to the moon or that artists paint a jug or a bottle "to get two guineas for it from the *London Mercury*."[44]

•

As Empson sees it, by complaining that analysis of merely "supposed" conflicts in the author leaves poetry completely behind, Smith "was striking at the roots of criticism."[45] It is not just that "critics have long been allowed to say that a poem may be something inspired which meant more than the poet knew"; according to Empson, "If critics are not to put up some pretence of understanding the feelings of the author in hand they must condemn themselves to contempt."[46] Empson recalls Graves's "Defence of Poetic Analysis" in *Poetic Unreason*: "Appreciation of a poem means nothing less than a certain intimate knowledge of the author."[47] Graves proves the axiom by reference to "any ... poem whose author is either anonymous or nothing but a name": "we find that our knowledge of the poet's politics, culture, nationality, his attitude to war, to love, to virtue, to truth, in fact all his important characteristics, is considerable."[48] Condemned to contempt is "the myopic literary historian who denies that we know anything at all about the author of an anonymous poem ... [I]f we had no knowledge the poem would convey to us as little as the as yet undeciphered inscriptions on Etruscan tombs or Mya tablets."[49]

According to Graves, "Emotional poetry demands that if the rhythmic hypnotism of the verse is to be effective or the symbolism intuitively understood ... then the reader must be in a mood analogous to the poet's when he wrote the poem ... To put it plainly, the only hopeful study of poetry is by examining the phase of mental conflict in the reader which allowed him to appreciate by analogy the emotional force of certain symbols and rhythms, and by then comparing this phase analytically with a phase of conflict in the mind of the poet, which historic research suggests as having given birth to the poem."[50] The first draft is precipitated out of this supposed mental conflict, and then it is elaborated through secondary and tertiary processes into a document of the poet's own extended experience of the poem, which is passed down through time as the poem of record. The words are the keystone that joins the reader's mood and the poet's mood, and so the literary critic must be capable of accounting for the words in terms of both the reader's mood and the poet's mood.

Graves predicted in the 1920s that "there are new analytic methods which literary criticism never had at its disposal before and … these reinforcing the merely emotional comprehension … may provide us with an intimate knowledge of certain phases of an obscure poet's life which before were mere blanks sparsely dotted with births, deaths, marriages and dates of publication"; in addition, this new method will lead to a new kind of literary criticism: "Research among dusty archives, and the sudden flashes of emotional recognition that come to the unscholarly general reader, are both methods of historic study and in the literary history of the future will tend towards a closer relation for a common end, and therewith lose their exclusive characters."[51] With these predictions, Graves seems to have foreseen the development in the late twentieth century of the "new historicism."

Empson accepts that "those who enjoy poems must in part be biographers."[52] Like Graves, who describes the poet's "more or less deliberate attempt, with the help of a rhythmic mesmerism, to impose an illusion of actual experience on the mind of others," Empson describes poetry as the poet's presentation of a definite human experience via the same sort of verbal magic: "As I understand it, there is always in great poetry a feeling of generalization from a case which has been presented definitely; there is always an appeal to a background of human experience which is all the more present when it cannot be named."[53] And Empson accepts that the biographical information about the poet that comes through reading poetry constitutes knowledge of an intimate kind. Less concerned than Graves to identify the experience in question as the poet's own (Empson explains that although "those who enjoy poems must in part be biographers … I am talking less about the minds of poets than about the mode of action of poetry"), Empson nonetheless insists, like Graves, that the reader's reaction to the poem be traceable to – and justified by – the words of the poem that represent the experience in question: "What I would suppose is that, whenever a receiver of poetry is seriously moved by an apparently simple line, what are moving him are the traces of a great part of his past experience and of the structure of his past judgments. Considering what it feels like to take great pleasure in verse, I should think it surprising … if even the most searching criticism of such lines of verse could find nothing whatever in their implications to be the cause of so straddling a connection and so broad a calm."[54]

•

When Empson quarrelled with Riding in the 1970s about her role in the birth of New Criticism, he "looked up some of the books concerned" and proceeded to cite chapter and verse in support of his argument that Graves alone deserved credit for inspiring the method of *Seven Types of Ambiguity*.[55] In 1946 and 1947, however, as he revised his book and wrote a new preface for it, he had no such spur to get out Graves's books once more. He seems instead to have relied on memory in citing Graves (a memory *slightly* faulty, as we have seen, insofar as Empson left a minor word out of the passage he cited, but a memory otherwise pretty accurate in recollecting particular observations and arguments in Graves's early works). And so the enduring memory of Graves that is traceable in the preface to the second edition is further evidence of how deeply his work had entered into Empson's mind by the end of the 1920s.

11

Richards and the Graves(t) Danger

Unlike William Empson, I.A. Richards had nothing good to say about Robert Graves – at least, not in print. Which is rather curious, for Graves exercised a demonstrably positive influence upon his work throughout the 1920s. As we shall see, Graves developed a psychological method of criticism that Richards would in many ways appropriate, even while attacking it; he listed topics for theorizing that Richards would accept by addressing, sometimes rather extensively; and he modelled a manner of close reading that Richards would adopt by adapting it to his ostensibly more scientific purposes. In the end, then, one might read Richards's animus against Graves as, at least in part, a sign of anxiety about the latter's influence.

•

Before his precocious student Empson spoke to him so excitedly about *A Survey of Modernist Poetry* in the fall of 1928, I.A. Richards was very much aware of Graves. Miranda Seymour observes that by the autumn of 1928, Richards "had collected all of Graves's prose works and poems."[1] She suggests that Richards knew Graves's poetry "well" and that without naming Graves in *Science and Poetry* (1926), Richards "evidently had him in mind when describing de la Mare's poems" – implying that unlike the best poet of the day, T.S. Eliot, a poet like Graves or de la Mare was "lost in a world of dreams and out of touch with his times."[2] As we have seen, Richards also associates Graves's literary criticism with the world of dreams, explicitly crossing swords with him in *Principles of Literary Criticism* (1924) on the question of the appropriateness of Graves's model of dream interpretation as a model for literary interpretation. In fact, he trashes Graves's attempt in *The Meaning of Dreams* (1924) to offer a psychoanalytical reading of Coleridge's poem "Kubla Khan." So Richards was aware of Graves both as poet and literary theorist, and he approved of neither.

That Richards was aware of Graves's work as literary theorist is not surprising. As part of his research for his own early works, *The Foundation of Aesthetics* (1922, co-authored with C.K. Ogden and James Wood), *The Meaning of Meaning* (1923, co-authored with C.K. Ogden), and *Principles of Literary Criticism* (1924), research that was all part of his project of establishing the new academic study of literature on a more scientific footing than it had ever had, he surveyed a wide range of contemporary work on aesthetics generally and poetics particularly.[3] No one was publishing more frequently and more substantially than Graves on this topic (there were six books in six years, and just as many articles as well), and no one was publishing to more provocative effect among the new generation of undergraduates studying English literature. So there were clearly professional reasons for collecting Graves.

Yet there were more personal reasons, too, for keeping an eye on Graves, for they were positioned as rivals in the 1920s, at least in a certain public's eye. Richards is today regarded as the more important theorist and the greater critic, and so it was by 1930. Yet, as George Watson observes, when contemporary English literary theory was born in the early 1920s, things were otherwise: "Theory was English, in those days, and the world knew it was. It was not wholly or even mainly academic, and perhaps all the livelier for that. In the 1920s Aldous Huxley and Robert Graves were both working excitedly in the field, and before Richards had published at all."[4] In fact, before the publication of Graves's *On English Poetry* (1922), his first work of theory and criticism, Richards had published a number of short but significant essays from 1919 onward that would find their way into his own first books, *The Foundation of Aesthetics* and *The Meaning of Meaning*, yet it is also true that Graves was well-known as a poet some years before Richards had published anything, so his name was the more familiar one in the early 1920s.[5]

The circumstance of their publishing histories placed them together in competition for the attention of readers interested in literary theory. Their earliest books of criticism and theory were often published in the same year and no doubt sat near each other on the bookstore shelves: *On English Poetry* was published in Britain in May of 1922, with Richards's co-authored *The Foundations of Aesthetics* appearing later the same year; *The Meaning of Dreams* was published in 1924, sufficiently before the publication of *The Principles of Literary Criticism* later that year for the former to have been quoted in the latter. Their essays sometimes appeared in the same British periodicals. Richards published early essays in *Athenaeum*, for instance, and Graves did likewise shortly thereafter in its successor *Nation & Athenaeum*.[6] Richards and Graves also published essays regularly in American periodicals throughout the 1920s. For instance, they both published essays in the *Saturday Review of Literature*: Graves in 1925, Richards in 1926.[7] As Richards was collecting Graves's books, it seems likely that he would have noticed these essays, too.

Watson is correct that Graves's notoriety as a theorist preceded (and for some time exceeded) that of Richards. Graves's books were more accessible to the average reader than Richards's, determinedly avoiding an academic style, and so they were more popular. As Richard Luckett confesses in his Introduction to *The Selected Letters of I.A. Richards*, he himself preferred Graves's theories to those of Richards in the 1920s.[8] Similarly, John Lehman traces the growth of his sophistication about poetry in the 1920s via the line extending from Graves to Empson: "*Seven Types of Ambiguity* ... I still consider one of the cardinal books of my initiation into the deeper mysteries of poetry, as important for me then as Robert Graves's *On English Poetry* had been at an earlier stage."[9] As we know, Empson himself read Graves carefully long before he first met with Richards in the fall of 1928, referring knowledgably to "'the Robert Graves' school of criticism" in a book review of 11 May 1928, and he recalled many years later that Graves seemed in the 1920s well ahead of the curve in bringing the science of psychology to bear on literary criticism.[10] Even Richards was reading Graves.

For many, Graves was a counter-balance to the relatively aggressive scientism of Richards, whose anatomy of literary criticism in *Principles of Literary Criticism* actually includes a diagram in which he depicts "the eye ... as reading a succession of printed words" by means of an illustration showing interactions amongst eyeball, cells, nerves, ganglia, and so on. Graves confesses in *On English Poetry* that "It is a heartbreaking task to reconcile literary and scientific interests in the same book. Literary enthusiasts seem to regard poetry as something miraculous, something which it is almost blasphemous to analyse ... [M]ost scientists on the other hand, being either benevolently contemptuous of poetry, or, if interested, insensitive to the emotional quality of words and their associative subtleties, themselves use words as weights and counters."[11] Explaining in *Poetic Unreason* his own sense of the virtue of his theoretical position, Graves also explains the appeal to others of his middle way between science and emotion: "the strength of my position lies ... in a synthesis suggested between modern analytic psychology and the reading of poetry 'emotionally,' if you like, and 'for its own sake.'"[12]

Whether or not Richards noted Empson's recommendation of "'the Robert Graves' school of criticism" to the readers of *Granta*, it is unlikely that, during his research into literary theory at this time, he managed to avoid noticing Graves's essays and also decided not to read the books by Graves that he was collecting. Moreover, it is quite likely that the salient points of Graves's literary theories were brought to his attention by his students in the Practical Criticism course of lectures that he was developing at Cambridge from 1923 to 1928. What Graves's theory lacked in the way of scientific method and disciplined scholarship, it made up for with a wit and ingenuity that provoked interest amongst the teens and twenty-somethings who were entering the new English literature programmes from Oxford and Cambridge to the University of Leeds. Richards was no doubt aware that Graves's literary theory was a rival to his own for the attention and allegiance of undergraduates.

Certainly Graves's reputation was not confined to Oxford. When Empson refers to the "'the Robert Graves' school of criticism" in May of 1928, he is writing a review of the book *Words and Poetry* by George Rylands, whom he characterizes as a follower of Graves who lacks the concentration necessary to achieve the "impressive" results of the master, and he is writing in *Granta*, the playful, irreverent student magazine dedicated to keeping Cambridge up-to-date about what is happening in the world of art and ideas.[13] So Empson's casual reference to the Graves school of criticism assumes that his readers will already have acquired some knowledge of Graves's conflict theory and his related practical literary analysis. The testimony of Luckett and Lehman about their own interest in Graves during the 1920s suggests that Empson's assumption was not unwarranted.

Richards might also have been aware of a parallel rivalry as to whether he or Graves was the most stimulating speaker. In terms of their notoriety in this regard, Graves's fame at Oxford was at least matched by Richards's at Cambridge. John Paul Russo's picture of Richards as lecturer in the early 1920s is instructive:

> Richards had a stunning impact in the lecture hall. Basil Willey audited the first lectures, which became *Principles of Literary Criticism* ... "I want to testify to their electrifying effect – on me, and on many others, including many senior lecturers" ... Joan Bennett said the lectures were "spell-binding," and Francis Partridge praises him as the "outstanding stimulus" in English studies ... Richards was the "prophet we had been waiting for," said Christopher Isherwood ... "he was our guide, our evangelist, who revealed to us, in a succession of astounding lightning flashes, the entire expanse of the Modern World" ... "We were terrifically thrilled at I.A. Richards's lectures," Edward Upward recalled... William Empson ... said that "more people would at times come to his lectures than the hall would hold, and he would then lecture in the street outside; somebody said that this had not happened since the Middle Ages."[14]

Graves and Richards drew both undergraduates and senior lecturers as members of the audiences; each came across as iconoclastic and ground-breaking; each astounded audiences with hitherto unimaginable interpretations of the role of literature in general and the meaning of certain poems in particular; each came across as speaking about and for – and even, in a sense, from – the future of English studies. Since *Principles of Literary Criticism* was based on Richards's early lectures at Cambridge, it is quite likely that the reference to Graves in Chapter Four of the book indicates that Richards included references to Graves in these lectures.

•

Yet however different contemporaries like Luckett and Empson might have perceived Graves and Richards to be, the passage of time allows us to see that their literary theories in the 1920s had much in common. We can appreciate now, for instance, the fact that they shared an intense interest in at least three major influences on the development of literary theory in the twentieth century: Coleridge, Eliot, and the new science of psychology in particular and the new social sciences more generally. These common interests mean that there are many points of convergence and agreement in their work, often where it was most influential on the development of New Criticism.

Graves suggests that "Biographia Literaria should be the poet's Bible."[15] As Elizabeth Friedmann points out, he and Riding shared an interest in Coleridge that became evident in their famous reading of Shakespeare's Sonnet 129 in *A Survey of Modernist Poetry*: "They had both read Coleridge on Shakespeare, and were drawn to his observations about a poem's 'multëity of integrated meanings.'"[16] Richards calls *Biographia Literaria* "that lumber-room of neglected wisdom which contains more hints towards a theory of poetry than all the rest ever written upon the subject."[17] Richards finds Coleridge full of such hints: "Coleridge drops the invaluable hint almost inadvertently," "luminous hints" that "seem to have dazzled succeeding spectators" ("How otherwise explain why they have been overlooked"?).[18] Richards is grateful to Coleridge for suggesting in Chapter XIV of *Biographia Literaria* that the poet is one who, in Richards's terms, experiences "the wholeness of the mind in the creative moment … without suppressions or restrictions."[19] Richards and Graves both accept that the fundamental act of the imagination is the reconciliation of opposites within an aesthetic whole, and, as we shall see, they both also regard this as the key to poetry's real-world impact: its psychotherapeutic reconciliation of conflicts in the emotional lives of its readers. Graves did not introduce Richards to Coleridge but he showed him how Coleridge in particular, and romantic literary theory in general, could be interpreted in terms of contemporary psychological theory.

Graves and Eliot campaigned together against poetry anthologies in 1920 and planned throughout 1925 and 1926 to collaborate on a critical study of modern poetry until Riding took Eliot's place in the project, shortly after which Graves quarrelled with Eliot about an insulting review of Riding's poetry that Eliot had allowed to be published in the *Criterion*.[20] This event marked the end of friendly relations between them for many years to come. From Eliot nonetheless descends Graves's engagement – individually and in collaboration with Riding – with the topics of modern poetry and anthologies, modern poetry and difficulty, modern poetry and wit, modern poetry and history, and modern poetry and anti-Semitism.[21] Indeed, Graves's work with Riding in *A Survey of Modernist Poetry* is implicitly an explanation and justification of Eliot's aesthetic.

Richards was an even closer friend of Eliot's during these years, having first sought him out in 1920 and thereafter hosting him occasionally at Cambridge. Important aspects of Richards's aesthetic theories are designed to make poetry like Eliot's comprehensible, and Eliot's own writings about impersonality, the poem as object, and significant emotion in poetry, as much as his poetic practice of radical disjunctions and obscure allusions, established many of the topics that Richards addressed throughout the 1920s. Graves and Richards both accepted that Eliot defined modern poetry – at least by his practice, if not by his critical prescriptions – and that therefore any definition of modernism and any theorization of criticism would have to comprehend his work.

Although Richards called Graves a "Freudian," Graves himself, as we know, preferred to think of himself as non-Freudian in important respects, championing the theories of W.H.R. Rivers as a corrective to Freud's primitivizing and sexualizing definition of the unconscious.[22] On the one hand, Graves knew Rivers personally and received direction from him as to how he might try to cope with the effects of shell-shock, and, on the other hand, he balked at Freud's conception of the unconscious: "The most general notion, which I cannot accept, is that every grown man and woman has a sort of hidden bogey inside them, with the uncontrolled emotion of a child or savage, and as little sense of the decencies or refinements of civilized life as this same child or savage, and that dreams are the work of this creature."[23] Here, as Watson notes, the views of Graves and Richards converge: "The new psychology went wide, and far beyond the demands of therapy. Richards had studied it at Cambridge, and like Rivers and Graves he felt that Freud's view of the unconscious, born of the cosseted, introspective world of late-nineteenth-century Vienna, had been excessively sexual and infantile in its emphasis."[24] Yet although Richards agreed with Graves in his criticism of Freud, Richards did not know Freud nearly as well as Watson implies. As Russo observes, "psychoanalysis entered England in 1913, but the war delayed its progress. By the early 1920s Richards had already formed his philosophical position and was too caught up in mapping out his own system to entertain anyone else's seriously, especially one constructed on entirely different foundations."[25] Although, as Russo also notes, "for many years Richards was tagged as a behaviourist in orientation, and for good reason: he used stimulus-response phraseology, toyed with Pavlov's conditioned reflex mechanism to depict sign interpretation, debated John B. Watson, and perhaps borrowed from Margaret Washburn's psychology," he is best described as following a "functionalist approach" to psychology, interested to trace the evolutionary dynamics by which consciousness is used by human organisms to adapt to their environment – the more efficient organization of attitudes through exposure to poetry representing a selective advantage.[26] And so, beyond their agreement that Freud's theories were not adequate to the task of explaining everyday psychology, let alone the traumas of the Great War, Graves (with his belief that "dreams ... have a value on their own account, quite apart from the light that they throw on the waking life") and Richards (with his "pragmatic psychologism") appear to follow quite different psychological paths.[27]

Still, just as we can see now that Coleridge's emphasis on the reconciling powers of the imagination and Eliot's conception of poetry as an impersonal act of creation stimulated both critics in the direction of what we now call New Criticism, so we can also see that, different though the psychological paradigms to which they subscribed proved to be, Graves and Richards were each convinced that the explanation of the way words and images become meaningfully associated in the writing and reading of poetry would be found in the study of psychology. And so whether students of literary theory in the 1920s favoured the approach of the one or the other, reading either Graves or Richards at this time confronted them with the suggestion that the modern social sciences would be necessary to a full understanding of the imagination.

According to Graves, in the poet as "spokesman" of the "group-mind of his culture," "men of smaller scope ... hear at times in his utterances what seems to them the direct voice of God."[28] Supplementing Shelley with Frazer and Durkheim, Graves aligns poetry with magic and religion as a development and expression of the group mind as conceived anthropologically and sociologically. What Graves has secularized, Richards further secularizes in language that Graves would later describe as "an uneasy mixture of Victorian literary incantation ... and bald modern laboratory exposition"[29]: "In the arts we find the record in the only form in which these things can be recorded of the experiences which have seemed worth having to the most sensitive and discriminating persons.

Through the obscure perception of this fact the poet has been regarded as a seer and the artist as a priest ... The arts, if rightly approached, supply the best data available for deciding what experiences are more valuable than others."[30]

That Graves balks in the 1940s at describing the arts as a record of scientific data should not obscure the fact that he and Richards both present themselves in the 1920s as amateur anthropologists able to demystify the origin and function of poetry. They take from *Biographia Literaria* the language of reconciliation and the conception of the imagination and adapt them to the twentieth-century – a post-Frazer and post-Durkheim context in which magic, religion, and poetry, diachronically and synchronically related, are conceived as a development and expression of the group mind.

•

Despite their being positioned by students as rival literary theorists, and despite there being significant points of contention between their literary theories, there remains an emotional energy expressed in Richards's engagement with Graves in *Principles of Literary Criticism* that is surplus to the requirements of his argument. He deploys a rhetoric of disdain against Graves that is deployed against no one else in the book, even though it is clear that Graves is a surrogate for Freud. And he does so in the context of an argument that is neither accurate nor effective: he misidentifies Graves as a follower of Freud, and he pretends to displace Graves's reading of "Kubla Khan" with a reading that merely supplements it. There is more sound and fury and less sense in Richards's dealing with Graves than with any other figure.

His complaint about Graves's thoroughgoing Freudian onslaught is based, at least in part, on misunderstanding: Richards refers to Graves as a "Freudian" yet Graves explicitly distances himself from both Freud and Jung (as Richards himself knows) and defines himself as inspired instead by W.H.R. Rivers. For example, Graves concludes *The Meaning of Dreams* with the reading of "Kubla Khan" that Richards notes, to demonstrate the interpretive potential available to literary critics who apply Rivers's understanding of the dream state to the literary state – the state of inspiration that produces illogical or fantastic romantic poetry. Moreover Graves opens *The Meaning of Dreams* explaining that: "Dr. Rivers ... traces the part played in dreams by what is called Dissociation, that is the breaking up of the human individual into two or more rival 'selves' under the stress of difficult circumstances … [W]hen we are up against a problem that has two possible ways out … we split up [into] two selves, each self standing for one of these opposing courses of action … *When a person is in a conflict between two selves, and one self is stronger than the other throughout the waking life, the weaker side becomes victorious in dream.*"[31]

By allowing expression to the repressed self, dreams of conflict balance the personality that has split in waking life. In case a reader thinks that he and Rivers follow Freud and Jung on this point, Graves hastens to add – as we have seen above in the section on Empson – that "the so-called 'unconscious self'… is not the sort of primitive bogey that people think, but is just the self which in conflict happens at the time to be beaten."[32] Further distancing himself from Freud and Jung, Graves suggests that "the usual claim of modern dream-interpreters is not justified, when they say that once a dream of conflict is interpreted the conflict thereby ends."[33] A symbol's effectiveness might thereby disappear, but not necessarily the conflict: "If a dream of conflict is interpreted and the conflict remains strong, the dream will merely change its symbols and come again in a new guise."[34]

Again, as we have already seen, the work of Rivers is the key to understanding all of Graves's criticism in the 1920s prior to his collaboration with Riding. In *On English Poetry*, which was dedicated to Rivers, Graves treats romantic poetry as analogous to dream, declaring that "emotional conflict is necessary for the birth of true poetry."[35] Poetry's usefulness for both the writer and the reader, in fact, consists of the way it deals with emotional conflict. For the poet, poetry is "the unforeseen fusion in his mind of apparently contradictory emotional ideas."[36] After this "spontaneous process … over which the poet has no direct control," it "becomes the duty of the poet as craftsman to present this nucleus ["the unforeseen fusion in his mind"] in the most effective way possible" so that the poem can function for the reader as it does for the poet: "Poetry … is a form of psycho-therapy. Being the transformation into dream symbolism of some disturbing emotional crisis in the poet's mind … poetry has the power of homeopathically healing other men's minds similarly troubled, by presenting them … with an allegorical solution of the trouble. Once the allegory is recognized by the reader's unconscious mind as applicable the affective power of his own emotional crisis is diminished."[37]

In his psychoanalytical account of "Kubla Khan," Graves suggests that the fact that the poem had "very few alterations after the first draft" marks it as an inspired poem better read as analogous to a dream of conflict (expressing conflicts about Coleridge's married life, his opium addiction, his disappointed ambitions) than as a poem that "had not and never could have any particular meaning attached to it" (appreciable only in terms of "its simple beauty of images and rhythm") or as a poem whose meaning might be found in a "literary source" (Graves implies that any such question has either been answered by Coleridge's declaration of Purchas's *Pilgrimage* and Maurice's *History of Hindoostan* as his sources or been frustrated by Coleridge's refusal to name other sources).[38]

According to Graves, Coleridge is Kubla, "making himself half-divine on the strength of his genius, not only to impress his friends who are losing confidence in him, but also as a weapon against his ambitious and disillusioned wife."[39] Chasms, caverns, and caves, as well as rivers that burst high, run mazy, and fall, all emerge as symbols from Coleridge's imagination as symbols in a dream emerge from the state of deep sleep: "What of the romantic chasm and the woman wailing for her demon lover? I would suggest that this refers to the former strong passion that Coleridge had felt for his wife who was now bitterly reproaching him for his supposed unfaithfulness ... The cave into which this river sinks to run underground in the lifeless ocean would represent ... his wife's [pregnant] condition at the time complicating his attitude towards her ... In a more general sense the river is probably also the life of man, from birth to death; we understand from the poem that Coleridge has determined to shun the mazy complications of life by retreating to a bower of poetry, solitude and opium."[40]

The apparently incredulous Richards does not dignify this reading with direct comment upon any particular point, regarding none of it as worth summarizing, but all of it as worthy of disdain: "The reader acquainted with current methods of analysis can imagine the results of a thoroughgoing Freudian onslaught."[41] According to Richards, readers can imagine whatever reading they like – as Graves has done – since "nearly all speculations as to what went on in the artist's mind are unverifiable, even more unverifiable than the similar speculations as to the dreamer's mind."[42] And so, "whatever psycho-analysts may aver, the mental processes of the poet are not a very profitable field for investigation. They offer far too happy a hunting-ground for uncontrollable conjecture."[43]

Of course Graves is not concerned that his conjecture be correct, nor is he very interested in controlling his conjecture. His primary purpose is to persuade readers that there is always a logic in the mental processes of poets even if it is only the logic of idiosyncratic personal associations, and that such logic accounts for a poem's words, images, ideas, and events no matter how fantastic these might seem. Thus in *Poetic Unreason,* Graves entertains the idea of Herbert as having been inspired to write a poem after listening to Donne's account of having been invited by a tavern girl to sleep with her. His point is not that we need to know what actually happened in Herbert's mind, but rather that we need to know that something of this sort – even if very different from this conjecture – will have happened in his mind. Similarly, advancing considerably more scholarly research, he constructs a picture in *The Meaning of Dreams* of Coleridge and Keats wrestling in their poetry with conflicts among physical disease, desire for women, and poetic ambition. Trained to control conjecture by the discipline of scientific method, Richards is disdainful of the psychoanalytical methodology that Graves proclaims in *The Meaning of Dreams*. Graves's method is determinedly "poetic," rather than scientific:

> I admit frankly that in certain cases for the sake of the argument I have run together two and even three records of dreams that have come to my notice, where the conflict was in outline similar. My reasons for doing so have been to make the argument clearer, the book less of a catalogue and the dreams themselves more interesting to the reader … In taking this course, I have availed myself of the licence readily allowed to poets and novelists, that of telling the truth by a condensation and dramatization of their experiences of life – which is, of course, the method of dreams themselves and a very good one. There is no reason that I can see for scientists to object to this way of writing so long as the general principles of classification satisfy them. Their method of recording each case minutely and conscientiously may be sure, but is at any rate extremely slow … [I]f occasionally in order to illustrate a point I have had … to embroider a bare outline of history with picturesque detail, such additions do not make the story any the

> less true as illustrating the general mechanism of the fantastic dream which arises out of the conflict; and indeed the easiness with which the images have formed in my mind with a complicated cross-reference existing between them ... is in itself proof of the constructive and direct powers of this fantastic method of thought, a proof of the value of dreams on their account.[44]

Richards can perhaps be forgiven for balking at Graves's displacement of proof according to the scientific method of thought by proof according to the fantastic method of thought. To him, Graves's reconciliation of scientific and emotional readings of poetry must have involved precious little science.

Yet because of what Graves avers about a possible psychological explanation of "Kubla Khan" in particular and about the value of his method for the interpretation of dreams in general, no one suffers harsher treatment in *Principles of Literary Criticism* than him. Although Richards also complains of the poor quality of the practical criticism of the arts produced by Freud and Jung – "to judge by the published work of Freud upon Leonardo da Vinci or of Jung upon Goethe ... psycho-analysts tend to be peculiarly inept as critics" – his whipping boy is Graves. The latter is not only named more often and criticized at greater length than either Freud or Jung, but he is also subject to a pun on his name: "the attempt to display the inner working of the artist's mind by the evidence of his work alone must be subject to the gravest dangers."[45]

Empson would be inspired by Graves's insights into "the constructive and direct powers" of the "fantastic method of thought" that Graves identified in poetry and dream in general (and identified often in his own poetry and dreams in particular – "images have formed in my mind with a complicated cross-referencing existing between them"), but Richards suggests that the only virtue of Graves's reading is a negative one: it makes it easy to show that in psychoanalytical speculations about what went on in the poet's mind "the most plausible explanations are apt to depend upon features whose actual causation is otherwise."[46] Richards himself claims to know the "actual causation" and "simple explanation" of many of the features of "Kubla Khan" that Graves makes the basis of his psychoanalytical interpretation, despite declaring that "nearly all speculations as to what went on in the artist's mind are unverifiable, even more unverifiable than the similar speculations as to the dreamer's mind."[47]

Richards points out that the appearance and function of Coleridge's river that rises in a fountain, then runs mazy for miles, and finally falls dispersingly into an ocean can be accounted for in other and more objectively verifiable ways – in fact, by the literary scholarship that Graves gives as short a shrift as scientific method. With great rhetorical flourish, Richards advises the reader how he might save himself from Graves's "thoroughgoing Freudian onslaught":

> If he will ... open *Paradise Lost*, Book IV, at line 223, and read onwards for sixty lines, he will encounter the actual sources of not a few of the images and phrases of the poem. In spite of –
>
> > Southward through *Eden* went a River large,
> > Nor changed his course, but through the shaggie hill
> > Pass'd underneath ingulft ...
>
> in spite of –
>
> > Rose a fresh Fountain, and with many a rill
> > Watered the Garden; thence united fell
> > Down the steep glade, and met the neather flood ...
>
> in spite of –
>
> > Rowling on Orient Pearl and Sands of Gold
> > With mazie error under pendant shades
> > Ran Nectar ...
>
> in spite of –
>
> > Meanwhile murmuring waters fall
> > Down the slope hills, disperst ...
>
> his doubts may still linger until he reaches
>
> > Nor where *Abassin* Kings their issue Guard,
> > Mount Amara.
>
> and one of the most cryptic points in Coleridge's poem, the Abyssinian maid, singing of Mount Abora, finds its simple explanation ... From one source or another almost all the matter of

> *Kubla Khan* came to Coleridge in a similar fashion ... This very representative instance of the unconscious working of a poet's mind may serve as a not inapposite warning against one kind at least of possible applications of psychology in criticism.[48]

It is odd that although his account of the unconscious factors at work in "Kubla Khan" is different from Graves's account of such unconscious factors, Richards does not see that the two accounts are not mutually exclusive. It remains open to Graves (or any member of the Graves school of criticism) to counter that the unconscious processes that he describes also account for the more text-based process of literary influence or verbal echoing that Richards documents.[49] As we have seen, for instance, Empson, anticipating resistance to his explanation that the word "enrolled" occurred to John Ford as the most fitting one for a certain passage in *'Tis Pity She's a Whore* because of several ambiguities in the meaning of the word that make for appropriate associations at this point in the play, argues as follows: "You may say this is fanciful, and he was only looking for a word that contained the letter 'r' which kept up the style, but in that case it is these associations which explain how that particular word came into his mind."[50] Similarly, Graves might just as easily have claimed that the state of mind that he describes in Coleridge (anxiety about his career, his marriage, his health) is responsible for the pattern of literary recollection of the particular passages from *Paradise Lost* to which Richards draws attention. In fact, Graves implies as much in *On English Poetry* when he announces his axiom: "'Poetry contains nothing haphazard,' which follows naturally on the theory connecting poetry with dreams. By this rule I mean that if a poem, poem-sequence or drama is an allegory of genuine emotional experience and not a mere cold-blooded exercise, no striking detail and no juxtaposition of apparently irrelevant themes which it contains can be denied at any rate a personal significance – a cipher that can usually be decoded from another context."[51] From Graves's point of view, Richards's reading implicitly reduces Coleridge's poem to a cold-blooded exercise, albeit an unconscious one. Graves regards information of the sort that Richards provides about Coleridge's literary sources as merely supplemental to his own kind of interpretation. Richards implies that his reading of the poem is objectively preferable to the one by Graves, celebrating his "simple explanation" of the poem in terms of its "actual sources." Yet he actually demonstrates nothing conclusive beyond his contempt for Graves's method.

One wonders, moreover, why Richards harpoons a minnow like Graves when he also tells us that he has equally serious criticisms to make of the leviathans Freud and Jung. Presumably the students to whom Richards was lecturing at Cambridge in the early 1920s cited Graves more often than they cited Freud or Jung when they posed questions to Richards, and did so far more credulously and approvingly than Richards could tolerate. Students like Luckett, Lehman, and Empson were clearly enamoured of conflict theory; Empson cannot have been the first student to have quoted Graves to Richards. One can hear in the rhetorical flourish of this passage about what Richards regards as the *actual* unconscious sources of Coleridge's poem something of the manner with which he dismissed the Robert Graves school of criticism. The dismissive punning on Graves's name probably comes right out of Richards's lectures, where it would have been sure to get a laugh – especially with just the right exaggerated pronunciation and intonation.

Richards's description of Graves as a "Freudian," in complete disregard of Graves's attempts to avoid such a label, suggests either that he does not know enough or, more likely, that he does not care enough, about the distinctions amongst Freud, Jung, and Rivers to be troubled by the inappropriateness of asserting the inadequacy of Freudian literary analysis by ostensibly demonstrating the inadequacy of Graves's literary analysis. To Richards, they are all cut from the same cloth: they promote the idea that one finds in poetry an overdetermination of meaning that can be traced to the most lawless and unaccountable of the human provinces: the unconscious. Richards's urging of a "simple explanation" of "Kubla Khan" in "actual sources" thus amounts to a reassertion of what Graves defines as the conventional, classical ideal for poetry: one word, one meaning – the very ideal for poetry that Graves enlists Rivers (and, less directly, Freud and Jung) to overturn.[52]

12

How Graves Shapes Richards's *Principles*

Perhaps the energy invested by Richards to distance himself so publicly from Graves is explicable by a sense of rivalry that he felt with Graves. Or perhaps the cavalier methodology by which Graves proposed to join psychology and literary criticism really did call for just such a sharply dismissive response as the more scientific Richards gave it. Or perhaps Richards writes in anxious misprision of the precursor critic: Graves was first upon the scene and therefore must be misread if Richards himself is to be a strong critic and theorist. Whatever the case, Richards's dismissal of Graves belies significant similarities and significant points of contact in the 1920s between their literary theories and their critical practice.

For instance, Richards's account of poetry as communication and his account of the value of poetry as "the two pillars upon which a theory of criticism must rest" in *Principles of Literary Criticism* are more like than unlike Graves's treatment of these topics in *On English Poetry* and *The Meaning of Dreams*.[1] In addition, a number of the ideas advanced in *On English Poetry* and *The Meaning of Dreams*, as well as ideas announced in the essays that would become chapters of *Poetic Unreason*, are also important stimuli for – if not the source of – Richards's account in *Principles of Literary Criticism* of the psychological dimensions of the writing and reading of poetry. Like Empson, Richards systematized and said better many things that Graves said first, and also like Empson, he usually did not bother to mention Graves by name as the one whose ideas he was engaging with.

•

The portrait of the artist as a reconciler of conflict is Graves's main claim to fame as a literary theorist by the mid-1920s. In *On English Poetry*, he defines "the typical poet" as follows:

> A poet in the fullest sense is … an intermediary between the small-group consciousness of particular sects, clans, castes, types and professions among whom he moves. To … many of these has he been formally enrolled as a member, and to … many more has he virtually added himself as a supernumerary member by showing a disinterested sympathy and by practicing his exceptionally developed powers of intuition … But the rival sub-personalities formed in him by his relation to these various groups, constantly struggle to reconciliation in his poetry, and in proportion as these sub-personalities are more numerous, more varied and more inharmonious, and his controlling personality stronger and quicker at compromise, so he becomes a more or less capable spokesman of that larger group-mind of his culture which we somehow consider greater than the sum of its parts.[2]

In *Principles of Literary Criticism*, Richards suggests that the poet represents the community or the race in the same way: the poet "is the point at which the growth of the mind shows itself. His experiences, those at least which give value to his work, represent conciliations of impulses which in most minds are still confused, intertrammelled and conflicting. His work is the ordering of what in most minds is disordered."[3] There is little to distinguish between the terms of the two passages; the shared language of conflict and (re)conciliation is notable. And there is even less to distinguish between their content.

As Graves sees it, the value of poetry's reconciling function, for the reader as well as for the poet, is medicinal or therapeutic: "Poetry … is a form of psycho-therapy. Being the transformation into dream symbolism of some disturbing emotional crisis in the poet's mind (whether dominated by delight or pain) poetry has the power of homoeopathically healing other men's minds similarly troubled, by presenting them under the spell of hypnosis with an allegorical solution of the trouble."[4] For poetry to serve as a cure for the reader, the latter must not only share the poet's emotional conflict, but must also be able to translate into his own experience the experience that the poet communicates to him in the form of the poem:

> The poet, once emotion has suggested a scheme of work, goes over the ground with minute care and makes everything sure, so that when his poem is presented to the reader, the latter is thrown off his balance temporarily by the novelty of the ideas involved ... He is carried away in spite of himself ... [T]he reader on recovering from the first excitement finds the implied conclusion laid for him to discover, and ... finally carries it off as his own. Even where a conclusion is definitely expressed in a poem the reader often deceives himself into saying, "I have often thought that before, but never so clearly," when as a matter of fact he has just been unconsciously translating the poet's experience into terms of his own.[5]

Richards also sees poetry as having the psychological value of advancing the reader "from a chaotic to a better organised state," "typically through the influence of other minds"; moreover, "Literature and the arts are the chief means by which these influences are diffused."[6] According to Richards, "the after-effects, the permanent modifications in the structure of the mind, which works of art can produce, have been overlooked ... [A]mong all the agents by which 'the widening of the sphere of human' sensibility may be brought about, the arts are the most powerful, since it is through them that men may most co-operate and in these experiences that the mind most easily and with least interference organises itself."[7] Graves is certainly not one of those who overlooked the after-effects of poetry on the mind. Indeed, he is in advance of Richards in celebrating poetry's power of reorganizing mental life in a more efficient way than the reader would otherwise be capable of achieving.

Just as for Graves poetry is a process of "healing other men's minds similarly troubled," a process depending on a reader's feeling himself so similar to the poet as to think, "I have often thought that before, but never so clearly," so for Richards a person achieves functional improvement through the reading of poetry by means of a circuit's being established between normal poet and normal reader.[8] According to Richards, if the poet's "experience does not tally with that of those with whom he communicates, there will be failure."[9] Despite the seemingly "utterly eccentric experience" that we often associate with "great innovating artists," "so much must be alike in the nature of all men, their situation in the world so much the same ... that variation both wide and successful is most unlikely."[10]

And so "the ways in which the artist will differ from the average will as a rule presuppose an immense degree of similarity. They will be further developments of organisations already well advanced in the majority ... We should not forget that finer organisation is the most successful way of relieving strain, a fact of relevance in the theory of evolution. The new response will be more advantageous than the old, more successful in satisfying varied appetencies."[11]

For both Richards and Graves, poetry "is the most successful way of relieving strain."[12] Richards prefers the terms of evolutionary psychology to the terms of psychoanalysis that Graves uses but the psychological mechanism is the same: poetry stimulates in the reader the reconciliation of contradictory, or opposed, or divergent impulses in an advantageously balanced system of emotional energies. For both Richards and Graves, it is a question of whatever gets you through the night, whether you are an individual facing personal conflicts, or whether you are all humanity, organizing yourself through an evolutionary process.

•

Richards not only follows Graves in describing response to poetry as a matter of unconscious affiliation of experiences between normal reader and normal poet, he also describes the same psychological process of emotional release, reconciliation, and reorganization: "The mind which is, so far as can be seen, least wasteful, we take as a norm or standard, and, if possible, we develop in our degree similar experiences. The taking of the norm is for the most part done unconsciously by mere preference, by the shock of delight which follows the release of stifled impulse into organised freedom. Often the choice is mistaken ... Little by little experience corrects such illusory preference, not through reflection – almost all critical choices are irreflective, spontaneous, as some say – but through unconscious reorganization of impulses. We rarely change our tastes, we rather find them changed."[13] There is little difference between the "release of stifled impulse into organized freedom," after "the shock of delight," for Richards's reader and the solution of emotional conflict for Graves's reader on "recovery from the first excitement," after "being thrown off his balance temporarily," and "being carried away in spite of himself."[14] Similarly, Richards's conclusion that a reader's "critical choices" are a function of an "irreflective, spontaneous ...

unconscious reorganization of impulses" is little different from Graves's suggestion that "the reader on recovering from the first excitement finds the implied conclusion laid for him to discover, and flattering himself that he has reached it independently, finally carries it off as his own … when as a matter of fact he has just been unconsciously translating the poet's experience into terms of his own, and finding the formulated conclusion sound, imagines that the thought is originally his."[15]

In fact, Richards's reference here to "some" who say that critical choices are "spontaneous" may well be an allusion to Graves's work. In *On English Poetry*, for example, the word "spontaneous" is prominent from the first page onward. Graves defines two types of poetry: "spontaneous Poetry over which the poet has no control" ("the unforeseen fusion in his mind of apparently contradictory emotional ideas"), and "Poetry over which he has a certain conscious control": "I would suggest that every poem worthy of the name has its central idea, its nucleus, formed by this spontaneous process; later it becomes the duty of the poet as craftsman to present this nucleus in the most effective way possible, by practising poetry more consciously as an art."[16] Partial more to the spontaneous form of poetry, and ultimately regarding all poetry as spontaneous in origin, Graves nonetheless acknowledges that each type has its weaknesses and that "each is helpless without the other": "The weakness of originally unspontaneous poetry seems to be that the poet has only the very small conscious part of his experience to draw upon, and therefore in co-ordinating the central images, his range of selection is narrower and the links are only on the surface. On the other hand, spontaneous poetry untested by conscious analysis has the opposite weakness of being liable to surface faults and unintelligible thought-connections."[17]

Graves explains that a spontaneous poem "is the surprise that comes after thoughtlessly rubbing a mental Aladdin's lamp," so the problem becomes how to communicate this surprise to the reader.[18] According to Graves, the poet "creates in passion, then by a reverse process of analyzing, he tests the implied suggestions and corrects them on common-sense principles so as to make them apply universally."[19] In terms of his original metaphor, "If spontaneous poetry is like the Genie from Aladdin's Lamp, this conscious part of the art is like the assemblage of sheet, turnip-head, lighted candle and rake to make the village ghost … The Genie is the most powerful magic of the two, and surest of its effect, but the turnip Ghost is usually enough to startle rustics who wander at night, into prayer, sobriety, rapid movement or some other unusual state."[20]

When the poet's magic is successful, the reader will experience the same unforeseen fusion of apparently contradictory emotional ideas that the poet experienced: "The power of surprise which marks all true poetry, seems to result from a foreknowledge of certain unwitting processes of the reader's mind, for which the poet more or less deliberately provides."[21] It is homoeopathic psychotherapy. In "spontaneous poetry," the "rhythm of emotions," "the mental bracing and relaxing on receipt of sensuous impressions" constitutes a "musical side of poetry" that is "not merely a hypnotic inducement to the reader to accept suggestions, but a form of psycho-therapy in itself."[22] According to Graves, "Wordsworth's lines 'I wandered lonely as a cloud' are ... an important poem only because Wordsworth has written spontaneously ... and recorded to his own satisfaction an emotional state which we can all recognize."[23] And so "bad poetry is simply the work of a man who solves his emotional problems to his own satisfaction but not to anybody else's."[24] In each case, a spontaneous overflow of powerful feelings is as fundamental to the creation of the poem as it is to the personally transformative reading of the poem by the reader that Graves imagines.

The language of Graves is simpler than that of Richards, and his images livelier and more amusing, but his point anticipates the one made by Richards: the shock of surprise produced by spontaneous poetry reorganizes the impulses and startles one into a new life.

•

In an address delivered at the University of Leeds in December of 1922, published in the *North American Review* as "What is Bad Poetry?" in September of 1923, Graves reflects further on the implications both for aesthetic theory and for literary history of the psychotherapeutic function that he locates at the heart of the writing and reading of poetry.[25] It turns out that the reader's response to poetry is as much responsible for bad poetry as bad poets are. Richards agrees, and he spares no effort throughout the 1920s to bring this point home to students and literary critics.

As noted above, denying that "there is somewhere already written a wholly good poetry ... that is always good poetry and always good medicine for any age," and denying that "there is a kind of poetry which does not and cannot serve any possible need either for the poet or the reader," Graves argues that "aesthetic canons of good and bad" are relative (a function of time and place) and pragmatic (a function of usefulness): "One age values emotional intensity, another values sophistication and emotional restraint; one age demands a high standard of craftsmanship, another demands an anarchic abandon of grammatical or logical control ... My suggestion is that these criteria are not accidental or foreseeable; they represent a need on the part of critics for poetry that will repair certain deficiencies or maintain certain successes not only in poetry of the past, but also in the social, religious and scholastic conditions at the time obtaining."[26] For Graves, a society's reaction to poetry is always changing, but it is not necessarily the case for Graves as it is for Richards that a society's reaction to poetry is an agent in the process of evolution, rather than merely an epiphenomenal shadow of such a process.

In *On English Poetry*, he had worked out the implications of such a reader-response determination of poetic value for the task of discriminating between genuine and fake poetry. On the one hand, "the theory that a conflict of emotional ideas is a necessary ingredient of verse to make it poetry, will satisfactorily explain why many kinds of verse, loosely called Poetry, such as Satire and Didactic verse are yet felt not to be the 'highest' forms of Poetry ... Where the writer is dominated by only one aim, in satire, the correction of morals; in didactic verse, instruction; there is no conflict and therefore no poetry."[27] Genuine poetry emerges from conflict; fake poetry does not emerge from conflict, but pretends to do so: "As in household economics, you cannot take out of a stocking more than has been put in, so in poetry you cannot present suffering or romance beyond your own experience. The attempt to do this is one of the chief symptoms of the fake poet; ignorance forces him to draw on the experience of a real poet who actually has been through the emotional crises which he himself wants to restate. The fake is often made worse by the theft of small turns of speech which though not in any sense irregular or grotesque, the poet has somehow made his own; it is like stealing marked coins, and is a dangerous practice when Posterity is a policeman."[28]

On the other hand, through the response of later generations of readers to a fake poem, it may come to be accepted as genuine: "A fake, then, is not a fake when lapse of time has tended to obscure the original source of the borrowing, and when the textural and structural competence that the borrower has used in synthesizing the occasional good things of otherwise indifferent authors is so remarkable that even the incorruptible Porter of Parnassus winks and says 'Pass Friend!'"[29] Thus "hard-working and ingenious conjurors are billed by common courtesy as 'magicians.'"[30] A non-policing Posterity, it seems, may project its own conflicts onto the poem in such a way as to turn a fake poem into a functionally genuine poem.

Graves makes a similar point in one of the passages in *Poetic Unreason* that caught Empson's eye, when he imagines a scenario by which a poem execrated in one age becomes celebrated later as the best poem that the age produced. The problem of the fake poem is the same as the problem of the bad poem: in the fullness of time, readers may put into the poem what the bad poet did not. And there would seem to be no reason why the good poem should not be liable to the same problem, for lapse of time will make it hard for posterity to tell whether the conflict that the poem represents is genuine or fake: "Poetry is the protective pearl formed by an oyster around the irritations of a maggot. Now if, as we are told, it is becoming possible to put synthetic pearls on the market, which not even the expert with his X-ray can detect from the natural kind, is not our valuation of the latter perhaps only a sentimentality?"[31]

Richards reflects on similar problems in his discussion of the stock responses that bad poets can invoke and that bad readers can project onto virtually any poem. The biggest problem that the stock response poses, according to Richards, is its disabling of the psychological mechanism of "unconscious reorganization of impulses" within the reader. It disables this process by an inappropriate and inefficient fixing of attitudes, emotions, and impulses in a closed circuit. "Stock conventional attitudes" are ideas that gain "fixity or privileged standing … not by any special suitability to circumstances … but much more by social suggestion and by accidents which withdraw us from actual experience."[32] These stock conventional attitudes, "as we dwell in them, become more and more difficult to pass."[33] Whether in the workaday world or in reading poetry, "the losses incurred by these artificial fixations of attitudes are evident. Through them the average adult is worse, not better adjusted to the possibilities of existence than the child. He is even in the most important things functionally unable to face facts: do what he will he is only able to face fictions, fictions projected by his own stock responses."[34]

Regular doses of good poetry might recover a person from such an artificial and limited existence, but such an outcome is not guaranteed. And so for Richards the "strongest objection" to a sonnet by Ella Wheeler Wilcox that he analyses – a poem that Richards finds to be dependent upon stock responses, a poem that Graves would call "fake" poetry – is that "a reader who ... thoroughly enters into and enjoys this class of verse, is necessarily so organized that he will fail to respond to poetry."[35] Poets of this sort keep a reader trapped within his stock responses. According to Richards, "Time and much varied experience might change him sufficiently, but by then he would no longer be able to enjoy such verse, he would no longer be the same person."[36] We do not so much change our taste, it seems, as find it spontaneously changed, with no way back.

For Richards, as for Graves, genuine poetry depends for its existence as much on the reader's response during the reading of it as on the poet's experience and expression during the making of it. And they both feel that good poetry has never before required a stronger, more comprehensive defence against the badness of fake poets and the badness of weak readers.

•

We recall that according to Richards, along with "an account of value," "an account of communication" is one of "the two pillars upon which a theory of criticism must rest."[37] One of the distinctive features of the mind is that it is "an instrument for communication," the emphasis that natural selection has placed on this human ability being "overwhelming."[38] And so "it is as a communicator that it is most profitable to consider the artist," although "the artist is not as a rule consciously concerned with communication, apparently regardless of its [art's] communicative efficacy."[39] According to Richards, the result of the artist's simply "getting it right" is that he communicates effectively, no matter how much he may have neglected the goal of communication: "The very process of getting the work 'right' has itself ... immense communicative consequences ... The degree to which it accords with the relevant experience of the artist is a measure of the degree to which it will arouse similar experiences in others."[40] In fact, "those artists and poets who can be suspected of close separate attention to the communicative aspect tend ... to fall into a subordinate rank."[41]

Graves presents virtually the same observations about the nature of communication in poetry in his essay "What is Bad Poetry?" According to Graves, the poet stands no chance of even knowing what he wants to communicate before the poem is written: "I wish to stress two important psychological phenomena: first, that no poet can ever rationally state beforehand what he is going to write about: second, that no poet can rationally state exactly what he has written and why; in effect, what the conflict is or what the new factor is that solves the conflict, until after completely emerging from the mood that made him write the poem."[42] He develops these points explicitly in relation to the question of poetry as communication: "the act of composition is primarily not communication between the individual poet and his neighbours, but an inter-communication of the different selves formed within the individual in relation to the various groups with which he has come in contact."[43] Generally, the poem's "primary function" is a making sure of the unforeseen fusion of emotional ideas for the benefit of the poet himself:

> Although there are a number of poems in which the communicative spirit is present from the start as a factor in the conflict, where the poet has missionary intentions or wishes to use the poem as a social weapon, yet in a vast number of cases the poem as it appears in first draft has no communicative intention at all ... [M]y experience of the first drafts of other poets' work and my own is that generally while the poem is what I might call a private poem not yet dispassionately viewed as a marketable commodity, the neat hand-writing, cleanliness, and orderliness of the communicative spirit are conspicuously absent. But when the poet wakes up to the poem as a poem ... he begins the secondary or tertiary elaboration ... But by then the poem has already fulfilled its primary function and has become a commodity or a record, nothing more.[44]

And so "poetry is in its first writing and first reading none but the poet's own business and afterwards is elaborated only for a limited group of readers."[45] Graves makes the very distinction that Richards makes between poets "not ... consciously concerned with communication" and poets paying "close separate attention to the communicative aspect."[46] Both agree that the poet's job is to get it right for himself – that is, to say to himself what needs to be said.

In fact, Graves's discussion of the balance between the poet's desire to produce something for himself and something for others is remarkably similar to Richards's later discussion of the same topic. According to Richards,

> How far desire actually to communicate, as distinguished from desire to produce something with communicative efficacy (however disguised), is an "unconscious motive" in the artist is a question to which we need not hazard an answer ... What concerns criticism is not the avowed or unavowed motives of the artist, however interesting these may be to psychology, but the fact that his procedure does, in the majority of instances, make the communicative efficacy of his work correspond with his own satisfaction and sense of its rightness ... In any case it is certain that no mere careful study of communicative possibilities, together with any desire to communicate, however intense, is ever sufficient without close natural correspondence between the poet's impulses and possible impulses in the reader. All supremely successful communication involves this correspondence, and no planning can take its place. Nor is the deliberate conscious attempt directed to communication so successful as the unconscious method.[47]

Virtually every point that Richards makes here has already been made by Graves in "What is Bad Poetry?"

In collaboration with Riding, Graves develops these ideas further in *A Survey of Modernist Poetry*. They suggest that the surest way for the poet to guarantee miscommunication is to try to write down to the reader for whom "clearness ... is really the suppression of everything in the poem over and above the average standard of comprehension": "A poem, therefore, that really is potentially superior to the average standard of comprehension and which nevertheless conforms to it actually obscures its real meaning the more it observes this standard."[48] Their further elaboration of Graves's original point brings it even closer to Richards's formulation of it when they suggest that "A poem that is potentially superior to the average standard of comprehension and which, disregarding it, fulfills all its potentialities, makes its real meaning clearer and clearer."[49] Just as for Richards the trick for the artist seems to be to please himself ("what he is making is something which is beautiful in itself, or satisfying to him personally, or something expressive, in a more or less vague sense, of his emotions, or of himself"), so for Graves, and for Riding and Graves, the only standard of comprehension that counts is that of the poem's best reader, the writer himself: "If a variable standard of comprehension were admitted, the poem would have the privilege of developing itself to the degree of clearness corresponding with the degree of comprehension in the reader most above the average. As the poet himself would thus be allowed as a possible reader of his own poem, it would be encouraged to attain its maximum, not its minimum, of real clearness."[50] As Riding goes on to say in *Contemporaries and Snobs*, developing Graves's point even further, "The poem itself is supreme, above persons; judging rather than judged; keeping criticism at a respectful distance; it is even able to make a reader of its author."[51] Graves and Richards and Riding all agree: to say that "the very process of getting the work 'right'" maximizes its communicative power is simply to recognize the poet as his own best reader, a recognition that Graves came to first.[52]

Richards, on the one hand, and the team of Riding and Graves, on the other, follow up on Graves by suggesting that compromise between the standards of the average reader and those of the poet as the reader of his own work is inadvisable. Riding and Graves suggest that Cummings's poem "Among/these/red pieces of/day" "combines two qualities of clearness: clearness of composition in the interests of the poem as a thing in itself, clearness of transmittance in the interests of the reader."[53] They imply that "the poet has been wrong in paying too much attention to the rendering of the poem for the reader" and that "if he had allowed it to be more difficult, if he had concentrated exclusively on the poem as a thing in itself, it would have seemed less freakish."[54] And so Riding and Graves announce that "When ... bare, undressed ideas are found in poetry instead of the rhetorical devices by which poets try to 'put over' their ideas ... the poet has cut off all his communications."[55] For Richards, of course, communication is all, and since "the deliberate conscious attempt directed to communication" is not "so successful as the unconscious indirect method," "the artist is entirely justified in his apparent neglect of the main purpose of his work."[56] They all agree that benignly neglecting his communications is the best poet's best way of ensuring them.

Interestingly, Richards's Graves-like observation that "the unconscious indirect method" of communicating meaning in poetry is more effective than "the deliberate conscious attempt directed at communication" immediately preludes his invocation of Graves in Chapter Four of *Principles of Literary Criticism*, "Communication and the Artist": "Since the poet's unconscious motives have been alluded to, it may be well at this point to make a few additional remarks. Whatever psycho-analysts may aver, the mental processes of the poet are not a very profitable field for investigation ... [T]he attempt to display the inner working of the artist's mind by the evidence of his work alone must be subject to the gravest dangers ... Mr Graves has attempted to analyse *Kubla Khan* ... The reader acquainted with current methods of analysis can imagine the results of a thoroughgoing Freudian onslaught."[57] It is as though Richards anticipates that readers will recognize that he has paraphrased in his preceding paragraphs Graves's observations regarding poetry as communication, requiring him next, therefore, to distance himself from Graves by explicit criticism of his conflict theory. Having summoned the spectre of Graves, an anxious Richards proceeds to exorcise an oppressive sense of belatedness – in part by "a not inapposite warning against one kind at least of possible applications of psychology in criticism" (as distinct from his own application of psychology in criticism), and in part by the kind of misreading of similarity as difference that occludes his own debt to Graves here.

•

Further evidence that Richards read Graves's essay "What is Bad Poetry?" very attentively is suggested by his comments on how poetic communication is facilitated by the special nature of the poet: "He is pre-eminently accessible to external influences and discriminating with regard to them. He is distinguished further by the freedom in which all these impressions are held in suspension, and by the ease with which they form new relations between themselves. The greatest difference between the artist or poet and the ordinary person is found, as has often been pointed out, in the range, delicacy, and freedom of the connections he is able to make between different elements of his experience."[58] However much it has "often been pointed out," Graves is the most recent to have defined the poet in print, both in *On English Poetry* and in "What is Bad Poetry?" by these very terms. In "What is Bad Poetry," he explains his assertion that the poet's primary responsibility is to communicate with himself by quoting his explanation in *On English Poetry* of how the poet's special nature facilitates the inter-communication within him of external influences from the community as a whole:

> the act of composition is primarily not communication between the individual poet and his neighbours, but an inter-communication of the different selves formed within the individual in relation to the various groups with which he has come in contact. I do not wish to retreat far from what I wrote in my previous volume:
>
> "A poet in the fullest sense is one whom some unusual complications of early environment or mixed parentage develop as an intermediary between the small group-minds of particular sects, clans, castes, types and professions, among whom he moves. To so many of these has he been formally enrolled as a member and to so many more has he virtually added himself as supernumerary member by showing a disinterested sympathy and by practising his exceptionally developed powers of intuition, that in any small group sense the wide diffusion of his loyalties makes him at first appear everywhere as a hypocrite and traitor. But the rival selves formed in him by this relation to these various groups constantly struggle to reconciliation in his poetry and in proportion as these selves are more numerous, more varied and more inharmonious and his controlling personality stronger and quicker at compromise (I should have said 'synthesis') so he becomes a more or less capable spokesman of that larger group mind of his culture."[59]

Richards's observations about the range, freedom, and discrimination of the poet's reconciling access to the experiences and perspectives of others are the same as Graves's.

Richards even follows Graves in his explanation of the mental state that enables the poet to communicate the special experiences facilitated by his poetic nature. In his chapter "The Availability of the Poet's Experience," Richards suggests that it is the "available possession of the past which is the first characteristic of the adept in communication, of the poet or the artist."[60] Observing that "persons to whom the past comes back as a whole are likely to be found in an asylum," and acknowledging the poet's "superficial resemblance to those who are merely mental chaoses, unorganised, without selective ability and of weak and diffused attention," Richards is concerned to distinguish the poet from lunatics and children.[61] He explains that "what is in question here is not memory ... but free reproduction. To be able to revive an experience is not to remember when and where and how it occurred, but merely to have that peculiar state of mind available."[62] He suggests that "how far an experience is revivable would seem to depend in the first place upon the interests, the impulses, active in the experience," and in the second place upon the "the difference between understanding a situation and the more usual reactions to it"; "the difference between a systematised complex response, or ordered sequence of responses, and a welter of responses."[63] The poet's responses to experiences are more complex and more organized: "In order to keep any steadiness and clarity in his attitudes the ordinary man is under the necessity on most occasions of suppressing the greater part of the impulses which the situation might arouse. He is incapable of organising them; therefore they have to be left out."[64] It is a question of mental vigilance:

> Contrast the behaviour of the sleepy and the fully awake, of the normal man with the lightly and more deeply anaesthetised patient ... To describe these differences in neural potency, and to mark the degree of physiological efficiency, Dr [Henry] Head has recently suggested the term *vigilance* ... In a high state of vigilance the nervous system reacts to stimuli with highly adapted, discriminating, and ordered responses; in a lowered state of vigilance the responses are less discriminating, less delicately adapted. Whether we are considering the decerebrate preparation or the intact poet, the simplest automatisms or the most highly conscious acts, what happens in a given stimulus situation varies with the vigilance of the appropriate portion of the nervous system ... The answer then, at least in part, to the problem of how the poet's experience is more than usually available to him is that it is, as he undergoes it, more than usually organised through his more than usual vigilance. Connections become established for him which in the ordinary mind, much more rigid and exclusive in its play of impulses, are never effected, and it is through these original connections that so much more of his past comes to be freely revivable for him at need.[65]

It is important to note, furthermore, that "to understand a situation in the sense intended here is not necessarily to reflect upon it, to inquire into its principles and consciously distinguish its characters, but to respond to it as a whole," and so we must not "make an artificial distinction between intellectual or theoretical and non-intellectual or emotional activities."[66]

Richards reproduces here the terms and perspectives foregrounded by Graves. That the poet is able to respond to a situation "as a whole" and that a critic's artificial distinctions within that whole between intellectual and theoretical elements and non-intellectual and emotional ones will thereby leave the critic incapable of appreciating the poem are points made first by Graves in the chapter of *Poetic Unreason* called "The Illogical Element in Poetry," first published in the *Spectator* in 1922.[67] Richards's definition of the poet's understanding of his experience as comprehending both thinking and feeling in a coherent whole echoes Graves's defence of apparently illogical romantic poetry (full of "illegitimate associations") in the face of the classical sensibility for which "thinking was a logical process of one continuous strand" and according to which "the poetry recommended was to pursue a steady course in which every image was to be deduced from the previous one."[68]

Similarly, Richards's concern to disavow the poet's resemblance to "the patient in the asylum" and "mental chaoses" echoes Graves's concern to counter the "false idea that the Romantic or emotional mode of thought has no place in civilized life and is merely a survival of the child or the savage."[69] According to Graves, the "method of Romantic poetry and the method of thought in fantastic dreams" is the "associative method of thought," "for which Logic has had for centuries nothing but the sneering patronage of the self-respecting citizen for the grotesque but cheerful village idiot."[70] Although he had sneered at the extremes of Graves's associational method of literary analysis earlier in the book, Richards now defends something very like that interpretive method.

Graves points out that the two modes of thought in which the poet specializes have equal integrity. He makes this point by means of his regular analogy between dreams and poetry, and also by means of a special analogy between the degree of consciousness observable in romantic and classical poetry, on the one hand, and the degree of consciousness observable in those who are sleepy and those who are fully awake, on the other, an analogy similar to that of Richards in the passage above. Graves quotes from W.H.R. Rivers's *Conflict and Dream*:

> the mind may be regarded as composed of a number of levels or strata comparable with the levels of neurological activity which

> are now widely held to furnish the best explanation of the mode of action of the nervous system. According to this view, the deeper the sleep the larger the number of these levels which are put out of activity, and the lower the level which finds expression in dream. The dreams of deep sleep in which many levels of activity are put out of action will reveal infantile modes of thinking, feeling, and acting; the dreams of less deep sleep in which fewer of the higher levels are inactive would express modes of mental function proper to childhood or youth; while the dreams of very light sleep would have a character but little different from that of the ordinary mental activities of the waking life … Dreams, or rather certain dreams, are readily forgotten because they are manifestations of levels of mental activity remote in character from those of later periods in life … [E]arly levels of mental activity are suppressed because they are incompatible with the activities of later life. The mental efficiency of a person would be greatly prejudiced if modes of thinking, feeling and acting proper to infancy or childhood were continually intruding into the activities of adult life.[71]

Graves agrees with much in this passage: "I can confirm Dr. Rivers' observations on the relation between the depth of sleep and the character of the dream, by the poetic analogy. Critical or Classical poems are written in a mood in which the poet is preoccupied perhaps, but aware of the conventional waking view of reality: when the emotional Kubla Khan kind of poem appears, it arises either from actual deep sleep or from a 'brown study' trance, disturbance in which will affect the poet with the same shock as if he had been actually asleep."[72]

Yet Rivers's "admirable observations on the mechanism of dreams, especially admirable where he makes the accompanying physiology plain, are disappointing where they do not allow that associative thought is as modern and reputable a mode as intellectual thought, and regard it as a return of infantility."[73] And so, he explains, "I only disagree with sentences like 'The *mental efficiency* of a person would be prejudiced if modes of thinking *proper to childhood* were continually intruding into the activities of adult life,' when the implications are that (a) dreams are not an integral part of adult life; (b) poetry and humour of the kind which corresponds with imaginative dreams are less reputable and of less value than, say, scientific thought."[74] So Graves looks forward to a day when the clash between intellectual and emotional modes of thought will end; a day when "either one or other method of thought employed for dealing with any conflict" will be respected; a day that will come only "once it is admitted by philosophers that though Romantic thought cannot be exactly foreseen, neither any more can intellectual thought; and further, when they admit that emotional poetry and thought, once it has appeared, has discernible an orderly orientation and inevitability; and when further they observe that such poetry and thought is not so primitive in the popularly accepted sense that it cannot use intellectual formulae for its own purposes, but is a method constantly employed unknown to themselves by the most sophisticated and Aristotelian minds, and of great service to them."[75] According to Graves, then, the two modes of thought in which the poet specializes are both necessary for mental order and for mental efficiency – the same point that Richards makes.

For Graves, the poet's mind is especially vigilant in terms of its associative ability. Richards agrees that the poetic mind capable of these associations or connections is one to be nurtured, especially given the more "rigid and exclusive" tendencies of the ordinary mind.[76] And so for both, the poetic mind's claim to fame in this regard is based upon its greater vigilance, whether that be a greater intellectual vigilance or a greater emotional vigilance. Of course Richards quotes Henry Head on the question of mental vigilance in waking life, whereas Graves quotes Rivers on the question of mental vigilance in states of dream as well as in waking life. Yet for all his determined acknowledgment of Rivers's work as fundamental to his conflict theory, Graves actually dedicates *Poetic Unreason* to Henry Head. Graves clearly recognizes that his work complements Head's research; it is not surprising that Richards should have recognized this fact too by adapting so many of Graves's insights to his own purposes – even before *Poetic Unreason* and its dedication to Head had appeared.

•

Richards's observation in the chapter of *Principles of Literary Criticism* called "Badness in Poetry" that critics who fail to receive the poem's communication have no right to call it bad and his more general observations about the responsibilities of critics in his chapter "The Definition of a Poem" seem to have come right out of Graves's essay "What is Bad Poetry?" According to Richards, "It would perhaps be best to restrict the term bad art to cases in which genuine communication does to a considerable degree take place, what is communicated being worthless, and to call the other cases defective art. But this is not the usual practice of critics, any work which produces an experience displeasing to the critic being commonly called bad, whether or not the experience is like that responsible for the work."[77] Graves puts this more succinctly: "where there is no contact there can be no criticism."[78] According to Richards:

> A critic should often be in a position to say, "I don't like this but I know it is good," or "I like this and condemn it," or "This is the effect which it produces upon me, and this quite different effect is the one it should produce." For obvious reasons he rarely makes such statements ... Any honest reader knows fairly well the points at which his sensibility is distorted, at which he fails as a normal critic and in what ways. It is his duty to take these into consideration in passing judgment upon the value of a work. His rank as a critic depends at least as much upon his ability to discount these personal peculiarities as upon any hypothetical impeccability of his actual responses.[79]

Declaring that "poetry is in its first writing and first reading none but the poet's own business and afterwards is elaborated only for a limited group of readers," Graves anticipates Richards in "What Is Bad Poetry" by calling for critics to observe the same principles:

> what right has the reviewer to tax the poet with carelessness, obscurity, pedantry, dullness, immorality, or any other similar failing where the interests which the poet has shown in the conflict or construction of his poetry are not represented in the experience of the reviewer?
>
> The most that a reviewer can sensibly say is, "So far as I can see, this poem represents such and such interests; it does not meet the demands of such and such other interests. The writer appears to take this or that philosophic position, to be in sympathy with this or that literary tradition ... [H]e uses certain symbols in different senses from the accustomed ones, arguing particular incidents in his life, which we can only guess at, connected with these

> symbols ..." But the time may come for him to admit honourably, "I cannot talk of this book dispassionately because the author has completely overcome me with one of the poems, which means far more to me than other people to whom I have shown it because the poet and myself have an emotional (or intellectual) experience of an unusual character in common." Or instead, "I cannot talk of this book dispassionately because it is written by a man who stands for everything I most detest, and the qualities which put me out of sympathy with him are best shown in the following passages. I admit that there must be a complementary quality for him to detest in myself and therefore this review must be regarded as only one side of an antinomial story."
>
> Every poem, I repeat, can only be fairly judged in its own context.[80]

Both Richards's duplication of the figure of the confessing critic and the similarity of the confessions that the critics make suggest that Richards recalled Graves's paragraphs when writing his own.

•

Similarly, Richards's discussion of the role of rhythm and metre closely follows Graves's discussion of this topic. Graves also considers the communicative impulse evident in the poet's "more-or-less deliberate attempt, with the help of mesmerism, to impose an illusion of actual experience on the mind of others."[81] He regards poetry "as being like Religion, a modified descendent of primitive magic."[82] According to Graves, poetry "originated" in "rhythmic dream utterances, intoxicating a primitive community to sympathetic emotional action for a particular purpose": "Primitive man was much troubled by the phenomenon of dreams ... [W]here it was felt that a dream was needed to confirm or reverse a decision, the peculiarly gifted witch doctor or priestess would induce a sort of self-hypnotism, and in the light of the dream so dreamed, utter an oracle which contained an answer to the problem proposed. The compelling use of rhythm to hold people's attention and to make them beat their feet in time, was known, and the witch doctor seems to have combined the rhythmic beat of a drum or gong with the recital of his dream."[83] And so "whoever it was who found it convenient that his word stresses should correspond with beat of drum or stamp of feet, thereby originated the rhythm that is common both to verse and to poetry."[84]

Whereas prose "does not trouble to keep rhythmic control over the reader," Graves suggests that "this constant control seems an essential part of Poetry proper."[85] Such control is not a matter of unvarying constancy in rhythm and sound: "In poetry proper our delight is in the emotional variations from a clearly indicated norm of rhythm and sound-texture; but in prose poetry there is no recognizable norm."[86] According to Graves, "the limitation of *Vers Libre*, which I regard as only our old friend, Prose Poetry, broken up in convenient lengths, seems to be that the poet has not the continual hold over his reader's attention that a regulated (this does not mean altogether 'regular') scheme of verse properly used would give him."[87] Suggesting that "there is some sort of rhythm in every phrase you write," in fact, "there is often a queer, broken-kneed rhythm running through whole sentences of standard prose," Graves points out that the key to the effect of rhythm is a reader's listening in a particular way out of the expectation of rhythm: "One doesn't 'listen' when reading prose, but in poetry or anything offered under that heading a submerged metre is definitely expected."[88]

The poet who answers this expectation faces a great obligation: since "in regulated verse the reader is compelled to accentuate as the poet determines," "the regulating poet must of course make sure at the beginning of the poem that there is no possible wrong turning for the reader to take."[89] Expectation answered becomes expectation established. The problem with *vers libre* is that it frustrates expectations: "In *vers libre* there is no natural indication as to how the lines are to be stressed ... [T]his seems to be leaving too much to chance."[90] So although "rhythmic control ... seems an essential part of Poetry proper," "to expect it in prose poetry" – or *vers libre*, "our old friend, Prose Poetry, broken up in convenient line lengths" – "is to be disappointed; we may take an analogy from the wilder sort of music where if there is continual changing of time and key, the listener often does not 'catch on' to each new idiom, so that he is momentarily confused by the changes and the unity of the whole musical form is thereby broken for him."[91]

As we shall see, as though addressing a list of topics distilled from Graves's early work, Richards sounds all these notes: rhythm and metre, when repeated, create anticipation; the key to establishing expectations is control and regulation of rhythm and metre; *vers libre* forgoes this control and regulation for the sake of other freedoms, sometimes at great cost; readerly pleasure is a function of varying the meeting of expectations by occasional departures from expectations; breaking the unity of the whole is a source of pain for the reader, and a sign of failure in the poet.

In the chapter "Rhythm and Metre" in *Principles of Literary Criticism*, Richards begins by observing that "rhythm and its specialized form, metre, depend upon repetition, and expectancy. Equally where what is expected recurs and where it fails, all rhythmical and metrical effects spring from anticipation. As a rule, this anticipation is unconscious."[92] Expectation is the key to rhythm, for without it "there can be no surprise and no disappointment" – a matter of some consequence, for "most rhythms perhaps are made up as much of disappointments and postponements and surprises and betrayals as of simple, straightforward satisfactions."[93] And so rhythm is the "tissue of expectations, satisfactions, disappointments, surprisals, which the sequence of syllables brings about."[94] According to Richards, "there is nothing arbitrary or out of the poet's control ... in the way in which an adequate reader will stress particular syllables."[95] Graves points out in *On English Poetry* that "The regulating poet must of course make sure at the beginning of the poem that there is no possible wrong turning for the reader to take."[96] Richards agrees: the poet brings about a proper stressing of syllables by "the modification of the reader's impulses by what has gone before."[97]

Drawing an analogy between poetry and "the plastic arts and ... architecture", Richards notes that "the difference in detail between a surprising and delightful variation and one which merely irritates and breaks down the rhythm ... is here, as elsewhere, a matter of the combination and resolution of impulses too subtle for our present means of investigation. All depends upon whether what comes can be an ingredient in the further response, or whether the mind must, as it were, start anew; in more ordinary language, upon whether there is any 'connection' between the parts of the whole."[98] Graves says something remarkably similar with analogy to music: "if there is continual changing of time and key, the listener often does not 'catch on' to each new idiom ... and the unity of the whole musical form is thereby broken for him."[99]

Graves finds occasion in *On English Poetry* to explain the inadequacies of the traditional method of marking syllables in terms of just long and short stresses, and so does Richards in *Principles of*

Literary Criticism. Graves suggests that "the Anglo-French theory of only two standardized sound values, long or short," is not subtle enough to indicate the full complexity of the whole that rhythm, metre, and sound form in a poem. What "many prosodists assume" – that "all words in daily speech [are] spoken at the same rate ... all stressed syllables and all unstressed syllables, similarly, [are] dwelt on for exactly the same length of time" – is simply not the case ("poetry would be a much easier art to practise" if it were).[100] According to Graves, however, "In true poetry the mental bracing and relaxing on receipt of sensuous impressions, which we may call the rhythm of emotions, conditions the musical rhythm. This rhythm of emotions also determines the sound texture of vowels and consonants, so that Metre, as schoolboys understand it ... has in spontaneous poetry only a submerged existence ... A far more subtle notation must be adopted, and if it must be shown on the blackboard, poetry will be marked out not in 'feet' but in convenient musical bars, with the syllables resolved into quaver, dotted crotchet, semibreve and all the rest of them."[101] In fact, "The musical side of poetry is, properly understood, not merely a hypnotic inducement to the reader to accepts suggestions, but a form of psycho-therapy in itself."[102]

Richards devotes several paragraphs of his chapter "Rhythm and Metre" to the same topic. Explaining the role of anticipation in the reader's response to the rhythm and metre of poetry, he suggests that "we do great violence to the facts if we suppose the expectations excited as we read verse to be concerned only with stress, emphasis, length, foot structure and so forth of the syllables which follow. Even in this respect the custom of marking syllables in two degrees only, long and short, light and full, etc., is inadequate ... The mind responds to subtler niceties than these. The obvious comparison with the difference between what even musical notation can record in music and the player's interpretation can usefully be made here."[103] Among the subtler niceties to which the mind responds are influences upon rhythm and metre of emotions stirred by the reading and the sense suggested by it: it is "impossible ... to consider rhythm or metre as though it were purely an affair of the sensory aspect of syllables and could be dissociated from their sense and from the emotional effects which come about through their sense."[104]

Richards develops this point further in *Practical Criticism*: "the rhythm which we admire, which we seem actually to detect *in* the sounds ... is something which we only *ascribe* to them and is, actually, a rhythm of the mental activity through which we apprehend not only the sound of words but their sense and feeling. The mysterious glory which seems to inhere in the sound of certain lines is a projection of the thought and emotion they evoke, and the peculiar satisfaction they give *to the ear* is a reflection of the adjustment *of our feelings* which has been momentarily achieved."[105] Richards's "rhythm of ... mental activity" that, by "projection," we "seem to detect actually *in* the sounds" of the words that we read parallels closely Graves's "rhythm of emotions" that "determines the sound-texture of vowels and consonants."[106] Richards even avails himself of a psychoanalytical term, "projection," that attributes to successful rhythm and metre the same psychotherapeutic function for it that Graves identifies. And to explain some of the more intense psychological effects of rhythm and metre, he also, like Graves, invokes one of the "more important powers" of rhythm and metre – hypnosis: "We need not boggle at the word 'hypnosis' ... [T]here is a change in the regime of consciousness, which is directly due to the meter ... [S]yllables, which in prose or in *vers libre* sound thin, tinny and flat, often gain an astonishing sonority and fullness even in verse which seems to possess no very subtle metrical structure."[107]

Richards also shadows Graves in his criticism of *vers libre*. Observing that *vers-libre* poets relinquish "the continual hold" over a reader's attention that "a regulated ... scheme of verse properly used" gives a poet, Graves suggests that "the temporary loss of control must be set off against the freedom which *vers libre*-ists claim from irrelevant or stereotyped images suggested by the necessity of rhyme or a difficult metre."[108] This "freedom" is "a serious limitation": "In *vers libre* there is no natural indication as to how the lines are to be stressed. There are thousands of lines of Walt Whitman's, over the pointing of which, and the intended cadence, elocutionists would disagree; and this seems to be leaving too much to chance."[109] Graves offers as "the most damaging criticism" of *vers libre* its failure to compensate for its serious formal limitations with greater virtuosity elsewhere: "with rhythmic freedom so dearly bought, one expects a more intricate system of interlacing implications than in closer bound poetry."[110]

Like Graves, Richards aligns *vers libre* with prose: syllables that "gain an astonishing sonority and fullness" in verse "in prose or in *vers libre* sound thin, tinny and flat."[111] He and Ogden write to similar effect in *The Meaning of Meaning*, observing "the greater sensitiveness to vowel and consonantal characters which accompanies metrical reading, and the flat or tinny effect of the same syllables occurring in *vers libre.*"[112] Criticizing a poem by H.D. that he regards as an example of failed *vers libre*, Richards complains that the poem leaves too much to chance not just in terms of elocution, but also in terms of sense: "The reader here supplies too much of the poem ... [W]hat results is almost independent of the author."[113] Richards agrees with Graves that relinquishing the responsibility of controlling the reader is a freedom dearly bought and likewise suggests that the relative simplicity of the rhythm and metre of *vers libre* requires that this formal deficit be supplemented by other virtues: "Not the brevity only of the vehicle, but its simplicity, makes it ineffective. The sacrifice of metre in free verse needs, in almost all cases, to be compensated by length. The loss of so much of the formal structure leads otherwise to tenuousness and ambiguity."[114]

Also like Graves, Richards traces the origin of rhythm and metre in poetry to its function in the religious practices of primitive times, and like Graves again he is interested in their "unconscious" effect, particularly in terms of their hypnotic power.[115] Graves suggests that insofar as poetry is "a modified descendant of primitive Magic," the poet is a descendent of "the peculiarly gifted witch doctor or priestess" who could "induce a sort of self-hypnotism," from which emerged "rhythmic dream utterances" capable of "intoxicating a primitive community to sympathetic emotional action."[116] Similarly, Richards observes that metre's "use as an hypnotic agent is probably very ancient"; its effect is similar to that of "much primitive music and dancing."[117] Graves notes "the compelling use of rhythm ... to make [people] beat their feet in time"; Richards suggests that "there can be little doubt that historically [metre] has been closely associated with dancing, and that connections of the two still hold."[118] Graves regards the hypnotic agency of rhythm as physical: "hypnotism, by the way, I regard as having a physical rather than a mental effect and being identical with the rhythmic hypnotism to which such animals as snakes, elephants or apes are easily subject."[119] Richards again concurs: "As with rhythm so with metre, we must not think of it as in the words themselves or in the thumping of the drum ... [I]ts effect is not due to our perceiving a pattern in something outside us, but to our becoming patterned ourselves. With every beat of the metre a tide of anticipation in us turns and swings ...

[T]he pattern is a vast cyclic agitation spreading all over the body, a tide of excitement pouring through the channels of the mind."[120]

Graves describes poets as assuming control of their readers' imaginations by "hypnotizing them into a receptive state by indirect sensuous suggestions and by subtle variations of verse-melody," the efficacy of the hypnotic strategies depending on limiting the field of attention ("the compelling use of rhythm to hold people's attention") and, because of "the greater emotional power on the average reader's mind of simple metres and short homely words with an occasional long strange one for wonder," avoiding "foreign or unusual prosody."[121] The ancient process involved "intoxicating a primitive community."[122] The poetic process involves "a constant appeal ... to the childish habits of amazed wondering, sudden terrors, laughter to signify mere joy, frequent tears and similar manifestations of uncontrolled emotion."[123] According to Graves, "the dream origin of Romantic poetry gives it the advantage of putting the audience in a state of mind ready to accept it; in a word, it has a naturally hypnotic effect."[124] This state of mind is the illogical mind of childhood: "dreams are illogical as a child's mind is illogical, and spontaneous undoctored poetry, like the dream, represents the complications of adult experience translated into thought-processes analogous to, or identical with, those of childhood."[125] This is a process that many "a grown man and especially an Englishman" dislikes, "the dislike being apparently founded on a feeling that to wake this child-spirit in the mind of a grown person is stupid and even disgusting, an objection that has similarly been raised to the indiscriminate practice of psycho-analysis, which involves the same process."[126]

Richards also addresses the topic of poetic hypnosis with Ogden in *The Meaning of Meaning*. Explaining the effects of words in evoking feelings and attitudes, they suggest that it "may be reasonably supposed" that "rhythms and especially metres have to a small degree an hypnotic effect."[127] Furthermore, "emotionality, exaggeration of belief-feelings, the occulting of the critical faculties, the suppression of the questioning – 'Is this so as a matter of fact?' – attitude, all these are characteristics of metrical experiences and fit in well with a hypnosis assumption."[128] In *Principles of Literary Criticism*, he argues that rhythms that are "too simple" will "grow cloying or insipid unless hypnoidal states intervene, as with much primitive music and dancing and often with metre."[129] In fact, "That certain metres, or rather that a certain handling of metre should produce in a slight degree a hypnoidal state is not surprising. Poetry produces a slight degree of hypnotic effect. But it does so not as Coleridge suggests, through the surprise element in metrical effects, but through the absence of surprise, through the lulling effects more than through the awakening."[130]

Principles of Literary Criticism accords the question of the role of hypnotism in poetry's effect both a more extended treatment and a more ambivalent status than in Richards's earlier text. We read that in addition to "giving an increased interconnection between words through an increased control of anticipation," metre has "even more important powers" – the "very ancient" powers of hypnosis.[131] But because Graves argued that "One may think of Poetry as being like Religion, a modified descendent of primitive Magic," Richards quickly acts to subordinate it to science: "We need not boggle at the word 'hypnosis.' It is sufficient to say ... that there is a change in the regime of consciousness, which is directly due to the metre, and that to this regime the above-mentioned characteristics attach."[132] Still, Richards notes the same effects that Graves notes: "Many of the most characteristic symptoms of incipient hypnosis are present in a slight degree. Among these susceptibility and vivacity of emotion, suggestibility, limitations of the field of attention, marked differences in the incidence of belief-feelings closely analogous to those which alcohol and nitrous oxide can induce."[133]

Between *The Meaning of Meaning* and *Principles of Literary Criticism*, Richards has discovered the need to address those who "boggle at the word 'hypnosis.'" In other words, he has discovered the need to reassure those who might think that his talk of poetry as hypnosis is evidence that he has gone over to the Graves school of criticism. Just as he is determined that his account of the imagination should not wander onto the theological shoals that consign Coleridge's account to neglect, he is also determined that the hypnotic effect of rhythm and metre not be occulted by association with anything magical or mysterious, let alone theological, in Graves's. In *Principles of Literary Criticism*, therefore, Richards implicitly does to Graves what he explicitly does to Coleridge: he removes the taint of an unscientific paradigm.[134]

Richards notes that "The history of science is full of mysterious unique entities which have gradually evaporated as explanation advanced ... The struggles of economists with 'utility,' of mathematical philosophers with 'points' and 'instants,' of biologists with 'entelechies,' and the adventures of psycho-analysts with 'the libido' and 'the collective unconscious' are instances in point."[135] Graves's popularizing psychoanalytical framework – "I am trying ... to avoid the use of any technical words at all, and so I shall explain Dr. Rivers' views and my own with as little quotation as possible from scientific works" – is the "theology" that Richards removes from Graves's work.[136]

As prelude to "the analysis of poetic experience," Richards suggests, "it is necessary to break away from the set of ideas by which popular and academic psychology alike attempt to describe the mind":

> We naturally tend to conceive it as a thing of a peculiar spiritual kind ... endowed with ... capacities ... for knowing, willing and feeling ... A violent shock to this entity comes when we are forced by a closer examination of the facts to conceive it as doing all these three unconsciously as well as consciously. An unconscious mind is a fairly evident fiction, useful though it may be, and goings on in the nervous system are readily accepted as a satisfactory substitute. From this to the recognition of the conscious mind as a similar fiction is no great step, although one which many people find difficult. Some of this difficulty ... wears off as we notice how many of the things which we believed true of the fiction can be stated in terms of the less fictitious substitute. But much of the difficulty is emotive, non-intellectual, more specifically religious, in origin.[137]

Richards concedes that "the account which we give must frankly be admitted to be only a degree less fictitious than one in terms of spiritual happenings," but he insists that "the kind of account which is likely to be substantiated by future research has become clear, largely through the work of Behaviourists and Psycho-analysts, the assumptions and results of both needing to be corrected."[138] We can see that vis-á-vis Graves, Richards acts as just such a corrector – purging psychoanalytical absolutes from Graves's insights about how poems, poets, and readers operate, and replacing them with a more functional psychological account of their operations. According to Richards, "the mind is the nervous system," so he has no need of such a ghost in the machine as Graves supplies.[139]

13

Conflict Theory in *Science and Poetry*

If the imprint that Graves's early work left in Richards's imagination is clear in *Principles of Literary Criticism*, it is even clearer in *Science and Poetry* (1926), where Richards presents the salient points of *Principles of Literary Criticism* in a more accessible and popular form. Richards adopts here what Graves calls in *The Meaning of Dreams* the "Theory of the Double Self" and adapts it to the more behaviourist, functionalist terms of his own literary theory. He is thereby put on the road to an appreciation of the overdetermination of meaning in poetry and an increasingly sophisticated appreciation of poetry's systematic reconciliation of overdetermined meanings. Paraphrasing Rivers, Graves explains the occurrence in dreams of

> Dissociation, that is the breaking up of the human individual into two or more rival "selves" under the stress of difficult circumstances ... When we discuss a man, one John Jones, and ... come to examine John Jones, it is possible that two or more John Jones's who are very hostile to each other may appear in the one person ... Now all ... examples of double-self are alike in this, that they show that there is a conflict in the man or woman's nature between different ideas or interests ... The so-called "unconscious self" ... is just the self which in conflict happens at the time to be beaten ... So long as the waking life is ruled by one interest or view at the expense of the other the defeated interest will appear in one form or another in every dream dreamed.[1]

As we have seen, Graves further explains the literary application of Rivers's conceptual framework in *Poetic Unreason*: "This book will principally show Poetry as a record of the conflicts between various pairs of Jekyll and Hyde, or as a record of the solution of these conflicts. In the period of conflict, poetry may be either a partisan statement ... of one side of the conflict; or else a double statement of both sides of the conflict, one side appearing in the manifest statement ... the other in the latent content ... In the period of solution there will be no discrepancy between latent content and manifest statement."[2] In a person's life, such a solution makes a "new individual" out of the conflicting sub-personalities: "Hyde and Jekyll co-exist in an individual as possibilities, but in relation to any given situation only one will appear at a time while the conflict continues. If a situation occurs in which they *can* sink their differences, the action of the individual will be neither Hyde-ish nor Jekyllesque but of such a nature that ... a single individual will emerge not predominantly Jekyll or Hyde ... but a new creation making the continuance of the conflicting elements unnecessary."[3]

Graves discusses the poet's sub-personalities in *On English Poetry*, regarding emotional conflict between them as so essential to poetry that should such conflict disappear, so would poetry. He suggests that the two ways in which poets overcome their conflicts and lose the ability to write poetry are when they "come to a dead end and stop writing" because "the poet's preoccupation with the clash of his emotions has been transmuted into a calmer state of meditation" or when "the conflict of the poet's sub-personalities has been finally settled, by some satisfaction of desire or removal of a cause of fear, in the complete rout of the opposing parties, and the victors dictate their own laws, uncontradicted."[4]

Like Empson, Richards uses the language of Graves's "conflict theory" without actually referring to the author of the theory: "Conflicts between different impulses are the greatest evils which afflict mankind."[5] Richards sketches the same picture of human psychology as a contest between conflicting impulses within a person, and he depicts the "good life" for such a person as "one in which ... as many of his impulses as possible" are engaged, "with as little conflict, as little mutual interference between different sub-systems of his activities as there can be."[6] The language of "conflict" is the same and the language of "sub-personalities" is merely replaced by the language of "sub-systems of ... activities," as Richards converts the terms of psychoanalysis to the terms of behaviourism.

Also like Graves, Richards observes that "there are two ways in which conflict can be avoided or overcome. By conquest and by conciliation. One or other of the contesting impulses can be suppressed, or they can come to a mutual arrangement, they can adjust themselves to one another."[7] Richards again avails himself of a psychoanalytical term, and he does so quite self-consciously: "We owe to psycho-analysis – at present still a rather undisciplined branch of psychology – a great deal of striking evidence as to the extreme difficulty of suppressing any vigorous impulse. When it seems to be suppressed it is often found to be really as active as ever, but in some other form, generally, a troublesome one."[8] Graves is not interested in describing this "so-called 'unconscious self'" as "the sort of primitive bogey" that Freud describes, preferring to regard it as "just the self which in conflict happens at the time to be beaten."[9] Similarly Richards avoids the Freudian paradigm, regarding a suppressed impulse not necessarily as primitive, but merely as defeated – "troublesome" not necessarily because it is transgressive but rather because it has been transgressed: "People who are always winning victories over themselves might equally well be described as always enslaving themselves."[10] Richards's view is closer to Jung's than it is to Freud's, and it is closer to Graves's than it is to Jung's.

Those who are always winning victories over themselves and so always enslaving themselves are legion, for, "unfortunately, most of us, left to ourselves, have no option but to go in for extensive attempts at self-conquest. It is our only means of escape from chaos. Our impulses must have some order, some organisation, or we do not live ten minutes without disaster."[11] Fortunately, however, we are not left entirely to ourselves to organize our impulses, for we have poetry. According to Richards, the "good life" requires that "experience ... be organized so as to give all the impulses of which it is composed the greatest possible degree of freedom"; after all, "conflicts between different impulses are the greatest evils that afflict mankind" and so "if it is asked, what does such a life feel like, how is it to live through? the answer is that it feels like and is the experience of poetry."[12]

Immediately after this passage, Richards outlines a psychotherapeutic function for literature. Poetry is our best response to the fact that "persistent mental imbalances are the source of nearly all our troubles."[13] Since "suppression is wasteful of life, conciliation is always to be preferred to conquest," and so we need a new "moral ordering of the impulses; a new order based on conciliation, not on attempted suppression."[14] Here, the poet leads: "Only the rarest individuals hitherto have achieved this new order, and never yet perhaps completely. But many have achieved it for a brief while, for a particular phase of experience, and many have recorded it for these phases ... Of these records poetry consists."[15] His position is similar to that outlined by Graves, first in *On English Poetry* (1922), where he declares poetry "a form of psycho-therapy ... homoeopathically healing other men's minds similarly troubled," and then in *Poetic Unreason* (1925), where he explains that: "Poetry is for the poet a means of informing himself on many planes simultaneously ... of the relation in his mind of certain hitherto inharmonious interests, you may call them his sub-personalities or other selves. And for the reader, Poetry is a means of similarly informing himself of the relation of analogous interests hitherto inharmonious on these same various planes. For the poet, the writing of poetry ... enables him to be rid of these conflicts between his sub-personalities. And for the reader ... the reading of poetry performs a similar service; it acts for him as a physician of his mental disorders."[16] So in *Science and Poetry*, despite his association of the psychoanalytical interpretation of literature with "the gravest dangers" in *Principles of Literary Criticism*, Richards now celebrates the psychological function of literature not just in terms of its organization of human impulses or the socially progressive development that it fosters, but also in terms of the psychotherapeutic effect that Graves has emphasized in three successive books.

•

Richards also follows Graves in drawing an analogy between the poetic reconciliation of tensions within the poet and reader and the process of reconciling political tensions through the diplomatic mediation practised at international conferences. According to Richards, poetry will lead us toward "a new order based on conciliation, not on attempted suppression," an allusion to hope after the Great War that Woodrow Wilson would lead the world to a new moral order based on the self-determination of peoples, a hope that was disappointed by the Treaty of Versailles: "In the past, Tradition, a kind of Treaty of Versailles assigning frontiers and spheres of influence to the different interests, and based chiefly upon conquest, ordered our lives in a moderately satisfactory manner. But Tradition is weakening. Moral authorities are not as well backed by beliefs as they were; their sanctions are declining in force. We are in need of something to take the place of the old order. Not in need of a new balance of power, a new arrangement of conquests, but a League of Nations for the moral ordering of the impulses."[17] However much, in the wake of twentieth-century history, one might be inclined to sneer, "Good luck to the League, and good luck to poetry," one can also nonetheless see how, in the 1920s, Isherwood could perceive a lecturer like Richards as "the prophet we had been waiting for ... our guide, our evangelist, who revealed to us, in a succession of astonishing lightning flashes, the entire expanse of the Modern World."[18]

Yet Richards has merely dressed up with contemporary political references an analogy developed by Graves at three different points in *On English Poetry*. First he suggests that "The mind of a poet is like an international conference composed of delegates of both sexes and every shade of political thought, which is trying to decide on a series of problems of which the chairman has himself little previous knowledge – yet this chairman, this central authority, will somehow contrive to sign a report embodying the specialized knowledge and reconciling the apparently hopeless disagreements of all factions concerned. These factions can be called, for convenience, the poet's sub-personalities."[19] Later he recalls this analogy in slightly different terms: "I have ... attempted to show Poetry as the Recorder's *précis* of a warm debate between the members of the poet's mental Senate on some unusually controversial subject."[20] He also offers a more colloquial version: "The poet is consciously or unconsciously always either taking in or giving out; he hears, observes, weighs, guesses, condenses, idealizes, and the new ideas troop quietly into his mind until suddenly every now and again two of them violently quarrel and drag into the fight a group of other ideas that have been loitering about at the back of his mind for years; there is great excitement, noise and bloodshed, with finally a reconciliation and drinks all round. The poet writes a tactful police report on the affair and there is the poem."[21] Given Graves's service as an officer in the Great War (often involved in military courts charged with disciplining soldiers for drunkenness, swearing, fighting, and so on), this final version of the analogy actually anticipates the allusion to the Great War constituted by Richards's reference to the Treaty of Versailles. And of course the language of "reconciliation" in Graves's analogy is directly echoed by the language of "conciliation" in Richards's version of the analogy.

•

In *The Philosophy of Rhetoric* (1936), Richards finally recognizes the affinity between his own perspective on the overdetermination of meaning in poetry and Freud's with respect to the unconscious: "Freud taught us that a dream may mean a dozen different things; he has persuaded us that some symbols are, as he says, 'over-determined.'"[22] Richards now accepts the extension of this paradigm to the study of literature that Graves was encouraging almost fifteen years earlier: Freud's "theorem goes further" than the study of dream symbols "and regards all discourse – outside the technicalities of science – as over-determined, as having multiplicity of meaning. It can illustrate this view from almost any of the great controversies. And it offers us – by restraining the One and Only One True Meaning Superstition – a better hope, I believe, of profiting from the controversies."[23] Of course it was the One and Only One True Meaning Superstition with which he had tried to restrain Graves's Freudian reading of "Kubla Khan." Now Richards advances via Freud's teaching a "controversy" theory that recalls Graves's "conflict theory" and the analogy by which he often explained it: "A controversy is normally an exploitation of a systematic set of misunderstandings for war-like purposes. This theorem suggests that the swords of dispute might be turned into plough shares."[24]

Russo suggests that Richards's recognition of the relation between his own work and Freud's came "rather late," yet I would suggest it is a case of "better late than never."[25] This is especially true when compared with the lack of any recognition at all by Richards of his position's affinities with Graves's insight that overdetermination of meaning can be found not just in English poetry, but also (as Richards notes ten years after the publication of *Impenetrability*, and fifteen years after Graves's letter to the Society for Pure English, reproduced as the final chapter of *On English Poetry*) in every non-scientific use of the English language generally.

Graves repudiates the possibility of any single, simple determiner of meaning in poetry: "I wish to stress two important psychological phenomena: first, that no poet can ever rationally state beforehand what he is going to write about: second, that no poet can rationally state exactly what he has written and why; in effect, what the conflict is or what the new factor is that solves the conflict, until after completely emerging from the mood that made him write the poem. In the second case he may find it impossible to trace even in outline the history of every emblem that occurs in the poem, and any explanation of the poem in terms of the logical reasoning that demands a single recognizable character for every statement made in the poem will be inadequate in face of the associative complexities and absurdities that the multiple vision of the poet produces."[26]

Graves restates here positions outlined in *On English Poetry*, where his oft-repeated claim is that overdetermination of meaning in dream and in inspired and fantastic romantic poetry is not just the norm, but is in fact the rule: "Prose in its most prosy form seems to be the art of accurate statement by suppressing as far as possible the latent associations of words; for the convenience of his readers the standard prose-writer uses an accurate logical phrasing in which … he only says what he at first appears to say. In Poetry the implication is more important than the manifest statement; the underlying associations of every word are marshalled carefully."[27] In "all true poetry," he insists, "the underlying associations of each word in a poem form close combinations of emotion unexpressed by the bare verbal pattern."[28] The carefully marshalled associations underlying the manifest content of the poem inevitably surprise readers incapable of the "fusion … of apparently contradictory emotional ideas" that the poet has achieved, and so "the power of surprise … marks all true poetry."[29] Graves offers his readers a further surprise by suggesting that the underlying associations of words is not something that can be kept out of language; they can only be controlled, for they are a property of language itself: whether the language is Chinese or English, the undercurrents of allusion contained in every word make possible in poetry a "pattern underneath."[30]

Russo goes on to observe that "although their intellectual tradition and approach are entirely different, there are parallels between Richards' comments on equilibrium and Freud … In both thinkers there is an awareness of the person's need for equilibrium and an equal awareness of the dangers of habit and entrapment."[31] This parallel need not be regarded as coincidence, for Graves is acknowledged by Richards as someone mediating to him certain aspects of Freud's work, and Graves foregrounds in his conflict theory the simultaneously balancing progressive functions of poetic consciousness. To recognize parallels between the work of Richards and the work of Freud is implicitly to note the effect of Graves's unrecognized and unacknowledged influence on Richards.

•

That Graves influenced Richards is clear. Graves did not always make sense for Richards, but Richards often found that there was sense enough to be recovered from what Graves said to make it worthwhile to say it again in his own words and on his own terms. Graves certainly introduced and explored topics in a fitful way, offering in *On English Poetry* a book divided into dozens of sections of what he called merely "notebook reflections" ("I have dispensed with a continuous argument, and so the sections either stand independently or are intended to get their force by suggestive neighbourliness rather than by logical force"), but Richards found in many cases the suggestive neighbourliness of topics like "*Vers Libre*," "Reading Aloud," and "On Writing Musically" were very much worth systematic and logical exposition in chapters of his own such as "Rhythm and Metre" in *Principles of Literary Criticism*. In essays by Graves such as "What is Bad Poetry?" Richards found a number of points concerning poetry as communication worth much further reflection and development. And, in the essays collected in *Poetic Unreason*, he found many ideas close to his own, which he later communicated more simply, especially in *Science and Poetry*.

Although the proportion of his early work that was influenced by Graves was not as large as that of Empson's, Richards nonetheless owed Graves a great deal, especially regarding his gradual acceptance that the ideal of a "simple explanation" for poetry, an explanation grounded in "actual sources," needed to be supplemented by a "Theory of the Double Self." Richards ultimately discovered that proper appreciation of poetry requires that one face "the gravest dangers" after all.

Acknowledgement of the debt that he owed Graves would not have gone amiss. But of course times were different then. And besides, Richards did not regard Graves's ideas as proper company for a serious academic to keep.

14

Riding Corrects Richards (and Graves)

As a literary theorist, Richards was increasingly a force in his own right throughout the 1920s. By the end of the decade, he was more famous and more influential than Graves – at least in academic circles. Graves must have been aware of his work. Richards's books were being reviewed in periodicals that Graves read and in which he published his own essays and reviews. Certainly his collaborator Laura Riding knew Richards's work. In fact, her strong reaction against Richards proved frequently to be the occasion for her explicit or implicit correction of Graves's early work. Graves was never the same afterwards. Nor, in a number of important respects, was Richards.

Graves was presumably aware that he had been singled out in *Principles of Literary Criticism* as representing one of "the gravest dangers" concerning the "possible applications of psychology in criticism."[1] Reading the section on Richards in *The Reader over Your Shoulder: A Handbook for Writers of English Prose* (1943), which Graves co-wrote with Alan Hodge, one suspects that he was not only aware of this, but also nursed a bit of a grudge about it. The sample of Richards's writing is one of the longest of the more than fifty chosen for examination and occurs just three paragraphs after Richards ridicules Graves's "thoroughgoing Freudian onslaught" on Coleridge's "Kubla Khan."[2]

If Graves's voice is the dominant one in the comments about Richards's prose (as it seems to have been dominant in comments about writing by other contemporaries such as T.S. Eliot, Ezra Pound, Ernest Hemingway, Aldous Huxley, F.R. Leavis, C. Day-Lewis, Desmond MacCarthy, J. Middleton Murry, George Bernard

Shaw, and Stephen Spender), one can certainly see what he says about Richards as payback. He rewrites Richards's paragraph as he claims it ought to have been written, and explains that any discrepancy between his own "Fair Copy" and the original paragraph is Richards's own fault:

> If I.A. Richards really finds the communication of simple experiences so much more difficult than most people do, this is probably because he avoids defining the terms he uses: here, for example, he does not explain what "the arts" are, what "values" are, who it is who decides about "values," or who is thought to have usurped the functions of the artist and the poet. Also, the argument is incomplete, repetitive and disordered, and the language an uneasy mixture of Victorian literary incantation ... and bald modern laboratory exposition ... Our alternative version may not represent exactly what I.A. Richards had in mind; but it is the nearest we can get to a coherent statement, with the materials supplied by him.[3]

Richards's rhetorical excess in his dismissal of Graves in *Principles of Literary Criticism* is matched here by Graves's rhetorical excess (relative to the other such comments in his book) in his dismissal of Richards. To complain that Richards neither fully defines terms nor fully explains issues in a particular paragraph found thirty pages into a book that clearly enough defines such terms and explains such issues elsewhere is not fair: certain terms appear undefined and certain issues seem unexplained only because the paragraph that Graves examines is removed from its context. No one who reads *Principles of Literary Criticism* would have any doubts about where in the book the answers to the questions that Graves poses are to be found.

But perhaps part of Graves's fun comes from re-issuing in his own voice – the "Fair Copy" into which he translates Richards's prose – a description of the nature and function of poetry that he must have believed Richards had originally borrowed from him. When Graves was reading Richards in preparation for treating him in *The Reader over Your Shoulder*, he actually wrote to a friend: "I had never read Richards before – not word for word – what a crook he seems to be!"[4] The "Fair copy" that he produces from Richards's paragraph would not have looked out of place in either *On English Poetry* or *Poetic Unreason*, which may be exactly his point:

> The working out of a theory by which to reckon, account for, and compare the intrinsic values of spiritual [?] experience, implies the study of poems and works of art – no other evidence being so helpful – in an investigation both of the circumstances in which they were produced and of the communicative power which they exercise. Poems and works of art are accurate and lasting records of certain tranquil hours in the lives of exceptionally sensitive people, when their vision has been keener, their range of observation wider, their faculty for co-ordinating intricate facts and possibilities stronger, and their power of expression more felicitous than usual ... The popular view that the poet's divinatory function has been usurped by the scientist, and the artist's priestly function by the philosopher, shows a vague understanding that, when properly consulted, poems and works of art yield the right answer to many questions about the comparative value of experiences.[5]

One recognizes here Graves's picture of the poet as a harmonizer of diverse experiences and interests within himself and within his community; one so good at this work that his words are often mistaken for those of God.

•

In this text of 1943, now that the relationship between Graves and Riding was over, Graves was free to show how little he had moved beyond his theorizing about literature in the 1920s. The first and second chapters of *The Reader over Your Shoulder* lift ideas and sentences right out of *Impenetrability*. Graves observes that "The vernacular freedom of English allows many meanings, complex and simple, to be struck from the interplay of words, which in Greek or Latin or even French would be ruled out by the formal relationships insisted on by grammatic logic."[6] In fact, when one compares English to other European languages, one finds that "none other admits of such poetic exquisiteness, and often the apparent chaos is only the untidiness of a workshop in which a great deal of repair and other work is in progress: the benches are crowded, the corners are piled with lumber, but the old workman can lay his hand on whatever spare parts or accessories he needs, or at least on the right tools and materials for improvising them."[7] "The English method," we read, "tends to ambiguity and obscurity of expression in any but the most careful writing"; in fact, "English writers of prose and poetry find that, so soon as a gust of natural feeling snatches away the merely verbal disguise in which their phrases are dressed, the pictorial images stand out sharply and either enliven and enforce the argument or desert it and go on a digressive ramble."[8]

Similarly, passages in the third chapter recall *On English Poetry*, *The Meaning of Dreams*, and *Poetic Unreason*. Graves finds occasion once more to observe that for Keats "La Belle Dame sans Merci" "seems to have been a mixture of Fanny Brawne, with whom he was hopelessly in love, Consumption, which had carried off his brother Tom and was to kill him too, and the intractable spirit of poetry."[9] Affirming that "Poetic meaning ... is contained in the complicated correspondence between the words used, regarding both as sense and as sound, and in latent meanings of the words evoked by the rhythmic spell," he also reminds readers of his great abilities as a close reader by analyzing a stanza of the poem that "presents a simple story situation" ("I saw pale kings and princes too,/Pale warriors, death pale were they all –/They cried 'La Belle Dame Sans Merci/Hath thee in thrall'"): "One notes how the conventional phrase 'She has enthralled you,' by being resolved into its original elements, recovers its metaphorical force of 'has you in slavery'; and how the internal rhyme of *merci* with *thee* echoes in the mind and gives 'thee' the force of 'thee too'; and how the variation of the vowel-sounds gives iridescence to the lines; and how well-suited to the sense the alliteration is; and what a shiver comes with the word 'warriors.'"[10]

Graves also recalls in this later work the importance in the 1920s of the development of "slow reading" techniques for poetry: "while the prose writer must nowadays assume his reader to be a busy person whose eye sweeps along the page at a fairly steady rate, seldom pausing long even at key passages, the poet ... still assumes his reader to have perfect leisure and patience for dwelling on each word in a poem and appreciating its relation with every other. Prose, in fact, is expected to reveal its full content at first reading; poetry only at third or fourth. The first glance at a poem takes in its prose sense as a base on which to build up the poetic sense ... The unusual juxtaposition of two words may carry a weight of meaning over which a thoughtful reader will spend as much time as over a page or more of prose argument."[11] As we shall see in chapters to follow, these ideas were at the heart of the conversation between the texts of Richards and those of Riding and Graves.

•

The question arises, however, as to when Graves *first* read *Principles of Literary Criticism*. One presumes that he would have read at least the offending pages shortly after they were published. Surely friends and acquaintances would have drawn his attention to them. Certainly Graves was very alert to how he was treated in print during the period of his collaboration with Riding. As we have seen, at the beginning of *A Pamphlet Against Anthologies* the two note how many reviewers have treated Graves as the sole author of *A Survey of Modernist Poetry*. They retained a clipping agency to forward references to their work when they left the country for Mallorca and, even in this out-of-the-way place, it took little time for them to learn that Empson had misrepresented *A Survey of Modernist Poetry* as having been written by Graves alone. (Empson's book was published in November of 1930, and by the end of January, 1931, their press clipping agency had sent them a copy of a review of *Seven Types of Ambiguity* in which this error was committed.)[12] Assuming that Graves was as attentive to references to his individual work as he was to references to his collaboration with Riding, and noting that he was part of the social network of both modernist writers and Oxford professors when *Principles of Literary Criticism* came out, news of his treatment in Richards's book must have reached him at least as fast as news of his treatment in Empson's, whether or not he employed a press clipping agency at this time.

Furthermore, given his growing stature as a literary theorist in the early 1920s, it is difficult to believe that Graves would not have read Richards's widely noted book on his own initiative. Just as students like Empson mentioned Graves to Richards at Cambridge, so students at Graves's talks at universities such as Oxford and Leeds may have asked Graves questions about Richards's early works like *The Foundation of Aesthetics* and *The Meaning of Meaning*. And of course others were talking and writing about Richards: T.S. Eliot, Graves's friendly acquaintance at this point, reviewed Richards's work favourably in *The Criterion*, a journal to which Graves contributed, and in which he tried throughout 1926 to place some of Riding's essays. Graves's explanation in *Poetic Unreason* that "there are few particular references in the present volume to other treatises on aesthetics because the philosophical and psychological premises to which these works invariably refer are not referred to here" implies that he is familiar with such treatises on aesthetics.[13]

However, it is unlikely that Graves read *Principles of Literary Criticism* in time for it to have influenced *Poetic Unreason*, for although it was published in 1925, the original essays first appeared between 1922 and 1923, well before Richards's book was published.[14] The first chapter of *Poetic Unreason* is a lecture delivered at Leeds University in 1922. Other chapters appeared in whole or in part in British and American reviews and journals between 1922 and 1923.[15] Arthur Clutton-Brock, who died on 8 January 1924, is referred to as having reviewed much of the book's contents and criticized its main argument.[16]

By the time that Graves began writing *A Survey of Modernist Poetry* in 1926, however, it is clear that even if he had not yet read *Principles of Literary Criticism*, Riding had read it. She was well aware of Richards's work when she was writing both *Contemporaries and Snobs* (published February 1928) and *Anarchism is Not Enough* (published May 1928). In the latter, Riding devotes extensive attention to the (mis)understanding of language generally, and of poetic language in particular, in *The Meaning of Meaning*, *Principles of Literary Criticism*, and *Science and Poetry*. The allusions to Richards in *Contemporaries and Snobs*, combined with internal evidence that indicates that she is writing the book during the fall of 1926, suggest that Riding is very familiar with Richards's work as she and Graves begin their collaboration on *A Survey of Modernist Poetry*. In fact, on the basis of her explicit engagement with Richards's work in *Anarchism is Not Enough*, one can see that Riding was working out her response to Richards while writing her essay "T.E. Hulme, The New Barbarism, and Gertrude Stein" in 1926 – the essay that Graves revised with her so that it could serve as their concluding chapter in *A Survey of Modernist Poetry*.

•

In *Anarchism Is Not Enough*, Riding scorns what she identifies as a systematic denigration of poetic language rooted in Richards's veneration of scientific knowledge. *The Meaning of Meaning* is a "science-proud collation of verbal niceties," a "confused mixture of philosophy, psychology, ethnology and literature": "To Mr. Ogden and Mr. Richards language is ideally a neutral region of literalness between reality and its human perception. Signs … being the closest the perceiving mind can come to reality, must for convenience be regarded as reality itself; the more faithfully they are defined as signs, the more literally they represent reality. There is no evidence anywhere in this book that perception is properly anything other than a slave of reality."[17] She complains that "the conclusion of this study … is that man has no right to meaning: meaning is the property of reality."[18] For Riding, Richards is an imperial agent of science and, as such, an enemy of poetry.

In the essay "Poetry and the Literary Universe," the first of three in the slightly earlier book *Contemporaries and Snobs*, Riding makes the same point about how the empire of concrete fact threatens poetry, but without mentioning Richards by name: "the victorious concrete intelligence seems to have taken possession of all the facts of actual experience."[19] The language in the earlier book – "the slaves of this knowledge-material can imagine no state of activity which shall not be dependent on it" – is the same as that in *Anarchism Is Not Enough*.[20] She celebrates in the latter a "disobedient perception" that can imagine activity not dependent on the knowledge-material of science, and complains that in *The Meaning of Meaning* "there is no hint that individual perception, instead of making a separate approximation of the general sign conveying the object, does in fact where originality is maintained experience a revulsion from the object or event concerned."[21] Similarly, she argues in "Poetry and the Literary Universe" that "the slaves of this knowledge-material … cannot understand that the poet can have experience of it as an independent mind reducing authoritative mass to unauthoritative ideas."[22] Riding may not have named Richards as her representative of this possessive and apparently "victorious concrete intelligence" until she writes *Anarchism Is Not Enough*, but it is clear that she has begun to quarrel with him in the essays of the earlier book *Contemporaries and Snobs*.[23]

Riding claims that it is the "snobbism" of literary critics who are "knowledge-slaves" (taking everything, and especially poetry, "with a grain of scientific salt") that "drives poets who stand in fear of the knowledge-hierarchy to profess only the single reality of the poetic mind – what we may call the apologetic absolute. The result is poetry whose only subject is the psychology of the poet and whose final value is scientific."[24] According to Riding, whether the poem is taken to refer to the collective reality of the ostensibly objective world described by the physical sciences or the individual reality of the ostensibly subjective world described by the psychological sciences, "in both cases the one belief from which the poetic mind must not disconnect itself is the belief in reality."[25] Richards is her primary target in this criticism of false paradigms for understanding and interpreting poetry, but she is also explaining here the problem she finds with Graves's conflict theory. From her point of view Graves partakes of "the apologetic absolute" of psychology, for the goal of his early books is to promote detailed analysis as a way of accommodating traditional emotional approaches to poetry to the new science of psychology. The distinction that Richards and Graves would make between their respectively behaviourist and more-or-less Freudian psychological paradigms makes no difference to her: in each case, the poem refers to a reality to be found in the psychological state of the poet at the time of composition.

Of course there is much that Riding accepts in Graves's early criticism, and much that she appropriates from it. She agrees with the terms by which Graves distinguishes between classicism and romanticism, for instance, celebrating the latter as representing the truly poetic mind because it is not subordinated to the world of logic, knowledge, and fact. Riding effectively appropriates Graves's characterization of the classical impulse as an Aristotelian project of establishing a knowledge-hierarchy within which poetry is subordinated to public, practical purposes. According to Graves, Aristotle "was intending to make poetry conform to an absolute system, to weed it of all the symbolic extravagances and impossibilities of the dream state from which romantic poetry has always originated, and to confine it within rational and educative limits. Drama was with him chiefly an intuitive imitation of how typical men think and react upon each other when variously stimulated; lyric poetry, apart from certain approved imitations of romantic characters, was logically harmonious and rational statement."[26]

She effectively accepts Graves's characterization of English as a romantically poetic language ready at the least lapse of a writer's attention to resist the paradigms by which the "knowledge-material" and the "knowledge-hierarchy" maintain hegemony in collective social reality and individual psychological reality.[27] Similarly, she agrees with Graves's assertion of "the rule that 'Poetry contains nothing haphazard'": "By this rule I mean that if a poem, poem-sequence or drama is an allegory of genuine emotional experience and not a mere cold-blooded exercise, no striking detail and no juxtaposition of apparently irrelevant themes which it contains can be denied at any rate a personal significance."[28] Regarding the poem's meaning as its own self-authorizing event (and not as an allegory of the poet's experience, or the reader's, or the critic's, or the scientist's, or anything else), Riding certainly agrees that there is nothing haphazard in any real poem, but she regards Graves's reference by rule to a foundation of "personal significance" as requiring correction: no striking detail and no juxtaposition of apparently irrelevant themes which a poem contains can be denied at any rate a *poetic* significance.

Riding develops as her own axiom Graves's suggestion that "Poetry is not as some people want it to be, a condensation and rearrangement of past events, according to a preconceived logical structure, not merely a combination of historic strands, but a new entity whose past is past."[29] She recognizes in statements like this what Graves does not: that he here disavows his earlier model of poetry as "a cipher that can usually be decoded from another context."[30] Riding finds the grounding of Graves's conflict theory in the psychological experience of the poet a product of "fear of the knowledge-hierarchy," a hierarchy "by which poetry may manage to survive" in the world of scientific fact and objective knowledge if the poet is willing "to profess only the single reality of the poetic mind."[31] But this is "to treat poetry as if it were a science," whereas "The poem itself is supreme, above persons; judging rather than judged; keeping criticism at a respectful distance; it is even able to make a reader of its author. It comes to be because an individual mind is clear enough to perceive it and then to become its instrument. Criticism can only have authority over the poem if the poet's mind was from the start not sufficiently clear, sufficiently free of criticism; if it obeyed an existing, that is, past order of reality."[32]

The work that obeys a past order of reality is a false poem: "The creative history of the false poem is the age, the author sensible of the age and the set of outer circumstances involved in his delicate adjustment to the age at a particular moment, in a particular place. Nothing remains beyond this, no life, no element, untranslatable except in the terms provided by the poem itself. In the true poem these terms form a measurement that hitherto did not exist."[33] The true poem is not a cipher to be decoded from another context. Riding sees it as nothing or "no thing" in the way Sartre sees a person as nothing or "no thing": in each case, existence precedes essence in such a way that *to do* is *to be*: "The word *poem* itself is an ever new meaning of an ever new combination of *doing* and *making* as one act, with a third inference of *being* perpetuating these in dynamic form. The only difference between a poem and a person is that in a poem *being* is the final state, in a person the preliminary state. These two kinds of realities, that of the person, that of the poem, stand at one end and the other of the poet's mind, which is but progressive experience made into a recurrent sequence circulating between one kind of reality and the other without destroying one reality in the other."[34] From Riding's point of view, Graves's conflict theory threatens to destroy the reality of the poem by subsuming it within the personal reality of the poet.

Richards is not the only representative of the imperialistic practical intellect. In T.E. Hulme and T.S. Eliot, Riding identifies two more dangerously influential contemporaries devoted to "knowledge-material" and the "knowledge-hierarchy." She notes that "T.S. Eliot observed some time ago that 'the conditions which may be considered to be unfavourable to the writing of good poetry are unfavourable to the writing of good criticism,'" complaining that "this implies that the reality of poetry is externally, not internally derived."[35] In *A Survey of Modernist Poetry*, she and Graves have Eliot's "Tradition and the Individual Talent" in mind when they complain that the atmosphere created by "this new primitive stage ... in contemporary poetry" hampers "those who are poets by nature ... with the considerations of all the poets who have ever written or may be writing or may ever write – not only in the English language but in all languages of the world under every possible social organization. It invents a communal poetic mind which sits over the individual poet whenever he writes; it binds him with the necessity of writing correctly in extension of the tradition, the world tradition of poetry; and so makes poetry internally an even narrower period activity than it is forced to be by outside influences."[36] The panopticon of tradition disciplines the individual talent by an interior colonization at the hands of the historical sense.

Similarly, Riding notes that T.E. Hulme "advocated a discipline that would control both time and the creator through the impersonal severity, the absoluteness, in which artistic forms might be conceived. The product of this 'objective' objectivity is therefore pure, hard, non-sympathetic. It is not intelligent: that is, it is not materialistically interpretative, but material. It is not emotional: that is, it is not imaginatively imitative but unimaginatively representational. It is a non-human object."[37] Whether from Richards, or Eliot, or Hulme, Riding will have none of this subordination of the human to the non-human, especially in poetry.

One can see that Riding works out her reaction to *The Meaning of Meaning*, *Principles of Literary Criticism*, and *Science and Poetry* in this analysis of Hulme and Eliot in *Contemporaries and Snobs*. Hulme's "unimaginatively representational ... non-human object" is an example of the attitude toward language endorsed, according to Riding, by Ogden and Richards: to them, words "are certified scientific representatives of the natural objects, or constructions of objects called events ... [T]he more faithfully they are defined as signs, the more literally they represent reality."[38] The conclusion of Ogden and Richards, Riding finds, is that "man has no right to meaning."[39] Eliot's poetry of a "reality ... externally, not internally derived" is another example of this attitude toward language according to which "meaning is the property of reality, which is to be known scientifically."[40]

According to Riding, for Richards, "evocative (poetic) speech is false *by itself* ... it is scientifically admissible only where it shows close dependence on symbols meaningless in themselves but showing close, scientific dependence on reality."[41] In *Science and Poetry*, she observes, "we are returned to the assumption scattered through the pages of *The Meaning of Meaning*, that man has no right to meaning ... [T]he one belief from which the poetic mind must not disconnect itself is the belief in reality; which proves itself ... to be only the most advanced 'contemporary background' appreciable."[42]

The language of Riding's analysis of Richards in *Anarchism Is Not Enough* is the same as the language of her analysis of Hulme and Eliot throughout *Contemporaries and Snobs*, the revised central essay of which serves as the concluding chapter of *A Survey of Modernist Poetry*. The latter observes that in Hulme's programme for a new barbarism in poetry, "Language ... had to be reorganized, used as if afresh, cleansed of its experience ... Words had to be reduced to their least historical value; the purer they could be made, the more eternally immediate and present they would be; they could express the absolute at the same time as they expressed the age. Or at any rate this was the logical effect of scientific barbarism if taken literally."[43] This reference to "scientific barbarism" (the only time the phrase is used) certainly hints at the influence of Ogden and Richards behind the critique of Hulme and Eliot in *A Survey of Modernist Poetry*. Ogden and Richards are invoked in *Anarchism Is Not Enough* as the ones who explain *scientifically* the theory according to which reality (whether collective or individual) is "the organ of communication and author of symbols": "The symbolism of the individual real in its scientific aspect is best explained in C.K. Ogden's and I.A. Richards' *The Meaning of Meaning*," a "confused mixture of philosophy, psychology, ethnology and literature," a "science-proud collation of verbal niceties."[44] They offer a scientific perspective on the vulgar artist's belief that his language is "not symbolic, but literal, not 'artistic' but natural. It ... makes everything it touches equally significant, physical, real" because "To Mr. Ogden and Mr. Richards language is ideally a neutral region of literalness between reality and its human perception."[45]

Later in *A Survey of Modernist Poetry,* Riding and Graves explain Hulme's programme to achieve a poetry of "direct communication," "direct communication referring to an immediate ideal of intelligibility," in similar terms: "since language had been tainted by false experiences, much of the energy ... had to be devoted to an attack on the ordinary language of communication."[46] This anticipates Riding's complaint a year later in *Anarchism is Not Enough* that Ogden and Richards regard language not regulated by their limited list of definitions as "disobedient"; an "Enchanted Wood of Words"; an unreformed grammar susceptible to the "treachery of words" that are liable to be "vulgar stage-players of images" rather than the reality that "man's mind, like a dust-cloud, is assumed to obscure from himself."[47]

•

It is just possible, I suppose, that before she read Richards's early works Riding evolved a critique of Hulme and Eliot as enslaved to "knowledge-material" and "the knowledge-hierarchy," and that she subsequently recognized that this also applied to Richards. Yet it seems much more likely that she acquired through reflection on Richards's work the metaphysical language of her critique of others who mistook knowledge as reflecting or indicating a hierarchy of reality. And it seems equally likely that it was her reaction to Richards that allowed her to recognize a subordination of poetry to an external reality as something that was common to the criticism of Hulme and Eliot as well – and even common to the conflict theory of her collaborator Graves.

In *Contemporaries and Snobs* and in *Survey*'s revised version of the *Contemporaries and Snobs* essay "T.E. Hulme, the New Barbarism, and Gertrude Stein," Riding actually refers to *The Meaning of Meaning* indirectly. She concludes of Hulme's "dry theory of historical objectivity" that "it shows the creator defeated by progress taking refuge in a petulant barbarism."[48] The "barbarism" to which she refers, the "new barbarism" of her essay's title, is a twentieth-century version of the ancient "barbaric absolute": the identification of an absolute as "the divine source of 'things.'"[49] She implies that Hulme and Eliot are new barbarians in their nostalgia for "the 'things' which are supposed to be revealed in direct communication ('things' in which apparently the first principle inheres)."[50]

Riding's term, "barbarism," and her understanding of it as designating a magically logocentric attitude toward language, allude to *The Meaning of Meaning*, wherein Ogden and Richards devote an early chapter, "The Power of Words," to the role of barbarism in ancient and contemporary understandings of the power and purpose of language. In particular, they review "the linguistic illusions of primitive man," warning that since "the verbal machinery on which we so readily rely ... was set up by him," and that since "from the structure of our language we can hardly even think of escaping," we may still be in the grip of "other illusions hardly less gross and not more easily eradicable" than those of "arboreal man."[51] Reviewing the superstitious attitude toward words and names in a wide variety of ancient sources including the religion of ancient Egypt, the thought of Greek philosophers from Heraclitus and Pythagoras to Plato, the Book of Revelation, and the fairy tales of Europe, the authors suggest that "it is clear that in the days before psychological analysis was possible the evidence for a special world of words of power, for *nomina* as *numina*, must have appeared overwhelming."[52] Noting that "in Frazer's *Golden Bough* numerous examples of word taboos are collected to show the universality of the attitude," they quote Frazer to the effect that this attitude is a barbarism that continues in the modern world: "Superstitions survive because, while they shock the views of enlightened members of the community, they are still in harmony with the thoughts and feelings of others, who, though they are drilled by their betters into an appearance of civilization, remain barbarians or savages at heart."[53] They then point out that the most enlightened members of their own community are not immune to this barbarism: "The persistence of the primitive linguistic outlook not only throughout the whole religious world, but in the work of the profoundest thinkers, is indeed one of the most curious features of modern thought. The philosophy of the nineteenth century was dominated by an idealist tradition in which the elaboration of monstrous symbolic machinery (the Hegelian Dialectic provides a striking example) was substituted for direct research, and occupied the centre of attention. The twentieth century opened with a subtle analysis of the mysteries of mathematics on the basis of a 'Platonism' even more pronounced than that of certain Critical Realists of 1921."[54]

One of Riding's pleasures by means of her phrase "the new barbarism" is to hoist Ogden and Richards with their own petard. Her point is that for all their disdain for barbarism, Ogden and Richards – even if only "for convenience" – treat signs "as reality itself," implying that "the more faithfully they are defined as signs, the more literally they represent reality."[55] What is this but a new barbarism? According to Riding and Graves, "Poetry in the past had found it expedient to accept barbaric philosophical or religious 'ideas' and to cast itself within the limits imposed by them. They were barbaric ideas because they were large but definite; infinite, yet fixed by the way that they fixed man; crude and unshaded but incontestable – such as the barbaric idea of God ... A barbaric view or order depends on the underlying conception of a crude, undifferentiated, infinite, all-contemporaneous time, and of a humanity co-existent with this time, a humanity consolidated as a mass and not composed of individuals."[56] In *Anarchism is Not Enough*, Riding rejects *The Meaning of Meaning* paradigm according to which "meaning is the property of reality" in favour of the "disobedient perception" of the "individual" dedicated to maintaining "originality": "the very genesis or *utterance* of a sign" is not "a separate approximation of the general sign conveying the object" but rather "a revulsion from the object concerned," "an assertion of the independence of the mind against what the authors call the sign situation."[57]

Riding and Graves characterise Hulme's theoretical project (one endorsed by Eliot in both his critical prose and his poetic practice) as that Nietzsche attributes to Socrates: correcting existence. Since "his concept of the absolute (the search for the absolute is the chief concern ... of 'pure' philosophy) derides any idea of relativity," Hulme "stumbled on the need which art – painting or sculpture or poetry – had to be philosophically organized and corrected."[58] "Entering a new artificially barbaric era," according to Riding and Graves, "painting and sculpture merely had to revert to barbaric modes – Negroid, Oceanic, Aztec, Egyptian, Chinese, archaic Greek – creating modern forms as if in primitive times; forms primitive, obedient to the conventions which they accepted, therefore final, absolute, 'abstract.'"[59] Riding and Graves criticize the new barbaric art in the same way Ogden and Richards criticise Bertrand Russell's "primitive linguistic outlook" in *The Principles of Mathematics*: here "the world of universals" "was rehabilitated," "a modern Platonism reconstructed" where "everything is 'unchangeable, rigid, exact, delightful to the mathematician, the logician, the builder of metaphysical systems, and all who love perfection more than life.'"[60] Agreeing with the criticism by Ogden and Richards of those whose outlook betrays that they love perfection more than life, Riding and Graves observe that Ogden and Richards themselves suffer from the same illusion.

However difficult the task that lies ahead, "what language already does," Ogden and Richards suggest, "is the ground for hope that it may in time be made fully to perform its functions."[61] The problem lies with those uninterested "to pass beyond the mere exchange of accepted and familiar phrases," those "who, having never been troubled by thought, have never found any difficulty expressing it," those with "an uncritical reliance upon speech" despite "the fruitless questionings and bewilderment caused by the irrelevancies and the intrinsic peculiarities of words."[62] Whereas poetry and sculpture can "revert to barbaric modes" as if the renaissance and romanticism had never occurred, "poetry could not seemingly submit itself to an *as if*, because its expressive medium, language, had been intrinsically affected not only by the works in which it had been used but also by the non-poetic uses of which language is capable."[63] Transposing the rhetoric of Ogden and Richards to their own characterization of the new barbarism, Riding and Graves suggest that Hulme and Eliot agree that "since language had been tainted by false experience," poetry "had to be devoted to an attack on the ordinary language of communication" if it were to recover the possibility of "direct communication."[64] And so "Language, therefore, had to be reorganized, used as if afresh, cleansed of its experience: to be as 'pure' and 'abstract' as colour or stone. Words had to be reduced to their least historical value; the purer they could be made, the more eternally immediate and present they would be; they could express the absolute at the same time as they expressed the age. Or this was at any rate the logical effect of scientific barbarism if taken literally."[65] The "scientific barbarism" in question is the attitude toward language of Ogden and Richards in *The Meaning of Meaning*, which Riding and Graves find Hulme and Eliot reflecting and refracting in the theories and practices of their modernist aesthetic.

So it is clear not only that Riding and Graves know well the work of Richards as they write *A Survey of Modernist Poetry*, but also that they organize the book so as to conclude it with a repudiation of the "scientific barbarism" that has crept into both literary theory and modernist poetry by means of Richards, Hulme, and Eliot. Otherwise, however, Graves seems to have been content to watch Riding tackle Richards on her own. She seems to have persuaded Graves that Richards's criticism of his psychological method of interpreting literature was an attack on a scientific barbarism from which they both suffered. To collaborate with Riding, he had to accept that defending his reading of "Kubla Khan" against Richards's attack would be retrograde. Only after Riding and Graves had separated did Graves have a go at Richards on *his* own in *The Reader over Your Shoulder*, and by then the history between them had already been made. It simply needed to be recorded and set straight.

15

Asserting the Poem's Autonomy contra Richards

By his criticism of H.D.'s poetry in the chapter "Badness in Poetry" in *Principles of Literary Criticism*, Richards implies a method for reading modernist poetry as a whole that Riding and Graves repudiate in *A Survey of Modernist Poetry*. Richards exposes the poverty of H.D.'s poetry: what results from its "tenuousness and ambiguity" "is almost independent of the author."[1] Riding and Graves – no fans of H.D. – may be somewhat thankful for this, but Richards exposes here assumptions about the nature of what is communicated in poetry that Riding and (now) Graves vigorously reject. They imply that Richards is representative of critics who fear the freedom that poems like H.D.'s confer on the reader and that he is at the head of those who prefer to find in poetry – to use Riding's phrase criticizing the conception of words that she finds in *The Meaning of Meaning* – a "neutral region of literalness between reality and its human perception."[2] Their point in *A Survey of Modernist Poetry* is that the freedom-fearing professional critic's valuation of poetry as a neutral conduit of concrete reality is wrong-headed. The poem is a reality in its own right, precisely the autonomous aesthetic entity, independent of the poet, that Richards fears in general and that he fears H.D. in particular tends to produce.

Just as Richards seems to have paid close attention in *Principles of Literary Criticism* to Graves's essay "What is Bad Poetry?", so in *A Survey of Modernist Poetry* Riding and Graves seem to have paid particular attention to Richards's chapter in *Principles of Literary Criticism* on "Badness in Poetry." They follow his analysis of H.D.'s poem "The Pool"–

Are you alive?
I touch you.

You quiver like a sea-fish.
I cover you with my net.
What are you – banded one?[3]

– which Richards foregrounds in explanation of his complaint about confusions in contemporary critical terminology: "Sometimes art is bad because communication is defective ... sometimes because the experience communicated is worthless; sometimes for both reasons. It would perhaps be best to restrict the term bad art to cases in which genuine communication does to a considerable degree take place, what is communicated being worthless, and to call the other cases defective art."[4] According to Richards, H.D.'s poem is "an instance of defective communication ... in which it is likely that the original experience had some value."[5]

Riding and Graves follow Richards in observing that questions of communication and questions of value are confused in contemporary criticism. Like Richards, they would prefer that the term "*Bad* ... be the only possible critical term by which a poem could be categorically dismissed."[6] And like Richards again, they note that many critics short-circuit their evaluation of the poem as good or bad by a smug, stultifying comment about its defective communication: "at the present time, regardless of the possible classification of a poem as *good* or *bad* according to the standard it suggests, it is enough for a critic to call a poem *obscure* to relieve himself of the obligation of giving a real criticism of it."[7]

For Riding and Graves, however, Richards is just such a confused critic. When he judges "The Pool" obscure (defective in communication), he shirks his real work as critic, for he relieves himself of the obligation of determining whether or not the experience communicated by H.D.'s poem has any worth by merely gesturing toward "the original experience" that "likely ... had some value." Riding and Graves insist that better criticism of H.D.'s work is possible and necessary. As we shall see, Riding and Graves react to the inadequacy of Richards's criticism of H.D. by proceeding to what they agree with Richards is a "real criticism" of poetry: her poems fail not because they are obscure – she is not "incomprehensible" so she is not failing to communicate experience – but rather they fail because they are bad, for the experience they communicate is worthless.[8]

As an example of poetry "in which communication is successful, where the objection lies to what is communicated," Richards offers Ella Wheeler Wilcox's sonnet "Friendship After Love."[9] According to Richards, Wilcox's poem communicates experience effectively but ought not to have done so, for the impulses that her sonnet evokes are not genuinely reorganized or balanced or reconciled. Comparing a couple's progress from feelings of love to feelings of friendship with the year's progress from the heat of summer to the coolness of autumn, the sonnet has achieved "the soothing effect of aligning the very active Love-Friendship groups of impulses with so settled yet rich a group as the Summer-Autumn simile brings in," and so "the restless spirit is appeased, one of its chief problems is made to seem as if ... it is no problem but a process of nature."[10] Or so at least it seems to the bad reader: "Only for those who make certain conventional, stereotyped maladjustments ... does the magic work."[11] Such readers are in the grip of "stock conventional attitudes."[12] The reaction of good readers to such bad poetry is very different, however, for "those who have adequate impulses as regards *any* of the four main systems involved, Summer, Autumn, Love, Friendship, are not appeased."[13] Sadly, we recall, saving bad readers from their stock responses is not as easy as simply introducing them to good poetry: "a reader who ... thoroughly enters into and enjoys this class of verse, is necessarily so organized that he will fail to respond to poetry. Time and much varied experience might change him sufficiently, but by then he would no longer be able to enjoy such verse, he would no longer be the same person."[14]

Richards's analysis of poems by H.D. and Wilcox foregrounds his conviction that the real value of poetry resides in its reorganization of the reader's experience. Against the background of psychological utilitarianism, Richards explains the function of literature in terms of its ability to reorganize readers towards "free, varied and unwasteful life": "the organization and systematization of which I have been speaking in this chapter are not primarily an affair of conscious planning or arrangement ... We pass as a rule from a chaotic to a better organized state by ways which we know nothing about. Typically through the influence of other minds. Literature and the arts are the chief means by which these influences are diffused."[15] Riding and Graves regard Richards as simply asserting here the superiority of what Riding calls the individual psychological real over what she calls the collective social real. They regard both what Richards defines as good poetry and what he defines as bad poetry as the product of a scientific imperialism that colonizes readers by planting the flag of objective reality. Richards enslaves readers and poems alike, thwarting discovery by readers both of their own independence of mind or originality and of the poem's own unreality or difference from reality.

•

Richards implies in his criticism of "The Pool" a method for reading modernist poetry that Riding and Graves dissect and reject. This is not to say that they were fans of H.D. On the contrary, they argue that "The only excuse for those who once found H.D. 'incomprehensible' is that her work was so thin, so poor, that its emptiness seemed 'perfection,' its insipidity to be concealing a 'secret,' its superficiality so 'glacial' that it created a false 'classical' atmosphere," so they were not necessarily unhappy to find Richards similarly unimpressed by her.[16] Speculating minimally about the experience that H.D. might be trying to communicate in this poem, Richards opines that "it is likely that the original experience had some value."[17] On this point, Riding and Graves disagree: they find in H.D.'s poetry only "a story of feeble personal indecision"; "She was never able ... to reach a real climax in any of her poems"; "the personal reality of the poet ... has been represented with false intensity to make a romantic appeal to the reader."[18]

As we have seen, Riding rejects "personal reality" as the basis of a true poem. The problem for Riding and Graves here is not that H.D.'s "personal reality" – the original experience to which Richards alludes – did not actually have the value that Richards assumes it did. Their point is actually that H.D.'s mistake is to confuse her personal reality with the poem's reality. She is twice in error: she not only infuses her poetry with the insipid, superficial personality that Riding and Graves insult, but she also perpetuates the mistake created by romanticism's appeal to the personal reality of the poet as the basis of poetry. The deficient personality is an incidental matter; the deficiency of the aesthetic is the real problem. Presumably H.D.'s devotion to such an aesthetic makes her personality fair game for *ad hominem* criticism, but it is also the case that Riding and Graves can be cruel in their criticism of other writers.

Riding and Graves repudiate the aesthetic of "personal appeal" as scientific. It seems that under Riding's tutelage Graves now recognizes that the refraction of romanticism through the new science of psychology simply makes it a new corruption of poetry before the altar of concrete fact. As antidote to H.D. in particular, and to the romantic aesthetic of "personal appeal" generally, they point to Emily Dickinson as an equally eccentric and extravagant poet "whose personal reality pervades her work, though she kept it strictly out of her work."[19] Their point, of course, is related to Eliot's assertion in "Tradition and the Individual Talent": the personality of the poet ought not to be confused with the personality of the poem.[20] According to Riding and Graves, "the important part of poetry is now not the personality of the poet as embodied in a poem … but the personality of the poem, its quality of independence from both the reader and the poet, once the poet has separated it from his personality by making it complete – a new and self-explanatory creature"[21] Therefore they can agree with Eliot that "the difference between art and the event is always absolute" and they can agree with Richards that just because "the original experience is presumably slight, tenuous and fleeting," the form of the poem does not have to be correspondingly slight, tenuous and fleeting.[22]

And they can also agree with Richards that H.D.'s poem is incomplete. Insisting that the value of the poem consists in its communication of the poet's original experience, Richards suggests that rather than translating the brevity and simplicity of the experience in question into the formal structure of the poem, H.D. ought to have compensated for the tenuous and ambiguous aspects of the original experience by making the poem longer, more specific, and more complex than it is. The point that Riding and Graves make, however, is not Richards's point, effectively a complaint that the reader's experience of the poem "is almost independent of the author," but rather the opposite of his: their point is that the reader's experience of the poem is *not sufficiently* independent of the author, for H.D. has not – like Dickinson – kept her personality strictly out of the poem: she has not completed the poem because she has not completed her separation from it.

The biggest problem for Riding and Graves here is that Richards's criticism of H.D.'s poem shows that however much he finds fault with this particular Imagist poem, he nonetheless accepts Imagism's main assumptions. His complaint is that the poem's five short lines constitute "the whole link which is to mediate between the experiences of the author and of the reader" and that the poem's "brevity" and "simplicity" make its communication of the poet's original experience "ineffective": "The experience evoked in the reader is not sufficiently specific."[23] On this point, Riding and Graves suggest that "Imagism took for granted the principle that poetry was a translation of certain kinds of subjects into the language that would bring the reader emotionally closest to them. It was assumed that a natural separation existed between the reader and the subject, to be bridged by the manner in which it was presented."[24]

They attribute to Imagism here the aesthetic theory of communication both at the heart of *Principles of Literary Criticism* and at the heart of Graves's own books and essays up to this point. Richards accepts that a poem (Imagist or otherwise) is a vehicle for communicating to the reader an experience outside and other than the poem itself, and so does the pre-Riding Graves. Now, however, Graves aligns himself with Riding in disagreement with such an aesthetic, and therefore with a central aspect of Richards's theory of communication. Moreover, the two of them represent modernist poetry as a whole as disagreeing with such an aesthetic. Although Imagism was associated in practice with H.D., whom many regarded as the purest Imagist, it was associated in theory with Hulme and so it serves Riding and Graves in *A Survey of Modernist Poetry* as an example of poetry gone wrong through the new barbarism. That they identify a sympathy between Richards and Imagism, as they define it, is therefore no surprise, for from their point of view this sympathy is simply a case of one new barbarism saluting and supporting another. They regard Imagism as falling far short of the achievement of modernist poetry: "the modernist poet does not have to talk about the use of images 'to render particulars exactly,' since the poem does not give a rendering of a poetical picture or idea existing outside the poem, but presents the literal substance of poetry."[25] Richards exposes the poverty of H.D.'s poetry just as Riding and Graves do, but he also exposes assumptions about the nature of what is communicated in poetry that Riding and (now) Graves vigorously reject.

Richards concludes his criticism of H.D. by complaining that "the reader here supplies too much of the poem."[26] He speculates about what kind of poem a reader might have come up with "had the poet said only, 'I went and poked about for rocklings and caught the pool itself.'"[27] Richards substitutes for the poem a prose paraphrase. Regarding the value of poetry as consisting in its reorganization of our attitudes and impulses, Richards declares that there is not much difference between a reader's experience of "The Pool" and a reader's experience of Richards's prose statement about a pool: "the reader, who converts what is printed above [the prose paraphrase above] into a poem, would still have been able to construct an experience of equal value; for what results is almost independent of the author."[28]

Noting that "The Pool" lacks "magnitude," suffers from "simplicity," and sacrifices metre and formal structure for the sake of free verse, Richards implicitly condemns it as prose that has been insufficiently poeticized (not much different from, and not really any better than, his own prose statement). Implicitly in the case of H.D.'s poem, that is, and explicitly in the case of his own prose paraphrase of it, Richards understands readers of certain kinds of minimalist modernist poetry to be mandated to turn prose into a poem on their own. That is, since in this exercise Richards does not raise the question of *whether* the reader ought to bring anything to the poem but only the question of just *how much* the reader ought to bring to it, he implies that the interpretive process requires that readers make their own poems out of the prose statement that such a modernist poem constitutes.

This is the very process that Riding and Graves object to as virtually guaranteeing the misunderstanding of modernist poetry. They complain that the tendency to supply a poetical summary of a poem is a recent invention of contemporary critics, an interpretive strategy necessitated by the so-called obscurity of modernist poetry. Echoing Richards's points about H.D.'s poem, they note that the modernist poem seems to the contemporary critic more prose than poetry – at best, a "prose idea in a slightly poetical form" – and so "the reader finds it necessary to make a poetical rather than a more strictly prose summary."[29]

Riding and Graves speculate about how such a person might react to the first two lines of Riding's poem: "The rugged black of anger/Has an uncertain smile border."[30] Perhaps the ostensible obscurity of these lines would lead readers to interpret them as concealing "an incidental satire on the popular poetical sentiment: 'Look around and you will find/Every cloud is silver-lined.'"[31] The point of such speculation is to declare that they do not accept what such an interpretation implies, that the two lines beginning "The Rugged Black of Anger" are "the prose idea as poem" that the reader needs "to amplify along suggested poetical lines."[32] Rather, they see "a discrepancy ... appear between the poem as it stands and the reader's poetical summary of it"; "we ... have not two equivalent meanings but one meaning and another gratuitous meaning derived from it."[33] In other words, there is the "one meaning" and there is the heresy of its paraphrase.

So much for Richards's claim that a reader who substituted the prose paraphrase "I went and poked about for rocklings and caught the pool itself" for the poem "would still have been able to construct an experience of equal value."[34] It would seem to be in response to Richards's disparagement of H.D. that Riding and Graves announce both the independence and autonomy of the poem and the correlative warning about the heresy of paraphrase. According to Riding and Graves, "the ideal modernist poem is its own clearest, fullest, and most accurate meaning."[35] Agreeing with Richards that H.D. should be the poster-girl for the failings of Imagism, however, Riding and Graves displace defence of both the communicative abilities of "obscure" modernist poetry and the value of the experience communicated therein from H.D.'s poetry to Riding's own. Perhaps alluding to Richards's complaint that "The Pool" suffers from "simplicity," they joust with an imaginary "advanced" critic whose criticism "is mere literary snobbery," and who is imagined as disliking "The Rugged Black of Anger" for being "too simple," "a common charge against the 'obscure' poem when its obscurity is seen to have been excessive clearness."[36]

Richards is fingered by Riding in *Anarchism Is Not Enough* as the critic responsible for the contemporary perversion of poetic language into a stooge of science, an obedient perception of reality, as opposed to language as "assertion of the independence of the mind against ... the sign situation."[37] According to Riding, "The difference between the collective-real and the individual-real as revealed by their respective methods of symbolism proves itself to be no more than a snobbish difference of degree: the art of the individual-real is self-appointed good art ... The symbolism of the individual-real in its scientific aspects is best explained in C.K. Ogden's and I.A. Richards's *The Meaning of Meaning*."[38] Richards is her whipping-boy for the failings of all contemporary critics who are too beholden to a scientifically validated reality – "critics who, like I.A. Richards, wish to find a place for literature and art 'in the system of human endeavours,' to prove the unreal to be but 'a finer organization of ordinary experiences'" – and he is also the type of the literary critic as snob that she excoriates in *Contemporaries and Snobs*.[39]

Moreover, "Mr Richards, we learn from his *Principles of Literary Criticism* (published in 1925, the first textbook of psychologico-literary criticism) is interested in value rather than purity. Criticism is to him a minute and comprehensive gradation of what T.E. Hulme called the world of religious and ethical values; purity, a social rather than aesthetic attribute; a moral term, by which a work is described as a public act of its author ... Mr. Richards ... is plainly trying to discover ... the laws of goodness in humanity."[40]

Mind you, although he is the one through whom she focuses her main complaints about contemporary trends in criticism, Richards is not the only critic that Riding castigates. Herbert Read and Wyndham Lewis, for instance, between them illustrate the new barbarism. Riding observes that to Read, "criticism should use the same language about art as it does about reality; it should unite philosophy and art in Reality. Reason is personal, direct, conscious traffic in reality. It is enlightened magic ('an inner conviction of necessity'). Primitive man, being more instinctively aware of reality, did not need to have his magic (his art) enlightened. The primitive artist was a seer, the civilized artist is a visionary."[41] She notes that "Mr. Lewis uses the same language of criticism ... 'For me art is the civilized *substitute* for magic.'"[42] According to Riding, "To both Mr. Read and Mr. Lewis purity means that magical intelligence, that inspired (rather than primitive, stupid 'objective') literalness which may be philosophically defined as the individual-real ... They are interested in getting man into proper focus in reality, and in his usefulness as an instrument of measurement: they are interested, that is, in psychology, in the language of criticism, the mathematics of synthesis."[43]

Yet Riding always returns to Richards, for his criticism epitomizes better than any other the new barbarism in its scientific aspect: "Mr. Richards ... condemns Beauty-and-Truth terminology – the criticism that treats civilized art as unintelligent magic, in fact. He not only recognizes Reason as man's participation in the patterns of reality; he insists on Reason as social duty; criticism is to him morality. The mathematics of synthesis by which morality may be accurately apprehended is to be developed by turning the human world into a world of values: making conduct (communication, relation) achieve significant pattern. Conduct is then the training of the community as a whole in the traffic of reality, with the artist as band-master – 'the arts are the supreme form of communicative activity.' Value (the graded necessity of reality) is to be discovered by a 'systematization of impulses.'"[44]

These critics are purveyors of "the nostalgic desire to reconstitute an illusory whole that has no integrity but the integrity of accident."[45] Oneness is their god, and knowing their god is their goal: "Deity to the collective-realist is reality as symbolic oneness; to the individual-realist, reality is rationalistic oneness. To the former therefore personality is an instrument for conceiving emotionally the mass character of this oneness; to the latter, an instrument for corroborating intellectually the individualistic character of this oneness."[46] Their criticism would make of the reader a "Simpleton" – in Richards's case, a "Moral Simpleton" – whose goal is not "to become unreal" (that is, to recognize his difference from reality) but rather "to become more real."[47] "Instead of freeing the self to self, it frees it to Reason, to prove merely that intelligent civilized individuals can be in closer touch with reality than a stupid civilized mob: that they can know more, conform more perfectly to customs of more perfect taste, control what is unreal self in them more systematically, respond more respectfully, regularly (classical-poetically) to the stimuli of accidental reality. That they can behave, that is, by finding a civilized substitute for magic, like a perfect primitive mob of philosophy-fed art students."[48]

And so "to the professional critic (Mr. Richards, for example) ... Art ... becomes a skilful thwarting of originality. The immediate shock to the consciousness which a work brings, which might be expected to encourage an independence in the consciousness, a dissociation from reality (influences) and a development of its differences from reality, is utilized to possess the consciousness for reality, to force it to organize itself according to its resemblances (responses) to the particular object-work by which it is attacked. Art is an exaggeration of the hostile operation of reality on the individual consciousness, an exaggeration proportioned to overcome the originality which offers a casual, disorganized resistance to ordinary objects."[49]

This is precisely the function of poetry as Graves initially conceived it in his conflict theory, so we can see that Riding's engagement with Richards on these points also functions as a displacement of her engagement with the early work of Graves. Empson ought not to have wondered why Graves did not develop his conflict theory further: Riding put an end to all that pseudo-scientific imperialism on behalf of objective reality.

Riding and Graves have Richards in mind as the kind of critic who would charge "The Rugged Black of Anger" with "obscurity," a complaint deriving from the theory of language that Riding identifies in

The Meaning of Meaning – the theory that "words ... are certified scientific representatives of the natural objects, or constructions of objects called events, which man's mind, like a dust-cloud, is assumed to obscure from himself."[50] Their point is that the critic's search for the "neutral region of literalness between reality and its human perception" is wrong-headed.[51] Poetry cannot be condemned as obscure because it fails at "making a separate approximation of the general sign conveying the object," for the mind is an obscuring "dust-cloud only when perceptively organized to define reality."[52] In the poem of "disobedient perception" (in disobedient perception there is "a revulsion from the object or event concerned"), "the very genesis or *utterance* of a sign is an assertion of the independence of the mind"[53]

When Riding and Graves mock the critic who will dismiss "The Rugged Black of Anger" as obscure out of "mere literary snobbery" they anticipate the language of *Contemporaries and Snobs* and also the way Riding castigates Richards in *Anarchism Is Not Enough* as asserting an "intelligent, superior, adult ... difference of degree in sophistication, manners" over "the stupidity, the hypocrisy of the fanatic mob."[54] Such a critic may dislike such a poem "because it is 'too simple' (a common charge against the 'obscure' poem when its obscurity is seen to have been only its excessive clearness)."[55] According to Riding and Graves, such a poem is "The Rugged Black of Anger" and such a critic is I.A. Richards.

•

Richards's complaint that H.D.'s poem not only allows but actually requires a response "almost independent of the author" leads Riding and Graves to affirm the autonomy of the poem as "the crucial complication in the adjustments to be made between poetry itself and the reader of poetry": the latter "is unable to have a free and straightforward personal intimacy with a poem but is continually haunted by the idea of the presence of the poet in the poem."[56] In his fear of the freedom that a poem like H.D.'s confers on the reader, Richards is the kind of critic-reader that Riding and Graves find inadequate to modernist poetry, the kind who "is not at his ease with the poem: it is never entirely his own ... The reader cannot get over the idea that the poet had designs on him in writing the poem, to which he must respond."[57] In short, for his complaint in the face of a poem that he mistakenly fears has become "independent of the author," Richards is mocked by Riding and Graves as a coward: "the plain reader does not really want to be left all alone with poetry ... The real discomfort to the reader in modernist poetry is the absence of the poet as his protector from the imaginative terrors lurking in it."[58]

16

From Slow Reading to Close Reading: Escaping the Stock Response

Although Riding seems to have had nothing good to say about Richards at this time, in collaboration with Graves in *A Survey of Modernist Poetry* she responds positively to a number of the points raised in *Principles of Literary Criticism,* without acknowledging the fact. Indeed, together they adapt many of Richards's ideas to the purposes of their apology for modernist poetry in general, and for Riding's own poetry in particular. Of course some of these ideas were originally appropriated from early work by Graves, so this back-and-forth influence is not surprising. In fact, we shall find not only that ideas originally worked out by Graves and Richards are modified in *A Survey of Modernist Poetry* according to the distinctive collaborative idioms of Riding and Graves, but also that the same ideas subsequently re-emerge in *Practical Criticism.* These literary theories and practices go on to shape the development of New Criticism for a long while to come.

•

Riding and Graves take up Richards's concern about the danger for poetry, and for the larger culture, of "stock responses" and "stock feelings." In *Principles of Literary Criticism*, Richards warns that bad poetry wins approval from readers because it presents them with "stock conventional attitudes."[1] These attitudes begin to inhabit us sometime after the age of ten, introduced initially "by social suggestion and by accidents," "*removing us from experience*," and becoming ever more fixed the more "we dwell in them."[2] The person in the grip of stock attitudes "is even in the most important things functionally unable to face facts: do what he will he is only able to face fictions, fictions projected by his own stock responses."[3] According to Richards, the stock response effectively marks the boundary in culture between reality and illusion.

In the world of art, the stock response marks the boundary between good and bad art, pure and impure writing, healthy and unhealthy reading. Although immersion in mediocre poetry can lead to "not only an acceptance of the mediocre in ordinary life, but a blurring and confusion of impulses and a very widespread loss of value," Richards most fears the debasing influence of "the screen" and the "best-seller": "They tend ... to develop stock attitudes and stereotyped ideas, the attitudes and ideas of producers: attitudes and ideas which can be 'put across' *quickly* through a medium that lends itself to crude rather than to sensitive handling."[4] The impact on the most intimate aspects of life can be profound, since "Even the decision as to what constitutes a pretty girl or a handsome young man, an affair apparently natural and personal enough, is largely determined by magazine covers and movie stars."[5] The artist, then, must choose for or against the stock response: "Against these stock responses the artist's internal and external conflicts are fought, and with them the popular writer's triumphs are made."[6]

Riding and Graves deploy these terms and express these values in their defence of modernist poetry. Concerned to account for "the 'freakishness' and abnormality of feeling with which the modernist poet is often charged," they suggest that the modernist poet is not the problem; "the trouble is rather that ordinary modern life is full of the stock-feelings and situations with which traditional poetry has continually fed popular sentiments."[7] These stock feelings inhabit poems and readers alike. Ostensibly modernizing poets like "the Imagists" and "the Vers Librists generally," on the one hand, or "the Georgians," on the other, managed to avoid "archaistic diction" and, "in reaction to Victorianism," "formally religious, philosophic or improving themes," but none of them was "capable of writing a new poetry within these revised forms. So in both cases all that happened was that the same old stock-feelings and situations were served up again."[8] Georgianism particularly became "principally concerned" with "stock-subjects": "Nature and love and leisure and old age and childhood and animals and sleep and other uncontroversial subjects."[9]

Concentrating on poetry rather than movies and pulp fiction, Riding and Graves conclude that contemporary readers who are fed a diet of stock feelings and stock subjects often recognize in a poem only the stock feelings and stock subjects they project upon it: "The reader should enter the life of the poem and submit himself to its conditions in order to know it as it really is; instead of making it enter his life as a symbol having no private reality, only the reality it gets by reflection from his world."[10] Richards expressed a larger concern about the disconnection between the real world and the subjective world of the person in the grip of stock attitudes, the person who "is even in the most important things functionally unable to face facts: do what he will he is only able to face fictions, fictions projected by his own stock responses."[11] They share this same larger concern, too, observing "that modern life is full of the stock-feelings and situations with which traditional poetry has continually fed popular sentiments; that the commonplaces of everyday speech are merely the relics of past poetry."[12]

The great attention that Riding and Graves paid to the chapter "Badness in Poetry" is suggested, then, not only by their attention to Richards's criticism of H.D. but also by their attention to his concern with both the reader's and the poet's reliance on stock responses. Suggesting that stock responses lie at the heart of "dead movements" in poetry not only builds on Richards's assertion that "no theory of criticism is satisfactory" that cannot explain the "wide appeal" of the stock response, but does so in language similar to Richards's own.[13] They agree that the person in the grip of the stock response is remote from genuine experience, trapped in a narcissistic hermeneutic (if projecting a stock response onto a poem that does not call for it), or trapped in a collective social fiction (if responding with the stock response actually solicited by the poem).

Furthermore, they adopt the very tropes by which Richards advances his analysis. Stock responses, says Richards, depend on "general Ideas ... certain of success ... if suitably advertised": "The critic and the Sales Manager are not ordinarily regarded as of the same craft, nor are the poet and the advertising agent ... But the written appeals which have the soundest financial prospects as estimated by the most able American advertisers are such that no critic can safely ignore them. For they do undoubtedly represent the literary ideals present and future of the people to whom they are addressed."[14]

Similarly, Riding and Graves are concerned to distinguish in modern poetry "between peculiarities resulting from a deliberate attempt to improve the status of poetry by jazzing up its programme and those resulting from concentration on the poetic process itself. The first class of peculiarities are caused by a desire to improve the popularity of poetry with the public and constitute a sort of commercial advertising of poetry."[15] They present "dead movements" in poetry as part of the wasteful disorganization of life that Richards associates with the stock response and its cynical economics: "A dead movement is one which never had or can have a real place in the history of poets and poems. It occurs because some passing or hitherto unrealized psychological mood in the public offers a new field for exploitation, as sudden fashion crazes come and go, leaving no trace but waste material."[16] The dead movements of the late nineteenth century and early twentieth century "were all merely modernized advertisements of the same old product of which the reader had grown tired."[17]

Imagism, for instance, was "a stunt of commercial advertisers of poetry to whom poetic results meant a popular demand for their work, not the discovery of new values in poetry"[18] According to Ridings and Graves, Imagists "could only go so far as to say everything that had already been said before in a slightly different way," putting themselves in the "position of selling one's ideas rather than of constantly submitting them to new tests."[19] In Imagism, and similar contemporary dead movements, "all that happened was that the same old stock-feelings and situations were served up again, only with a different sauce."[20]

By contrast, "authentic 'advanced' poetry of the present day differs from such programmes for poetry in this important respect: that it is concerned with a reorganization of the matter (not in the sense of subject-matter but of poetic thought as distinguished from other kinds of thought) rather than the manner of poetry."[21] Like Richards, they present the stock response as a function of the subordination of poetic values to commercial values – evidence of the degeneration of twentieth-century Western culture.

Accepting Richards's suggestion that "Against these stock responses the artist's internal and external conflicts are fought, and with them the popular writer's triumphs are made," Riding and Graves offer modernist poetry as the antidote.[22] Richards points out that the disease is viciously circular, and Riding and Graves agree: "the general reading public … gets its excitement from literature and literary feelings instead of life"; "traditional poetry has continually fed popular sentiments" with "stock-feelings and situations"; literary stock feelings thus overflow literary bounds into "the commonplaces of everyday speech," which "are the relics of past poetry."[23] In the face of such a narrowly circumscribed discursive reality, "the only way for a modern poet to have an original feeling or experience that may become literature is to have it outside of literature."[24] Consequently, "the modernist poet is often charged" with "'freakishness' and abnormality of feeling": to plain readers residing in a literary world that they mistake for reality, modernist poets seem to have left both literature and reality behind in their quest to invest poetry with experience beyond stock feelings and situations.[25]

Like Richards, Riding and Graves recognize in authentic poetry a means of breaking the vicious commercial circle that sustains poet and reader in their exchange of de-realizing stock responses. They present modernist poetry as challenging the plain reader by means of its reorganized thought: "This is why the plain reader feels so balked by it: he must enter into the matter without expecting a cipher-code to the meaning."[26] Poetry of "cipher-code" is poetry that is to be interpreted in relation to the reality of science, a conception of poetry that Riding and Graves repudiate. Poetry that serves up stock feelings and situations to the reader – including the kind of poetry that does this in a new way (Imagism, *vers libre*, Georgianism), poetry thereby "designed to recapture his interest" from "other forms of social entertainment" – is poetry that depends on a stock reality as key to the cipher-code that will explain it.[27]

Modernist poetry, according to Riding and Graves, is as indifferent to the requirements of commerce as to the requirements of soothing stock responses, and so "The plain reader has an exaggerated antagonism toward poetry of this ... sort because it is too serious to permit of a merely neutral attitude in him and because, instead of presenting him with the benefits of its improvements, the poet seems impudently intent on advertising poetry for its own sake rather than for the reader's."[28] Yet the reader's salvation resides in modern poetry's challenges ("challenges which his self-respect does not permit him to overlook"): "it would be wise to refrain from critical comments such as 'that is incomprehensible' unless he is willing to make the effort of criticism. If he does this, much that at first glance antagonized him will appear not incomprehensible but only perhaps difficult, or if not difficult, only different from what he has been accustomed to consider poetical."[29]

This reference to the "neutral attitude" that modernist poetry prevents anticipates Riding's language in *Anarchism Is Not Enough* when she charges Richards with misconceiving language as a "neutral region of literalness between reality and its human perception," just as the representation of poetry here as existing for its own sake anticipates her upbraiding of Richards and his ilk in both *Anarchism Is Not Enough* and *Contemporaries and Snobs*.[30] Nonetheless, like Richards, Riding and Graves depict recovery from the circle of stock responses as not only a possibility offered by authentic poetry but also a potential achievement by individual readers – an achievement uncertain as to its efficacy and duration. Making "the effort of criticism" in good faith, the reader "may even train himself to read certain contemporary poets with interest or, if he persists in keeping the critical process separate from the reading process, have at least a historical sense of what is happening in poetry."[31]

•

Riding and Graves also seem to have followed with interest Richards's notorious distinction between two broad uses of language: the scientific and the emotive. In *Anarchism Is Not Enough*, Riding summarizes what she regards as the offensive claims of *The Meaning of Meaning*, *Principles of Literary Criticism*, and *Science and Poetry*, quotes from each book, and opposes to them a counter-vision of her own.[32] Much of this counter-vision is already evident in *A Survey of Modernist Poetry*.

In *Anarchism Is Not Enough*, Riding reviews – in order to reject – the paradigm in *Science and Poetry* according to which Richards accords the "stabilizing of the scientific or symbolic use of words" priority over poetry's "deliberately unscientific use of words" whether as "evocative speech" or as "figurative speech." She complains that, according to Richards, "Poetry as evocative speech takes its cue from external (scientific) symbols of reality rather than from internal (imaginative) symbols of reality – it means, in Mr. Richards' words, 'The transference from the magical view of the world to the scientific.'"[33] And so, Riding concludes, "evocative speech is in fact not an independent speech of its own but a persuasive quality that may be added to symbolic speech … evocative (poetic) speech is false *by itself* (in opposition to symbolic speech), it is scientifically admissible only where it shows close dependence on symbols meaningless in themselves but showing a close, scientific dependence on reality"[34] According to Riding, Richards sees poetry as a cipher whose value is determined by reality.

Of course Graves did not require Riding's tutelage to work out his own opposition to the hierarchy that placed logical above illogical modes of thought. As we have seen, he addresses the problem explicitly in "The Illogical Element in Poetry," and he does so in terms that Riding takes up in her own work:

> The scholastic tradition as finally systematized in the textbooks makes no allowance for associative thinking, finds no virtue in a spoonerism or a pun suggested by the homophonic association of, say, 'horse' and 'hoarse,' or in fantastic slips either of pen or tongue; ridicules the ancient notion that medical bane and salve are always to be found growing together, or that between the crescent moon and the horseshoe nailed over the lintel a sympathy can exist by means of resemblance in shape; denies to a ghost any real existence unless the camera or barometer under the surveillance of a body of sceptics can be affected by the ghost's entry into the haunted corridor.
>
> Poetry of the kind which we recognize as Romantic or Fantastic or Inspired being, as Coleridge first showed, dependent on associative thought, its symbolism bound up with a vast number of logical false premises, a defiance of the ordered spatio-temporal structure which the civilized intellect has built for its habitation – this Poetry when Logic was first achieving pre-eminence under the Greeks, either had to be banned altogether from the ideal republic of the philosophers as Plato wished it banned, or had to submit itself to a severe examination and systematization – hence Aristotle's Poetics. For centuries since, philosophical speculation about emotional poetry, dreams and phantasy has been silent or found only illogic in them.[35]

However partial to the method of romantic poetry he might be, Graves accepts that just as partisans of the logical method might claim that "the logical method is the only right method, and all others are useless because illogical," so "the romantic method has a similar scorn for the logical method," and so "both may therefore be suspect when they advance these mutually exclusive claims."[36] Graves understands himself merely to be urging the righting of an imbalance: "associative thought is as modern and reputable a mode as intellectual thought."[37] In fact, it is "a method constantly employed unknown to themselves by the most sophisticated and Aristotelian minds and of great service to them."[38] Graves therefore looks forward to a time when "the clash" between these modes of thought "can end and these terms can be used to qualify the forms of poetry alternately appearing as either one or other method of thought employed for dealing with any conflict."[39]

Of course Riding not only regarded Graves's psychoanalytical perspective on conflict in poetry as subordinating poetry to a meaning outside it, but also regarded the claim that there need not be a distinction between logical and illogical uses of language as belying the significance of the distinctive unreality of poetry. Since for Richards – and for the pre-Riding Graves – "the one belief from which the poetic mind must not disconnect itself is the belief in reality," "Poetry is according to such criticism ... a socially beneficial affirmation of reality."[40] However much Graves would have objected to Richards's assertion that in *Science and Poetry* he was describing "the transference from the magical view of the world to the scientific," since Graves regards the associational thought that underlies the magical view of the world as just "as modern and reputable as intellectual thought," he did not recognize before his collaboration with Riding that conflict theory subordinated poetry to scientific reality in the same way.[41]

A Survey of Modernist Poetry, however, shows that Riding and Graves have already worked out this problem, and that they have done so in response to Richards's scientism: "Experiment ... may be interpreted in two ways. In the first sense it is a delicate and constantly alert state of expectancy directed toward the discovery of something of which some slight clue has been given ... The important thing in the whole process is the initial clue, or, in old-fashioned language, the inspiration. The real scientist should have an equal power of genius with the poet."[42] To this point, the passage in *A Survey of Modernist Poetry* is in agreement with what Graves writes in *Poetic Unreason*. Yet the influence of Riding's point of view soon becomes evident: "the real scientist should have an equal power of genius with the poet," but there is "the difference that the scientist is inspired to discover things which already are (his results are facts), while the poet is inspired to discover things which are made by his discovery of them (his results are not statements about things already known to exist, or knowledge, but truths, things which existed before only as potential truth)."[43] Riding's sense of poetry as an existential nothing is present here.

As we have seen, according to Riding, the scientist is a slave obedient to reality; the true poet is disobedient to reality and free to experiment in unreality. Not every scientist is a "real scientist," however, and not every poet is a true poet:

> Experiment in the second sense is the use of a system for its own sake and brings about, whether in science or poetry, no results but those possible to the system. As it is only the scientific genius who is capable of using experiment in the first of these senses … experiment in the second sense is the general method of the labouring, as against the inventive, side of science … Poets, then, who need the support of a system (labourers pretending to be inventors, since in poetry, unlike science, there is no place for labourers) are obliged to not only the workshop method of science, but the whole philosophical point of view of science, which is directly opposite to the point of view of poetry.[44]

We find here in general terms about the relationship between poetry and science the same terms that Riding applies more particularly in *Anarchism Is Not Enough* to *The Meaning of Meaning*, *Principles of Literary Criticism*, and *Science and Poetry*.

Riding and Graves clearly impute to their "plain reader" Richards's hierarchical distinction between "figurative" and "evocative" language: "The plain reader makes two general categories for poetry; the realistic (the true), which is supposed to put the raw poetry of life felt dumbly by him into a literary form, a register of the nobler sentiments of practical life; and the non-realistic or romantic (the untrue), which covers his life of fantasia and desires, the world he is morally obliged to treat as unreal."[45] This passage echoes Richards's characterisation of poetry's relationship to practical life throughout *Principles of Literary Criticism*, and it anticipates Riding's complaints about his definitions of "figurative" and "evocative" uses of poetic language in *Anarchism Is Not Enough*: "Poetry as symbolic speech is only figurative speech; it invents a fairy-story of reality. Poetry as evocative speech takes its cue from external (scientific) symbols of reality rather than from internal (imaginative) symbols of reality – it means, in Mr. Richards' words, 'The transference from the magical view of the world to the scientific.'"[46]

•

It is clear, then, that engagement by Riding and Graves with the work of Richards shapes a number of aspects of their discussion, definition, and defence of poetry in general and of modernist poetry in particular, yet of all the insights they derive from him perhaps the most practical is his recommendation that readers of poetry read poems more slowly. Richards writes about this in *Science and Poetry* (1926), which was published a year before *A Survey of Modernist Poetry*. Believing that "in nearly all poetry the sound and feel of the words, what is often called the *form* of the poem in opposition to its *content*, get to work first, and the senses in which the words are later more explicitly taken are subtly influenced by this fact," Richards does not here recommend the slow reading of the poem as a method of interpreting its sense or meaning, but rather as a way of mastering the sound of the poem – a necessary preliminary step on the way towards the interpretation of its sense that will follow.[47] He continues: "Let us begin by reading it very slowly, preferably aloud, giving every syllable time to make its full effect upon us. And let us read it experimentally, repeating it, varying our tone of voice until we are satisfied that we have caught its rhythm as well as we are able, and … that we … are certain how it should 'go.'"[48] Just as poetry begins to communicate upon the poet's "getting it 'right,'" so readers begin to understand poetry once they "are certain how it should go."[49] Reading poetry slowly to get the sound right was linked from the beginning to reading slowly to get the sense right. However, Riding and Graves recognized the importance of this link before Richards did.

•

Graves would write a letter to the editor of the *Times Literary Supplement* in 1955 claiming that the analysis of Hopkins's poem "Hurrahing in Harvest" in *A Survey of Modernist Poetry* began the influence of Hopkins on modern poetry, yet Richards's earlier attention to Hopkins was at least as influential in this regard.[50] Empson refers to it in *Seven Types of Ambiguity*, and Riding and Graves seem to have noticed it themselves.

Russo notes that "in 1927, Richards introduced Hopkins by defending poetry 'with some slight obscurity.' He applauded writers who 'can compel slow reading'; the 'effort' and 'heightened attention' may 'brace the reader'; the 'peculiar intellectual thrill which celebrates the step-by-step conquest of understanding may irradiate and awaken other mental activities more essential to poetry' such as intellectual inquiry, perception of the wider 'equilibrium,' and freedom."[51] In fact, the first version of Richards's essay on Hopkins in which he makes these claims was actually published the year before.[52] This fact is important, for it shows that Richards begins to associate slow reading with "the step-by-step conquest of understanding" even before he can have read *A Survey of Modernist Poetry*. Yet, as his dismissal of the slow reading of Shakespeare's sonnet by Riding and Graves as a mere game of interpretation shows, Richards remained a long way from understanding slow reading as a close reading by which to detect a systematic overdetermination of semantic, syntactic, and tonal ambiguities.

Determined to make Richards the inventor of close reading, Russo suggests that Richards's treatment in *Practical Criticism* of a poem by Luce "exemplifies the close reading method as it stood in 1929."[53] As Haffenden points out, however, Russo is both incorrect in this claim and inaccurate in his account of Richards's writing about Luce: "Russo, intent upon proving that Richards had it in mind to illuminate an ambiguity in Luce's line of poetry, has no compunction about supplying rather more than the gloss that Richards offered ... [I]t is clear that Russo makes a different point from the original. Richards ... was really not explaining the workings of ambiguity in poetry."[54] In 1929, in fact, not only was Empson well beyond any such half-hearted engagement with ambiguity as Richards shows in *Practical Criticism* at this time, but so were Riding and Graves.

Richards does refer to slow reading as enabling "the step-by-step conquest of understanding" what a poem means, but he never demonstrates in *Principles of Literary Criticism* or *Science and Poetry* or even *Practical Criticism* the step-by-step process of appreciating the competing, complementary, contradictory, and conciliating meanings of the words of a poem that we see in the work of first Graves, and then Riding-and-Graves, and finally Empson. That Riding and Graves were indeed familiar with Richards's reading of Hopkins is implied by the fact that they demonstrate by a *slow reading* of six lines of a sonnet by Hopkins that the reader "must use his wits" in a step-by-step analysis of the possible meanings of the ambiguous words to be able to "appreciate the accuracy" of the poet's use of "exactly the proper association" as "the neatest possible way of combining" effects and "reconciling the two seemingly opposed qualities" of his subject.[55] Their language is very similar to that employed by Richards.

Hopkins's editor Robert Bridges complains that there is in certain of his poems "some perversion of feeling" – in the "nostril's relish of incense along the sanctuary side," for instance, and in the image of "the Holy Ghost with warm breast" – that is more repellent to him than "the rude shocks of his purely artistic wantonness."[56] Ridings and Graves respond to this charge by arguing that the value of Hopkins's poetry is in its "reconciling" of such "seemingly opposed qualities," a defence that recalls Graves's interest in the same implicitly sexual and spiritual conflict at the heart of similar imagery in poems by Herbert.[57] Just as Herbert's poem "The Bag" reconciles in language simultaneously sexual and spiritual the conflict between the two Donnes, John and Jack, so Hopkins's poem "Hurrahing in Harvest" can be "appreciated as ... reconciling the two seemingly opposed qualities of mountains, their male, animal-like roughness and strength and at the same time their ethereal quality under soft light."[58] One can take the poet's psychological reality out of a conflict theory of poetry, it seems, but one can't take psychological conflict out of the poetry itself – especially religious poetry.

Of course it is precisely in reaction to the claim that they presume their anonymous professional critic (Richards) would make that Riding's poetry suffers from "so-called obscurity" that Riding and Graves recommend "increasing the time-length of reading."[59] Their prime example of a poem that needs greater attention than might customarily be given it is Riding's "The Rugged Black of Anger," a poem whose so-called "'obscurity' ... would probably cause it to be put aside by the critic after he had allowed it the customary two-minute reading (for if the poet has obeyed all the rules, this is long enough to give a rough idea of what the poem is all about – and that is all that is generally wanted)."[60] Of course such a rough idea will not do, for "if it were possible to give the complete force of a poem in a prose summary, then there would be no excuse for writing the poem": a poem is more than prose, and it is more than an idea. Reader and critic must "let it interpret itself, without introducing any new associations or, if possible, any new words."[61] They offer an example of a possible slow reading of Riding's poem – repeating lines, inverting lines, making up transitional lines from the poem's own words and phrases until, "as a sufficient illustration of the method of letting the poem interpret itself," "the poem interpreted is practically itself repeated to three times its own length."[62] The time invested in reading is the key to better reading: "The important thing that would be revealed by a wide application of this method to the reading of poems ... would be that much of the so-called obscurity of poems was created by the laziness of the plain reader, who wishes to hurry through poetry as quickly as he does through prose, not realizing that he is dealing with a kind of thought which, though it may have the speed of prose to the poet, he must follow with a slowness proportionate to how much he is not a poet."[63] And so "increasing the time-length of reading is one way of getting out of the prose and into the poetic state of mind, of developing a capacity for minuteness, for seeing all there is to see at a given point and for taking it all with one as one goes along."[64]

Riding and Graves transform the literally (that is, temporally) slow reading that Richards recommends (conceiving it as something of a vocal exercise preliminary to attempting to understand the meaning of a poem) into New Criticism's close reading. For Riding and Graves, whatever the actual time-length of the reading, the important thing in reading slowly is to develop "a capacity for minuteness, for seeing all there is to see at a given point and for taking it all with one as one goes along."[65] The phrase "capacity for minuteness" indirectly acknowledges the role of Richards in this aspect of the thinking of Riding and Graves. When Riding complains in *Anarchism Is Not Enough* that Richards's "meticulous poetic" is merely an expression of "the nostalgic desire to reconstitute an illusory whole" of reality, she recalls Richards's declaration that art deals with "minute particulars."[66] Riding and Graves are not above adapting a phrase that betrays Richards's wrong-headed meticulousness ("minute particulars") into a phrase ("capacity for minuteness") by which they can define a proper reader's meticulousness.[67]

According to Riding, there is no such whole of reality for Richards's "minute particulars" to reconstitute beyond the one nostalgically remembered by the new barbarism. The minute particulars of "The Rugged Black of Anger" constitute a new reality that emerges from and is created by the artist's revulsion from conventional reality. Like Foucault, who declares history a matter of chance that discourse is determined to control, Riding declares that the reality that Richards's "meticulously poetic" instinct would make "whole" actually "has no integrity but the integrity of accident."[68]

And so Riding and Graves react against Richards by defining an existentialist, rather than essentialist, understanding of poetry. Their slow reader's "capacity for minuteness" reveals "as one goes along" just as much a dissociation of minute particulars as an association of them, for poetry is just as much a disintegration of existing reality as an integration of a new reality. Order, pattern, system: these are projections of the labouring scientific mind – projections that can become functions – functions both in the mind of the poet as labourer "who needs the support of a system" and in the mind of the professional critic who subordinates poetry to scientific reality.[69] According to Riding and Graves, the proper reader must develop a capacity for minuteness because poetry creates not more of the same, but always a "more" that is ever new and never simple.

17

Taking New Stock of Stock Responses

As mentioned above, Russo argues that Richards's early work is the most important influence on the development of New Criticism and that one can identify in the reading of Luce in *Practical Criticism* the most important early example of close reading. As we have also seen, Haffenden effectively refutes the latter half of this claim. Yet *Practical Criticism* is certainly one of the founding documents of New Criticism, if for no other reason than that it makes the case overwhelmingly, through its many examples of readings gone wrong, that a new method of reading poetry more carefully – one that attends very closely to the meaning of the words on the page – is necessary.

John Crowe Ransom makes this point about the influence of *Practical Criticism* in the first chapter of the book that unintentionally gave the new close-reading method its name, *The New Criticism* (1941): "the protocols revealed dismal deficiencies in the power of supposedly trained students to cope with poetry. In criticizing the students' ability to read the meaning of poetry, Richards reveals himself as an astute reader. He looks much more closely at the objective poem than his theories require him to do. His most incontestable contribution to poetic discussion, in my opinion, is in developing the ideal or exemplary readings, and in provoking such readings from other scholars."[1] Whatever the value of any of his own readings as a "contribution to intensive reading," Richards provokes intensive reading of great value from others, especially Empson.[2] And so, since "a brilliant pupil is presumptive evidence of a brilliant teacher," Ransom combines attention to *Practical Criticism* in his first chapter with attention to *Seven Types of Ambiguity*: "I believe it is the most imaginative account of readings ever printed, and Empson the closest and most resourceful reader that poetry has yet publicly had."[3]

Thus conflating the work of Empson and Richards, Ransom says of Empson's analysis of a poem by Sidney that "writings as acute and at the same time as patient and consecutive as this have not existed in English criticism, I think, before Richards and Empson. They become frequent now; Richards and Empson have spread quickly."[4] Yet Ransom curiously contradicts his own suggestion that no example of such analysis existed before *Seven Types of Ambiguity* and *Practical Criticism* when he notes that Empson's "debt to Richards (and to others) is acknowledged as follows": "Mr. I.A. Richards, then my supervisor for the first part of the English Tripos, told me to write this essay, and various things to put in it; my indebtedness to him is as great as such a thing should ever be. And I derive the method I am using from Miss Laura Riding's and Mr. Robert Graves' analysis of a Shakespeare sonnet."[5] Ransom quotes Empson in such a way as to mention also the work of Riding and Graves, although this contradicts his assertion of Empson's uniqueness. Since he asserts that the kind of analysis that he celebrates is original to teacher Richards and student Empson, either he ought not to have mentioned Empson's debt "to others" at all – even parenthetically – or he ought not to have asserted the uniqueness of Richards and Empson. By doing so, Ransom acknowledges that there is more to the story of this new criticism than he tells.

And there is more to the story than he knew. Second only to *Seven Types of Ambiguity*, I suggest, *Practical Criticism* is the founding document of New Criticism that is the most influenced by Riding and Graves. Richards's report on his experiments with his Cambridge students in the practical criticism of poems takes the shape it does in part because of his reaction to *A Survey of Modernist Poetry*. Like Empson's book, *Practical Criticism* serves as something of a Trojan Horse – an influential work welcomed by American New Critics like Ransom who either did not notice or chose not to acknowledge that it contains the influence of Riding and Graves within it. Like *Seven Types of Ambiguity*, *Practical Criticism* is thereby a tremendous multiplier of the influence of Riding and Graves on New Criticism.

•

Stanley Fish observes that "Richards's theories and his prejudices weigh heavily on his protocols."[6] Indeed, Richards is an informing presence in his analysis of the anonymous protocols that he received from his students. Richards not only makes of the protocols submitted by the dull and the witless a platform from which to expound his own corrective views, but he also often finds in the protocols of the brilliant and the witty a point of view with which he can agree. His selection of which protocols to discuss is guided by their usefulness in these respects. Moreover, Richards often finds aspects of his own point of view reflected back to him; some of the writers offer critiques of poetry based on their (mis)understanding of the principles and practices of his books and lectures at this time. Such protocols constitute a significant number of those he selects for discussion.

One notices in particular that many protocol writers echo Richards's belief that "the arts are the supreme form of communicative activity."[7] Richards argues that whether or not the artist aims at communicating his experience to others, "the very process of getting the work 'right' has ... immense communicative consequences ... The degree to which it accords with the relevant experience of the artist is a measure of the degree to which it will arouse similar experience in others."[8] He also explains bad poetry in these terms: "sometimes art is bad because communication is defective ... sometimes because the experience is worthless ... It would perhaps be best to restrict the term bad art to cases in which genuine communication does to a considerable degree take place, what is communicated being worthless, and to call the other cases defective art."[9]

In a large number of the protocols, writers offer judgments of the communicative efficacy of the poems put before the class: "communication extraordinarily successful"; "confusion in thought has failed to establish, in the reader, communication, and even comprehension"; "failure of communication"; "the whole idea is well communicated"; "The communication is not quite clear"; "The communication of this is bad"; "Perfect communication"; "The communication is excellent."[10] The comments quoted here are all from the 1925–26 class. The same thing can be observed in the 1927–28 class: "If he had anything to say it is likely that he would communicate it effectively: unfortunately he has next to nothing"; "This one seems to me a successful communication of an experience whose value is dubious."[11] Presumably Richards's gratification at finding in these protocols evidence that his students had been listening to his lectures, and perhaps even reading his books, was tempered by the lack of interpretive skills that so many of his students showed.

•

One can also see in some of the protocols that students were following both the work of Graves and the work of Riding and Graves. For instance, the protocol writer that Richards describes as "on his guard" against "mnemonic irrelevance" walks a walk modeled by Graves.[12] He explains why he cannot trust himself to provide an honest, objective criticism of Christina Rossetti's "Spring Quiet": "I fear I am not an impartial judge, as the lines inevitably associate themselves with a scene and experience I value."[13] This writer seems to have taken Graves's advice: "the time may come for him to admit honourably, 'I cannot talk of this book dispassionately because … the poet and myself have an emotional (or intellectual) experience of an unusual character in common'" – a point that we have seen Richards adapt to his own purposes in *Principles of Literary Criticism*.[14] The language and the logic of the student's passage and that by Graves are interchangeable.

The member of the 1927–28 class who complains of the obscurity of Henry Wadsworth Longfellow's "In the Churchyard at Cambridge" combines a point made by Riding and Graves in *A Survey of Modernist Poetry* with one made by Richards in *Principles of Literary Criticism*: "Don't think I mind obscurity, because I *don't; but I do like to get some meaning sooner or later, and this poem seems very muddled and confused*. At all events the poem is not worth much effort on the part of the reader because the underlying emotion is not of sufficient value."[15] One recognizes the influence here of Richards's distinction between poetry that is "bad because communication is defective" and poetry that is bad "because the experience is worthless."[16] And one can see that the writer's defensiveness about criticizing the poem as obscure has been prompted by someone's suggestion to him that to complain of obscurity in a poem is a sign of incompetence as a critic – perhaps Riding and Graves.[17] Similarly, whether or not Richards read "The Anthologist in Our Midst" by Riding and Graves when it appeared in the spring of 1927, he encountered its contempt for anthologies from at least one protocol writer in the autumn of 1927. Richards begins his analysis of the protocols about G.H. Luce's poem "Climb, cloud, and pencil all the blue" with examples of opinions demonstrating "mnemonic and other irrelevancies": "The poem *is the type which invades school anthologies* though it is a disreputable offspring of Shelley (misunderstood) and a woolly sentimental mind ... It is such and not the Goths nor the classics that desolate Europe."[18] Richards supplies the italics here, indicating his suspicion as to the source of the bad memories recalled for the reader by the poem. The italics recall both his introductory point concerning the inadequate training he associates with anthology reading and his summary remark about the bewilderment experienced by protocol writers required to evaluate poetry lacking "the sanction of an anthology."[19] Yet this protocol writer does more than recall a bad personal memory from his school days. He also alludes to the analysis by Riding and Graves in *A Survey of Modernist Poetry* of disastrous contemporary methods of teaching English in British schools by modifying Blake's line in "On Homer's Poetry" – it is "the Classics & not Goths nor Monks, that desolate Europe with Wars" – so as to suggest that it is not the classics that desolate Europe, but anthology poems. Richards's selection of this piece to reinforce his point about the dangers of anthology culture is rooted in the much more vociferous warnings of Riding and Graves from "The Anthologist in Our Midst" (April 1927) to *A Survey of Modernist Poetry* (November 1927) and *A Pamphlet Against Anthologies* (July 1928).[20]

•

The hitherto undetected influence of Riding and Graves in *Practical Criticism* is evident less in the particular protocols that echo their topics and views than in Richards's own echoing of such topics and views. It would seem that in the midst of writing up the results of his experiment in interpretation by means of his practical criticism classes – an experiment he designed and implemented entirely on his own, before Riding and Graves had set collaborative pen to paper– Richards found himself investigating and supporting many of the claims made by Riding and Graves. Richards, that is, finds that the results of his serious classroom experiment support the results of work that he previously thought mere "games of interpretation."

Although published in 1929, *Practical Criticism* was a long time in preparation. In a May 1928 preface to a subsequent edition of *Principles of Literary Criticism*, Richards explains that he is "preparing a companion volume, *Practical Criticism*. Extremely good and extremely bad poems were put *unsigned* before a large and able audience. The comments they wrote at leisure give, as it were, a stereoscopic view of the poem and of possible opinion on it. This material, when systematically analysed, provides not only interesting commentary on the state of contemporary culture but a new and powerful educational instrument."[21] As early as 1923, however, Richards had begun experimenting with students' interpretation of poetry by placing unsigned poems before them for analysis. When he complains in *Principles of Literary Criticism* (1924), for instance, that for those who have little understanding of poetry, "a defective rime – bough's house, bush thrush, blood good – is sufficient ground for condemning a poem in neglect of all other considerations," it is clear that he has already put Christina Rossetti's poem "Spring Quiet" before his students and received responses just like those he later cites in *Practical Criticism*: "The writer has *only got to find twelve rhyming words* to express very trivial thoughts so why 'thrush,' 'bush,' 'boughs,' 'house'"; "the rhyme 'thrush' with 'bush' *is almost bearable*. When 'boughs' and 'house' come next however, the attempt to enjoy the poem fails"; "I laughed at the rhyming of thrush and bush; and boughs and house."[22] He also mentions in *Principles of Literary Criticism* that he has put poems by Ella Wheeler Wilcox before students in the same way, referring to "the response made by well-educated persons, who read it without being aware of the authorship."[23]

Richards developed this teaching strategy into a formal course called "Practical Criticism", the work of the 1925–26 class serving as the basis of the protocols analyzed in connection with poems I to VIII of *Practical Criticism*. Richards was away from Cambridge (traveling in Japan and China) during the 1926–27 school year, but he taught this course one final time in 1927–28, the work of the new class serving as the basis of the protocols analyzed in connection with poems IX to XIII. He supplemented the protocols of high-achieving Cambridge undergraduates such as F.R. Leavis, Alastair Cooke, Muriel Bradbrook, Christopher Isherwood, and E.E. Phare (later Duncan-Jones) with others by eminent literary figures such as Professor Mansfield Forbes of Clare College, Cambridge, and even T.S. Eliot, by now a good friend. It is possible that certain of the protocols were written by William Empson, who recalled that when he was "a math student," he "attended one or two of the lectures which became *Practical Criticism*."[24]

Whereas Richards had assembled in his classes over several years more than a hundred students who produced for him about a thousand protocols, from which he distilled a detailed portrait of the contemporary reader, Riding and Graves defined the contemporary "plain reader" they were commissioned to teach how to read modernist poetry by a process that seems, by comparison, rather arbitrary. The reader pictured by Riding and Graves is a composite sketch generated, on the one hand, from their assessment of the deficient literary standards evident in reviews with which they disagree and, on the other hand, from the just as deficient literary standards implied by contemporary book sales. And yet the deficient reader that Riding and Graves conjure up illustrates the most significant failings of the protocol writers that Richards analyzes and corrects. It must have been somewhat galling for Richards to find the results of his hard work anticipated by a pair of critics that he could not take seriously.

We recall that Richards's new pupil, Empson, drew his attention to *A Survey of Modernist Poetry* at the beginning of the fall term at Cambridge in 1928, presumably in October. Richards probably knew of the book independently of Empson's reference to it, yet even if he did not, he certainly would have looked it up after Empson's enthusiastic recommendation of its interpretive methods. As Miranda Seymour points out, he was collecting all of Graves's publications.

In fact, there is considerable circumstantial evidence that Richards read and responded to *A Survey of Modernist Poetry* before Empson recommended it to him. It consists, first, of the ways in *Practical Criticism* that he returns to topics that he first raised in *Principles of Literary Criticism*, for his further development here of his earlier ideas shows the influence of Riding and Graves. And it consists, second, of the new topics that he takes up in *Practical Criticism* – topics that Riding and Graves introduce to him.

•

In the chapter of *Practical Criticism* that concludes with recommendation of "very slow" reading, one finds the influence of Riding and Graves on discussion of the role in poetry of the sounds of words. Although Richards declares in *Science and Poetry* that "a good deal of poetry and even some great poetry exists … in which the sense of the words can be *almost* entirely missed or neglected without loss," his position on this question in both *Principles of Literary Criticism* and *Practical Criticism* is much less open to this possibility.[25] In the former, he acknowledges that there is "no such thing as *the* effect of a word or a sound. There is no one effect which belongs to it. Words have no intrinsic literary characters";[26] in the latter, he explains that "The mysterious glory which seems to inhere in the sound of certain lines is a projection of the thought and emotion they evoke, and the peculiar satisfaction they seem to give *to the ear* is a reflection of the adjustment *of our feelings* which has been momentarily achieved."[27]

Riding and Graves make a similar point about problems arising from the "great deal of emphasis on the phonetic sense of words" in "modern French poetic theory" generally, and in Valéry's poetry particularly.[28] Denying that sounds have intrinsic values, they demonstrate their argument by a simple experiment. Taking Tennyson's "immemorial elms / And murmur of innumerable bees," they "improvise a line of the same musical character but with a totally different meaning": "More ordure never will renew our midden's pure manure."[29] Richards undertakes the same experiment in *Practical Criticism*: if "the mere sound of verse has *independently* any considerable aesthetic virtue," then "it should be possible to take some masterpiece of poetic rhythm and compose, with nonsense syllables, a double or dummy which at least comes recognizably near to possessing the same virtue."[30] This Richards does, turning Milton's "On the Morning of Christ's Nativity," xv, into "J. Droostan-Sussting Benn / Mill-down Leduren N."[31]

Riding and Graves are by no means opposed to "picture-making in poetry by the help of sounds" – certain "sound-combinations may be very wittily employed" in a poem – but "musical meaning" must not "get the upper hand in a poem" over "word-meaning."[32] That "musical meaning" and "word-meaning" must work together is shown by the transformation of Tennyson's "murmur" into "pure manure": "This line will show how misleading to the sense letters can be, and makes us suspect that the aim of such poetry as Valéry's is to cast a musical enchantment unallied with the meaning of a poem. The meaning becomes merely a historical setting for the music."[33] Richards concludes his experiment with the same acknowledgment of the potential power of sound, and the same insistence that sound work with meaning: "Such arguments … do not tend to diminish the power of the sound (the inherent rhythm) *when it works in conjunction with sense and feeling*."[34]

Similarly, in *Practical Criticism*, Richards takes up the subject of stock responses once more, but this time in a way that shows he has been paying attention to what Riding and Graves have to say on this topic in *A Survey of Modernist Poetry*. He expands the approximately five-page treatment of the stock response in *Principles of Literary Criticism* into a discussion that begins in the Introduction, is continued thereafter on many pages throughout the book, culminates in a chapter of its own, "Irrelevant Associations and Stock Responses," and returns yet again in the Summary chapter that concludes the book. As in *Principles of Literary Criticism*, he attributes much of the problem to a certain kind of poem produced by a certain kind of poet: "Here ... the stock response actually is in the poem."[35] As an example of poems that depend on stock responses from readers, Richards points to poems that seem familiar, even on first acquaintance: "The familiarity of these poems belongs to them as we first read them, it is not an acquired familiarity but native. And it implies, I think, that the mental movements out of which they are composed have long been parts of our intellectual and emotional repertory."[36] This aspect of his discussion of stock responses clearly emerges from his analysis in *Principles of Literary Criticism* of the responses by his protocol writers to the sonnet by Ella Wheeler Wilcox.

But the focus of his analysis shifts. He emphasizes in his original treatment of the dangers of the stock response *the bad effect upon the reader* of the poem that the poet has built up as an invocation of stock responses. Such an emphasis is not surprising, for Richards is interested to define the role of poetry in systematizing the impulses of readers in a healthy, life-enabling equilibrium. In *Practical Criticism*, however, he emphasizes *the bad effect upon the poem* of the reader who imposes his own stock responses on it.

Richards now notices that a predisposition toward stock responses corrupts the interpretation even of poems without them: "the critical traps that surround what may be called *Stock Responses* ... have their opportunity whenever a poem seems to, or does, involve views and emotions already fully prepared in the reader's mind, so that what happens appears to be more of the reader's doing than the poet's. The button is pressed, and then ... the record starts playing in quasi- (or total) independence of the poem which is supposed to be its origin or instrument."[37] Falling into this trap, the reader is often "brought to object to a poem for not being quite a different poem, without regard paid to what it is *as itself*."[38] In this case, "it is the *difference* between the poem and the stock poem the reader has in mind that is the objection."[39] Such misreading involves "distorting the poem or setting up an irrelevant external standard."[40]

Practical Criticism argues that "Intelligent critics ... realize that no poem can be judged by standards external to itself."[41] In *Principles of Literary Criticism*, however, Richards regards judging a poem as a question of measuring its efficiency in stimulating a "supremely fine and complete organization" in the reader.[42] This organization, best evidenced in tragedy but not peculiar to it, consists of "balanced poise, stable through its power of inclusion, not through the force of its exclusions," and "it is a general characteristic of all the most valuable experiences of the arts."[43] Characteristic of experience of the arts, this inclusive balance of differences is a psychological property of the person, not the work of art: "We must resist the temptation to analyse its cause into sets of opposed characters in the object ... The balance is not in the structure of the stimulating object, it is in the response."[44] And so "Keats ... is a more efficient poet than Wilcox, and that is the same thing as saying that his works are more valuable."[45] In *Principles of Literary Criticism*, that is, the poem is judged entirely by standards external to itself: its efficiency in stimulating adequate attitudes and organizing impulses in economical and useful ways.

As John Paul Russo notes, however, whereas one can trace in Richards's earlier works such as *The Foundation of Aesthetics*, *The Meaning of Meaning*, and *Principles of Literary Criticism* his conception of the aesthetic experience as an equilibrium of opposed impulses in a reader, "soon he was asking not how a reader completes himself, but how the model poem ... completes itself."[46] Ransom points out that "Richards always holds ... that the heart of the aesthetic experience is the affective activity," but "in later books he will stop reiterating ... this dogma."[47] In fact, according to Ransom, *Practical Criticism* is the first occasion for the muting of this dogma because Richards has discovered that the best defense against stock responses – and the only cure for them once infection has set in – is precise cognition:

> In this connection it will be interesting to look at Richards' remarks on Sentimentality. For him, a sentimental reader is a person too facile, or too copious, in his affective responses to the object; his show of affections (as in those protocols which were "gushing"') seems to exceed the object. But this must mean that it exceeds the objective occasion, which is the "communicated" one. He is adding out of his own imagination to the occasion, or in his lack of experience he is

> misconstruing it; his reading is off the text. A sentimental poet, similarly, must be a poet who neglects a complete communication of his occasion, and for a short-cut pronounces the affective words that the reader should pronounce for himself, and then only on the understanding that they were appropriate to a communication that had been received. Whether of reader or poet, the error seems to reduce to Richards' idea of Stock Response: the affective activity is not grounded in precise cognition.[48]

The practical result of a critic's precise cognition of poetry, of course, is an ideal or exemplary reading.

•

For all their duplication in *A Survey of Modernist Poetry* of Richards's analysis of stock responses in *Principles of Literary Criticism*, Riding and Graves nonetheless inflect Richards's terms and concerns with their own idiom, which allows one to trace Richards's response to their work when he in turn adopts such idioms himself. For instance, according to Riding and Graves, the modernist poet has left the stock-feelings of literature for a psychological reality nearer to life: "it must be realized that it is always the poets who are the real psychologists, that it is they who break down antiquated literary definitions of people's feelings and make them or try to make them self-conscious about formerly ignored or obscure mental processes; for which an entirely new vocabulary has to be invented. The appearance of freakishness generally means: poetry is not in a 'poetical' period, it is in a psychological period. It is not trying to say 'Things often felt but ne'r so well expressed' but to discover what it is we are really feeling."[49] One recognizes Richards's explanation in *Principles of Literary Criticism* that the stock response fixes in place "immature and actually inapplicable attitudes to most things," with the result of "*removing us from experience.*"[50] He makes the case again in *Practical Criticism* for good poetry's power to redeem readers from stock reality: "The only corrective [to "stock inappropriate responses"] in all cases must be a closer contact with reality, either directly, through experience of actual things, or mediately through other minds which are in closer contact. If good poetry owes its value in large measure to the closeness of its contact with reality, it may thereby become a powerful weapon for breaking up unreal ideas and responses."[51]

The 1929 book seems in many ways to be taking up the argument developed in the 1924 book. Noting that even good poetry cannot prevail against stock responses "if we read into it just what we happen to have already in our minds, and do not use it as a means for reorganising ourselves," notwithstanding the fact that "most good poetry ... resists this kind of misusage," Richards laments that today "the emotional and intellectual habits of the readers are too strong for the poet. Moreover, the official doctrine of the eighteenth century that 'True wit is nature to advantage dress'd,/What oft was thought, but ne'er so well express'd' is still firmly entrenched in many minds."[52] It may be merely a coincidence that Richards follows Riding and Graves in associating the psychological inertia induced in contemporary readers by the stock response with an eighteenth-century aesthetic that he represents by the same quotation from Pope, but it is consistent with other evidence of how thoroughly he absorbed their book.

Similarly, Richards follows Riding and Graves in suggesting that stock responses are the result of bad parenting. For Riding and Graves, the reader who makes the poem "enter his life as a symbol having no private reality, only the reality it gets by reflection from his world," is paralleled by the poet who will not grant the poem independence, believing that "the important part of poetry is ... the personality of the poet as embodied in the poem, which is its style."[53] Between them, such a reader and such a poet maintain the vicious hermeneutic circle of the stock response: "Style may be defined as that old-fashioned element of sympathy with the reader which makes it possible for the poem to be used as an illustration to the text of the reader's experience."[54] To break this circle, the modernist poet aims at the poem's "independence from both the reader and the poet" – a sign of proper parenting.[55] According to Riding and Graves, "a new sense has arisen of the poem's rights comparable with the new sense in modern times of the independence of the child, and a new respect for the originality of the poem as for the originality of the child. One no longer tries to keep a child in place by suppressing its personality or laughing down its strange questions, so that it turns into a rather dull and ineffective edition of the parent; and modernist poetry is likewise freeing the poem of stringent nursery rules and, instead of telling it exactly what to do, is encouraging it to do things, even queer things, by itself ... The most that the poet can do is be a wise, experimenting parent."[56] As in modern parenting, what is needed is "a new kind of relationship between the parent and the child, the poet and the poem, a feeling of mutual respect favourable to the independent development of each and therefore to a maximum of benefit of one to the other. Of course, if the poem is left to shift entirely for itself and its independence is really only a sign of the irresponsibility of the poet, then its personality, by its wildness, is likely to be as indecisive as the personality of the formalized poem is by its reliance on discipline."[57]

According to Riding and Graves, in the attempt "to make a radical change in a tradition within the memory of that tradition," the modern poet must not address himself in the first instance to the education of the reader: "The problem of preventing poetry from sinking into rapid decline and disuse does not seem to point ... to a sense of responsibility in the poet toward the reader as shown in the use of a carefully designed 'style'" (and so, "much modernist poetry may be said to be literally without style").[58] The problem "points rather to the responsibility which the poet owes to the poem because of its dependence on him until it is complete, a dependence which shall not, however, be reflected as a weakness in the poem after it has been completed; as childhood should survive in a person as the element of continuous newness in him, not as the permanent bad effect of discipline that made him less, rather than more, independent as he grew."[59] And so the modern poet must first address himself to "the education of the poem (literally, the 'drawing out' of it)."[60]

Writing not metaphorically about the relationship between the poem as child and the poet as parent, but literally about the relationship between the child as bad reader and the parent as producer of the bad reader, Richards nonetheless traces the origin of "inappropriate stock responses" to the same source. As in *Principles of Literary Criticism*, so in *Practical Criticism* he declares that "the chief cause of ill-appropriate, stereotyped reactions is *withdrawal from experience*," yet he is no longer content to pass over the process by which this happens as though it were the natural outcome of a "deliberate organization of attitudes" consequent upon "general reflection," "social suggestion," and "accidents."[61] Instead, he blames bad reading on the kind of parenting that creates just "such moral disasters as produce timidity" as Riding and Graves describe.[62]

According to Richards, the "*withdrawal from experience*" that founds and funds the stock response "can come about in many ways. Physically, as when a London child grows up without ever seeing the country or the sea; morally, as when a particularly heavy parent deprives a child of all the adventurous expansive side of life; through convention and inculcation, as when a child being too easily persuaded what to think and to feel, develops parasitically; intellectually, as when insufficient experience is theoretically elaborated into a system that hides the real world from us."[63] Richards sounds the same notes as Riding and Graves: bad discipline makes a child less, rather than more, independent; the bad parent tells a child what to think; the bad parent restricts the child's play. The effect in a person is the same as the effect in a poem: bad parenting hinders and obstructs the proper relationship of each with reality.

Richards also traces in *Practical Criticism* the impact of bad pedagogy on the personality of the poem, following Riding and Graves in granting the poem a certain independence from writer and reader.[64] The more we examine the details of poems that seem familiar to us on first reading, he suggests, "the more we shall notice, I believe, their extreme impersonality – the absence of any personal individual character either in their movement as verse or in their phrasing ... Such impersonality, like the familiarity, is a sign that they are composed of stock responses."[65] Like the reader given to stock responses, the poem composed of stock responses cannot speak for itself or act on its own initiative: it thinks and feels only parasitically. The poet must not be so heavy a parent as by instilling conventional attitudes in general, and by inculcating the parent's own attitudes in particular, to leave the poem so easily persuaded what to think and feel that "The only touches of character that anyone can point to are the echoes of other poets."[66]

Such an attribution of personality to the poem cannot be explained by reference to *Principles of Literary Criticism*; it can, however, be explained as the consequence of, on the one hand, a sympathetic and appreciative reading of the development and extension of his ideas as undertaken by Riding and Graves in *A Survey of Modernist Poetry* and, on the other hand, as an acknowledgment of the force of the arguments that lead Riding and Graves to a wholesale repudiation of certain other of his ideas.

In the words of Riding and Graves, the poet who produces the poem of stock feelings and situations has not only refused to grant the poem independence, but has also made it "a rather dull and ineffective edition of the parent."[67] Riding and Graves use the word "edition" both figuratively and literally, for earlier in *Survey* they suggest that behind Cummings's poem "Sunset" – "at the back of the poet's mind," as it were – is the conventional sunset poem that Cummings is systematically avoiding, a poem thereby recoverable from the traces left by the efforts to erase it, so "Just as the naturalist Cuvier could reconstruct an extinct animal in full anatomical detail from a single tooth, let us restore this extinct poem from what Cummings has permitted to survive."[68] They come up with "Sunset Piece," a poem that "it is difficult to feel respect for" because it "is full of reminiscences not only of Remy de Gourmont, but of Wordsworth ... Milton ... Messrs. Belloc and Chesterton ... and Tagore in English translation."[69] The poem is an abridged edition of the work of popular precursors and contemporaries – in effect, a miniature anthology.

Of course Riding and Graves have composed a poem of "reminiscences" to show how the poem of stock feelings and situations finds its stock ready-to-hand in the warehouse of literary tradition. They make the abnormal personality of the original poem by Cummings disappear into impersonality and they allow no character to the poem beyond echoes of other poets. Richards may recall this playful exercise when, after identifying four of the poems that he gave his students as "composed of stock responses," he suggests that "Each of them might well have been written by a committee," as was "Sunset Piece" in *A Survey of Modernist Poetry*.[70]

In the inflection of his ideas with the idioms of Riding and Graves, I suggest, we can trace their influence in alerting Richards to the idea that what a poem means is a function of words on a page. In *Practical Criticism*, that is, Richards adapts a principle that Riding and Graves identify in modernist poetry into a principle applicable to all poetry: that poems must be judged by the standards that they imply. In *Principles of Literary Criticism* he had already accepted Graves's suggestion that poetry must be judged by its communication of experience, but he now shows the influence of Riding and Graves's assertion that poetry communicates an experience independent of the poet's experience. He apparently accepts their repudiation of his claim that H.D.'s poem, her personal experience prompting the poem, and his own paraphrase of poem and experience ought to converge in an experience of equal value.

18

Poetry, Interpretation, and Education

And so pedagogy's the thing. Does it promote the stock response, the stock feeling, the stock situation, the stock poem, or does it promote the independence and the individuality of the poem, the poet, and the reader? On these fronts, Richards's main concern in *Practical Criticism* is the same as that of Riding and Graves in *A Survey of Modernist Poetry*: how to educate people to become better readers of poetry, for better reading of poetry has the potential to make people better citizens of a democracy. Each book, furthermore, explores this problem in terms of its implications for classroom culture, literary culture, and political culture.

Riding and Graves trace resistance to modernist poetry back to the classroom, for the plain reader's "introduction to poetry is generally not through personal compulsion or curiosity, but through the systematic requirements of his education."[1] The "old-fashioned" school system ("which on the whole was preferable"), often using "poetry as a means of teaching grammar, or as so many lines to be learned by heart as a disciplinary task or penalty," at least tended to "leave poetry alone as poetry."[2] Riding and Graves dislike the new "liberal school-system," which "attempts to interest the child in the 'values' of poetry"; "'Beauty' is the term of approval which the schoolmaster applies to the 'values' of poetry; character-formation is their expressed practical end, or if not character-formation, at least a wholesome relief from its ardours."[3] In the new system, the young reader "will subscribe to these values and accept poetry through them, or he will not subscribe to these values but reject poetry through them."[4]

Either way the reader is alienated from poetry as poetry. In the old system, "the reader either discounts poetry for ever as a dreary pedagogical invention or he can perhaps rediscover it as something so different from the classroom exercise as to be unaffected by the unpleasant associations attached to it as such."[5] Riding and Graves prefer "the elder system" not just because it leaves poetry alone as poetry, but also because it leaves a way for the reader to escape the system "unaffected" as a reader of poetry. As they explain in *A Pamphlet Against Anthologies*, "There was this to be said for the old-fashioned straight-classical education, that what corresponded in the curriculum to the modern Poetry Lesson, the making of Latin Verses on the model of Ovid and Virgil, was never felt by the child to have any connection with poetry and was rather an amusing game, like the cross-word puzzle ... [S]o poetry was spared from the school-boy as he from it; and if in the play-hour he read or even wrote English poetry, the shadow of the blackboard did not darken the page."[6]

Riding and Graves support their assertions by analysis of Henry Newbolt's "official report on 'The Teaching of English in England' (1919)."[7] The full title of the document is "The teaching of English in England, being the Report of the Departmental Committee appointed by the President of the Board of Education to inquire into the position of English in the educational system of England."[8] The reference to this report by Riding and Graves is not quite accurate: the Committee was struck in 1919 but did not publish its report until 1921. It included the popular poet Sir Henry Newbolt as chairman, as well as a wide range of eminent members such as Arthur Quiller-Couch, John Dover Wilson, F.S. Boas, Caroline Spurgeon, and George Sampson, author of the almost-as-often quoted book *English for the English* (1921).[9] Graves reviewed the Newbolt Report for *The Daily Herald* in December of 1921.[10]

It was regarded in its own time as a progressive document, for it recognized the inappropriateness of using Latin grammar as a model for teaching English grammar, the need to distinguish both in textbooks and in teaching between prescriptive grammar and descriptive grammar, and the fundamental role of teaching English language and literature in forming a student's cultural knowledge and social sensibility. But the report has since been criticized for (among other things) its promotion of nationalistic cultural and moral values (to teach English literature is to teach "the native experience of men of our own race and culture," which will "form a new element of national unity, linking together the mental life of all classes by experiences which have hitherto been the privilege of a limited section"), its promotion of the best thoughts of the best minds as a weapon in the fight against the powerful influences of evil habits of speech contracted in home and street ("among the vast mass of the population, it is certain that if a child is not learning good English he is learning bad English, and probably bad habits of thought"), and its imperialistic celebration of the universal value of English language and literature (anticipating English's becoming the international language post-1919, the report suggests that "the position of the English language in the world affords an argument for all English children being taught English as distinct from a dialect of English").[11]

Riding and Graves identify the Newbolt Report as their prime target in their criticism of the new "liberal school-system" that has "generally superseded" the old one "in England and America."[12] They criticize its recommendations that teachers present a canon of literature espousing fundamental moral and spiritual values as a principle of selection and instruction by means of which "All poetry ... tends toward the same general tone and the same general purpose."[13] Emphasis on Englishness and class in poetry also makes for sameness because "sameness is accentuated by the nationalistic element: every poet wrote as an Englishman first, bound by his very use of the language to a policy of increasing the national heritage of song rather than the development of a strictly personal idiom. He also wrote as a member of a class, the governing class."[14] After Newbolt, "The emphasis that the educational system lays on personal and literary similarities in poets makes it still more difficult to appraise them separately."[15]

In the end, all poems become one poem and all poets become one poet. Just as lines from Remy de Gourmont, Wordsworth, Milton, Belloc, Chesterton, and Tagore can anonymously and impersonally combine in a collective stock sunset piece, so a selection by Riding and Graves of six "typical schoolroom passages" (by Shelley, Byron, Keats, Tupper, Wordsworth, and Coleridge) reflects such "extraordinary sameness" that one cannot ascribe them correctly to these six poets, poets who, encountered otherwise than in this universalizing schoolroom setting, are "of such entirely different personal character."[16]

Furthermore, with the stock subject and the stock setting – whether a natural sunset or a natural value – working to impersonalize both the poet and the poem, the new method of teaching English also works to impersonalize the reader. In the new system, teachers are encouraged to use the student essay to ensure that stock poems and stock values receive stock treatment, and so, according to Riding and Graves, the common specimen poem celebrated by the Newbolt Report goes hand-in-hand with the "common specimen-essay" it recommends:

> One of the stock essay-subjects in the schools is "The Uses of Poetry"; and when the essay comes up to be "corrected" and the humanistic teacher prepares a specimen-essay on the subject, the "uses" are found to be as follows:
>
> 1 Poetry gives the reader joy.
> 2 Poetry gives relief to sorrow, pain or weariness.
> 3 Poetry teaches the reader to love the Good.
> 4 Poetry is the concentrated wisdom of former ages.
> 5 Poetry teaches other-worldliness.
>
> and so on until the final summing-up …
> Poetry's uses may be expressed in a single phrase: Spiritual Elevation.[17]

According to Riding and Graves, teaching poetry in the Newbolt way condemns poetry to sameness by conflating its value as poetry with the religious, social, and national values that it is made to represent, and such teaching condemns to sameness the people educated to read poetry in this way.

Richards observes the same totalitarian potential in the misuse of poetry to promote stock responses – the "tendency of our acquired responses to intervene in situations to which they are not appropriate," a tendency that arises these days with "fatal facility."[18] He goes on, "If we wish for a population easy to control by suggestion we shall decide what repertory of suggestions it shall be susceptible to and encourage this tendency except in the few. But if we wish for a high and diffused civilization, with its attendant risks, we shall combat this form of mental inertia. In either case … we shall do well to recognize how much of the value of existence is daily thrust from us by our stock responses."[19]

Like Riding and Graves, he refers readers who want to know how English is now being taught in school to the Newbolt Report: "Those who wish to acquaint themselves with the methods employed in the schools could hardly do better than to consult the Report of the Departmental Committee appointed by the President of the Board of Education into the position of English in the educational system of England, entitled *The Teaching of English in England.*"[20] He also notes that "George Sampson's *English for the English* should on no account be overlooked. It says some things in a plain way, with passion and with point."[21] Richards repeats in his own conclusion in *Practical Criticism* the conclusion of the Newbolt Report that "every teacher in English is a teacher of English"[22]: "It is self-evident," the Report suggests, "that until a child has acquired a certain command of the English language, no other educational development is even possible ... Merely from this point of view English is plainly no matter of inferior importance, nor even one among other branches of education, but the one indispensable preliminary and foundation of all the rest."[23] He also adopts Sampson's bolder formulation of the same idea, that "Before the English child can awaken to any creative fullness of life he must become proficient in the use of his native tongue, the universal tool of all callings and of all conditions."[24] He concurs that "English is by far the most important subject," observing that "It is a condition of school life"; in fact, "English is really not a subject at all. It is a condition of existence rather than a subject of instruction. It is an inescapable circumstance of life, and concerns every English-speaking person from cradle to grave. The lesson in English is not merely one occasion for the inculcation of knowledge; it is part of the child's initiation into the life of man."[25] Richards emphasizes that instruction in proper understanding of English needs to be recognized as one of the most important aspects of this subject:

> The only improvements in training that can be suggested must be based upon a closer study of meaning and of the causes of unnecessary misunderstanding ... However incomplete, tentative, or, indeed, speculative we may consider our present views on the subject, they are far enough advanced to justify some experimental applications, if not in the school period then certainly at the Universities. If it be replied that there is no time for an additional subject, we can answer by challenging the time at present spent in extensive reading. A very slight improvement in the capacity to understand would so immensely increase the value of this time that part of it would be exchanged with advantage for direct training in reading. This applies quite as much to such studies as

> economics, psychology, political theory, theology, law or philosophy, as to literature ... [Q]uite as many readers blunder over intricate argumentation and exposition as poetry. And a direct study of interpretation here can be made quite as useful. The incidental training that everyone is supposed to receive in the course of studying other subjects is too fragmentary, accidental and unsystematic to serve this purpose. Sooner or later interpretation will have to be recognized as a key-subject.[26]

And so Richards supplements the Newbolt Report's claim that every teacher in English is a teacher of English with the suggestion that every teacher of English is a teacher of interpretation. Richards thus justifies *Practical Criticism*: although "no one would pretend that the theory as it is propounded in this book is ready, as it stands, for immediate and wide application," nonetheless "a very strong case can, I think, be made out, both for the need and the possibility of practical steps towards applying it," and so "we ought to hesitate before deciding that a Theory of Interpretation in some slightly more advanced and simplified form ... may not quite soon take the foremost place in the literary subjects of all the ordinary schools."[27]

Just as Newbolt and Sampson recognize the importance of teaching English not just as a lesson but also as "an initiation into the corporate life of man," Richards concedes that "Language is primarily a social product."[28] Yet he also recognizes, like Riding and Graves, that it is important to teach English in such a way as to enable not just corporate understanding, but also individual understanding. Like Riding and Graves, he objects to the Newbolt schoolmaster's reduction of poetry to a simple, single, sameness: "I have not heard of any schoolmaster who may have attempted to make a *systematic* discussion of the forms of meaning and the psychology of understanding part of his teaching. I have met not a few, however, who would treat the suggestion with an amused or indignant contempt. 'What! Fill the children's heads with a lot of abstractions! It is quite hard enough already to get them to grasp *one* meaning – THE MEANING – let alone four or sixteen, or whatever it is! They couldn't understand a word you were talking about.'"[29]

Like Riding and Graves, he refuses to accept that the plain reader must languish in the realm of the simple stock response: "the widespread inability to construe meaning" in poems is evidence that "this construing ... is not nearly so easy and 'natural' a performance as we tend to assume. It is a craft ... It can be taught ... The best methods of instruction remain to be worked out ... No attempt at imparting a reasoned general technique for construing has yet been made ... But it is not doubtful that ... this poor capacity to interpret complex and unfamiliar meanings is a source of endless loss, for those whose lives need not be narrowly standardized at a low level. If anything *can* be done, educationally, that is not already being done to improve it, the attempt would be worth much trouble."[30]

It is not clear whether or not Richards would have directed readers to the Newbolt Report had he not recently had it recalled for him by Riding and Graves in *A Survey of Modernist Poetry*. But Richards's agreement with much that Riding and Graves say is certainly clear. He agrees with them that the political consequences of teaching a generic sameness in poetry will be disastrous. He agrees with them that good poetry's ability to train a mind to be attentive to – and even feel at home in – ambiguity of meaning, and even ambiguity of syntax, is essential to a liberal democratic state. Riding and Graves present modernist poetry as the educational instrument that can improve the reader's ability to interpret complex and unfamiliar meanings in the world of human experience more generally. And they do so in a way that provides Richards with the main outlines of his own model for a properly modern human consciousness. For all three, the nature of present society and the future of humankind are at stake in the question of how to interpret poetry.

•

The Chapter "Variety in Modernist Poetry" in *A Survey of Modernist Poetry* is dedicated to the discovery of an antidote to the "sameness" that threatens poems, poets, and readers should the attitudes toward poetry promoted in the Newbolt Report come to hold sway. Riding and Graves imply that the Newbolt Report is the latest incarnation of a regular feature of the history of poetry; one tends to find "a tacit or written critical agreement as to the historical form proper to the poetry of any period," and also agreement on "the necessity of having socially secure convictions."[31] In short, there has always been a poetry "of the school-room tradition": "Poetry was to poets of the school-room tradition the instrument, the illustration of their convictions, whether ... patriotic ... moral ... religious ... 'philosophical'... social ... 'artistic' ... Even the decadents at the end of the last century were decadent from conviction ... Decadence introduced no variety. It merely substituted self-satisfied pessimism for self-satisfied optimism; and one nationalism for another by moving the poetical center from London to Paris."[32] Agreeing with Riding and Graves that the sole aim of a poem is "becoming what in the end it has become" and that the sole aim of the reader and critic is to recognize "what it is," Richards disavows as a poem's aim the same list of goals and standards external to it they formulate: "I do not mean by its 'aim' any sociological, aesthetic, commercial or propagandistic intentions or hopes of the poet."[33]

According to Riding and Graves, poetry of the school-room tradition flourishes in the marketplace of a mass society, the efficiency of its large-scale reproduction of sameness answering with appropriate supply the very demand that its miseducation of plain readers creates. "The sameness of poetry is likewise accentuated rather than diminished by the spirit of competition. Once there is a tacit or written critical agreement as to the historical form proper to the poetry of any period, all the poets of fashion or 'taste' vie with each other in approximating to the perfect period manner ... willing to polish away every vestige of personal eccentricity from their work. Period monotony is further increased by imitation of the most successful 'period' poets."[34] Acknowledging the influence of just such a marketplace upon poets, Richards half-jokingly anticipates a similar misuse of the information to be gleaned from *Practical Criticism*: "A strange light ... is thrown upon the sources of popularity for poetry. Indeed I am not without fears that my efforts may prove of assistance to young poets (and others) desiring to increase their sales. A set of formulae for 'nation-wide appeal' seems to be a just possible outcome."[35]

For Riding and Graves, contemporary resistance to the impersonal, commodifying, and imperial tendencies of the schoolroom tradition is centred in modernism: "The school-room may still remain the citadel of convictions ... But the modernist poet does not write for the school-room: if for anything at all, for the university."[36] They celebrate "the lack of narrow schoolroom purposiveness shown by modernist poets," arguing that for the modernist, "poetry ceases to be the maintenance of a single idealistic tone; it has a less obvious, a more complicated consistency."[37] Opposing the interest in sameness in "the old world of poetry ... going on at the same time," modernism offers "alternatives" to the "single idealistic tone":

"This refinement of conviction, this maturing of social purposiveness, contributes more than any other cause to the raising of the barriers of poetical monotony."[38]

According to Riding and Graves there are three degrees of modernist poet, descending from the "free-lance modernist" to the "professional modernist," and then finally to the "pseudo-modernist."[39] They are distinct in terms of their attitude towards one of the qualities that distinguishes modernism: "individuality." The free-lance modernist sets the standard: "Free-lance modernists do not make 'individuality' their object: their object is to write each poem in the most fitting way. But the sum of their works has individuality because of their natural variousness; like the individuality of the handwriting of all independent-minded men or women, however clearly and conventionally they form their actual letters."[40] Other modernists deploy individuality purposefully: "To professional modernists individuality is the earnest of a varied social purposiveness. To pseudo-modernists individuality is the earnest of a narrow literary purposiveness."[41]

The professional modernist poet purposes by his "individuality" an alternative to the schoolroom monotony of sameness in poem, poet, and reader. In such cases, "modernism is a professional conscience rather than a personal trait."[42] Pseudo-modernists are shaped by the schoolroom tradition. Ironically, "Individuality" is even more their object than it is for the professional modernists, its object being to show that they have identified and followed the "formula" of the modernist period style: "In this they are not dissimilar from those eighteenth-century poets whose sole object was to write correctly, to conform to the manner of the period. In practice, this conforming individualism means an imitation, studiously concealed, merely of the eccentricities of poetry that is really individual."[43]

Misshaped by the schoolroom tradition, the conscience of professional and pseudo-modernist alike is further misshaped by their constant attention to their competitive position in the marketplace. In a poetic environment where "modernism is a professional conscience rather than a personal trait ... the modernist poetry-producing world has the look of a complicated hierarchy," for there will always be "a certain sifting and grading of personalities and groups," both by the professional modernists and by the pseudo-modernists.[44] And "the complication is increased by the efforts of professional modernists to enroll free-lance modernists in their socially purposive movement, and of pseudo-modernists to enroll themselves in it by literary forgery."[45]

According to this valuation of genuine individuality by Riding and Graves, the free-lance modernist will try to evade imitation, even changing his signature to prevent forgery: "The only legitimate use of the word 'style' in poetry is as the personal handwriting in which it is written; if it can be easily imitated or defined as a formula it should be immediately suspect to the poets themselves."[46] Of course "'Groups' may spring up in the old style around any poet; but in general, the free-lance modernist who had by accident become popular or notorious and still retained a sense of personal dignity would shrink from being made a '*cher maître*' ... Indeed, as soon as any imitation is made of his work, and his style by imitation becomes a formula of mannerisms, he may even be inclined to change them to preserve his integrity."[47]

Richards also follows Ridings and Graves in identifying the ironic modernist state of mind as the best resource for coping with an increasingly complex political future. He presents poetry like Eliot's as a welcome incitement to the development of new methods of reading poetry that will make us better citizens of the liberal democratic state. Once upon a time, Richards observes, one could run a business or speak a language without much formal knowledge of business and without much formal knowledge of the language: "Some generations ago, when businesses were simpler and more separate, the owner could carry one on by rule of thumb or by mere routine proficiency without troubling himself much about general industrial or economic conditions. It is not so now. Similarly, when man lived in small communities, talking or reading, on the whole, only about things belonging to his own culture, and dealing only with ideas and feelings familiar to his group, the mere acquisition of his language through intercourse with his fellows was enough to give him a good command of it."[48] Of course it is not so now: "Our everyday reading and speech now handles scraps from a score of different cultures ... [W]e are forced to pass from ideas and feelings that took their form in Shakespeare's time or Dr. Johnson's time to ideas and feelings of Edison's time or Freud's time and back again ... The result of this heterogeneity is that for all kinds of utterances our performances, both as speakers (or writers) and listeners (or readers), are worse than those of persons of similar natural ability, leisure and reflection a few generations ago."[49]

To avoid the confusion and misunderstanding that arise from the fact that words have multiple, ambiguous referents in the cosmopolitan culture of the twentieth century ("And this threat ... can only grow worse as world communications, through the wireless and otherwise, improve"), a new mind must be developed.[50] This will be a "mind that can shift its view-point and still keep its orientation, that can carry over into quite a new set of definitions the results gained through experience in other frameworks, the mind that can rapidly and without strain or confusion perform the systematic transformations required by such a shift."[51] The mind that can shift from the ideas and feelings of Shakespeare's time to those of Freud's time and back again ("descending from the scholar's level to the kitchen-maid's," says Richards), looks a lot like the mind that composed *The Waste Land,* shifting from *The Tempest*'s "Those are pearls that were his eyes!" to Cockney gossip about Albert and Lil and then to Ophelia's farewell, "Goodnight sweet ladies" (via a barbershop quartet's version of a similar lyric). There are "few such minds" at present, however, because "The whole linguistic training we receive at present is in the other direction, towards supplying us with one or other of a number of frameworks of doctrine into which we are taught to force all the material we would handle."[52]

The "fameworks of doctrine" into which poetry is fitted are particularly damaging to this future mind. So far as poetry is concerned, "our educational methods are glaringly at fault, creating a shibboleth situation that defeats its purpose": "Our traditional ideas as to the values of poetry – given us automatically if poetry is set apart from life, or if poems are introduced to us from the beginning as either good or bad, as 'poetry' or 'not poetry' – misrepresent the facts and raise unnecessary difficulties. It is less important to like 'good' poetry and dislike 'bad,' than to be able to use them both for ordering our minds ... So long as we feel that the judgment of poetry is a social ordeal, and that our real responses to it may expose us to contempt, our efforts ... will not take us far. But most of our responses are not real, are not our own, and this is just the difficulty."[53]

All is not lost, however, for new ways of reading poetry can lead us into the future with precisely the kind of mind that the future will require. On the one hand, "As the finer parts of our emotional tradition relax in the expansion and dissolution of our communities, and as we discover how far out of our intellectual depth the flood-tide of science is carrying us ... we shall increasingly need every discipline that can be devised."[54] On the other hand, "If we are neither to swim blindly in schools under the suggestion of fashion, nor to shudder into paralysis before the inconceivable complexity of existence, we must find means of exercising our power of choice."[55] This discipline and this power of choice can be found in studying poetry. "The critical reading of poetry is an arduous discipline; fewer exercises reveal to us more clearly the limitations under which, from moment to moment, we suffer. But, equally, the immense extension of our capacities that follows a summoning of our resources is made plain. The lesson of all criticism is that we have nothing to rely upon in making our choices but ourselves. The lesson of good poetry seems to be that, when we have understood it, in the degree in which we can order ourselves, we need nothing more."[56] It is poetry that will enable the free man to choose, and teach him how to do so.

•

Richards finds in many of his protocol writers precisely the fearful, risk-averse, self-protection that contemporary educational methods promote, but once again Riding and Graves have beaten Richards to the punch. They identify the same failings in the plain reader, who is "the timid victim of orthodox criticism on the one hand, and unorthodox poetry on the other"; "His attitude toward poetry has … to be one of self-defence. He must be cautious in his choice of what he reads. He must not make a fool of himself by reading anything in which he may be called on to rely on his own critical opinion."[57] Such a reader resists the poem's call to authentic engagement: "Poetry … in its more exacting side, makes … no demands which exceed the private intimacy of the reader and the poem … But the plain reader is … afraid of the infringements that poetry may make on his private mental and spiritual ease … And undoubtedly the way that anything can interfere most with an individual's privacy is by demanding criticism (complete attention, complete mental intimacy and confidence) for itself from him."[58] Above all, the plain reader avoids difficult poetry, "for if it is difficult it means that he must think in unaccustomed ways, and thinking to the plain reader, beyond the range necessary for the practical purposes of living, is unsettling and dangerous; he is afraid of his own mind."[59] Consistent with these principles, "he will prefer an unoriginal but undisturbing poem to an original but disturbing one … [N]o common poetry reader could bring himself without great effort to meet the demands of thought put upon him by an authentic poem."[60]

Richards generalizes about the contemporary "critical act" in similar terms: "The personality stands balanced between the particular experience which is the realized poem and the whole fabric of its past experiences and developed habits of mind. What is being settled is whether this new experience can or cannot be taken into the fabric with advantage ... Often it must be the case that ... too much reconstruction would be needed. The strain, the resistance, is too great, and the poem is rejected."[61] Readers of this sort frustrate Richards, and so he gives least representation among the protocols that he quotes to "that great body of readers whose first and last reaction to poetry ... is bewilderment" – "the havering, non-committal, vague, sit-on-the-fence, middle-body of opinion."[62] The average reader too often "feels himself distressingly at a loss before a poem. Too sheer a challenge to his own unsupported self seems to be imposed ... Without *some* objective criteria, by which poetry can be tested, and the good distinguished from the bad, he feels like a friendless man deprived of weapons and left naked at the mercy of a treacherous beast."[63]

Richards's metaphor is similar to the one that Riding and Graves use to depict the discomfort of the self-confronting modern poems in which the poet has abjured the tradition of writing poetry "formed with an eye to its serviceability as reading matter": "the reader does not really want to be left alone with poetry. The mental ghosts, which only poets are supposed to have commerce with, assail him. The real discomfort to the reader in modernist poetry is the absence of the poet as his protector from the imaginative terrors lurking within it."[64] The one's "treacherous beast" descends from the "imaginative terrors" of the others' "mental ghosts."

Riding and Graves declare that such a reader "is afraid of his own mind," and so does Richards: "We decided that the treacherous beast was within him, that critical weapons ... would only hurt him, that his own experience – not as represented in a formula, but in its available entirety – was his only safeguard, and that if he could rely sufficiently upon this, he could only profit from his encounter with the poem."[65] As Riding and Graves put it, "if the plain reader could conquer his initial self-consciousness ... it should be possible to be on completely unembarrassed and impersonal terms with poetry."[66] Richards too depicts poetry as calling the reader to an intimate engagement with that reader's own mind, an intimacy and an engagement in which the reader risks his sense of himself and his reality: "When we have the poem in all its minute particulars as intimately and as fully present to our minds as we can contrive ... then our acceptance or rejection of it must be *direct*. There comes a point in all criticism where a sheer choice has to be made without the support of any arguments, principles, or general rules ... [I]t is in these moments of sheer decision that the mind becomes most plastic, and selects ... the direction of its future development."[67] And in the liberal capitalist democracy that Richards imagines, of course, this plastic mind's choices will existentially found and fund collective future development of human being.

19

Anthology Culture, Self-Reliance, and Self-Development

Another of the "chief difficulties of criticism" that Richards identifies and explains in a way that suggests the influence of Riding and Graves concerns "the effects of *technical presuppositions*" ("whenever we attempt to judge poetry from outside by technical details") and the effects of "*general critical preconceptions* (prior demands made upon poetry as a result of theories – conscious or unconscious – about its nature and values)."[1] According to Richards, these preconceptions and preconditions are a function of anthology culture, which impedes a reader's abilities to rely on his own wit to interpret poetry and to develop himself through the reading of poetry. By 1928, there was no issue in contemporary literary criticism more distinctly the preserve of Riding and Graves than such criticism of anthology culture.

Riding and Graves deal at length with the problems that these "theories" about the nature and value of poetry create for poetry and its readers. They suggest, on the one hand, that "No genuine poet or artist ever called himself after a theory or invented a name for a theory," and, on the other hand, that any fairly good poet can be used to justify any practicable theory of poetry, however inadequate a theory it may be by which to write poetry."[2] Shakespeare, for instance, "was independent of poetic theory" and yet "can be used to justify … any … poetic theory simply because he was such a good poet."[3] Theories are the creation of poets who lack genius and critics who lack poetic sense: "An undue prominence is given to poetic theories either when people who are not real poets are encouraged by the low state of poetry to try to write it themselves … Or when critics without any poetic sense attempt to explain changes in poetry to themselves and to the reading public."[4] The reading public is most vulnerable to the bad effects of poetic theories because "it is surely criticism which has always stood between poetry and the plain reader, made possible the writing of so much false poetry and, by granting too much respect to theories, lost the power of distinguishing between what is false and what is true."[5]

In *Practical Criticism*, Richards notes that "The protocols show ... how entirely a matter of authority the rank of famous poets, as it is accepted and recognized by public opinion, must be."[6] For "a great body" of protocol writers, the task of judging an anonymous poem produced only "bewilderment": "Without further clues (authorship, period, school, the sanction of an anthology, or the hint of a context) the task of 'making up their minds about it,' or even of working out a number of possible views from which to choose, was felt to be really beyond their powers."[7] The cause of the "despairing helplessness" that "haunts the protocols" is a dependence fostered by anthology culture.[8] From the point of view of even the well-educated protocol writer, it is a "mysterious, traditional authority" that determines "the rank of famous poets."[9] And so "the sanction of an anthology" takes the place of self-reliant evaluation and effectively makes up the reader's mind about poetry.

Richards seems to register here the argument of Riding and Graves against the lazy reading habits encouraged by anthology culture. According to Richards, the contemporary reader's "despairing helplessness" when faced with the task of distinguishing between good and bad poetry without the unholy ghost of traditional authority to guide him "should lead us to question very closely the quality of the reading we ordinarily give to authors whose rank and character have been officially settled ... Far more than we like to admit, we take a hint for our response from the poet's reputation. Whether we assent or dissent, the traditional view runs through our response like the wire upon which a hanging plant is trained ... The attempt to read without this guidance puts a strain upon us that we are little accustomed to ... We learn how much we are indebted to the work of other minds that have established the tradition ... And we discover what a comparatively relaxed and inattentive activity our ordinary reading of established poetry is."[10] This is precisely the point of Riding and Graves's exercise of reading beyond the relaxed and inattentive reading of Shakespeare's sonnet encouraged by the anthology tradition.

•

In his explanation in *Practical Criticism* of how much time his students spent preparing their protocols, Richards suggests that "on the whole it is fairly safe to assert that the poems received much more thorough study than, shall we say, most anthology pieces get in the ordinary course."[11] The archness of his "shall we say" construction perhaps acknowledges the campaign against anthology culture waged by Riding and Graves, the culture most responsible for the plain reader's expectation that a proper poem ought to be understandable on a first, quick reading.

The incidental sniping in *A Survey of Modernist Poetry* at Louis Untermeyer's *Anthology of Modern American Poetry* as "an anthology whose principal aim is to soothe, not irritate" – a typical aspect of the anthology's preference for "simplicity" – and the sustained criticism of the mangling of Shakespeare's "Th' expense of Spirit in a waste of shame" by "the *Oxford Book of English Verse* and other popular anthologies which have apparently chosen this sonnet from all others as being particularly easy to understand" express Riding and Graves's concern that readers have been so thoroughly trained by anthology reading to expect poetry to be comprehensible at a glance that they will not spend more than a few minutes reading a poem.[12] As we have seen, they offer Riding's "The Rugged Black of Anger" as an example of a modernist poem the difficulty of "which would probably cause it to be put aside by the critic after he had allowed it the customary two-minute reading."[13] As they note in *A Pamphlet Against Anthologies*, "The reader whose first approach to poetry is through anthologies usually acquires the anthology habit for life ... He has never read a long poem ... He cannot read any poem which presents the slightest difficulty of thought, which demands, that is, more than one reading."[14]

Richards's familiarity with *A Pamphlet Against Anthologies* is suggested by his discussion of "the general question of the place of the plain prose sense, or thought, in poetry."[15] Riding and Graves read Wordsworth's "A slumber did my spirit seal" very closely in terms of its plain prose sense: "As a prose fancy this poem is confused and illogical ... [F]rom the prose point of view ... the details are even more illogical than the main argument."[16] Their point is that the poem "is not logical," was not meant to be, and certainly ought not to have been: "It has rather a supra-logical harmony, by identity of the theme, which shows the inability of the mind to face the actual reality of death, with the expression, which shows an inability to get the right words to pair off in a logical prose manner. Had the mind been able to face lyrically the fact of Lucy's death and had the words been illogically placed; or had the mind not been able to face the fact and had the words been logically placed – it would not have been as true a poem as it is now in its distortion."[17]

Richards presents similar observations about the potential virtuosity of departing from plain prose sense. On the one hand, he offers the example of Swinburne as "a very suitable poet in whom to study the subordination, distortion and occultation of sense through the domination of verbal feeling" because in his poetry, "the argument, the interconnection of the thought, has very little to do with the proper effect of the poem, where the thought may be incoherent and confused without harm, for the very simple reason that the poet is not using the argument as an argument."[18] One notes here the word that Riding and Graves use to describe poetry's departure from prose sense: "distortion." On the other hand, Richards acknowledges distortion of the prose sense in a poem as a proper way of accurately depicting "desperate or sublime" feelings: "There are types of poetry ... where the effect of the poem may turn upon irrationality, where the special feelings which arise from recognizing incompatibility and contradiction are essential parts of the poem."[19] This is the point that Riding and Graves make about Wordsworth's poem.

Similarly, in his own anthological presentation to his students of poems arbitrarily grouped together for protocol analysis, Richards notes the same intertextual confusions that Riding and Graves identify in the effect of anthologies upon readers. The latter complain that anthologized poems infect readings of each other where common themes, images, settings, events, and so on, can be identified: "We could show how, in alphabetical anthologies ... Wordsworth's 'Lucy' will get somehow identified with Rogers' 'Lucy' poem ... and how in a subject anthology, under the heading of 'Lost Maidens,' the 'Lucy of the Springs of Dove' will get confused with Kingsley's 'Mary of the sands of Dee.'"[20] It gets worse. "Once these confusions start, there is no checking them. Byron's praise of his mistress ... is infected by and infecting Sir Henry Wotton's praise of his ... Shirley and Shakespeare, alphabetically allied, get entangled ... Through likeness of title and nearness of date poems so fundamentally unlike as Keats' *Nightingale* and Shelley's *Skylark* affect each other strangely."[21]

Richards is similarly bemused by his students' tendency to compare and contrast the poems in the sets of four that he has grouped together quite arbitrarily for their perusal, speculating that "the collocation of this set of four poems ... may be thought to have acted rather unfairly as a trap" to induce such comparison and contrast, and yet confessing that "this mutual influence between poems that are presented together is as difficult to calculate as to avoid."[22]

•

And so Richards attributes precisely the same function to poetic theories and observes precisely the same vulnerabilities in contemporary readers as Riding and Graves. He too holds that "Most critical dogmas, preconceptions of the kind that can be and are applied to poetry ... rest upon our desire for explanation, our other desires, our respect for tradition, and to a slight degree upon faulty induction."[23] He traces to our desire for explanation and our "predilection" for certain experiences in poetry the same loss of power to distinguish between true and false poetry that Riding and Graves complain of: "The result of a highly ambiguous though simple-seeming doctrine, when it collaborates with our well ascertained capacity to read poems as we wish to read them, is to disable our judgment to a point well below its normal unindoctrinated level."[24] In fact, according to Richards, "All critical doctrines are attempts to convert choice into what may seem a safer activity – the reading [of] evidence and the application of rules and principles. They are an invasion into an inappropriate sphere of that modern transformation, the displacement of the will by observation and judgment."[25] "On the whole," he concludes, critical doctrines "make us much more stupid than we would be without them."[26]

In their rewriting of E.E. Cummings's poem "Sunset" as "Sunset Piece," Riding and Graves identify ways in which the poem fails to satisfy the plain reader's expectations concerning proper poetic techniques and ways in which it fails to express the values expected of a poem called "Sunset": "With so promising a title, what barriers does the poem raise between itself and the plain reader? In what respects does it seem to sin against the common intelligence? To begin with, the lines do not begin with capitals. The spacing does not suggest any regular verse form ... No punctuation marks are used. There is no obvious grammar ... But even overlooking these technical oddities, it still seems impossible to read the poem as a logical sequence. A great many words essential to the coherence of the ideas suggested have been deliberately omitted; and the entire effect is so sketchy that the poem might be made to mean almost anything or nothing."[27] They interpret Cummings's poem as an attempt to avoid the kind of sunset poem by means of which anthologies "have indulged" the plain reader's "lazy reading habits" and thereby contributed to the degradation of the common intelligence ("our common intelligence is the mind in its least active state").[28] "Sunset" is "a case of making the lazy reader think and work along with the poet."[29]

Since "stale phrases" that "have come to mean so little that they scarcely do their work" in a poem "cannot be avoided" if one is to write "the poem for the plain man," and since in the face of the "stalenesses in traditional poetry" Cummings feels "obliged to attack them or escape from them," the poem "Sunset" strikes Riding and Graves as itself running the danger of becoming a formulaic anti-poem.[30] "Cummings' technique, indeed, if further and more systematically developed, would become so complicated that poetry would be no more than mechanical craftsmanship, the verse patterns growing so elaborate that the principal interest in them would be mathematical."[31] Although "in their present experimental stage, and only in their experimental stage, these patterns are undoubtedly suggestive," Cummings must beware the poem with no more than "a technical soul" because "excessive interest in the mere technique of the poem can become morbid in both the poet and the reader, like the composing and solving of cross-word puzzles."[32]

As things stand, however, one of the most important ways in which this poem by Cummings is "suggestive" is pedagogically: "The important thing to recognize, in a time of popular though superficial education, is the necessity of emphasizing to the reading public the differences between good and bad poems."[33] In "Sunset," according to Riding and Graves, Cummings accepts the obligation "in such a time ... to teach the proper approach to poetry."[34] If we consider sunset poems as a whole, "we may not accept the Cummings version, but once we have understood it we cannot return with satisfaction to the standardized one."[35] An experimental poem of this sort proposes to stimulate active reading, to raise the level of common intelligence, and thereby to reduce the market for anthologies. "It is not suggested here that poets should imitate Cummings, but that poems like Cummings' and the attention they demand should make it harder for the standardized article to pass itself off as poetry."[36]

When they later set for the plain reader the task of determining who amongst contemporary poets is a free-lance modernist, a professional modernist, and a pseudo-modernist, Riding and Graves suggest that the first step is to move beyond all technical presuppositions and critical preconceptions. They claim that "Criticism in the simplest literary scenes has never been able to recognize who are authentic contemporary poets and how much of each poet is authentic."[37] Quantity overwhelms critics; the contemporary scene confronts them not just with too many poets, but more disconcertingly with too many varieties of poetry: "Criticism (even advanced criticism), reared for centuries on the faith of the technical and philosophical consistency of poetry (a faith continuously derived and revised from Aristotle), cannot cope with poetry in quantity; as it could a hundred years ago, when the possible varieties of poetical composition were countable on the fingers."[38] Critics simply know too much; "the usual type of orthodox critic is more equipped with prejudices than the plain reader, if only because his position forces him to know quantitatively more, and ... he therefore has a less reliable instinct than the plain reader for determining what is genuine and what is not."[39] Paradoxically, then, an even more ignorant reader than the one castigated for his inactive intelligence offers some hope for the future of poetry: "The reader, even the critic, does not have to trouble to plot out a literary chart, to develop a carefully graded technical vocabulary. All that either of them needs is a simple and instinctive recognition of the real, which is easily discovered if all other personal or critical questions are brushed aside as irrelevant."[40]

This course of analysis and argument is the same as Richards's:

> We should be better advised to acknowledge frankly that, when people put poems in our hands ... what we say, in nine cases out of ten, has nothing to do with the poem ... It cannot arise from the poem if the poem is not yet there in our minds, and it hardly ever, in fact, is there ... It would be an excellent thing if all the critical chitchat which we produce on these occasions were universally recognized to be what it is, social gesture, "phatic communion" ... [T]he sincere and innocent reader is much too easily bounced into emptying his mind by any literary highwayman who says, "I want your opinion," and much too easily laid low because he has nothing to produce on these occasions. He might be comforted if he knew how many professionals make a point of carrying stocks of imitation currency, crisp and bright, which

> satisfy the highwaymen and are all that even the wealthiest critic in these emergencies can supply.[41]

Richards employs the colourful metaphor of the professional critic as counterfeiter where Riding and Graves simply speak of the "orthodox critic" as "more equipped with prejudices," but the task, as Richards sees it, is to escape the preconceptions that Riding and Graves identify in favour of the personal engagement with the poem that they recommend. On the successful completion of this task depend the personal future of the reader, the future of poetry within British culture – and perhaps the future of civilization itself.[42]

Although in *Principles of Literary Criticism* the guidance of the reader's mind towards an efficient organization of energies that the minds of poets have achieved is the greatest value that literature offers, Richards takes the position of Riding and Graves in *Practical Criticism*, warning of the "dangers" of the average reader's dependence for "guidance" in reading, understanding, and valuing literature on the "other minds that have established the tradition."[43] By the experiment conducted in *Practical Criticism*, "we discover what a comparatively relaxed and inattentive activity our ordinary reading of established poetry is."[44] This is the common mind in its least active state, the tired mind of lazy reading habits that Riding and Graves decry. There is no hint in *Principles of Literary Criticism* of anger, or even impatience, towards Richards's first students, whose inadequate readings of poems are occasionally acknowledged in this book. By their disdain for the plain reader, Riding and Graves may have emboldened Richards to take a similarly bare-knuckled approach to his protocol writers.

Richards also identifies a reader's preoccupation with what Riding and Graves call "personal or critical questions" as the greatest impediment to what they call "a simple and instinctive recognition of the real": "simple-seeming doctrine … collaborates with our well ascertained capacity to read poems much as we wish to read them" in a "degradation" of the reading process.[45] In many of the protocols, Richards notes, "certain tests, criteria and presuppositions as to what is to be admired or despised in poetry proved their power to hide what was actually present … [A] serious … reader, unprovided with any such criteria, theories and principles, often feels himself distressingly at a loss before a poem … The desire to condense his past experience, or to invoke doughty authority, is constantly overwhelming."[46]

Like Riding and Graves, Richards prefers that the reader be "left naked" before the poem, rather than clothed in the presuppositions of others. Since critical dogmas "make us much more stupid than we would be without them" (they "disable our judgment to a point well below its normal unindoctrinated level"), our task is to escape them. According to Richards, the reader's "own experience – not as represented in a formula but in its available entirety – [is] his only safeguard, and ... if he could rely sufficiently upon this, he could only profit from his encounter with the poem."[47] Once again Richards characterizes the experience as the same sort of "simple and instinctive recognition of the real" that Riding and Graves describe: "When we have the poem in all its minute particulars as intimately and as fully present to our minds as we can contrive – no general description of it but the very experience itself present as a living pulse in our biographies – then our acceptance or rejection of it must be direct. There comes a point in all criticism where a sheer choice has to be made without the support of any arguments, principles, or general rules."[48] In fact, "*critical* certainties, convictions as to the value, and kinds of value, of kinds of poetry, might safely and with advantage decay, provided there remained a firm sense of the critical act of choice, its difficulty, and the supreme exercise of all our faculties that it imposes."[49]

Richards now conceives of a reader's proper, authentic engagement with poetry as rather existential: no longer is it merely a vaguely evolutionary exercise in organizational efficiency, but rather it is an exercise of will in the making of human being. As "a sheer choice ... made without the support of any arguments, principles, or general rules," the critical act is for Richards "the starting-point, not the conclusion, of an argument. The personality stands balanced between the particular experience which is the realized poem and the whole fabric of its past experiences and developed habits of mind. What is being settled is whether this new experience can or cannot be taken into the fabric with advantage."[50]

Richards here applies to the reader language that Riding and Graves apply to the poem: "Modern poetry ... is groping for some principle of self-determination to be applied to the making of the poem – not lack of government, but government from within."[51] They authorize this shift by their valuation of a poem like "Sunset" by Cummings, whose "method turns the reader into a poet": "This *Sunset* poem of Mr. Cummings, then, is not, strictly speaking,

Mr. Cummings' poem, but the poem of anybody who will be at pains to write it ... The poet blends the subject of the poem with the feelings that the subject arouses into one expression. This unity makes the poem a living whole."[52] Reading a certain kind of modern poem properly, in other words, is an existential exercise. According to Riding and Graves, the genuinely creative poet – "the making poet" – does not repeat a method; indeed, "The making poet ... has no method, but a faculty for allowing things to invent themselves."[53] It is this "'obsession with making' ... that the reader will have to reckon with if poetry continues in its present tendency of forcing him inside the framework of the poem and making him repeat the steps by which it came to be. So that technique in the modernist definition does not refer to the method by which a poem is written but that evolutionary history of the poem which is the poem itself."[54] To read such a modernist poem in the way it requires, in other words, is for the reader to participate in the poem's self-governed creation. The poem's biography becomes part of the reader's biography: a vicarious experience of self-creation, self-explanation, self-government.

Richards makes very similar points: first, that when one lives at the level where one's impulses are most organized, life is a poem; second, that a poem's effect on a reader can cascade over all other aspects of his life. He explains in *Principles of Literary Criticism* that aesthetic experiences

> are the most formative experiences, because in them the development and systematization of our impulses goes to the furthest lengths. In our ordinary life a thousand considerations prohibit for most of us any complete working out of our response ... But in the "imaginative experience" these obstacles are removed. Thus what happens here, what precise stresses, preponderances, conflicts, resolutions and interanimations, what remote relationships between different systems of impulses arise, what before unapprehended and inexecutable connections are established, is a matter which, we see clearly, may modify all the rest of his life. As a chemist's balance to a grocer's scales, so is the mind in the imaginative moment to the mind engaged in ordinary intercourse or practical affairs.[55]

In *Practical Criticism*, when discussing the opportunity for "self-completion" that the proper criticism of poetry allows, Richards expresses frustration that a number of quite formidable critics have misinterpreted his interest in poetry's ability to organize a reader's impulses as an interest in something like a mechanical order rather than in the unified, living whole:

> I have in several other places made prolonged and determined efforts to indicate the types of mental order I have in mind, but without escaping certain large misunderstandings ... Thus Mr Eliot, reviewing *Science and Poetry* in *The Dial*, describes my ideal order as "Efficiency, a perfectly-working mental Roneo Steel Cabinet System," and Mr Read performing a similar service for *Principles* in *The Criterion*, seemed to understand that where I spoke of "the organisation of impulses" I meant that kind of deliberate planning and arrangement which the controllers of a good railway or large shop must carry out. But "organisation" for me stood for that kind of interdependence of parts which we allude to when we speak of living things as "organisms"; and the "order" which I make out to be so important is not tidiness.[56]

And so, although concentrating on the meaning of poetry from the perspective of the reader's psychological experience of it, rather than from the perspective of the poem (the perspective that Riding and Graves attempt to present), Richards nonetheless describes a process similar to the one that Riding and Graves outline. Reading a poem ought to make "the very experience itself present as a living pulse in our biographies."[57] As he explains, when asserting that "the aim of the poem comes first, and is the sole justification of its means ... its success in doing what it set out to do, or, if we like, in becoming what in the end it has become," "I ... mean by this the whole state of mind, the mental condition, which in another sense *is* the poem. Roughly the collection of impulses which shaped the poem originally, to which it gave expression, and to which, in an ideally susceptible reader it would again give rise."[58] Richards virtually paraphrases Riding and Graves, when they say: "The poet blends the subject of the poem with the feelings that the subject arouses into one expression. This unity makes the poem a living whole."[59] For Richards now, as for Riding and Graves from the beginning, good reading is for the reader to live the living whole that is the good poem.

Since the whole that the poem comprises ought to be experienced by the reader, a "blunder in all cases is the attempt to assign marks *independently* to details that can only be judged fairly with reference to the whole final result to which they contribute."[60] Ideally, then, we should "have the poem in all its minute particulars as intimately and as fully present to our minds as we can contrive."[61] Since "value in poetry turns nearly always upon differences and connections too minute and unobtrusive to be directly perceived," "we recognize them only in their effects."[62] The proper response to poetry is more than an application of rules and principles, and it is more than a discretely intellectual or emotional exercise; it is the response of one living whole to another. And "so the differences between good and bad poetry may be indiscernible to direct attention yet patent in their effects upon feeling. The choice of our whole personality may be the only instrument we possess delicate enough to effect the discrimination."[63]

Direct acceptance or rejection of a poem is the making of a person, literally, because "it is in these moments of sheer decision that the mind becomes most plastic, and selects, at the incessant multiple shifting cross-roads, the direction of its future development."[64] The effect of the good poem is to share its self-completing spirit with the good reader: "The critic himself, of course, in the moment of choice knows nothing about all this. He may feel the strain. He may notice the queer shifts of emotional perspective – that may affect all his other thoughts – as his mind tries, now in one way now in another, to fit itself to the poem. He will sense an obscure struggle as the poem's secret allies and enemies manoeuvre within him ... But when the conflict resolves itself ... the mind clears, and new energy wells up; after the pause a collectedness supervenes; behind our rejection or acceptance (even of a minor poem) we feel the sanction and authority of the self-completing spirit."[65] And so Richard declares true of any good poem what Riding and Graves declare true of Cummings's: it "turns the reader into a poet"; it becomes "the poem of anybody who will be at pains to write it."[66] The good reader of such a poem – a poem "forcing him inside the framework of the poem and making him repeat the steps by which it came to be" – can choose to make the poem a step in his own coming to be.[67]

Of course not all readers are good readers. The reader beholden to stock feelings tends to reject the good poem precisely because of its potential to transform him. According to Riding and Graves, "The chief condition the reader makes about the poetry he reads is that it shall not be difficult. For if it is difficult it means that he must think in unaccustomed ways, and thinking to the plain reader, beyond the range necessary for the practical purposes of living, is unsettling and dangerous; he is afraid of his own mind."[68] Richards makes the same point. When, in reading, "The personality stands balanced between the particular experience which is the realized poem and the whole fabric of its past experiences and developed habits of mind," he notes, "Often it must be the case that the new modification of experience would improve the fabric if it could be taken in, but too much reconstruction would be needed. The strain, the resistance, is too great, and the poem is rejected."[69] Among the causes of this strain and resistance, according to Richards, "inadequate critical theories, withholding what we need and imposing upon us what we do not need, are sadly too frequent in our minds."[70] As Riding and Graves note, "A certain convention has existed until recently restraining the poet from troubling the public with the more unsettling forms of thought, which are vaguely known to be involved in the making of poetry but not supposed to be evident in the reading of poetry ... [I]t is the shock of this contact that the plain reader cannot bear."[71]

And so although Riding and Graves begin their book by proposing to investigate whether modernist poetry means "to withdraw itself from the plain reader" and "to keep the public out," allowing that "If, after a careful examination of poems that seem to be only part of the game of high-brow baiting low-brow, they still resist all reasonable efforts, then we must conclude that such work is, after all, merely a joke at the plain reader's expense and let him return to his newspapers," one learns very soon that they have no intention of allowing the plain reader to return to his newspapers.[72] Low-brow newspaper readers (with their "tired minds" and "lazy reading habits") are the threat, expecting poetry to be something that "common intelligence" can understand "without difficulty."[73] Like Richards, Riding and Graves fear the degenerative influence of capitalism on literary culture, especially as realized in the reader of newspapers. According to Richards, "a decline can be noticed in perhaps every department of literature."[74] According to Riding and Graves, "the reading public insists that no poetry is clear except what it can understand at a glance."[75] Insisting "that what is called our common intelligence is the mind in its least active state" and "that poetry obviously demands a more vigorous imaginative effort than the plain reader has been willing to apply to it," Riding and Graves assert that "the important thing to recognize, in a time of popular though superficial education, is the necessity of emphasizing to the reading public the difference between good and bad poems."[76]

Richards outlines a similar context for his work in *Practical Criticism* and announces similar educational objectives. Overwhelmed by the "reckless, desperate character" of the protocols written by "that great body of readers whose first and last reaction to poetry (it is hardly a response) is bewilderment," Richards plaintively suggests that "It should surely be possible, even without devoting more time or trouble to the reading of English than is given at present, to prepare them better, and make them more reasonably self-reliant."[77] This is no small matter: "It is natural to inquire how far insensitiveness, poor discrimination, and a feeble capacity to understand poetry imply a corresponding inability to apprehend and make use of the values of ordinary life."[78] To the problems of ordinary life that Richards spies, better training in the reading of poetry indeed promises help: "It is possible that the burden of information and consciousness that a growing mind has now to carry may be too much for its natural strength ... Therefore, if there be any means by which we may artificially strengthen our minds' capacity to order themselves, we must avail ourselves of them. And of all possible means, Poetry, the unique, linguistic instrument by which our minds have ordered their thoughts, emotions, desires ... in the past, seems to be the most serviceable."[79]

The Meaning of Meaning justifies the need to study "how words work" by reference to the fact that "New millions of participants in the control of general affairs must now attempt to form personal opinions upon matters which were once left to a few"; *Principles of Literary Criticism* suggests that it is "a contribution towards ... choices of the future" because "The thought, 'What shall we do with the powers, which we are so rapidly developing, and what will happen to us if we cannot learn to guide them in time?' already marks for many people the chief interest of existence. The controversies which the world has known in the past are as nothing to those which are ahead." For Richards, the mind educated to be at home in the ambiguities of poetry will be best placed to cope with the uncertainties of the future.[80]

In this regard, Richards again follows the lead of Riding and Graves, for the mind he celebrates is the mind that they suggest is both represented within modernist poetry and developed in readers by their engagement with it: "The mind that can shift its viewpoint and still keep its orientation, that can carry over into quite a new set of definitions the results gained through past experience in other frameworks, the mind that can rapidly and without strain and confusion perform the systematic transformations required by such a shift, is the mind of the future."[81]

Riding and Graves point to John Crowe Ransom's "Captain Carpenter" as exemplary of the ironic consciousness that modernist poetry demands of its readers: "to such a poem as this a variety of reactions is possible; and it is the balance of these various possible reactions that should form the reader's critical attitude toward the poem."[82] In Ransom's poem, "fact and fancy have equal value as truth. Captain Carpenter is both the realistic hero or knight-errant, who is bit by bit shorn of his strength until there is nothing left but his hollow boasts, and the fairy-tale hero who is actually reduced bit by bit to a tongue; and the double meaning has to be kept in mind throughout. The ordinary psychology, therefore, of the reader trained to look for a single reaction in himself is upset, and modernist poetry becomes the nightmare from which he tries to protect his sanity."[83] Riding and Graves present as the chief virtue of the poem precisely what the plain reader will advance as "the chief feeling against the poem": "that Captain Carpenter is not an easily defined or felt subject, neither a particular historical figure nor yet a complete allegory. He confounds the emotions of the reader instead of simplifying them and provides no answer to the one question which the reader will ask himself: 'Who or what, particularly, is Captain Carpenter?'"[84]

In the extensive Appendix to his book, Richards points particularly to the study of literary ambiguity as a place where the development of the flexible, plastic mind of the future can be encouraged:

> A word ... can equally and simultaneously represent vastly different things. It can therefore effect extraordinary combinations of feelings. A word is a point at which many very different influences may cross or unite. Hence its dangers in prose discussions and its treacherousness for careless readers of poetry, but hence at the same time the peculiar quasi-magical sway of words in the hands of a master. Certain conjunctions of words – through their history partly and through the collocations of emotional influences that *by their very ambiguity* they effect – have a power over our minds that nothing else can exert or perpetuate ... It is easy to be mysterious about these powers, to speak of the "inexplicable" magic of

> words and to indulge in romantic reveries about their semantic history and immemorial past. But it is better to realize that these powers can be studied, and that what criticism most needs is less poeticizing and more detailed analysis and investigation.[85]

Of course Richards's discussion of ambiguity in *Practical Criticism* suggests lines of influence between himself and Empson at this time on this topic. Empson recalled that during his meetings with Richards in the fall of 1928, "Two hours may have been spent on ambiguity, but not more."[86] Does this Appendix about the need for literary theorists to undertake more detailed analysis and investigation of literary ambiguity indicate Richards's attitude before he met Empson, and so perhaps represent his advice to his student during their famous meeting? Or is what we read about ambiguity in the Appendix an echo of Empson's view of the importance of Graves's attitude toward ambiguity as evidenced by his 30,000-word typescript on the topic some weeks after their talk? Perhaps the Appendix emerges from a combination of the two scenarios in question.

Russo suggests that Richards's attitude toward ambiguity develops from suspicion to celebration between 1923 and 1929 and that "in view of subsequent trends – Empson's ambiguity, Cleanth Brooks and William Wimsatt's wit and paradox, Allen Tate's tension, Philip Wheelwright's 'plurisignifications,' Paul De Man's 'free presence' of the word, Jacques Derrida's floating signifiers – Richards' promotion of ambiguity from a minor to a major – *the* major – literary device was a historic moment in criticism."[87] As Haffenden shows, this assertion is not quite convincing, and the argument that supports it is not quite accurate. Richards's genuine celebration of the systematic overdetermination of meaning represented by certain kinds of literary ambiguity would have to wait until *The Philosophy of Rhetoric* (1936), where he aligns himself with Freud as an explorer of this phenomenon. Russo is right, however, to say that Richards's mind is changing during these years; he simply misses the fact that the attention bestowed on literary ambiguity by, first, Graves, then by Riding and Graves, and, finally, by Empson are important factors in a number of these important changes of mind.

20

Slow Wit, Slow Close Reading, and Paraphrase

Finally, another significant influence of Riding and Graves is evident in Richards's observations about the contemporary reader's response to humour in poetry. A whole chapter of *A Survey of Modernist Poetry* is devoted to the topic of "The Humorous Element in Modernist Poetry." For the modernist poet, representing "a generation that the War came upon at its most impressionable stage and taught the necessity for a self-protective skepticism of the stability of all human relationships, particularly of all national and religious institutions, of all existing moral codes, of all sentimental formulas for future harmony," Riding and Graves suggest that "everything that would ordinarily seem serious to him now seems a tragic joke."[1] So pervasive is this skepticism that "the historically-minded modernist poet is uncertain whether there is any excuse for the existence of poets at all."[2] Humour is this distressed poet's response: "he brazens out the dilemma by making cruel jokes at his own expense ... [H]e is able to do what no generation of poets before has been able to do – to make fun of himself when he is at his most serious."[3]

The problem is that the plain reader is not likely to get the joke: "The poet's self-mockery is that feature of modernist poetry most likely to puzzle the reader or the critic."[4] In effect, "The probable failure of wit in the reader, whether plain reader or critic, removes from the poet that measure of address which an audience imposes."[5] So the poet makes "jokes which he expects no one to see or not to be laughed at if seen."[6] The poet becomes a clown without an audience: "The modernist clown, feeling a want in his audience, turns his back on it and performs his ritual of antics without benefit of applause."[7] According to Riding and Graves, the consequences of this failure of wit on the reader's part and this disdain for the audience on the poet's part are far-reaching: "Limitations in the sense of humour of the critic-reader have ... the effect of making the modernist poem more and more difficult. For, the poet tells himself, if the reading public is bound anyhow to be a limited one, the poem may as well take advantage of its isolation by using references and associations which are as far out of the ordinary critic's reach as the modernist sense of humour."[8]

On the whole, Riding and Graves approve of this disdain for the relatively witless critic-reader. They call once more on the poetry of John Crowe Ransom to make their point. Although they generally cite his poetry approvingly, this time they offer "Winter Remembered" as an example of how too much respect for the audience can lead to too much of the self-mockery that is a staple of the modernist poet's technique: "He insists upon the wit of his reader; he makes an appeal which it is impossible that the reader shall overlook: if the reader be slow in discovering the clues to the poet's clownishness, the poet forces his clownishness in a way that the reader cannot mistake. It is as if a performing clown had made a deep but delicate joke against himself which the audience had missed. Bound to have his audience appreciate his mood, the clown slaps himself very hard and makes a long face. The audience now sees the joke and laughs."[9] Riding and Graves regret that Ransom "was obliged to brutalize his joke in order to soften his audience to him" and worry that he is "overstepping the disrespect which the poet wishes to do himself" by adding to the poem "a pathetic element, a tearfulness, which rarely is entirely sincere."[10]

Richards takes note of this image of the poet forced by his reader's failure of wit to signal his sense of humour in an obvious and exaggerated way. His students' responses to Henry Wadsworth Longfellow's "In the Churchyard at Cambridge" prompt him to comment in just such terms on the limitations of the sense of humour of "modern readers."[11] Richards presents this poem, the last of the thirteen to be discussed, as an example of the danger that stock responses can cause:

> If the easiest way to popularity is to exploit some stock response, some poem already existent, fully prepared, in the reader's mind, an appearance of appealing to such stock responses, should the reader happen to have discarded them, is a very certain way of courting failure. So that a poet who writes on what appears to be

> a familiar theme, in a way which, superficially, is only slightly unusual, runs a double risk. On the one hand, very many readers will not really read him at all. They will respond with the poem they suppose him to have written and then, if emancipated, recoil in horror to heap abuse on the poet's head. On the other hand, less emancipated readers, itching to release their own stock responses, may be pulled up by something in the poem which prevents them. The result will be more abuse for the hapless author.[12]

Longfellow's poem is just such a poem. Because it is set in a churchyard and contemplates the grave that awaits us all, "It was very generally assumed that since the subject of the poem is solemn the treatment must be solemn."[13] What baffles readers, according to Richards, is an unexpected change in tone mid-way through the poem from solemn to humorous – a change in tone that does not register with most readers because of their stock response to graveyard poetry.

Richards hypothesizes that despite most readers' assumptions to the contrary, "the poet is not trying to be impressive, to inflate the reader with swelling sentiments and a gaseous 'moral'"; rather, readers in the grip of a stock response project these motives onto lines that they do not understand.[14] The poet is actually trying to keep his contemplation of the levelling effect of death "cool and sober."[15] The poem, then, is "not a grim warning, or an exhortation, but a cheerful realization of the situation, not in the least evangelical, not at all like a conventional sermon, but on the contrary extremely urbane, rather witty, and *slightly* whimsical."[16] The problem that a modern reader's failure of wit makes for the proper appreciation of a modern poem is not a small one, and it is not a problem confined to a few: "if there is any character in poetry that modern readers … are unprepared to encounter, it is this social, urbane, highly cultivated, self-confident, temperate and easy kind of humour."[17] This is the same point made by Riding and Graves.

Richards concludes his analysis of G.H. Luce's "Climb cloud, and pencil all the blue" with a similar observation about his students' failure to appreciate the change of tone at the end of the poem: "Exactly how seriously the grandiloquence of the last three verses is to be taken, is the problem. That a slightly mocking tone comes in … was not noticed. Humour is perhaps the last thing that is expected in lyrical poetry, above all when its theme is nature. If the poet is going to smile he is required to give clear and ample notice of his intention."[18] Richards focuses on the very fracture between the poet's humour and the audience's humour that Riding and Graves mark as a characteristic feature of modernism, and he makes the same point about the need to signal clearly the poet's antic disposition if the contemporary reader is to see his jokes and laugh. He has clearly found much more than mere "games of interpretation" in *A Survey of Modernist Poetry*.

•

Although I have suggested above that one of the most important insights into the problems with the contemporary reader's understanding of poetry that Riding and Graves derive from Richards is his recommendation that people read poems more slowly, it seems also to be the case that Riding and Graves influenced Richards in turn by their development of this concept beyond Richards's original formulation of it. In all of Richards's discussions of "slow reading" at this time, he writes as though he has in mind the act of reading poetry aloud. Even fifty-five years after the essay on Hopkins was published, Richards was reminded in rereading it of the problem that he originally set out to address of how "to bring out the sense and the movement" of Hopkins's verse "as fully as" a "voice might."[19] Certainly, in *Practical Criticism*, he continues to use the word "reading" as he does in *Science and Poetry* – that is, to indicate the phonological articulation of poetry: "By bad reading I suggest that we should mean ... reading that prevents the reader himself from entering into the poem ... Nothing more easily defeats the whole aim of poetry than ... to read out a poem in public before it has given up most of its secrets ... One piece of advice which has proved its usefulness may perhaps be offered: to remember that we are more likely to read too fast than to read too slow. Certainly ... a *very slow* private reading gives a better chance for the necessary interaction of form and meaning to develop than any number of rapid perusals."[20]

As in his essay on Hopkins, Richards emphasizes that good reading of a poem aloud requires it to have "given up most of its secrets" already, and that appreciation of form cannot be separated from appreciation of meaning – significantly revising the assumption in *Science and Poetry* that "a good deal of poetry and even some great poetry exists ... in which the sense of the words can be *almost* entirely missed or neglected without loss."[21] But he now believes that recognizing and respecting the virtues of slow reading is not primarily about making poetry sound good; it "would probably more than anything else help to make poetry understood."[22] And so Richards explains the process and the benefits of slow reading in a way that further aligns it with the incremental, cumulative appreciation of the poem's meaning that Riding and Graves describe.

In his "Introductory" remarks about "the conditions of the experiment" in his practical criticism classes, Richards implies that he explained his definition of what constituted a *reading* of a poem in the same way to both the 1925–26 class and the 1927–28 class. Yet it is clear that in *Practical Criticism* he develops the concept of "reading" beyond the one presented in his 1926 book *Science and Poetry* and his 1926 essay on Hopkins.[23] He now explains reading as a process more about making proper sense of the poem than about making proper sound out of it. Richards has come to regard determining the sense of a poem, whether or not one reads it aloud to oneself, as involving the same slow reading necessary to determining its phonological articulation: "I asked each writer to record on his protocol the number of 'readings' made of each poem. A number of perusals made at one session were to be counted together as one 'reading' provided that they aroused and sustained one single growing response to the poem."[24] Richards explains and justifies "this description of a 'reading'" as a necessary "measure of indirect suggestion" to his students. Without interfering too much with the existing reading habits that he proposes to study, he wishes to indicate that rapid perusals do not qualify as readings of poetry – the point, of course, that Riding and Graves emphasize in their instruction as to how to read "The Rugged Black of Anger."

In *Science and Poetry*, however, one finds that the "perusal" of a poem is not some initial engagement with a poem that is a mere step towards a reading, but rather, ideally, the occasion of the poem's understanding: "A poem, let us say Wordsworth's 'Westminster Bridge' sonnet, is ... the experience the right kind of reader has when he peruses the verses ... And the first step to an understanding of the place and future of poetry in human affairs is to see what the general structure of such an experience is. Let us begin by reading it very slowly."[25] Slow reading is clearly less than a perusal; in fact, it is merely a preliminary step toward the perusal that animates the poem as meaningful experience for the reader. "Perusal" here implicitly constitutes a more comprehensive and sophisticated response to the poem than any available through the "slow reading" described in *Science and Poetry*. Through its appreciation of phonological form, slow reading offers, at most, "an inexplicable premonition of a meaning which we have not yet grasped."[26] In *Practical Criticism*, however, "any number of rapid perusals" clearly promises less understanding of the poem than one "*very slow*" reading, and "one 'reading'" easily comprises "a number of perusals."[27] Between 1926 and 1929, the relationship in Richards's work between perusals and slow readings has reversed itself.

What counts for Richards as a *reading* in *Practical Criticism* is just what Riding and Graves recommend as a reading in *A Survey of Modernist Poetry*: not a two-minute perusal, but a time-length of engagement with the poem that enables what Richards calls a growing response to it and what Riding and Graves describe as a seeing of all that one can see at a given point and a taking of it all with one as one goes along, a model for the way of being in the world that the future will demand, according to Richards.

•

Riding and Graves's slow reading for sense is fundamental to Richards's concept of close reading in *Practical Criticism*. Observing that the sound of a poem can actually obscure the co-operation within it between sound and sense ("for many readers the metre and the verse-form of poetry is itself a powerful distraction" into "misreading," leaving them in the position of those "trying to do sums in the neighbourhood of a barrel-organ or a brass band"), Richards makes the same point as Riding and Graves: "most poetry needs several readings – in which its varied factors may fit themselves together – before it can be grasped. Readers who claim to dispense with this preliminary study, who think that all good poetry should come home to them in entirety at a first reading, hardly realize how clever they must be."[28]

Neither slow reading for meaning nor close reading for meaning should be confused with summary or paraphrase of the poem. Riding and Graves complain that the plain reader assumes "that the poet is not saying what he means but something *like* what he means in prettier language than he uses to himself about it."[29] Consequently, the reader searches for "the prose idea from which the real poem, apparently unwritten, is derived."[30] In "the ordinary translation system of poetry," that is, poetry begins as the "Poet's prose idea," is then expressed as the "Poem," and is finally interpreted via the "Reader's prose summary."[31] In a modernist poem like Riding's "The Rugged Black of Anger," however, "bare, undressed ideas are found … instead of the rhetorical devices by which poets try to 'put over' their ideas," and so "the ordinary translation system of poetry … is assumed to have been reversed."[32] Riding's poem, that is, is assumed to express the "Prose idea as poem," a dereliction of duty that leaves the reader searching for the real poem – the "Poem (suppressed)" – which can emerge only by the "Reader's poetical summary."[33]

In the "ordinary translation system," "the extravagant use of metaphor and simile in poetry is … seen to be governed by the necessity of making a poem … equal the prose summary which really is dictating it"; in the modernist translation system, according to the plain reader, one finds in a poem like Riding's "the prose idea in a slightly poetic form which the reader ha[s] to amplify along suggested poetical lines" into a "poetical summary of it."[34] For the benighted plain reader, poetry is either "prose summary" or "poetical summary."

In his chapter on "Figurative Language," Richards notes similar "misconceptions as to how the sense of words in poetry is to be taken."[35] Since "a good poet – to express feeling, to adjust tone and to further his other aims – may play all manner of tricks with his sense," readers baffled by figurative language tend to succumb to "twin dangers – careless, 'intuitive' reading and prosaic, 'over-literal' reading."[36] Adopting the terms introduced by Riding and Graves, Richards explains "the difference … between a 'poetic' and a 'prosaic' reading."[37] On the one hand, because of the assumption that the poet is playing tricks with his sense, "an obscure notion is engendered in the reader that syntax is somehow less significant in poetry than in prose, and that a kind of guess-work – likely enough to be christened 'intuition' – is the proper mode of apprehending what a poet may have to say."[38] The result is an intuitive or poetic reading. On the other hand is "the habit of regarding poetry as capable of explanation" – a laudable habit so long as it does not become the misconceived "literalism" of "those who see nothing in poetical language but a tissue of ridiculous exaggerations, childish 'fancies,' ignorant conceits and absurd symbolizations."[39] In this case, the result is the prosaic reading.

For Riding and Graves, the poem is neither the prose summary nor the poetic summary. They regard the critic-reader's regular question, "What, in so many words, is this all about?" as nonsensical. "If it were possible to give the complete force of a poem in a prose summary, then there would be no excuse for writing the poem: the 'so many words' are, to the last punctuation mark, the poem itself."[40] Either the prose summary and the poem are identical, or there is a discrepancy between them. In the former case, for instance, "If ... the author of the lines beginning 'The rugged black of anger' were asked to explain their meaning, the only proper reply would be to repeat the lines."[41] In the latter case, "to tell what a poem is all about in 'so many words' is to reduce the poem to so many words, to leave out all that the reader cannot at the moment understand to give him the satisfaction of feeling that he is understanding it."[42] Here, the prose summary of a poem is implicitly "the common-sense substitute for a piece of poetical extravagance."[43] It "cannot *explain* a poem, else the poet, if he were honest, would give the reader only a prose summary, and no poem."[44] In fact, "where such a prose summary does render the poem in its entirety, except for rhymes and other external dressings, the poem cannot have been a complete one; and indeed a great deal of what passes for poetry is the rewriting of the prose summary of a hypothetical poem in poetical language."[45] Of course Richards makes the same point via his observation about the relationship between H.D.'s poem and its prose paraphrase. Regarding the best reading of a poem as "one embracing as many meanings as possible, that is, the most difficult meaning," Riding and Graves conclude that "no prose interpretation of poetry can ever have complete finality, can be difficult enough."[46]

The "poetical summary" of a poem is a recent invention of the contemporary critic, an interpretive strategy necessitated by the so-called obscurity of modernist poetry. The modernist poem seems more prose than poetry, a "prose idea in a slightly poetical form," and so "the reader finds it necessary to make a poetical rather than a more strictly prose summary."[47] They speculate that the first two lines of Riding's poem – "The rugged black of anger/Has an uncertain smile border" – may lead readers to interpret the lines as concealing "an incidental satire on the popular poetical sentiment: 'Look around and you will find/Every cloud is silver-lined.'"[48] But of course Riding and Graves do not accept what such an interpretation implies, that the two lines beginning "The Rugged Black of

Anger" are "the prose idea as poem" that the reader needs "to amplify along suggested poetical lines."[49] Rather, in such an interpretation they see "a discrepancy ... appear between the poem as it stands and the reader's poetical summary of it"; "we ... have not two equivalent meanings but one meaning and another gratuitous meaning derived from it."[50] Again, one can compare this point to the one made by Richards about H.D.'s poem.

In his chapters on "Figurative Language" and "Sense and Feeling," Richards follows Riding and Graves in their emphasis on the "discrepancy" between what the poem says and any paraphrase of it that might be attempted, whether as a poetical or prose summary. Warning against the "careless," "intuitive," "poetic" "kind of guesswork" by which people misread, Richards hastens to add that he does not mean "to say that we can wrench the sense free from the poem, screw it down in a prose paraphrase, and then take the doctrine of our prose passage, and the feelings this doctrine excites in us, as the burden of the poem."[51] Riding and Graves say the same thing about the dangers inherent in the doctrine (and the feelings excited by it) that the poetical summary of "The Rugged Black of Anger" introduces: although "*anger* means just anger, *smile-border* just smile-border," "if we ... accept the silver-lined cloud explanation, we find that we are brought into a sentimental personal atmosphere in which *anger* is anger as felt by someone, or bad-luck seen as the anger of providence or fate, and in which *smile-border* is either personal happiness or good luck. Any such interpretation of *anger* and *smile-border*, indeed, would involve us in some such sympathetic history of the poem."[52] Here is the sense of the poem wrenched free from it, screwed down in a poetic paraphrase, the doctrine of the paraphrase then made the burden of the poem. Similarly, whereas Riding and Graves describe their own attempt to put a poem by Cummings "into ordinary prose," and then to explain this prose version of the poem, as "the expansion, the dilution, even the destruction of the poem which one reader may perform for another if the latter is unable to face the intensity and compactness of the poem," Richards recalls "the atrocities which teachers sometimes permit themselves" when "making a paraphrase or gloss" of a poem and acknowledges that "the risk of supposing that the feelings which the logical expansion of a poetic phrase excites must be those which the phrase was created to convey is very great."[53] Richards finds in his protocol writers the same tendency to replace the poem with a prose idea of it that Riding and Graves find in the contemporary critic-reader: "We easily substitute a bad piece of prose for the poem – a peculiarly damaging form of attack upon poetry"; the very kind of attack that Richards himself had made upon H.D.'s poem "The Pool" in *Principles of Literary Criticism*.[54] The argument in each case is the same, and so is much of the language by which it is articulated: the logical expansion of the poetic phrase into prose and the intuitive expansion of the poetic phrase into a parallel poem each constitute a destructive attack upon poetry.

The problem that Riding and Graves describe of being "brought into a sentimental personal atmosphere in which *anger* is anger as felt by someone" recalls Richards's complaint about what is missing in H.D.'s poem, and recalls Riding and Graves's complaint of H.D. generally that she does not eliminate her personality from her poetry the way Emily Dickinson does from hers.[55] Richards also agrees with Riding and Graves as to just what it is that distinguishes a poem from any summary or paraphrase of it. According to Riding and Graves, treating the first two lines of "The Rugged Black of Anger" as though they "mean what they say" and "mean just what they are" (right down to each word, and each punctuation mark) will reveal that what Riding has offered the reader is not "the prose idea as poem, but the poem itself."[56] "If ... without the addition of any associations not provided in the poem, or of collateral interpretations, it could reveal an internal consistency strengthened at every point in its development and free of the necessity of external application, that is, complete without criticism – if it could do this, it would have established an insurmountable difference between prose ideas and poetic ideas, prose facts and poetic facts. The difference would mean the independence of poetic facts, as real facts, from any prose or poetical explanation in the terms of practical workaday reality which would make them seem unreal, or poetical facts."[57]

One can understand the appeal of such a passage to the critic who asserts both the independence of poetic belief from scientific belief ("The bulk of the beliefs in the arts are ... provisional acceptances, holding only ... in the state of mind which is the poem or the work of art ... The difference between these emotive beliefs and scientific beliefs is not one of degree but of kind") and also the insufficiency of logic and prose in explanations of poetry ("There are few metaphors whose effect, if carefully examined, can be traced to the logical relations involved ... Those who look only to the ostensible purposes for the explanation of effects, who make prose analyses of poems, must inevitably find them a mystery").[58] Indeed, one can see that Richards finds his own earlier convictions developed so much further and expressed so much more forcefully by Riding and Graves that he virtually paraphrases the passage above from *A Survey of Modernist Poetry* in *Practical Criticism*: "All respectable poetry invites close reading. It encourages attention to its literal sense up to the point ... at which liberty can serve the aim of the poem better than fidelity to fact or strict coherence among fictions. It asks the reader to remember that its aims are varied and not always what he unreflectingly expects. He has to refrain from applying his own external standards ... We cannot legitimately judge its means by external standards (such as accuracy of fact or logical coherence) which may have no relevance to its success in doing what it set out to do, or, if we like, in becoming what in the end it has become."[59] Richards has adopted the language of Riding and Graves that celebrates in poetry the "principle of self-determination," "its quality of independence from both the reader and the poet," its "self-explanatory" nature.[60] Their observation that a poem ideally "corresponds in every respect with its own governing meaning" ("in this foreshadowing, inevitable meaning the poem really exists even before it is written"), and that in writing "The Rugged Black of Anger" Riding "has made the poem out of itself: its final form is identical in terms with its preliminary form in the poet's mind," appears in Richards's note explaining that by "the aim of the poem" "I ... mean ... the whole state of mind, the mental condition, which in another sense *is* the poem."[61]

Notes

INTRODUCTION

1 Donald J. Childs, "New Criticism," *The Encyclopedia of Contemporary Literary Theory*, ed. Irena R. Makaryk (Toronto: University of Toronto Press, 1993), 120–4.
2 John Crowe Ransom, *The New Criticism* (Norfolk, Connecticut: New Directions, 1941; repr. Westport, Connecticut: Greenwood Press, 1979).
3 T.S. Eliot, "Tradition and the Individual Talent" (1919), in *Selected Essays*, 3rd ed. enlarged (London: Faber and Faber, 1951), 17.
4 I.A. Richards, *Principles of Literary Criticism* (London: Kegan Paul, Trench, Trubner and Co., 1924; New York: Harcourt, Brace and Co., 1925); *Science and Poetry* (New York: W.W. Norton, 1926); and *Practical Criticism: A Study of Literary Judgment* (London: Routledge and Kegan Paul, 1929).
5 René Wellek and Austin Warren, *Theory of Literature* (London: Jonathan Cape, 1949).
6 Cleanth Brooks, *The Well Wrought Urn: Studies in the Structure of Poetry* (New York: Harcourt, Brace and World, 1947; repr. New York: Harvest Books, 1975), ix.
7 William K. Wimsatt, Jr, and Monroe C. Beardsley, "The Intentional Fallacy," *Sewanee Review* 54.3 (Summer 1946): 468–88.
8 Allen Tate, "Literature as Knowledge," in *Reason in Madness: Critical Essays by Allen Tate* (New York: G.P. Putnam, 1941), 20–61.
9 John Crowe Ransom, *The World's Body* (New York: Charles Scribner's Sons, 1938).
10 F.R. Leavis, *New Bearings in English Poetry: A Study of the Contemporary Situation* (London: Chatto and Windus, 1932).
11 Brooks, *The Well Wrought Urn*, 192.

12 Ibid., 203.
13 R.P. Blackmur, *The Double Agent: Essays in Craft and Elucidation* (1935; repr. Gloucester, Mass.: Peter Smith, 1962), 300.
14 Richards, *Practical Criticism*, 180.
15 T.S. Eliot, "The Metaphysical Poets," in *Selected Essays*, 287; Samuel Taylor Coleridge, *Biographia Literaria; or Biographical Sketches of My Literary Life and Opinions*, 2 vols (London: Rest Fenner, 1817), 1: 157.
16 Brooks, *The Well Wrought Urn*, ix, 194.
17 Robert Penn Warren, "Pure and Impure Poetry" (1942), in *Selected Essays* (New York: Random House, 1958), 29.
18 Brooks, *The Well Wrought Urn*, 209.
19 Ibid., 212.
20 Richards, *Practical Criticism*, 203.
21 Leavis published *Scrutiny: A Quarterly Review* from 1932 to 1953.
22 William Empson, *Seven Types of Ambiguity: A Study of Its Effects in English Verse*, 1st ed. (London: Chatto and Windus, 1930; New York: Harcourt, Brace and Company, 1931), 1.
23 Chris Baldick, *The Concise Oxford Dictionary of Literary Terms* (Oxford: Oxford University Press, 1991), 149–50.
24 Charles E. Bressler, *Literary Criticism: An Introduction to Theory and Practice*, 3rd ed. (New Jersey: Prentice Hall, 2003), 57–8.
25 Meyer Abrams, *A Glossary of Literary Terms*, 5th ed. (Fort Worth, Texas: Holt, Rinehart and Winston, 1985), 223.
26 Cleanth Brooks, "New Criticism," *The Princeton Encyclopedia of Poetry and Poetics*, ed. Alex Preminger, 2nd ed. enlarged (Princeton, New Jersey: Princeton University Press, 1974), 567–8.
27 David Robey, "Anglo-American New Criticism, in *Modern Literary Theory: A Comparative Introduction*, ed. Ann Jefferson and David Robey, 2nd ed. (London: B.T. Batsford, 1986), 79.
28 David Daiches, *Critical Approaches to Literature*, 2nd ed. (London: Longman, 1981), 299.
29 Ransom, *The New Criticism*, 44, 45.
30 Ibid., 101–31.
31 J.A. Cuddon, *The Penguin Dictionary of Literary Terms and Literary Theory*, 4th ed. (London: Penguin, 1999), 694, 694, 694, 142, 30.
32 William Van O'Connor, "Ambiguity," *The Princeton Encyclopedia of Poetry and Poetics*, 19.
33 John Paul Russo, *I.A. Richards: His Life and Work* (Baltimore: The Johns Hopkins University Press, 1989), 279.
34 Richards, *Practical Criticism*, 9.

35 John Haffenden, *William Empson: Among the Mandarins* (Oxford: Oxford University Press, 2005), 202–3.
36 Ibid., 202.
37 William Empson, letter to Laura Riding (25 Aug 1970), in *Selected Letters of William Empson*, ed. John Haffenden (Oxford: Oxford University Press, 2006), 430; Empson, *Seven Types of Ambiguity*, 1st ed., vii.
38 Haffenden, *William Empson*, 208.
39 Ibid., 228.
40 William Harmon and Hugh Holman, *A Handbook to Literature*, 10th ed. (New Jersey: Pearson Prentice Hall, 2006), 337.
41 Laura Riding and Robert Graves, *A Survey of Modernist Poetry* (1927; repr. New York: Haskell House, 1969).
42 Haffenden, *William Empson*, 217.
43 Laura (Riding) Jackson, "Some Autobiographical Corrections of Literary History," *Denver Quarterly*, 8.4 (Winter 1974): 12.
44 Haffenden, *William Empson*, 607n146; Deborah Baker, *In Extremis: the Life of Laura Riding* (London: Hamish Hamilton, 1993), 143–5.
45 Elizabeth Friedmann, *A Mannered Grace: The Life of Laura (Riding) Jackson* (New York: Persea Books, 2005), 97–8.
46 Ibid., 98.
47 Ibid., 100.
48 Jahan Ramazani, "Introduction," *The Norton Anthology of Modern and Contemporary Poetry*, 2 vols (New York: W.W. Norton, 2003), 1: lvi.
49 Harold Fromm, "Myths and Mishegaas: Robert Graves and Laura Riding," *Hudson Review* 44.2 (summer 1991): 194.
50 Cleanth Brooks writes that he dates his awareness of the "inner workings of poetry" to his reading of the early works of Richards and Empson between 1929 and 1931, shortly after his arrival at Oxford. See "William Empson: A Tribute," *The New Criterion*, 3 (September 1984): 84. John Crowe Ransom devotes the first chapter of *The New Criticism* to the work of Richards and Empson.
51 Laura (Riding) Jackson, letter to the editor (14 November 1971), *Modern Language Quarterly*, 32 (1971): 447–8.
52 Robert Graves, quoted by Martin Seymour-Smith, *Robert Graves: His Life and Work* (London: Hutchinson, 1982), 147.
53 Christopher Norris, *William Empson and the Philosophy of Literary Criticism* (London: Athlone Press, 1978), 33.
54 William Empson, "Still the Strange Necessity," in *Argufying: Essays on Literature and Culture*, ed. John Haffenden (Iowa City: University of Iowa Press, 1988), 123–5.

55 I.A. Richards, *The Philosophy of Rhetoric* (New York and London: Oxford University Press, 1936), 39; I.A. Richards, "Semantic Frontiersman," in *William Empson: The Man and His Work*, ed. Roma Gill (London: Routledge and Kegan Paul, 1974), 98.
56 T.S. Eliot, "The Frontiers of Criticism," in *On Poetry and Poets* (London: Faber and Faber, 1957), 113.
57 Terry Eagleton, *Literary Theory: An Introduction* (Oxford: Basil Blackwell, 1983), 43–4.
58 Ibid., 45–6.
59 Ibid., 46–7.
60 Ibid., 52–3.
61 Richard Palmer, *Hermeneutics: Interpretation Theory in Schleiermacher, Dilthey, Heidegger, and Gadamer* (Evanston: Northwestern University Press, 1969), 225–7.
62 Ibid., 174–5.
63 Ibid., 158–9.
64 Gerald Graff, *Literature Against Itself: Literary Ideas in Modern Society* (Chicago: University of Chicago Press, 1979), 133–5.
65 Ibid., 135.
66 Norris, *William Empson and the Philosophy of Literary Criticism*, 5, 3, 3.
67 John Guillory, "The Ideology of Canon-Formation: T.S. Eliot and Cleanth Brooks," *Critical Inquiry* 10 (September 1983): 194, 186, 194.
68 Tim Dean, "T.S. Eliot, Famous Clairvoyante," in *Gender, Desire, and Sexuality in T.S. Eliot*, ed. Cassandra Laity and Nancy K. Gish (Cambridge: Cambridge University Press, 2004), 43–4.
69 Ibid., 45.
70 Michele Tepper, "'Cells in One Body': Nation and Eros in the Early Work of T.S. Eliot," in *Gender, Desire, and Sexuality in T.S. Eliot*, 66, 80, 67, 80.
71 Colleen Lamos, *Deviant Modernism: Sexual and Textual Errancy in T.S. Eliot, James Joyce, and Marcel Proust* (New York: Cambridge University Press, 1998), 24; Dean, "T.S. Eliot, Famous Clairvoyante," 45.
72 Guillory, "The Ideology of Canon Formation," 194.
73 Tepper, '"Cells in One Body,'" 80.
74 Patricia E. Chu, *Race, Nationalism and the State in British and American Modernism* (Cambridge: Cambridge University Press, 2006), 16, 13, 8, 8, 9.
75 Ibid., 15, 15, 14.
76 See, for instance, the discussion of the interconnections in the work of Riding and Graves among the ideas and values they associate with close reading, modernism, and anti-Semitism in Donald J. Childs, "Generating

Modernism and New Criticism from Antisemitism: Laura Riding and Robert Graves Read T.S. Eliot's Early Poetry," in *Modernism and Race*, ed. Len Platt (Cambridge: Cambridge University Press, 2011), 77–96.

77 Riding and Graves, *A Survey of Modernist Poetry*, 5.

78 Empson, *Seven Types of Ambiguity*, 1st ed., 142.

79 Eliot, "The Metaphysical Poets," 287.

80 Robert Graves, *The Meaning of Dreams* (London: Cecil Palmer, 1924), 111.

81 Robert Graves, *On English Poetry: Being an Irregular Approach to the Psychology of This Art, from Evidence Mainly Subjective* (London: William Heinemann, 1922); Robert Graves, *Poetic Unreason: And Other Studies* (London: Cecil Palmer, 1925); Richards, *Principles of Literary Criticism*, 25.

82 Graves, *The Meaning of Dreams*, 19.

83 Laura Riding, *Contemporaries and Snobs* (Garden City, New York: Doubleday Doran and Company, 1927).

84 Richards, *Principles of Literary Criticism*, 200.

85 Ibid., 16, 17, 17.

86 Riding and Graves, *A Survey of Modernist Poetry*, 145.

87 Ibid., 47, 124, 124.

CHAPTER ONE

1 William Empson, letter to Laura Riding (25 August 1970), *Selected Letters of William Empson*, ed. John Haffenden (Oxford: Oxford University Press, 2006), 430.

2 William Empson, *Seven Types of Ambiguity: A Study of Its Effects in English Verse*, 1st ed. (London: Chatto and Windus, 1930; New York: Harcourt, Brace and Company, 1931), vii.

3 Empson, letter to Riding (25 August 1970), *Selected Letters*, 431.

4 Laura (Riding) Jackson, letter to the editor (14 November 1971), *Modern Language Quarterly*, 32 (1971): 447–8.

5 I.A. Richards, "William Empson," *Furioso*, 1.3 (1940), supplement following p. 44, quoted in John Haffenden, *William Empson: Among the Mandarins* (Oxford: Oxford University Press, 2005), 207.

6 Robert Graves, *Impenetrability; or the Proper Habit of English* (London: The Hogarth Press, 1926).

7 Empson, letter to Riding (5 February 1931), quoted in Elizabeth Friedmann, *A Mannered Grace: The Life of Laura (Riding) Jackson* (New York: Persea Books, 2005), 97.

8 Laura Riding and Robert Graves, *A Pamphlet Against Anthologies* (1928; repr. New York: AMS Press, 1970), 7.
9 Riding, quoted by Haffenden, *Selected Letters*, 425.
10 Empson, letter to Riding (25 August 1970), *Selected Letters*, 430. The length of the enormous letter by Graves grew in Empson's memory from the nineteen pages he reported to William H. Matchett, the editor of *Modern Language Quarterly* in 1966, to the forty pages that he reported to Riding in 1971. See Haffenden, *Selected Letters*, 430n8, and Empson, letter to Riding (29 April 1971), *Selected Letters*, 433.
11 James Jensen, "The Construction of *Seven Types of Ambiguity*," *Modern Language Quarterly*, 27.3 (1966): 243–59.
12 Robert Graves, letter to the editor, *Modern Language Quarterly*, 27.3 (1966): 256.
13 William Empson, "Preface to the Second Edition," *Seven Types of Ambiguity*, 3rd ed. (1953; repr. London: Hogarth Press, 1984), xiv.
14 Riding, letter to Susan Daniell (12 June 1970), quoted by Haffenden, *Selected Letters*, 428, and Riding, letter to Susan Daniell (8 August 1970), quoted by Haffenden, *Selected Letters*, 428.
15 Empson, letter to Riding (25 August 1970), *Selected Letters*, 429.
16 Ibid., 430.
17 Empson, letter to Riding (29 April 1970), *Selected Letters*, 433.
18 Empson, letter to Riding (25 August 1970), *Selected Letters*, 431.
19 Empson, letter to Riding (29 April 1970), *Selected Letters*, 435.
20 Riding, letter to Empson (13 December 1970), quoted by Haffenden, *Selected Letters*, 432.
21 Riding, letter to Empson (7 May 1971), quoted by Haffenden, *Selected Letters*, 436.
22 Empson, letter to Riding (29 April 1971), *Selected Letters*, 433.
23 Robert Graves, letter to the editor, *Modern Language Quarterly*, 27.3 (1966): 256.
24 Laura Riding and Robert Graves, *A Survey of Modernist Poetry* (1927; repr. New York: Haskell House, 1969), 5.
25 Ibid., 63.
26 Ibid., 11.
27 Ibid., 66–7.
28 Ibid., 67.
29 Ibid.
30 Ibid., 73–4.
31 Ibid., 69.
32 Ibid.

33 Ibid., 25, 27.

34 Robert Graves, letter to T.S. Eliot (16 February 1926), *In Broken Images: Selected Letters of Robert Graves*, ed. Paul O'Prey (London: Hutchinson, 1982), 164. Eliot suggested American poets to be discussed in the book, and strategies for classifying them, in letters of 27 October 1925 and 2 November 1925. See *The Letters of T.S. Eliot: Volume 2: 1923–1925*, ed. Valerie Eliot and Hugh Haughton (London: Faber and Faber, 2009), 764, 768–9.

35 Graves, letter to Eliot (24 June 1926), *In Broken Images*, 166.

36 Riding and Graves, *A Survey of Modernist Poetry*, 74.

37 Empson, *Seven Types of Ambiguity*, 1st ed., 102.

38 Ibid., 102, 102–3.

39 Ibid., 103.

40 Ibid.

41 Ibid., 103, 103, 104.

42 Ibid., 103.

43 William Empson, *Seven Types of Ambiguity*, 3rd ed. (1953; repr. London: Hogarth Press, 1984), 202, note.

44 Riding and Graves, *A Survey of Modernist Poetry*, 74.

45 Empson, *Seven Types of Ambiguity*, 1st ed., 104.

46 Ibid., 103.

47 Ibid., 104.

48 Riding and Graves, *A Survey of Modernist Poetry*, 149.

49 Empson, *Seven Types of Ambiguity*, 1st ed., 114, 115.

50 Graves, letter to Eliot (24 June 1926), *In Broken Images*, 166.

51 Empson, *Seven Types of Ambiguity*, 1st ed., 202.

52 Riding and Graves, *A Survey of Modernist Poetry*, 149.

53 Ibid., 138.

54 Ibid., 148.

55 Ibid., 149.

56 Ibid.

57 Empson, *Seven Types of Ambiguity*, 1st ed., 105–6.

58 Ibid., 157.

59 Ibid., 102.

60 Ibid.

61 Haffenden, *William Empson*, 217.

62 Haffenden, *William Empson*, 217–18. The essays by Empson to which Haffenden refers are the following: "Ambiguity in Shakespeare: Sonnet XVI," *Experiment* 2 (February 1929): 33, and "Some Notes on Mr. Eliot," *Experiment* 4 (November 1929): 6–8.

63 Empson, *Seven Types of Ambiguity*, 1st ed., 102, 62.
64 See Haffenden, *William Empson*, 218.
65 Richards, "William Empson," in Haffenden, *William Empson*, 207.
66 Empson, *Seven Types of Ambiguity*, 1st ed., 65.
67 Ibid., 66.
68 Ibid.
69 Ibid., 71.
70 Ibid., 102, 112.
71 Riding and Graves, *A Survey of Modernist Poetry*, 67, 74.
72 Empson, *Seven Types of Ambiguity*, 1st ed., 112.
73 Riding and Graves, *A Survey of Modernist Poetry*, 79–80.
74 Empson, *Seven Types of Ambiguity*, 1st ed., 112.
75 Ibid., 113.
76 Riding and Graves, *A Survey of Modernist Poetry*, 79, 80, 80.
77 Ibid., 79.
78 Ibid., 79–80.
79 Ibid., 79.
80 Ibid., 80; Empson, *Seven Types of Ambiguity*, 1st ed., 62.
81 Empson, *Seven Types of Ambiguity*, 1st ed., 63.
82 Riding and Graves, *A Survey of Modernist Poetry*, 72.
83 Ibid.
84 Empson, *Seven Types of Ambiguity*, 1st ed., 65, 65, 65, 169–70.
85 Riding and Graves, *A Survey of Modernist Poetry*, 67.
86 Ibid.
87 Empson, *Seven Types of Ambiguity*, 1st ed., 102.
88 I.A. Richards, *Principles of Literary Criticism* (London: Kegan Paul, Trench, Trubner and Co., 1924; New York: Harcourt, Brace and Co., 1925), 29.

CHAPTER TWO

1 Robert Graves, letter to Martin Seymour-Smith (1944), quoted in Martin Seymour-Smith, *Robert Graves: His Life and Work* (London: Bloomsbury Publishing, 1995), 147.
2 John Haffenden, *William Empson: Among the Mandarins* (Oxford: Oxford University Press, 2005), 217. The article that Haffenden refers to is William Empson, "Curds and Whey," *The Granta* (11 May 1928): 419.
3 Haffenden, *William Empson*, 217.
4 Robert Graves, *Impenetrability; or the Proper Habit of English* (London: The Hogarth Press, 1926), 55–6; Empson quotes this very passage in his letter to Riding of 25 August 1970 in justification of his assertion that

Graves had reached "a theory of poetical ambiguity" by 1926; see *Selected Letters of William Empson*, ed. John Haffenden (Oxford: Oxford University Press, 2006), 429.

5 Graves, *Impenetrability*, 58–9.

6 Robert Graves, *Poetic Unreason: And Other Studies* (London: Cecil Palmer, 1925), 33–4, 31, 33, 33, 31.

7 Robert Graves, *On English Poetry: Being an Irregular Approach to the Psychology of This Art, from Evidence Mainly Subjective* (London: William Heinemann, 1922), 23.

8 William Empson, *Seven Types of Ambiguity: A Study of Its Effects in English Verse*, 1st ed. (London: Chatto and Windus, 1930; New York: Harcourt, Brace and Company, 1931), 197.

9 Ibid., 197.

10 William Empson, *Seven Types of Ambiguity*, 3rd ed. (1953; repr. London: Hogarth Press, 1984), 113, note.

11 Empson, "Preface to the Second Edition," *Seven Types of Ambiguity*, 3rd ed., xiv.

12 Ibid. The full quotation reads as follows: "Mr. Robert Graves (I ought to say in passing that he is, so far as I know, the inventor of the method of analysis I was using here) has remarked that a poem might happen to survive which later critics called 'the best poem the age produced,' and yet there had been no question of publishing it in that age, and the author had supposed himself to have destroyed the manuscript."

13 Graves, *Poetic Unreason*, 3.

14 Ibid., 255.

15 Ibid., 255, 263, 263.

16 Ibid., 30.

17 Empson, letter to Riding (25 August 1970), *Selected Letters*, 430.

18 Empson, quoted by Haffenden, *Selected Letters*, 431n10.

19 Empson, *Seven Types of Ambiguity*, 1st ed., 142.

20 Graves, *Poetic Unreason*, 82.

21 Haffenden, *William Empson*, 228.

22 Empson, *Seven Types of Ambiguity*, 1st ed., 241.

23 Graves, *On English Poetry*, 123–4.

24 Ibid., 123, 123, 124.

25 Haffenden, *William Empson*, 228.

26 Robert Graves, *The Meaning of Dreams* (London: Cecil Palmer, 1924), 19–20. See W.H.R. Rivers, *Instinct and the Unconscious* (Cambridge: Cambridge University Press, 1920) and W.H.R. Rivers, *Conflict and Dream* (London: Kegan, Paul, Trench, Trubner and Co., 1923).

27 Graves, *The Meaning of Dreams*, 23.
28 Ibid., 90.
29 Ibid.
30 Haffenden, *William Empson*, 228, 229.
31 Graves, *On English Poetry*, 22.
32 Ibid., 13.
33 Ibid., 13, 13, 13, 85.
34 Graves, *Poetic Unreason*, xi.
35 Ibid.
36 Ibid., 1–2.
37 Ibid., 2.
38 Ibid., 2, 3.
39 Laura Riding and Robert Graves, *A Survey of Modernist Poetry* (1927; repr. New York: Haskell House, 1969), 73.
40 See Empson, letter to Riding (29 April 1971), *Selected Letters*, 434.
41 Empson, *Seven Types of Ambiguity*, 1st ed., 142.
42 Ibid., emphasis added.
43 Empson, "Preface to the Second Edition," xiii.
44 Graves, *On English Poetry*, 22, 18, 17.
45 Empson, letter to Riding (25 August 1970), *Selected Letters*, 428–9.
46 Ibid., 430.
47 Ibid.
48 Empson, *Seven Types of Ambiguity*, 1st ed., 1.
49 Ibid.
50 Ibid., 2, emphasis added.
51 Favell Lee Mortimer, *Reading without Tears, or A Pleasant Mode of Learning to Read* (London: Hatchard and Company, 1866).
52 Empson, *Seven Types of Ambiguity*, 1st ed., 142, 142, 142, 130, 144–5.
53 Ibid., 145.
54 Ibid., 145, 146.
55 Ibid., 146.
56 Ibid., 168.
57 Ibid., 146–7.
58 Ibid., 244.
59 Ibid., 147.
60 Ibid., 284.
61 Ibid, 287.
62 Graves, *Poetic Unreason*, 2; Empson, *Seven Types of Ambiguity*, 1st ed., 287.
63 Empson, *Seven Types of Ambiguity*, 1st ed., 244.
64 Ibid., 244, 246, 248.

65 Ibid., 245–6.
66 Ibid., 286.
67 Graves, *On English Poetry*, 13; Graves, *Poetic Unreason*, 1–2.
68 Empson, *Seven Types of Ambiguity*, 1st ed., 142, emphasis added.
69 Ibid., 255.
70 Empson, letter to Riding (25 August 1970), *Selected Letters*, 429.
71 Empson, *Seven Types of Ambiguity*, 1st ed., 102.

CHAPTER THREE

1 William Van O'Connor, "Ambiguity," *The Princeton Encyclopedia of Poetry and Poetics*, ed. Alex Preminger, 2nd ed. enlarged (Princeton, New Jersey: Princeton University Press, 1974), 19.
2 Department of English, Cornell University, accessed 1 December 2012, http://www.arts.cornell.edu/english/about/history/.
3 Elizabeth Friedmann, *A Mannered Grace: The Life of Laura (Riding) Jackson* (New York: Persea Books, 2005), 78. See 480n4. Friedmann speculates that they were written in May and June of 1925.
4 Frederick Clark Prescott, *The Poetic Mind* (New York: Macmillan, 1922), 36, 36, 36, 38.
5 Ibid., 53.
6 Ibid., 69.
7 Ibid., 94.
8 Robert Graves, *Impenetrability; or the Proper Habit of English* (London: The Hogarth Press, 1926), 55–8.
9 Prescott, *The Poetic Mind*, 169.
10 Ibid., 171–80.
11 Empson, letter to Laura Riding (25 August 1970), *Selected Letters of William Empson*, ed. John Haffenden (Oxford: Oxford University Press, 2006), 430, 429, 429.
12 Prescott, *The Poetic Mind*, 173–4.
13 Laura Riding and Robert Graves, *A Survey of Modernist Poetry* (1927; repr. New York: Haskell House, 1969), 11.
14 Ibid., 63.
15 Ibid., 81.
16 Coincidentally, Empson defines his first type of ambiguity, and begins his extensive analysis of ambiguity in Shakespeare's works generally, with close attention to the ambiguities in this line. See *Seven Types of Ambiguity: A Study of Its Effects in English Verse*, 1st ed. (London: Chatto and Windus, 1930; New York: Harcourt, Brace and Company, 1931), 3.

17 Prescott, *The Poetic Mind*, 230–1.
18 Riding and Graves, *A Survey of Modernist Poetry*, 80.
19 Ibid., 149.
20 Ibid., 74.
21 Empson, *Seven Types of Ambiguity*, 1st ed., 102.
22 Ibid., 102, 102–3.
23 Ibid., 103, 103, 104.
24 Ibid., 103.
25 Prescott, *The Poetic Mind*, 174.

CHAPTER FOUR

1 William Empson, *Seven Types of Ambiguity: A Study of Its Effects in English Verse*, 1st ed. (London: Chatto and Windus, 1930; New York: Harcourt, Brace and Company, 1931), 287.
2 Ibid., 298.
3 Ibid., 298.
4 Robert Graves, *Poetic Unreason: And Other Studies* (London: Cecil Palmer, 1925), 49.
5 Ibid., 49–50.
6 Ibid., 50.
7 Ibid.
8 Empson, *Seven Types of Ambiguity*, 1st ed., 308.
9 Ibid., 309.
10 Ibid.
11 Ibid.
12 Graves, *Poetic Unreason*, 50–1.
13 Ibid., 50.
14 Ibid., 51.
15 Ibid.
16 Laura Riding, *Contemporaries and Snobs* (Garden City, New York: Doubleday Doran and Company, 1927), 58.
17 Ibid., 61.
18 Ibid., 62–3.
19 Ibid., 60.
20 See Jean Paul Sartre, *Existentialism Is a Humanism* (1946), translated by P. Mairet, in *Existentialism*, ed. Robert C. Solomon (New York: Modern Library, 1974), 198.
21 Laura Riding, *Anarchism Is Not Enough* (London: Jonathan Cape, 1928), 16–17.

22 W.H. Auden, "In Memory of W.B. Yeats," in *The English Auden: Poems, Essays and Dramatic Writings 1927–1939*, ed. Edward Mendelson (London: Faber and Faber, 1977), 242. Robert Graves drew attention to Auden's borrowing from Riding. According to Martin Seymour Smith, in *Robert Graves: His Life and Work* (London: Hutchinson, 1982), 297, Graves had Alan Hodge write a letter to the editor of the *Times Literary Supplement* complaining about borrowings from Riding and himself. Graves also ran side-by-side passages from the poems of Riding and Auden in "These Be Your Gods, O Israel," *Essays in Criticism*, 5.2 (April 1955): 129–50.
23 Empson, *Seven Types of Ambiguity*, 1st ed., 131.
24 Graves, *Poetic Unreason*, 49.
25 Ibid., 50.
26 Empson, *Seven Types of Ambiguity*, 1st ed., 142.
27 Empson, *Seven Types of Ambiguity*, 1st ed., 285, 286. See I.A. Richards, "Gerard Hopkins," *The Dial*, 81 (1926): 195–203, repr. in *Complementarities: Uncollected Essays*, ed. John Paul Russo (Cambridge, Mass.: Harvard University Press, 1976), 139–47.
28 Empson, letter to Riding (25 August 1970), *Selected Letters*, 429.
29 I.A. Richards, *Principles of Literary Criticism* (London: Kegan Paul, Trench, Trubner and Co., 1924; New York: Harcourt, Brace and Co., 1925), 29.
30 Empson, *Seven Types of Ambiguity*, 1st ed., 131
31 Ibid.; Richards, *Principles of Literary Criticism*, 82.
32 Richards, *Principles of Literary Criticism*, 30, 29.
33 Empson, *Seven Types of Ambiguity*, 1st ed., 130.
34 Ibid.
35 Ibid., 153.
36 Ibid., 130, 132.
37 Ibid., 131, 131–2.
38 Graves, *Poetic Unreason*, 49, 51.
39 Empson, *Seven Types of Ambiguity*, 1st ed., 130–1.
40 Ibid., 130.
41 Ibid., 130–1.
42 Ibid., 131–2.
43 Ibid., 151, 152.
44 Ibid., 153.
45 Ibid., 167.
46 Ibid., 130.
47 Ibid., 166.

48 Ibid., 130.
49 Ibid., 166, 130, 130, 167, 167, 166, 167.
50 Ibid., 131.
51 Graves, *Poetic Unreason*, 55–6.
52 Ibid., 50.
53 Ibid.
54 Ibid.
55 Ibid.
56 Empson, *Seven Types of Ambiguity*, 1st ed., 3.
57 Graves, *Poetic Unreason*, 50.
58 Ibid., 51.
59 Ibid.
60 Empson, *Seven Types of Ambiguity*, 1st ed., 244.
61 Ibid.
62 Ibid.
63 Ibid., 249–51.
64 Ibid., 250.
65 Ibid., 166.
66 Ibid.
67 Ibid., 166, 141, 141, 166.
68 Ibid., 166.
69 Ibid.
70 Ibid., 167.
71 Ibid.
72 Robert Graves, *Impenetrability; or the Proper Habit of English* (London: The Hogarth Press, 1926), 55–8.
73 Empson, *Seven Types of Ambiguity*, 1st ed., 167.
74 Graves, *Poetic Unreason*, 92.
75 Ibid.
76 Ibid., 51
77 Ibid.
78 Empson, *Seven Types of Ambiguity*, 1st ed., 166.
79 Ibid., 135, 136.
80 Ibid., 136.
81 Ibid., 137, 138.
82 Ibid., 145.
83 Graves, *Poetic Unreason*, 51; Empson, *Seven Types of Ambiguity*, 1st ed., 131.
84 Empson, *Seven Types of Ambiguity*, 1st ed., 131, 131, 131, 132.
85 Ibid., 132.

86 Graves, *Poetic Unreason*, 49.
87 Robert Graves, *On English Poetry: Being an Irregular Approach to the Psychology of This Art, from Evidence Mainly Subjective* (London: William Heinemann, 1922), 99.
88 Ibid., 98, 99.
89 Ibid., 99.
90 Empson, *Seven Types of Ambiguity*, 1st ed., 136.
91 Graves, *On English Poetry*, 24.
92 Ibid., 13.
93 Ibid.
94 Ibid., 16.
95 Ibid., 24–5.
96 Empson, *Seven Types of Ambiguity*, 1st ed., 130.
97 Ibid., 166, 167.

CHAPTER FIVE

1 Empson, letter to Laura Riding (25 August 1970), *Selected Letters of William Empson*, ed. John Haffenden (Oxford: Oxford University Press, 2006), 429.
2 Both Tate and Brooks concentrate their attention on the conflicted poetry of John Donne. See, for instance, Allen Tate's essays "Literature as Knowledge," "A Note on Donne," and "The Point of Dying: Donne's 'Virtuous Men,'" in *Collected Essays* (Denver: Alan Swallow, 1959), 16–48, 325–32, 547–52, and Cleanth Brooks's chapters "The Language of Paradox" and "The Heresy of Paraphrase" in *The Well Wrought Urn: Studies in the Structure of Poetry* (1947; repr. New York: Harvest Books, 1975).
3 Robert Graves, *Poetic Unreason: And Other Studies* (London: Cecil Palmer, 1925), 57, 2, 57.
4 Ibid., 51–2, 53.
5 Ibid., 57, 62.
6 Ibid., 58–9.
7 Miranda Seymour, *Robert Graves: Life on the Edge* (New York: Henry Holt and Co., 1995), 115.
8 W.K. Wimsatt, Jr, and Monroe C. Beardsley, "The Intentional Fallacy," in *The Verbal Icon: Studies in the Meaning of Poetry* (Lexington: University of Kentucky Press, 1954), 5.
9 Graves, *Poetic Unreason*, 31; also see Robert Graves, "How Many Miles to Babylon? An Analysis," *The Spectator*, 129 (22 July 1922): 117–18.
10 Graves, *Poetic Unreason*, 30.

11 Ibid., 32–3.
12 Ibid., 33.
13 Ibid.
14 Ibid., 34.
15 William Empson, *Seven Types of Ambiguity: A Study of Its Effects in English Verse*, 1st ed. (London: Chatto and Windus, 1930; New York: Harcourt, Brace and Company, 1931), 63.
16 Ibid., 63–4.
17 Graves, *Poetic Unreason*, 31.
18 Robert Graves, *On English Poetry: Being an Irregular Approach to the Psychology of This Art, from Evidence Mainly Subjective* (London: William Heinemann, 1922), vii–viii.
19 T.S. Matthews, *Under the Influence: Recollections of Robert Graves, Laura Riding, and Friends* (London: Cassell, 1977), 118.
20 Graves, *Poetic Unreason*, 70–1.
21 I.A. Richards, "William Empson," *Furioso*, 1.3 (1940), supplement following p. 44, quoted in John Haffenden, *William Empson: Among the Mandarins* (Oxford: Oxford University Press, 2005), 207.
22 Graves, *Poetic Unreason*, 77.
23 Graves, *On English Poetry*, viii.
24 Graves, *Poetic Unreason*, 59.
25 Ibid., 58.
26 Ibid., 57–8.
27 Ibid., 58, 59, 59, 60–1
28 Ibid., 59.
29 Ibid., 69–70.
30 Ibid., 63.
31 Ibid.
32 Ibid., 64.
33 Ibid., 63.
34 Graves, *Poetic Unreason*, 68–9, quoting Allen Upward, *The Divine Mystery: A Reading of the History of Christianity down to the Time of Christ* (Letchworth: Garden City Press, 1913).
35 Graves, *Poetic Unreason*, 49.
36 Empson, *Seven Types of Ambiguity*, 1st ed., 132, 132, 130, 141.
37 Ibid., 141–2.
38 Ibid., 157.
39 Ibid., 142.
40 Ibid.

41 Ibid., 144.
42 Ibid., 162.
43 Ibid., 162, 162; Empson, *Seven Types of Ambiguity*, 3rd ed. (1953; repr. London: Hogarth Press, 1984), 128.
44 Laura Riding and Robert Graves, *A Survey of Modernist Poetry* (1927; repr. New York: Haskell House, 1969), 141, 142; Robert Graves, *The Meaning of Dreams* (London: Cecil Palmer, 1924), 142.
45 Empson, *Seven Types of Ambiguity*, 1st ed., 146.
46 Ibid., 130, 168, 244.
47 Ibid., 147.
48 Ibid., 148.
49 Ibid.
50 Empson, *Seven Types of Ambiguity*, 3rd ed., 118.
51 Empson, *Seven Types of Ambiguity*, 1st ed., 142.
52 Ibid., 148; Empson, *Seven Types of Ambiguity*, 3rd ed., 119.
53 Empson, *Seven Types of Ambiguity*, 1st ed., 165, 142, 165, 166.
54 Graves, *Poetic Unreason*, 52.
55 Empson, *Seven Types of Ambiguity*, 1st ed., 142, 166, 166, 166.
56 Graves, *Poetic Unreason*, 54.
57 Empson, *Seven Types of Ambiguity*, 1st ed., 284.
58 Graves, *Poetic Unreason*, 59.
59 Ibid.
60 Empson, *Seven Types of Ambiguity*, 1st ed., 147.
61 Ibid., 287.
62 Ibid., 163.
63 Ibid., 150; Empson, *Seven Types of Ambiguity*, 3rd ed., 119, 119. See also Riding and Graves, *A Survey of Modernist Poetry*, 240.
64 Empson, *Seven Types of Ambiguity*, 1st ed., 147.
65 Ibid., 244.
66 Graves, *The Meaning of Dreams*, 140.
67 Ibid., 144–5.
68 Empson, *Seven Types of Ambiguity*, 1st ed., 271.
69 Graves, *On English Poetry*, 51–2.
70 Graves, *The Meaning of Dreams*, 144.
71 Graves, *On English Poetry*, 54.
72 Ibid., 53–4.
73 Empson, *Seven Types of Ambiguity*, 1st ed., 272–3.
74 Ibid., 273.
75 Graves, *Poetic Unreason*, 2.

76 Empson, *Seven Types of Ambiguity*, 1st ed., 273.
77 Ibid., 279.

CHAPTER SIX

1 T.S. Eliot, "Tradition and the Individual Talent," in *Selected Essays*, 3rd ed. enlarged (London: Faber and Faber, 1951), 16, 13, 13, 13.
2 Robert Graves, *On English Poetry: Being an Irregular Approach to the Psychology of This Art, from Evidence Mainly Subjective* (London: William Heinemann, 1922), vii–viii.
3 Robert Graves, *Poetic Unreason: And Other Studies* (London: Cecil Palmer, 1925), ix.
4 William Empson, *Seven Types of Ambiguity: A Study of Its Effects in English Verse*, 1st ed. (London: Chatto and Windus, 1930; New York: Harcourt, Brace and Company, 1931), 21.
5 Ibid., 312.
6 Ibid., 315–16.
7 Ibid., 315.
8 Ibid., 312.
9 Graves, *Poetic Unreason*, 52–3.
10 Ibid.
11 Ibid., 56.
12 Empson, *Seven Types of Ambiguity*, 1st ed., 318.
13 Ibid., 320.
14 Graves, *Poetic Unreason*, 92.
15 Ibid.
16 Empson, *Seven Types of Ambiguity*, 1st ed., 314.
17 Graves, *Poetic Unreason*, 92.
18 Empson, *Seven Types of Ambiguity*, 1st ed., 315.
19 Graves, *Poetic Unreason*, 92–3.
20 Empson, *Seven Types of Ambiguity*, 1st ed., 316.
21 Graves, *Poetic Unreason*, 92, 93.
22 Ibid., 93, 92, 92.
23 Ibid., 93.
24 Ibid.
25 Empson, *Seven Types of Ambiguity*, 1st ed., 303.
26 Ibid.
27 Ibid.
28 Ibid.
29 Ibid.

30 Graves, *Poetic Unreason*, 94–5.
31 Empson, *Seven Types of Ambiguity*, 1st ed., 303, 303–4.
32 Empson, letter to Laura Riding (29 April 1971), *Selected Letters of William Empson*, ed. John Haffenden (Oxford: Oxford University Press, 2006), 432–3.
33 Graves, *Poetic Unreason*, 94.
34 Empson, *Seven Types of Ambiguity*, 1st ed., 207–8.
35 Graves, *Poetic Unreason*, 78.
36 Empson, *Seven Types of Ambiguity*, 1st ed., 12.
37 Graves, *Poetic Unreason*, 78–82.
38 Empson, *Seven Types of Ambiguity*, 1st ed., 12, 297–8.
39 Graves, *Poetic Unreason*, 16.
40 Ibid., 25–6.
41 Ibid., 78–9.
42 Ibid., 79.
43 Ibid., 81–2.
44 Empson, *Seven Types of Ambiguity*, 1st ed., 256.
45 Ibid., 296, 302.
46 Graves, *On English Poetry*, 14.
47 Empson, *Seven Types of Ambiguity*, 1st ed., 319.
48 Ibid., 301.
49 Laura Riding and Robert Graves, *A Survey of Modernist Poetry* (1927; repr. New York: Haskell House, 1969), 147–8.
50 Ibid., 143.
51 Empson, *Seven Types of Ambiguity*, 1st ed., 202.
52 Riding and Graves, *A Survey of Modernist Poetry*, 144.
53 Ibid., 145.
54 Ibid., 145, 146.
55 Empson, *Seven Types of Ambiguity*, 1st ed., 302.
56 Riding and Graves, *A Survey of Modernist Poetry*, 147, 146.
57 Ibid., 146.
58 Ibid., 149.
59 Ibid., 146.
60 Empson, *Seven Types of Ambiguity*, 1st ed., 319.
61 Empson, quoted by Haffenden, *Selected Letters*, 431n10; Graves, *On English Poetry*, vii, vii–viii.

CHAPTER SEVEN

1 T.S. Eliot, “The Metaphysical Poets,” in *Selected Essays*, 3rd ed. enlarged (London: Faber and Faber, 1951), 287, 289, 287, 287, 287.

2 William Empson, *Seven Types of Ambiguity: A Study of Its Effects in English Verse*, 1st ed. (London: Chatto and Windus, 1930; New York: Harcourt, Brace and Company, 1931), 26.
3 Ibid.
4 Robert Graves, *Poetic Unreason: And Other Studies* (London: Cecil Palmer, 1925), 83.
5 Ibid.
6 Ibid., 84.
7 Ibid.
8 Ibid., 84–5.
9 Ibid., 85.
10 T.E. Hulme, "Romanticism and Classicism," in *Speculations: Essays on Humanism and Art* (1924; repr. London: Kegan Paul, Trench, Trubner, 1936), 113–40.
11 Ford Madox Ford, "Modern Poetry," in *The Critical Attitude* (1911; repr. London: Books for Libraries Press, 1967), 187.
12 T.S. Eliot, "The Metaphysical Poets," in *Selected Essays*, 288, 289, 289, 289.
13 Empson, *Seven Types of Ambiguity*, 1st ed., 27.
14 Ibid.
15 Ibid.
16 Ibid.
17 T.S. Eliot, "Tradition and the Individual Talent," in *Selected Essays*, 17.
18 Empson, *Seven Types of Ambiguity*, 1st ed., 307.
19 Ibid., 306.
20 Ibid., 307.
21 Ibid., 306, 306; Robert Graves, *On English Poetry: Being an Irregular Approach to the Psychology of This Art, from Evidence Mainly Subjective* (London: William Heinemann, 1922), 62.
22 Graves, *On English Poetry*, 117–18.
23 Ibid., 121–2.
24 Ibid., 99, 99–100.
25 Ibid., 100.
26 Ibid.
27 Empson, *Seven Types of Ambiguity*, 1st ed., 319.
28 Graves, *On English Poetry*, 100.
29 Graves, *Poetic Unreason*, 89.
30 Empson, *Seven Types of Ambiguity*, 1st ed., 307.
31 William Empson, "Preface to the Second Edition," *Seven Types of Ambiguity*, 3rd ed. (1953; repr. London: Hogarth Press, 1984), xv–xvi.
32 Graves, *Poetic Unreason*, 89.

33 Graves, *On English Poetry*, 51–2; Robert Graves, *The Meaning of Dreams* (London: Cecil Palmer, 1924), 144.
34 Empson, *Seven Types of Ambiguity*, 1st ed., 273, 26.
35 Graves, *On English Poetry*, 44.
36 Empson, *Seven Types of Ambiguity*, 1st ed., 26.
37 Graves, *On English Poetry*, 68.
38 Ibid., 68–9.
39 Ibid., 69.
40 Empson, *Seven Types of Ambiguity*, 1st ed., 26.
41 Ibid.
42 Ibid., 27, 26, 26, 26.
43 Graves, *Poetic Unreason*, 106, 106, 106, 108–9, 109.
44 Ibid., 22–3.
45 Ibid., 24.
46 Ibid., 126, 119, 117.
47 Graves, *On English Poetry*, 69, 69; Graves, *Poetic Unreason*, 126–7.
48 Graves, *On English Poetry*, 141.
49 Ibid.
50 Empson, *Seven Types of Ambiguity*, 1st ed., 191.
51 Ibid., 22.
52 I.A. Richards, "Emotion and Art," in *Complementarities: Uncollected Essays*, ed. John Paul Russo (Cambridge, Mass.: Harvard University Press, 1976), 9.
53 Empson, *Seven Types of Ambiguity*, 1st ed., 27.
54 I.A. Richards, "Emotion and Art," 9.
55 Empson, *Seven Types of Ambiguity*, 1st ed., 27.
56 Ibid., 194.
57 Ibid., 191.
58 Ibid., 27.
59 Ibid., 191.
60 Ibid.
61 Ibid., 27.
62 Ibid., 26.
63 Empson, "Preface to the Second Edition," xv.
64 Empson, *Seven Types of Ambiguity*, 1st ed., 298.
65 Graves, *Poetic Unreason*, 120.
66 Ibid.
67 Ibid., 119.
68 Empson, "Preface to the Second Edition," xv.
69 Ibid., emphasis added.
70 Empson, *Seven Types of Ambiguity*, 1st ed., 196.

71 Ibid., 247, 248, 249, 249.
72 Ibid., 196, 196, 175, 175, 175.
73 Ibid., 201.
74 Graves, *Poetic Unreason*, 117–8.
75 Ibid., 121, 120–1.
76 Ibid., 119.
77 Ibid., 121.
78 Ibid., 122, 122, 123, 123–4.
79 Empson, *Seven Types of Ambiguity*, 1st ed., 196, 175.
80 Graves, *Poetic Unreason*, 117.
81 Empson, *Seven Types of Ambiguity*, 1st ed., 246.
82 Ibid., 246–9.
83 Ibid., 247, 248.
84 Ibid., 26.
85 Empson, "Preface to the Second Edition," viii.
86 Ibid., 195–204.
87 Ibid., 27, 26, 27, 27, 27.
88 Empson, "Preface to the Second Edition," viii.
89 Empson, *Seven Types of Ambiguity*, 1st ed., 208, 209, 209.
90 Ibid., 220, 208, 208.
91 Ibid., 222.
92 Ibid, 273.
93 Graves, *The Meaning of Dreams*, 158–9.
94 Empson, *Seven Types of Ambiguity*, 1st ed., 168.
95 Ibid., 194.
96 Graves, *On English Poetry*, 45.
97 Empson, *Seven Types of Ambiguity*, 1st ed., 192–4.
98 Ibid., 194.
99 Ibid., 241.
100 Graves, *On English Poetry*, 45.
101 Ibid.
102 Ibid.
103 Empson, *Seven Types of Ambiguity*, 1st ed., 241–2.
104 Eliot, "The Metaphysical Poets," in *Selected Essays*, 289.
105 Empson, *Seven Types of Ambiguity*, 1st ed., 27.

CHAPTER EIGHT

1 William Empson, *Seven Types of Ambiguity: A Study of Its Effects in English Verse*, 1st ed. (London: Chatto and Windus, 1930; New York: Harcourt, Brace and Company, 1931), 296.

2 W.H. Auden and Cecil Day-Lewis, preface to *Oxford Poetry* (1927), quoted by Empson, *Seven Types of Ambiguity*, 1st ed., 296. Blending ideas from Eliot's "Tradition and the Individual Talent" and "The Metaphysical Poets" with Graves's "conflict theory," Auden and Day-Lewis also foreground the idea of poetry as an experience of psychological "conflict" that produces a "new harmony": "Emotion is no longer necessarily to be analysed by 'recollection in tranquillity'; it is to be prehended emotionally and intellectually at once. And this is of most importance to the poet; for it is his mind that must bear the brunt of the conflict and may be the first to realize the new harmony which would imply the success of this synchronization." See the preface to *Oxford Poetry* (1927), in *The Complete Works of W.H. Auden: Prose and Travel Books in Prose and Verse: Volume 1. 1926–1938*, ed. Edward Mendelson (Princeton: Princeton University Press, 1997), 3.
3 Robert Graves, *Poetic Unreason: And Other Studies* (London: Cecil Palmer, 1925), 119; *On English Poetry: Being an Irregular Approach to the Psychology of This Art, from Evidence Mainly Subjective* (London: William Heinemann, 1922), 14; and *Poetic Unreason*, 120.
4 Robert Graves, "The Illogic of Stoney Stratford and of Poetry," *Spectator*, 129 (15 July 1922): 87; Graves, "How Many Miles to Babylon? An Analysis," *The Spectator*, 129 (22 July 1922): 117.
5 Graves, *On English Poetry*, viii.
6 Ibid., 14.
7 Ibid., 71.
8 Graves, *Poetic Unreason*, 117.
9 Ibid., 118, 132.
10 Ibid., 119, 120, 120.
11 Ibid., 127.
12 Empson, *Seven Types of Ambiguity*, 1st ed., 114.
13 Ibid., 115.
14 Ibid., 116.
15 Graves, *Poetic Unreason*, 117.
16 Empson, quoted by Haffenden, *Selected Letters of William Empson*, ed. John Haffenden (Oxford: Oxford University Press, 2006), 431n10.
17 Ibid.
18 Graves, *Poetic Unreason*, 117, 117, 127, 127.
19 Ibid., 121, 131, 132.
20 Ibid., 125, 125, 120.
21 Ibid., 120, 12, 125.
22 Ibid., 120, 135, 132.
23 Ibid., 124
24 Ibid., 123, 125, 124, 124, 125, 123–4.

25 Auden and Day-Lewis, preface to *Oxford Poetry*, 3.
26 Empson, *Seven Types of Ambiguity*, 1st ed., 296.
27 Graves, *Poetic Unreason*, 118.
28 Ibid., 137, 137, 135, 137, 137–8.
29 Graves, *On English Poetry*, 73–5.
30 Graves, *Poetic Unreason*, 133.
31 Empson, *Seven Types of Ambiguity*, 1st ed., 111.
32 Ibid.
33 Ibid.
34 Graves, *On English Poetry*, 143.
35 Ibid., 146.
36 Ibid., 147.
37 Ibid., 146.
38 Ibid., 148.
39 Ibid., 148–9.
40 Ibid., 146, 149.
41 Ibid., 144; Empson, *Seven Types of Ambiguity*, 1st ed., 299.
42 Empson, *Seven Types of Ambiguity*, 1st ed., 299.
43 Graves, *Poetic Unreason*, 120.
44 Empson, *Seven Types of Ambiguity*, 1st ed., 299, 300, 299, 299, 298.
45 Ibid., 300–1.
46 Ibid., 299, 299, 306.
47 Ibid., 297–8.
48 Ibid., 296.
49 Graves, *On English Poetry*, 32–3.
50 Ibid., 143–4.
51 Ibid., 149, 145.
52 Ibid., 147, 143.
53 Ibid., 146.
54 Ibid., 147–8.
55 Ibid., 148–9.
56 Ibid., 143, 42.
57 Ibid., 24–5.
58 Robert Graves, *Impenetrability; or the Proper Habit of English* (London: The Hogarth Press, 1926), 40.
59 Ibid., 39.
60 Ibid., 39–40.
61 Ibid., 40.
62 Ibid., 11.

63 Ibid., 55.
64 Empson, *Seven Types of Ambiguity*, 1st ed., 86–7.
65 Graves, *Impenetrability*, 55–9.
66 Ibid., 57.
67 Empson, *Seven Types of Ambiguity*, 1st ed., 314.
68 Graves, *Impenetrability*, 9–11
69 Empson, *Seven Types of Ambiguity*, 1st ed., 32–3.
70 Graves, *On English Poetry*, 33–4, 113, 26.
71 Empson, *Seven Types of Ambiguity*, 1st ed., 118–19, 119.

CHAPTER NINE

1 Robert Graves, *Poetic Unreason: And Other Studies* (London: Cecil Palmer, 1925), 147.
2 Ibid., 147, 141, 140.
3 Ibid., 141.
4 Ibid., 142.
5 Ibid., 52–3.
6 Ibid., 147–8.
7 Ibid., 148.
8 Ibid.
9 Ibid.
10 James Jensen, "The Construction of *Seven Types of Ambiguity*," *Modern Language Quarterly*, 27.3 (1966): 243–59.
11 Graves, *Poetic Unreason*, 1.
12 Jensen, 252–3.
13 William Empson, *Seven Types of Ambiguity: A Study of Its Effects in English Verse*, 1st ed. (London: Chatto and Windus, 1930; New York: Harcourt, Brace and Company, 1931), 168, 195, 244, 245, 245.
14 Graves, *Poetic Unreason*, 150.
15 Ibid., 152–3.
16 Empson, *Seven Types of Ambiguity*, 1st ed., 284, 147.
17 Ibid., 195; Graves, *Poetic Unreason*, 167–71.
18 Empson, *Seven Types of Ambiguity*, 1st ed., 202, 195; and "Preface to the Second Edition," *Seven Types of Ambiguity*, 3rd ed. (1953; repr. London: Hogarth Press, 1984), vi.
19 Graves, *Poetic Unreason*, 171.
20 Ibid, 172, 172, 172, 173.
21 Ibid., 172.

CHAPTER TEN

1 William Empson, "Preface to the Second Edition," *Seven Types of Ambiguity*, 3rd ed. (1953; repr. London: Hogarth Press, 1984), viii–ix.
2 Empson, "Preface to the Second Edition," viii–ix.
3 Empson, "Preface to the Second Edition," ix.
4 Robert Graves, *On English Poetry: Being an Irregular Approach to the Psychology of This Art, from Evidence Mainly Subjective* (London: William Heinemann, 1922), 84–5.
5 Robert Graves, *The Meaning of Dreams* (London: Cecil Palmer, 1924), 165, 163.
6 Robert Graves, *Poetic Unreason: And Other Studies* (London: Cecil Palmer, 1925), 82.
7 Empson, letter to Laura Riding (25 April 1971), *Selected Letters of William Empson*, ed. John Haffenden (Oxford: Oxford University Press, 2006), 434.
8 Empson, "Preface to the Second Edition," ix.
9 Empson, "Preface to the Second Edition," ix.
10 Graves, *Poetic Unreason*, 1–2.
11 Empson, "Preface to the Second Edition," ix.
12 Graves, *Poetic Unreason*, 2.
13 James Smith, "Books of the Quarter," *The Criterion*, 10.41 (July 1931): 741, quoted by Empson, "Preface to the Second Edition," xii.
14 Ibid.
15 Miranda Seymour, "Robert Graves, Laura Riding, and William Empson," accessed 1 December 2012, http://www.robertgraves.org/issues/37/2632_article_16.pdf.
16 Ibid.
17 Smith, "Books," xii–xiii.
18 Empson, "Preface to the Second Edition," xiii.
19 Smith, "Books," xii, xii; Empson, "Preface to the Second Edition," xiv.
20 Empson, "Preface to the Second Edition," xiv.
21 Graves, *On English Poetry*, 13.
22 Ibid.
23 Ibid.
24 Ibid., 128.
25 Ibid., 69.
26 Empson, "Preface to the Second Edition," ix; Graves, *Poetic Unreason*, 27.
27 Graves, *Poetic Unreason*, 26.
28 Graves, *On English Poetry*, 16.

29 Ibid., 24–5.
30 Ibid., 25.
31 Ibid.
32 Ibid., 16, 25.
33 Graves, *Poetic Unreason*, 17.
34 Ibid.
35 Ibid., 19, 18.
36 Graves, *Poetic Unreason*, 30.
37 Empson, "Preface to the Second Edition," xiv, xiv–xv.
38 Ibid., xiv, xv.
39 Graves, *On English Poetry*, 42–43.
40 Ibid., 42.
41 Empson, "Preface to the Second Edition," xiv, xiv, xiv.
42 Graves, *On English Poetry*, 42, 13, 13.
43 Empson, "Preface to the Second Edition," xi.
44 Graves, *On English Poetry*, 43.
45 Empson, "Preface to the Second Edition," xiii.
46 Ibid., xiv, xiii–xiv.
47 Graves, *Poetic Unreason*, 89.
48 Ibid.
49 Ibid.
50 Ibid., 92–3.
51 Ibid., 89–90.
52 William Empson, *Seven Types of Ambiguity: A Study of Its Effects in English Verse*, 1st ed. (London: Chatto and Windus, 1930; New York: Harcourt, Brace and Company, 1931), 307.
53 Graves, *On English Poetry*, 13; Empson, "Preface to the Second Edition," xv.
54 Empson, *Seven Types of Ambiguity*, 1st ed., 307; Empson, "Preface to the Second Edition," xv.
55 Empson, letter to Riding (29 August 1970), *Selected Letters*, 428.

CHAPTER ELEVEN

1 Miranda Seymour, "Robert Graves, Laura Riding, and William Empson," accessed 1 December 2012, http://www.robertgraves.org/issues/37/2632_article_16.pdf.
2 Miranda Seymour, *Robert Graves: Life on the Edge* (New York: Henry Holt and Co., 1995), 124.
3 I.A. Richards, C.K. Ogden, James Wood, *The Foundation of Aesthetics* (London: George Allen and Unwin,1922); C.K. Ogden and I.A. Richards,

The Meaning of Meaning: A Study of the Influence of Language upon Thought and of the Science of Symbolism (London: Kegan Paul, Trench, Trubner and Co., 1923).

4 George Watson, *Never Ones for Theory: England and the War of Ideas* (Cambridge: Lutterworth Press, 2001), 14.

5 See, for example, "Art and Science," *The Athenaeum*, (27 June 1919): 534–5, "Emotion and Art," *The Athenaeum* (18 July 1919): 630–1, and "The Instruments of Criticism: Expression," *The Athenaeum* (31 October 1919): 1131, all three essays repr. in I.A. Richards, *Complementarities: Uncollected Essays*, ed. John Paul Russo (Cambridge, Mass.: Harvard University Press, 1976), 3–15.

6 See, for example, the essays by I.A. Richards mentioned in the preceding note; and also Robert Graves, "Mr Hardy and the Pleated Skirt," *Nation & Athenaeum*, 33 (7 July 1923): 451–2.

7 See, for example, I.A. Richards, "Science and Poetry," *Saturday Review of Literature*, 2.45 (5 June 1926): 833–4, and Robert Graves, "Sensory Vehicles of Poetic Thought," *Saturday Review of Literature*, 1 (31 January 1925): 489–90.

8 Richard Luckett, introduction to *The Selected Letters of I.A. Richards*, ed. John Constable (Oxford: Clarendon Press, 1990), xii.

9 John Lehman, *The Whispering Gallery* (London: Longmans, 1955), 151.

10 Empson, "Curds and Whey," *The Granta* (11 May 1928): 419, quoted by John Haffenden, *William Empson: Among the Mandarins* (Oxford: Oxford University Press, 2005), 217; Empson, quoted by Haffenden, *Selected Letters of William Empson*, ed. John Haffenden (Oxford: Oxford University Press, 2006), 431n10.

11 Robert Graves, *On English Poetry: Being an Irregular Approach to the Psychology of This Art, from Evidence Mainly Subjective* (London: William Heinemann, 1922), vii–viii.

12 Robert Graves, *Poetic Unreason: And Other Studies* (London: Cecil Palmer, 1925), x.

13 William Empson, "Curds and Whey," 217.

14 John Paul Russo, *I.A. Richards: His Life and Work* (Baltimore: The Johns Hopkins University Press, 1989), 92–3.

15 Graves, *On English Poetry*, 132.

16 Elizabeth Friedmann, *A Mannered Grace: the Life of Laura (Riding) Jackson* (New York: Persea Books, 2005), 98.

17 I.A. Richards, *Principles of Literary Criticism* (London: Kegan Paul, Trench, Trubner and Co., 1924; New York: Harcourt, Brace and Co., 1925), 140.

18 Ibid., 189, 191, 191.

19 Ibid., 191.
20 See Paul O'Prey's account of the letters exchanged between Graves and Eliot in 1927 in *In Broken Images: Selected Letters of Robert Graves 1914–1946*, ed. Paul O'Prey (London: Hutchinson, 1982), 176–9.
21 On this latter topic, see Donald J. Childs, "Generating Modernism and New Criticism from Antisemitism: Laura Riding and Robert Graves Read T.S. Eliot's Early Poetry," in *Modernism and Race*, ed. Len Platt (Cambridge.: Cambridge University Press, 2011), 77–96.
22 Richards, *Principles of Literary Criticism*, 30.
23 Robert Graves, *The Meaning of Dreams* (London: Cecil Palmer, 1924), 16.
24 Watson, *Never Ones for Theory*, 16.
25 Russo, *I.A. Richards*, 189–90.
26 Ibid., 174.
27 Graves, *The Meaning of Dreams*, 105; Russo, *I.A. Richards*, 273.
28 Graves, *On English Poetry*, 123, 123, 124.
29 Robert Graves and Alan Hodge, *The Reader Over Your Shoulder: A Handbook for Writers of English Prose* (London: Cape, 1943), 406.
30 Richards, *Principles of Literary Criticism*, 33.
31 Graves, *The Meaning of Dreams*, 19–20.
32 Ibid., 23.
33 Ibid., 90.
34 Ibid.
35 Graves, *On English Poetry*, 22.
36 Ibid., 13.
37 Ibid., 13, 13, 13, 85.
38 Graves, *The Meaning of Dreams*, 146, 145, 145, 156, 156.
39 Ibid., 156.
40 Ibid., 157–8.
41 Richards, *Principles of Literary Criticism*, 30.
42 Ibid.
43 Ibid., 29.
44 Graves, *The Meaning of Dreams*, 109–11.
45 Ibid., 29–30, 29.
46 Graves, *The Meaning of Dreams*, 111; Richards, *Principles of Literary Criticism*, 30.
47 Richards, *Principles of Literary Criticism*, 30.
48 Ibid., 30–1.
49 Ibid., 31, 30.
50 William Empson, *Seven Types of Ambiguity: A Study of Its Effects in English Verse*, 1st ed. (London: Chatto and Windus, 1930; New York: Harcourt, Brace and Company, 1931), 196.

51 Graves, *On English Poetry*, 32.
52 Richards, *Principles of Literary Criticism*, 31.

CHAPTER TWELVE

1 I.A. Richards, *Principles of Literary Criticism* (London: Kegan Paul, Trench, Trubner and Co., 1924; New York: Harcourt, Brace and Co., 1925), 25.
2 Robert Graves, *On English Poetry: Being an Irregular Approach to the Psychology of This Art, from Evidence Mainly Subjective* (London: William Heinemann, 1922), 123–4.
3 Richards, *Principles of Literary Criticism*, 61.
4 Graves, *On English Poetry*, 84–5.
5 Ibid., 30–1.
6 Richards, *Principles of Literary Criticism*, 57.
7 Ibid., 132–3.
8 Graves, *On English Poetry*, 84–5, 30–1.
9 Richards, *Principles of Literary Criticism*, 190.
10 Ibid., 195, 194, 195–6.
11 Ibid., 196–7.
12 Ibid., 196.
13 Ibid., 198.
14 Ibid., 198, 198; Graves, *On English Poetry*, 30–1.
15 Richards, *Principles of Literary Criticism*, 198; Graves, *On English Poetry*, 30–1.
16 Graves, *On English Poetry*, 13.
17 Ibid., 16.
18 Ibid., 13.
19 Ibid.
20 Ibid., 81.
21 Ibid., 24–5.
22 Ibid., 83, 83, 83, 85.
23 Ibid., 43.
24 Ibid., 21.
25 Robert Graves, "What is Bad Poetry?" *North American Review* 218 (September 1923): 353–68.
26 Robert Graves, *Poetic Unreason: And Other Studies* (London: Cecil Palmer, 1925), 17, 17, 19, 18.
27 Graves, *On English Poetry*, 99.
28 Ibid., 97–8.

29 Ibid., 101.
30 Ibid.
31 Ibid., 101–2.
32 Richards, *Principles of Literary Criticism*, 197–8, 202.
33 Ibid., 202.
34 Ibid., 203.
35 Richards, *Principles of Literary Criticism*, 204–5. See Ella Wheeler Wilcox, "Friendship after Love," in *Principles of Literary Criticism*, 200–1.
36 Richards, *Principles of Literary Criticism*, 204–5.
37 Ibid., 25.
38 Ibid.
39 Ibid., 26.
40 Ibid., 27.
41 Ibid.
42 Graves, *Poetic Unreason*, 4–5.
43 Ibid., 27.
44 Ibid., 26.
45 Ibid., 28.
46 Richards, *Principles of Literary Criticism*, 26, 27.
47 Ibid., 28–9.
48 Laura Riding and Robert Graves, *A Survey of Modernist Poetry* (1927; repr. New York: Haskell House, 1969), 136, 137.
49 Ibid., 137.
50 Richards, *Principles of Literary Criticism*, 26; Riding and Graves, *A Survey of Modernist Poetry*, 137.
51 Laura Riding, *Contemporaries and Snobs* (Garden City, New York: Doubleday Doran and Company, 1927), 60.
52 Richards, *Principles of Literary Criticism*, 27.
53 Riding and Graves, *A Survey of Modernist Poetry*, 88.
54 Ibid., 89.
55 Ibid., 142.
56 Richards, *Principles of Literary Criticism*, 29.
57 Ibid., 29–30.
58 Ibid., 181.
59 Graves, *Poetic Unreason*, 27–8.
60 Richards, *Principles of Literary Criticism*, 181.
61 Ibid., 181, 185.
62 Ibid., 181.
63 Ibid., 182, 183, 183.
64 Ibid., 184.

65 Ibid., 183–4.
66 Ibid., 183.
67 Robert Graves, "The Illogic of Stoney Stratford and of Poetry," *Spectator* 129 (15 July 1922): 87.
68 Graves, *Poetic Unreason*, 133, 132, 132–3.
69 Richards, *Principles of Literary Criticism*, 182, 185; Graves, *Poetic Unreason*,127.
70 Graves, *Poetic Unreason*, 119.
71 Ibid., 129–30.
72 Ibid., 131.
73 Ibid., 127.
74 Ibid., 131.
75 Ibid., 133.
76 Richards, *Principles of Literary Criticism*, 184.
77 Ibid., 199.
78 Graves, *Poetic Unreason*, 37.
79 Richards, *Principles of Literary Criticism*, 224.
80 Graves, *Poetic Unreason*, 28–9.
81 Graves, *On English Poetry*, 13.
82 Ibid., 19.
83 Ibid., 20.
84 Ibid.
85 Ibid., 14.
86 Ibid., 15.
87 Ibid., 45–6.
88 Ibid., 48, 48, 49.
89 Ibid., 46, 47.
90 Ibid., 46.
91 Ibid., 14, 14, 45, 14.
92 Richards, *Principles of Literary Criticism*, 134.
93 Ibid., 137, 137–8.
94 Ibid., 137.
95 Ibid., 142.
96 Graves, *On English Poetry*, 47.
97 Richards, *Principles of Literary Criticism*, 142.
98 Ibid., 138.
99 Graves, *On English Poetry*, 14.
100 Ibid., 83.
101 Ibid., 83–4.
102 Ibid., 85.

103 Richards, *Principles of Literary Criticism*, 140–1.
104 Ibid., 142.
105 Ibid., 229.
106 Ibid., 229; Graves, *On English Poetry*, 83.
107 Richards, *Principles of Literary Criticism*, 144.
108 Graves, *On English Poetry*, 45–6.
109 Ibid., 46.
110 Ibid., 48.
111 Richards, *Principles of Literary Criticism*, 144.
112 C.K. Ogden and I.A. Richards, *The Meaning of Meaning: A Study of The Influence of Language upon Thought and of The Science of Symbolism* (London: Kegan Paul, Trench, Trubner and Co., 1923), 239–40. .
113 Richards, *Principles of Literary Criticism*, 200. Richards criticizes H.D.'s poem "The Pool," which he reproduces in full in *Principles of Literary Criticism*, 199.
114 Ibid.
115 Ibid., 134.
116 Graves, *On English Poetry*, 19, 20, 20, 20.
117 Richards, *Principles of Literary Criticism*, 143, 138.
118 Graves, *On English Poetry*, 20; Richards, *Principles of Literary Criticism*, 144.
119 Graves, *On English Poetry*, 31.
120 Richards, *Principles of Literary Criticism*, 139–40.
121 Graves, *On English Poetry*, 31, 20, 68, 68.
122 Ibid., 20.
123 Ibid., 69.
124 Ibid., 74.
125 Ibid., 68.
126 Ibid., 69.
127 Ogden and Richards, *The Meaning of Meaning*, 239.
128 Ibid., 240.
129 Richards, *Principles of Literary Criticism*, 138.
130 Ibid., 143.
131 Ibid.
132 Ibid., 144.
133 Ibid., 143.
134 Quite enamoured of Coleridge's literary theory, Richards is nonetheless determined to remove hints of Coleridge's God from it – "There is nothing peculiarly mysterious about imagination … [O]ur account will be devoid of theological implications" and thereby "avoid part of the fate which

befell Coleridge" through his mystification of imagination in chapter XIII of *Biographia Litteraria* as "a repetition in the finite mind of the eternal act of creation in the infinite I AM": the fate of being overlooked by people for whom God is dead. Richards, *Principles of Literary Criticism*, 191, 191; Samuel Taylor Coleridge, *Biographia Literaria; or Biographical Sketches of My Literary Life and Opinions*, 2 vols (London: Rest Fenner, 1817), 1: 295–6.

135 Richards, *Principles of Literary Criticism*, 43.
136 Robert Graves, *The Meaning of Dreams* (London: Cecil Palmer, 1924), 20.
137 Richards, *Principles of Literary Criticism*, 82–3.
138 Ibid., 83.
139 Ibid.

CHAPTER THIRTEEN

1 Robert Graves, *The Meaning of Dreams* (London: Cecil Palmer, 1924), 20–4.
2 Robert Graves, *Poetic Unreason: And Other Studies* (London: Cecil Palmer, 1925), 52–3.
3 Ibid., 52.
4 Robert Graves, *On English Poetry: Being an Irregular Approach to the Psychology of This Art, from Evidence Mainly Subjective* (London: William Heinemann, 1922), 36–7.
5 I.A. Richards, *Science and Poetry* (New York: W.W. Norton, 1926), 42.
6 Ibid.
7 Ibid., 43.
8 Ibid.
9 Graves, *The Meaning of Dreams*, 23, 23.
10 Richards, *Science and Poetry*, 43, 43–4.
11 Richards, *Science and Poetry*, 44.
12 Ibid., 42, 42, 42, 43.
13 Ibid., 43.
14 Ibid., 43, 45.
15 Ibid., 45.
16 Graves, *Poetic Unreason*, 1–2.
17 Richards, *Science and Poetry*, 44–5.
18 Chistopher Isherwood, *Lions and Shadows: An Education in the Twenties* (Norfolk, Conn.: New Directions, 1947, 121–2, quoted by John Paul Russo, *I.A. Richards: His Life and Work* (Baltimore: The Johns Hopkins University Press, 1989), 93.

19 Graves, *On English Poetry*, 33–4.
20 Ibid., 113.
21 Ibid., 26.
22 I.A. Richards, *The Philosophy of Rhetoric* (New York and London: Oxford University Press, 1936), 38.
23 Ibid., 39.
24 Ibid.
25 Russo, *I.A. Richards*, 280.
26 Graves, *Poetic Unreason*, 4–5.
27 Graves, *On English Poetry*, 14.
28 Ibid., 25.
29 Ibid., 24.
30 Ibid., 25.
31 Russo, *I.A. Richards*, 196–7.

CHAPTER FOURTEEN

1 I.A. Richards, *Principles of Literary Criticism* (London: Kegan Paul, Trench, Trubner and Co., 1924; New York: Harcourt, Brace and Co., 1925), 29, 31.
2 Ibid., 30.
3 Robert Graves and Alan Hodge, *The Reader Over Your Shoulder: A Handbook for Writers of English Prose* (London: Cape, 1943), 405–6.
4 Robert Graves, letter to Alun Lewis (26 November 1941), in *In Broken Images: Selected Letters of Robert Graves 1914-1946*, ed. Paul O'Prey (London: Hutchinson, 1982), 309.
5 Graves and Hodge, *The Reader Over Your Shoulder*, 405.
6 Ibid., 21.
7 Ibid., 10.
8 Ibid., 10, 11.
9 Ibid., 35.
10 Ibid.
11 Ibid., 34–5.
12 See Elizabeth Friedmann, *A Mannered Grace: the Life of Laura (Riding) Jackson* (New York: Persea Books, 2005), 97, and recall the account of the correspondence between Empson and Riding in Chapter1 above.
13 Robert Graves, *Poetic Unreason: And Other Studies* (London: Cecil Palmer, 1925), v.
14 The only exception to the early date of the essays making up *Poetic Unreason* is the last chapter, a version of which was published as "Sensory Vehicles of Poetic Thought" in *The Saturday Review of Literature*, 1 (31 January 1925): 489–90.

15 Graves acknowledges this fact: "Two of these chapters have appeared in the *North American Review* and the *Saturday Review of Literature* (New York), parts of others in the *Spectator, New Republic* and elsewhere" (*Poetic Unreason*, v). A version of the first chapter was published as "What Is Bad Poetry?" *The North American Review* (September 1923) 218: 353–68. Parts of the sixth chapter, "The Illogical Element in Poetry," were published as "The Illogic of Stoney Stratford and of Poetry," *The Spectator* (15 July 1922) 129: 87, and "Poetic Catharsis and Modern Psychology," *The Spectator* (29 July 1922) 129: 151–2. Part of the thirteenth chapter, "Succession," was published as "Mr Hardy and the Pleated Skirt," *Nation & Athenaeum* (7 July 1923) 33: 451–2 (also published in *The New Republic* [12 March 1924]).

16 Graves, *Poetic Unreason*, 85–6.

17 Laura Riding, *Anarchism Is Not Enough* (London: Jonathan Cape, 1928), 55, 54, 54–5.

18 Ibid., 55.

19 Laura Riding, *Contemporaries and Snobs* (Garden City, New York: Doubleday Doran and Company, 1927), 46.

20 Ibid., 57.

21 Riding, *Anarchism Is Not Enough*, 55.

22 Riding, *Contemporaries and Snobs*, 57.

23 Ibid., 46.

24 Ibid., 58.

25 Riding, *Anarchism Is Not Enough*, 57.

26 Graves, *Poetic Unreason*, 120–1.

27 Or as Graves puts it, there is in the English language a "rebellious tendency to form illicit assemblies that might affect the argument," such that "for English writers of prose or verse, so soon as a gust of natural feeling snatches away the typographical disguise in which their words are dressed, the conceits appear in all freedom: at first they enliven and enforce the argument, but after a while, if the author is not wary, they desert it and begin a digressive dance of their own." See *Impenetrability; or the Proper Habit of English* (London: The Hogarth Press, 1926), 11.

28 Robert Graves, *On English Poetry: Being an Irregular Approach to the Psychology of This Art, from Evidence Mainly Subjective* (London: William Heinemann, 1922), 32.

29 Graves, *Poetic Unreason*, 124.

30 Graves, *On English Poetry*, 33.

31 Riding, *Contemporaries and Snobs*, 58.

32 Ibid., 58, 60–1.

33 Ibid., 61.
34 Ibid., 62–3. See also Jean Paul Sartre, *Existentialism Is a Humanism* (1946), translated by P. Mairet, in *Existentialism*, ed. Robert C. Solomon (New York: Modern Library, 1974), 197–8.
35 Riding, *Contemporaries and Snobs*, 63.
36 Laura Riding and Robert Graves, *A Survey of Modernist Poetry* (1927; repr. New York: Haskell House, 1969), 263–4.
37 Riding, *Contemporaries and Snobs*, 88.
38 Riding, *Anarchism Is Not Enough*, 54.
39 Ibid., 55.
40 Ibid.
41 Ibid., 56.
42 Ibid., 57.
43 Riding and Graves, *A Survey of Modernist Poetry*, 274.
44 Riding, *Anarchism Is Not Enough*, 53, 54, 54, 55.
45 Ibid., 53, 54.
46 Riding and Graves, *A Survey of Modernist Poetry*, 278.
47 Riding, *Anarchism Is Not Enough*, 55, 55, 55, 54, 54.
48 Riding, *Contemporaries and Snobs*, 88.
49 Ibid., 188.
50 Ibid., 187.
51 C.K. Ogden and I.A. Richards, *The Meaning of Meaning: A Study of The Influence of Language upon Thought and of The Science of Symbolism* (London: Kegan Paul, Trench, Trubner and Co., 1923), 35, 35, 35, 35, 34.
52 Ibid., 36.
53 Ibid., 37, 33. For Ogden and Richards's quotation from Frazer, see James George Frazer, *Psyche's Task: A Discourse Concerning the Influence of Superstition on the Growth of Institutions* (London: Macmillan, 1909).
54 Ibid., 39.
55 Riding, *Anarchism Is Not Enough*, 54.
56 Riding and Graves, *A Survey of Modernist Poetry*, 266–7.
57 Riding, *Anarchism Is Not Enough*, 55.
58 Riding and Graves, *A Survey of Modernist Poetry*, 272.
59 Ibid., 273.
60 Ogden and Richards, *The Meaning of Meaning*, 39, 40, 40, 40, 41. Ogden and Richards quote here Bertrand Russell, *The Problems of Philosophy* (London: The Home University Library, 1912), 156.
61 Ogden and Richards, *The Meaning of Meaning*, 380.
62 Ibid.
63 Riding and Graves, *A Survey of Modernist Poetry*, 273.

64 Ibid., 278.
65 Ibid., 274.

CHAPTER FIFTEEN

1 I.A. Richards, *Principles of Literary Criticism* (London: Kegan Paul, Trench, Trubner and Co., 1924; New York: Harcourt, Brace and Co., 1925), 200.
2 Laura Riding, *Anarchism Is Not Enough* (London: Jonathan Cape, 1928), 54.
3 H.D., "The Pool." Richards reproduces the poem in full in *Principles of Literary Criticism*, 199.
4 Richards, *Principles of Literary Criticism*, 199.
5 Ibid.
6 Laura Riding and Robert Graves, *A Survey of Modernist Poetry* (1927; repr. New York: Haskell House, 1969), 137–8.
7 Ibid., 138.
8 Ibid., 122.
9 Richards, *Principles of Literary Criticism*, 200. See Ella Wheeler Wilcox, "Friendship After Love." Richards reproduces the poem in full in *Principles of Literary Criticism*, 200–1.
10 Richards, *Principles of Literary Criticism*, 201.
11 Ibid., 202.
12 Ibid.
13 Ibid.
14 Ibid., 204–5.
15 Ibid., 57.
16 Riding and Graves, *A Survey of Modernist Poetry*, 122.
17 Richards, *Principles of Literary Criticism*, 199.
18 Riding and Graves, *A Survey of Modernist Poetry*, 123, 122, 121–2.
19 Ibid., 122.
20 See T.S. Eliot, "Tradition and the Individual Talent," in *Selected Essays*, 3rd ed. enlarged (London: Faber and Faber, 1951), 21.
21 Riding and Graves, *A Survey of Modernist Poetry*, 124.
22 Eliot, "Tradition and the Individual Talent," 19; Richards, *Principles of Literary Criticism*, 200.
23 Richards, *Principles of Literary Criticism*, 200.
24 Riding and Graves, *A Survey of Modernist Poetry*, 118.
25 Riding and Graves, *A Survey of Modernist Poetry*, 118. Riding and Graves quote Amy Lowell's "Preface" in *Some Imagist Poets: An Anthology*, ed.

Amy Lowell (Boston and New York: Houghton Mifflin Company, 1915), vii.

26 Richards, *Principles of Literary Criticism*, 200.

27 Ibid.

28 Ibid.

29 Riding and Graves, *A Survey of Modernist Poetry*, 145.

30 Laura Riding, "The Rugged Black of Anger," in *The Laura (Riding) Jackson Reader*, ed. Elizabeth Friedmann (New York: Persea Books, 2005), 24.

31 Riding and Graves, *A Survey of Modernist Poetry*, 143.

32 Ibid., 144, 145.

33 Ibid., 145.

34 Richards, *Principles of Literary Criticism*, 200, 199, 200.

35 Riding and Graves, *A Survey of Modernist Poetry*, 118.

36 Richards, *Principles of Literary Criticism*, 200; Riding and Graves, *A Survey of Modernist Poetry*, 138.

37 Riding, *Anarchism Is Not Enough*, 55.

38 Ibid., 53–4.

39 Ibid., 63.

40 Ibid., 95.

41 Ibid., 101–2.

42 Ibid., 102.

43 Ibid., 102–3.

44 Ibid., 103.

45 Ibid., 104.

46 Ibid., 67.

47 Ibid., 104, 104, 104, 104

48 Ibid., 105.

49 Ibid., 113.

50 Ibid., 54.

51 Ibid.

52 Ibid., 55.

53 Ibid.

54 Riding and Graves, *A Survey of Modernist Poetry*, 138; Riding, *Anarchism Is Not Enough*, 103, 104–5.

55 Riding and Graves, *A Survey of Modernist Poetry*, 138.

56 Ibid., 134.

57 Ibid., 135.

58 Richards, *Principles of Literary Criticism*, 200; Riding and Graves, *A Survey of Modernist Poetry*, 136.

CHAPTER SIXTEEN

1 I.A. Richards, *Principles of Literary Criticism* (London: Kegan Paul, Trench, Trubner and Co., 1924; New York: Harcourt, Brace Co., 1925), 202.
2 Ibid.
3 Ibid., 203.
4 Ibid., 230, 231, 231.
5 Ibid., 203.
6 Ibid.
7 Laura Riding and Robert Graves, *A Survey of Modernist Poetry* (1927; repr. New York: Haskell House, 1969), 89.
8 Ibid., 119.
9 Ibid., 119, 120, 119.
10 Ibid., 123.
11 Richards, *Principles of Literary Criticism*, 203.
12 Riding and Graves, *A Survey of Modernist Poetry*, 89.
13 Riding and Graves, *A Survey of Modernist Poetry*, 115; Richards, *Principle of Literary Criticism*, 203, 203.
14 Ibid., 203, 203, 203, 203–4.
15 Riding and Graves, *A Survey of Modernist Poetry*, 114–15.
16 Ibid., 115–16.
17 Ibid., 116.
18 Ibid., 117.
19 Ibid.
20 Ibid., 119.
21 Ibid., 117–18.
22 Richards, *Principles of Literary Criticism*, 203.
23 Riding and Graves, *A Survey of Modernist Poetry*, 89.
24 Ibid.
25 Ibid.
26 Ibid., 118.
27 Ibid., 118, 115, 110.
28 Ibid., 115.
29 Ibid., 114.
30 Laura Riding, *Anarchism Is Not Enough* (London: Jonathan Cape, 1928), 54;
31 Riding and Graves, *A Survey of Modernist Poetry*, 114.
32 Riding, *Anarchism Is Not Enough*, 54–7.
33 Ibid., 57.
34 Ibid., 56.

35 Robert Graves, *Poetic Unreason: And Other Studies* (London: Cecil Palmer, 1925), 117–18.
36 Ibid., 118.
37 Ibid., 127.
38 Ibid., 133.
39 Ibid.
40 Riding, *Anarchism Is Not Enough*, 57.
41 I.A. Richards, *Science and Poetry* (New York: W.W. Norton, 1926), quoted in Riding, *Anarchism Is Not Enough*, 57; Graves, *Poetic Unreason*, 127.
42 Riding and Graves, *A Survey of Modernist Poetry*, 125.
43 Ibid., 125–6.
44 Ibid., 126.
45 Ibid., 106.
46 Riding, *Anarchism Is Not Enough*, 57.
47 Richards, *Science and Poetry*, 22–3.
48 Ibid.
49 Richards, *Principles of Literary Criticism*, 27; Richards, *Science and Poetry*, 23.
50 Robert Graves, "Gerard Manley Hopkins," letter to the editor (29 April 1955), *Times Literary Supplement* 2774 (29 April 1955): 209.
51 John Paul Russo, *I.A. Richards: His Life and Work* (Baltimore: The Johns Hopkins University Press, 1989), 278.
52 See I.A. Richards, "Gerard Hopkins," *The Dial* 81 (1926): 195–203, reprinted in *Complementarities: Uncollected Essays*, ed. John Paul Russo (Cambridge, Mass.: Harvard University Press, 1976), 139–47.
53 Russo, *I.A. Richards*, 280. The poem by G.H. Luce is "The Summer Cloud." Richards prints the poem in full in *Practical Criticism: A Study of Literary Judgment* (London: Routledge and Kegan Paul, 1929), 130.
54 John Haffenden, *William Empson: Among the Mandarins* (Oxford: Oxford University Press, 2005), 202.
55 Riding and Graves, *A Survey of Modernist Poetry*, 91, 92, 93, 92, 93.
56 See Robert Bridges, "Preface to Notes," in *Poems of Gerard Manley Hopkins*, ed. Robert Bridges (London: Humphrey, 1918).
57 Riding and Graves, *A Survey of Modernist Poetry*, 93.
58 Ibid., 93.
59 Ibid., 149.
60 Ibid., 138.
61 Ibid., 147.
62 Ibid., 148.
63 Ibid., 149.
64 Ibid.

65 Ibid.
66 Riding, *Anarchism Is Not Enough*, 104.
67 Ibid.
68 Ibid.
69 Riding and Graves, *A Survey of Modernist Poetry*, 126.

CHAPTER SEVENTEEN

1 John Crowe Ransom, *The New Criticism* (Norfolk, Connecticut: New Directions, 1941; repr. Westport, Connecticut: Greenwood Press, 1979), 44–5.
2 Ibid., 45.
3 Ibid., 101, 102.
4 Ibid., 111.
5 Ibid., 102. When writing *The New Criticism* between 1938 and 1941, Ransom must have referred to a copy of *Seven Types of Ambiguity* that included the erratum slip of 1931. Ransom spent the academic year 1931–32 in England on a Guggenheim fellowship and could have purchased the book then, bringing it back to the United States with him.
6 Stanley Fish, *Is There A Text in This Class?: the Authority of Interpretive Communities* (Cambridge, Mass. Harvard University Press, 1980), 56.
7 I.A. Richards, *Principles of Literary Criticism* (London Kegan Paul, Trench, Trubner and Co., 1924; New York: Harcourt, Brace and Co., 1925).
8 Ibid., 26.
9 Ibid., 199.
10 I.A. Richards, *Practical Criticism: A Study of Literary Judgment* (London: Routledge and Kegan Paul, 1929), 37, 44, 64, 66, 66, 88, 101,115.
11 *Practical Criticism*, 123,163.
12 Richards, *Practical Criticism*, 37.
13 Ibid.
14 Robert Graves, *Poetic Unreason: And Other Studies* (London: Cecil Palmer, 1925), 29.
15 Richards, *Practical Criticism*, 166.
16 Richards, *Principles of Literary Criticism*, 199.
17 Laura Riding and Robert Graves, *A Survey of Modernist Poetry* (1927; repr. New York: Maskell House, 1969).
18 Richards, *Practical Criticism*, 131.
19 Ibid., 315.
20 T.S. Eliot and Robert Graves had launched this criticism of anthology culture in letters to the *Times Literary Supplement* in 1921. See T.S. Eliot,

letter to the editor (24 November 1921), *Times Literary Supplement*, 746, and Robert Graves, letter to the editor (1 December 1921), *Times Literary Supplement*, 789.

21 I.A. Richards, "Preface to Third Edition," *Principles of Literary Criticism* (New York: Harcourt, Brace, 1968), 4.
22 Richards, *Practical Criticism*, 133.
23 Richards, *Principles of Literary Criticism*, 201.
24 Empson, "Remembering I.A. Richards," *Argufying: Essays on Literature and Culture*, ed. John Haffenden (Iowa City: University of Iowa Press, 1988), 226–7. See also John Haffenden, *William Empson: Among the Mandarins* (Oxford: Oxford University Press, 2005), 180–1.
25 I.A. Richards, *Science and Poetry* (New York: W.W. Norton, 1926), 31.
26 Richards, *Principles of Literary Criticism*, 136.
27 Richards, *Practical Criticism*, 229.
28 Riding and Graves, *A Survey of Modernist Poetry*, 35.
29 Ibid., 37.
30 Richards, *Practical Criticism*, 232.
31 Ibid.
32 Riding and Graves, *A Survey of Modernist Poetry*, 35, 37, 35, 37, 35.
33 Ibid., 38.
34 Richards, *Practical Criticism*, 233.
35 Ibid., 244.
36 Ibid.
37 Ibid., 15–16.
38 Ibid., 243.
39 Ibid.
40 Ibid., 244.
41 Ibid., 243.
42 Richards, *Principles of Literary Criticism*, 248.
43 Ibid.
44 Ibid.
45 Ibid., 206.
46 John Paul Russo, *I.A. Richards: His Life and Work* (Baltimore: The Johns Hopkins University Press, 1989), 265.
47 Ransom, *The New Criticism*, 51.
48 Ibid., 50–1.
49 Riding and Graves, *A Survey of Modernist Poetry*, 89–90.
50 Richards, *Principles of Literary Criticism*, 205, 204.
51 Richards, *Practical Criticism*, 251.
52 Ibid., 252.

53 Riding and Graves, *A Survey of Modernist Poetry*, 123, 124.
54 Ibid., 123–4.
55 Ibid., 124.
56 Ibid., 124–5.
57 Ibid., 129.
58 Ibid., 124, 130, 124.
59 Ibid., 130.
60 Ibid., 128.
61 Richards, *Practical Criticism*, 246; Richards, *Principles of Literary Criticism*, 202, 202, 202.
62 Richards, *Practical Criticism*, 246.
63 Ibid., 245, 246, 246, 246.
64 Richards, *Principles of Literary Criticism*, 58.
65 Richards, *Practical Criticism*, 244.
66 Ibid.
67 Riding and Graves, *A Survey of Modernist Poetry*, 125.
68 Ibid., 13.
69 Ibid., 17.
70 Richards, *Practical Criticism*, 245, 244.

CHAPTER EIGHTEEN

1 Laura Riding and Robert Graves, *A Survey of Modernist Poetry* (1927; repr. New York: Haskell House, 1969), 189.
2 Ibid.
3 Ibid., 189–90.
4 Ibid., 190.
5 Ibid., 189.
6 Laura Riding and Robert Graves, *A Pamphlet Against Anthologies* (1928; repr. New York: AMS Press, 1970), 166–7.
7 Riding and Graves, *A Survey of Modernist Poetry*, 190.
8 Henry Newbolt, John Bailey, K.M. Baines, F.S. Boas, H.M. Davies, D. Enright, C.H. Firth, J.H. Fowler, L.A. Lowe, Sir Arthur T. Quiller-Couch, George Sampson, Caroline F.E. Spurgeon, G. Perrie Williams, J. Dover Wilson, *The Teaching of English in England* (London: His Majesty's Stationery Office, 1921).
9 George Sampson, *English for the English: A Chapter on National Education* (London: Cambridge University Press, 1921).
10 See Robert Graves, "How English is Taught," *The Daily Herald* (14 December 1921): 7.

11 Newbolt, et al., *The Teaching of English*, 14, 15, 10, 67.
12 Riding and Graves, *A Survey of Modernist Poetry*, 190.
13 Ibid., 191.
14 Ibid., 194.
15 Ibid., 192.
16 Ibid., 192, 193, 194.
17 Ibid., 190–1.
18 I.A. Richards, *Practical Criticism: A Study of Literary Judgment* (London: Routledge and Kegan Paul, 1929), 313.
19 Ibid., 314.
20 Ibid., 33.
21 Ibid., 334.
22 Newbolt, et al., *The Teaching of English*, 63. The same sentence appears in Sampson, *English for the English*, 25.
23 Ibid., 10.
24 Sampson, *English for the English*, 14.
25 Ibid., 16, 24, 25.
26 Richards, *Practical Criticism*, 337–8.
27 Ibid., 337, 337, 336–7.
28 Newbolt, et al., *The Teaching of English*, 60; Richards, *Practical Criticism*, 336.
29 Richards, *Practical Criticism*, 334.
30 Ibid., 312–13.
31 Riding and Graves, *A Survey of Modernist Poetry*, 196, 197.
32 Ibid., 197.
33 Richards, *Practical Criticism*, 204.
34 Riding and Graves, *A Survey of Modernist Poetry*, 196–7.
35 Richards, *Practical Criticism*, 19.
36 Riding and Graves, *A Survey of Modernist Poetry*, 199.
37 Ibid., 200, 199.
38 Ibid., 199.
39 Ibid., 204.
40 Ibid., 205.
41 Ibid., 205.
42 Ibid., 206.
43 Ibid., 205–6.
44 Ibid., 206.
45 Ibid., 206–7.
46 Ibid., 205.
47 Ibid., 206.

48 Richards, *Practical Criticism*, 339.
49 Ibid., 339–40.
50 Ibid., 340.
51 Richards, *Practical Criticism*, 343.
52 Ibid., 343–4.
53 Ibid., 349.
54 Ibid., 350.
55 Ibid.
56 Ibid., 350–1.
57 Riding and Graves, *A Survey of Modernist Poetry*, 96.
58 Ibid., 99.
59 Ibid., 108.
60 Ibid., 97–8.
61 Richards, *Practical Criticism*, 303.
62 Ibid., 315, 18.
63 Ibid., 314.
64 Riding and Graves, *A Survey of Modernist Poetry*, 135, 136.
65 Riding and Graves, *A Survey of Modernist Poetry*, 108; Richards, *Practical Criticism*, 314–15.
66 Riding and Graves, *A Survey of Modernist Poetry*, 136.
67 Richards, *Practical Criticism*, 302–3.

CHAPTER NINETEEN

1 I.A. Richards, *Practical Criticism: A Study of Literary Judgment* (London: Routledge and Kegan Paul, 1929), 16, 17, 17.
2 Laura Riding and Robert Graves, *A Survey of Modernist Poetry* (1927; repr. New York: Haskell House, 1969), 46, 43–4.
3 Ibid., 44.
4 Ibid., 46.
5 Ibid., 46.
6 Richards, *Practical Criticism*, 315.
7 Ibid.
8 Ibid.
9 Ibid.
10 Ibid., 315–16.
11 Ibid., 4.
12 Riding and Graves, *A Survey of Modernist Poetry*, 26, 11, 63. See Louis Untermeyer, *Modern American Poetry: an introduction* (New York: Harcourt, Brace, and Howe, 1919).

13 Riding and Graves, *A Survey of Modernist Poetry*, 138.
14 Laura Riding and Robert Graves, *A Pamphlet Against Anthologies* (1928; repr. New York: AMS Press, 1970), 81.
15 Richards, *Practical Criticism*, 64.
16 Riding and Graves, *A Pamphlet Against Anthologies*, 128.
17 Ibid., 129–30.
18 Richards, *Practical Criticism*, 195, 64.
19 Ibid., 64.
20 Riding and Graves, *A Pamphlet Against Anthologies*, 76.
21 Ibid., 77–9.
22 Richards, *Practical Criticism*, 93.
23 Ibid., 299–300.
24 Ibid., 301.
25 Ibid.
26 Ibid., 300.
27 Riding and Graves, *A Survey of Modernist Poetry*, 12–13.
28 Ibid., 10.
29 Ibid., 54.
30 Ibid., 17, 17, 17, 17, 20, 20.
31 Ibid., 20.
32 Ibid., 20, 25, 25.
33 Ibid., 19–20.
34 Ibid., 20.
35 Ibid., 22.
36 Ibid., 21–2.
37 Ibid., 209.
38 Ibid., 208.
39 Ibid., 219.
40 Ibid., 218.
41 Richards, *Practical Criticism*, 318.
42 Riding and Graves, *A Survey of Modernist Poetry*, 219.
43 Richards, *Practical Criticism*, 316.
44 Ibid.
45 Riding and Graves, *A Survey of Modernist Poetry*, 218, 218; Richards, *Practical Criticism*, 301, 301.
46 Richards, *Practical Criticism*, 314.
47 Ibid., 314–15.
48 Ibid., 302.
49 Ibid., 305.
50 Ibid., 303.

51 Riding and Graves, *A Survey of Modernist Poetry*, 47.
52 Ibid., 41.
53 Ibid., 153.
54 Ibid., 134.
55 I.A. Richards, *Principles of Literary Criticism* (London: Kegan Paul, Trench, Trubner and Co., 1924; New York: Harcourt, Brace and Co., 1925), 237–8.
56 Richards, *Practical Criticism*, 285–6.
57 Ibid., 302.
58 Ibid., 204.
59 Riding and Graves, *A Survey of Modernist Poetry*, 41.
60 Richards, *Practical Criticism*, 295.
61 Ibid., 302.
62 Ibid.
63 Ibid.
64 Ibid., 303.
65 Ibid., 303–4.
66 Riding and Graves, *A Survey of Modernist Poetry*, 41.
67 Ibid., 134.
68 Ibid., 108.
69 Richards, *Practical Criticism*, 303.
70 Ibid.
71 Riding and Graves, *A Survey of Modernist Poetry*, 108–9.
72 Ibid., 9, 10, 10.
73 Ibid., 10.
74 Richards, *Practical Criticism*, 339.
75 Riding and Graves, *A Survey of Modernist Poetry*, 84.
76 Ibid., 10, 10, 19–20.
77 Richards, *Practical Criticism*, 315.
78 Ibid., 319.
79 Ibid., 320.
80 C.K. Ogden and I.A. Richards, *The Meaning of Meaning: A Study of the Influence of Language upon Thought and of the Science of Symbolism* (London: Kegan Paul, Trench, Trubner and Co., 1923), ix, x; Richards, *Principles of Literary Criticism*, 4, 4.
81 Richards, *Practical Criticism*, 343.
82 Riding and Graves, *A Survey of Modernist Poetry*, 106.
83 Riding and Graves, *A Survey of Modernist Poetry*, 106–7.
84 Ibid., 107, 108.
85 Richards, *Practical Criticism*, 364.
86 Empson, quoted by James Jensen, "The Construction of *Seven Types of Ambiguity*," *Modern Language Quarterly*, 27.3 (1966): 257–8.

87 John Paul Russo, *I.A. Richards: His Life and Work* (Baltimore: The Johns Hopkins University Press, 1989), 280.

CHAPTER TWENTY

1 Laura Riding and Robert Graves, *A Survey of Modernist Poetry* (1927; repr. New York: Haskell House, 1969), 226, 227.
2 Ibid., 227.
3 Ibid., 228–9.
4 Ibid., 229.
5 Ibid.
6 Ibid., 228.
7 Ibid., 230.
8 Ibid., 233–4.
9 Ibid., 230.
10 Ibid., 230.
11 I.A. Richards, *Practical Criticism: A Study of Literary Judgment* (London: Routledge and Kegan Paul, 1929), 176.
12 Riding and Graves, *A Survey of Modernist Poetry*, 163.
13 Ibid., 174.
14 Richards, *Practical Criticism*, 175.
15 Ibid.
16 Ibid.
17 Ibid., 176.
18 Riding and Graves, *A Survey of Modernist Poetry*, 143–4.
19 I.A. Richards, Preface to "Gerard Hopkins," in *Complementarities: Uncollected Essays*, ed. John Paul Russo (Cambridge, Mass.: Harvard University Press, 1976), 139.
20 Richards, *Practical Criticism*, 233–4.
21 I.A. Richards, *Science and Poetry* (New York: W.W. Norton, 1926), 31.
22 Richards, *Practical Criticism*, 234.
23 Ibid, ix.
24 Ibid., 4.
25 Richards, *Science and Poetry*, 22.
26 Ibid., 31.
27 Richards, *Practical Criticism*, 234, 4.
28 Ibid., 190.
29 Riding and Graves, *A Survey of Modernist Poetry*, 142.
30 Ibid., 144.
31 Richards, *Practical Criticism*, 144.
32 Riding and Graves, *A Survey of Modernist Poetry*, 142, 144.

33 Ibid., 144.
34 Ibid., 142, 145, 145.
35 Richards, *Practical Criticism*, 192.
36 Ibid., 190, 91.
37 Ibid., 191.
38 Riding and Graves, *A Survey of Modernist Poetry*, 191.
39 Richards, *Practical Criticism*, 216, 192,193.
40 Riding and Graves, *A Survey of Modernist Poetry*, 139.
41 Ibid., 143.
42 Ibid., 139.
43 Ibid., 87.
44 Ibid.
45 Ibid., 139–40.
46 Ibid., 74–5.
47 Ibid., 145.
48 Ibid., 143.
49 Ibid., 144, 145.
50 Ibid., 145.
51 Richards, *Practical Criticism*, 191.
52 Riding and Graves, *A Survey of Modernist Poetry*, 146.
53 Ibid., 87; Richards, *Practical Criticism*, 216.
54 Richards, *Practical Criticism*, 216.
55 Riding and Graves, *A Survey of Modernist Poetry*, 146.
56 Ibid., 146, 147, 146.
57 Ibid., 146.
58 Richards, *Principles of Literary Criticism* (London: Kegan Paul, Trench, Trubner and Co. 1924; New York: Harcourt, Brace and Co., 1925), 278, 240–1.
59 Richards, *Practical Criticism*, 203–4.
60 Riding and Graves, *A Survey of Modernist Poetry*, 47, 124, 124
61 Ibid., 133, 133–4, 142; Richards, *Practical Criticism*, 204.

Index